seashore. There is one motor vehicle to every three inhabitants in the County. In addition to contributing to the pleasure of two million people of this Country, these highways are a great factor in the commercial life of this region, making for rapid, economical transportation.

The Nearest Faraway Place

Also by Timothy White

Rock Lives: Profiles and Interviews
Catch a Fire: The Life of Bob Marley

The Nearest Faraway Place

Brian Wilson,
the Beach Boys,
and the
Southern California
Experience

Timothy White

Henry Holt and Company • New York

Henry Holt and Company, Inc.
Publishers since 1866
115 West 18th Street
New York, New York 10011

Henry Holt® is a registered
trademark of Henry Holt and Company, Inc.

Library of Congress Cataloging-in-Publication Data

White, Timothy
The nearest faraway place : Brian Wilson, the Beach Boys, and the
Southern California experience / Timothy White. — 1st ed.
p.   cm.
Includes bibliographical references and index.
1. Wilson, Brian, 1942–   . 2. Rock musicians—United States—
Biography.   3. Beach Boys.   4. California, Southern—Social life and
customs.   I. Title.
ML420.W5525W45 1994   94-42620
782.42166′092—dc20   CIP
[B]   MN

ISBN 0-8050-2266-X

Henry Holt books are available for
special promotions and premiums.
For details contact: Director, Special Markets.

First Edition—1994

Designed by Paula R. Szafranski
Photo insert designed by Kate Nichols

Printed in the United States of America
All first editions are printed on acid-free paper.∞

10 9 8 7 6 5 4 3 2 1

Frontispiece: SS *Anchoria*, which brought Brian Wilson's mother's family to
America; Alta Chitwood Wilson and her husband, William Henry Wilson,
Ohio, 1880s, just prior to their move to Kansas; the Beach Boys go collegiate,
mid-1960s: Mike Love, Al Jardine, Brian Wilson, Carl Wilson, and Dennis
Wilson; cover of *The Surfer Quarterly*, Vol. 2, No. 2, Summer 1961. *Endpaper
map:* 1929 motorist map, reprinted by permission of the Los Angeles Area
Chamber of Commerce.

To my sons Alexander and Christopher

Contents

"Life is heredity plus environment."
—Luther Burbank

1

● ● ● ●

Long-Promised Road

There would be no exceptions. Fred Morgan was adamant about that. As music instructor at Hawthorne High School, located just outside Los Angeles in the small South Bay community of Hawthorne, California, Morgan had warned students in his twelfth-grade piano and harmony course—especially the college-bound members of the class of 1960—that they must complete all the course requirements if they expected to earn a final mark of "B" or better.

Brian Wilson, a tall, timorous but attentive boy with wavy brown hair, aquamarine eyes, and a sad smile, was one of Morgan's most promising pupils, despite Wilson's handicap of deafness in his right ear. The seventeen-year-old's hearing had been damaged in an accident that occurred in early childhood, yet he was still having difficulty accepting his monaural existence. Morgan had been understanding, even allowing Brian to sit closer to the piano during class, but Morgan felt there was no excuse for Wilson's senior slump.

The truth was that Brian had allowed his position on the Hawthorne

1

Cougars varsity baseball team (he was a center fielder) and his involve-ment in a rock combo to distract him from his music homework. He was also spending too many evenings hanging out at Foster's Freeze on the corner of 120th Street and Hawthorne Boulevard when he should have been home studying. Morgan wouldn't have minded so much if Brian had been an average student, but the boy had demonstrated considerable musical aptitude in his grasp of Bach and Beethoven, and his knack for arranging was particularly impressive.

"Brian was the most quiet one of the bunch in his class," said Fred Morgan. "He was a nice boy and a good student and was fairly popular with his classmates because he had a good laugh. There was a portion of each class during which I would sit at the piano and play something, and everyone had to write down the notes. I remember Brian was very good at that; he had a quick mind."

Nevertheless, Brian had adopted a cavalier attitude toward his piano and harmony course during the last quarter, and so what could have been a uniformly meritorious final report card was subsequently marred:

English	B
Government	B
Physical Education	A
Spanish III	B
Senior Problems (Personal Psychology)	B
Piano and Harmony	C

"I had to give him a 'C' for the year because he did not do what he was supposed to do," said Morgan. "He did not finish his harmony exer-cises, for one thing. The exercises consisted of blocking in additional harmonic parts in a piece of music after the soprano part, let's say, had been supplied.

"Most important, he did not write a sonata. The major requirement of the course was to compose a piano sonata before the year was out; the project took the place of a final examination. Brian did not do a piano sonata, and so I gave him an 'F' for the project and a 'C' for the course. Instead of writing a sonata, he wrote [a melody that later became] the song called 'Surfin'.' I had nothing against the song; it was nice, but it just wasn't what I asked him for."

Nearly two years later, Brian Wilson was again bending the rules, talking Daniel Finnegan, an English teacher at Hawthorne's Lennox High School, into excusing Brian's girlfriend, Judy Bowles, from her class so he could say good-bye to her. At that point "Surfin'" was a rising hit on the national pop record charts, and Brian's Beach Boys were leaving to do a promotional tour in Chicago.

Lennox High was a conservative school in a conservative town, and its faculty was unaccustomed to granting special dispensations to burgeoning rock-and-rollers. However, as with many of the newly settled tract townships on the fringes of the Los Angeles basin, most of Hawthorne's natives knew the value of California boosterism (even if dispensed by a pop group); Judy Bowles was set free to briefly neck and nuzzle with her departing beau.

Although it began as a local favorite, "Surfin'," a bleating hymn to the Hawaii-derived sport sweeping Southern California, gained a countrywide foothold on airwaves via frequent rotation play on radio stations in gloomy Detroit and landlocked Phoenix. As far as the history of the Southland was concerned, this was business as usual: The further one was from the fabled locale, the greater its charms in the imaginations of the freshly smitten.

Brian Wilson, though a native Californian, was not a surfer; indeed, he had a lifelong fear of the water. In his music was a longing that somehow dismantled such ironies while addressing the immigrant essence in the region's state of mind. As a product of struggling midwestern sojourners who came west intent on personal renewal, Brian and his ingenuous songs ("Surfer Girl," "Surfin' U.S.A," "Be True to Your School," "Fun, Fun, Fun," "Wouldn't It Be Nice," "God Only Knows") retained the ingrained pieties, rural folkways, and tidy wisdoms once imparted by Chautauqua lecturers. But it was a Southern Californian belief—that there was a purity of purpose in the honest expression of pleasurable needs—which made them exhilarating, moving, and universal.

Brian Wilson did not sing about who he was—he sang about who he wished he might someday become. From all he had been taught, from every risk taken in his own family tree, from what he could see and guess about the pain in his own milieu and its sources, he believed he had no choice but to trust in the power of improvisation.

Southern California was itself an improvisation. As a Los Angeles newspaper columnist of decades past once quipped, in these parts "tomorrow isn't another day, it's another town." Like his sunshine-bound forebears, Brian Wilson believed in the idea of California more than the fact of himself, feeling that the energy focused on the romantic concept could carry over into the substance of his existence.

The impossible hope that runs through this story like a river, bending, swerving, and nearly reversing itself over the course of five generations, is that California could eventually expand to become more than a mere destination, that the land of sun would finally fulfill its unreal promise as Improvisation Rewarded—the shortcuts of heart songs alchemized into the intricate accomplishment of a sonata.

Even Paradise requires promoters, marketing salesmen to herald not only its ethereal splendors but also its mundane perks. In the beginning, the potential for plunder was always the surest lure to recruits for the Southern California Elysium. The promise of profiting from the misfortunes of the privileged was all it took in the 1860s, for instance, to draw a bumper crop of land speculators to the balmy Los Angeles basin. A protracted drought had by 1864 nearly destroyed the arid region's overextended cattle industry, causing the breakup of the great ranchos. (A decade earlier the predatory rancheros had themselves prospered within the state by selling beef to the San Francisco "forty-niners" at gold dust–gouging fees, the dons spending the lavish proceeds on French rugs for the clay floors of their *salas*.) The aggressive land-grabbing and subdivision that attended the cattlemen's reversals were as widespread as they were reckless. But buyers gambled, amid the general real estate chaos, that social stability would eventually resume.

Such restabilization would require cannier strategies, however, because Los Angeles was considered a backwater extraordinaire, the "city of lost demons" and the "port of missing men." San Francisco earned all the accolades as the West Coast repository of cultural and cosmopolitan verve; it was there that the gold of the Golden State was assayed, banked, and regularly funneled into edifying urban development and artistic expression.

San Francisco fit the "Paris of the West" image of an urbane, all-American window on the modern free market of civilization. Budding fortunes and journalistic freebooting fueled its smoke-filled rooms, and newspaper-chain owner William Randolph Hearst lined the path to wealthy Nob Hill with banner-headlined pulp benedictions. The city's wharfs were piled prodigiously with the most durable and outlandish wares of two hemispheres, a waterside groaning board unequaled in the continental states. Chocolate titan Domingo Ghirardelli, pants manufacturer Levi Strauss, and paper mogul Anthony Zellerbach called San Francisco home. And the city's Big Four financiers—Leland Stanford, Charles Crocker, Mark Hopkins, and Collis Huntington—all beamed as the Central Pacific Railroad was conjoined by golden spike to the Union Pacific in 1869, allowing seven hundred thousand passengers per annum to fan out from San Mateo to Sonoma.

The Bay Area's broody fog-bound mornings were catalysts for writers Bret Harte, Ambrose Bierce, Frank Norris, and Gertrude Atherton; its crystalline afternoons inspired barefoot dancer Isadora Duncan and genteel architect Willis Jefferson Polk to create astute paeans to the purity of form. It could have been the ethereal craftsmanship and classical eclecticism of Arthur and Lucia Mathews's California Decorative Style of painting and furnishings that Willis Polk was extolling when he wrote, in 1915, "Here among the poppy-covered hills, where purplish shadows cast their tinge upon the eucalyptus aisles, where palm and cypress stand out upon the ocean cliffs, a new art springs into blossom."

In comparison, Los Angeles was a lightly populated community of stubby buildings, dusty clay streets, paltry cultural life, and a steadily mounting crime rate. Politicians, landowners, and artists all conceded that its selling points were, at best, atmospheric. As travel writer Steven Powers commented in 1871: "It is true there is a great deal of dust in the streets; but that helps to suppress the flies. The flies are very numerous in the restaurants—very numerous indeed; but then you can keep them out of your wine by drinking it." And so forth.

Mere sunshine—constant cascades of the golden stuff—might strike outsiders as a pale attraction in a place experiencing forty-four homicides (out of a citizenry of eight thousand) in a single fifteen-month period in the mid-1800s. Indeed, a party of eastern land surveyors visiting the area in 1860 would later record that locals apologized for the queer quiet in the sun-drenched municipality—"because there have been no violent deaths during the two weeks that we have been here."

Reasons for the homicidal frictions in Los Angeles were rife. Lingering allegiances from the Mexican-American War (1846–48) had led to stubborn squatterism by Yankees, banditry by Mexicans, and vigilante sorties by disfranchised Californios. Added to this was the entrenched cross fire of the human residue of the gold rush: gamblers, cutthroats, and conniving vagrants who had headquartered along the main traffic lanes between Los Angeles and Northern California.

Nor were there any bright new breakthroughs on the economic front following the fall of the cattle kings. A visiting Frenchman named Louis Prevost sparked interest in a homegrown silk industry, and the California legislature passed an act in 1867 offering a subsidy of $250 for every field of five thousand mulberry trees two years old, and a purse of $300 for every one hundred thousand salable silkworm cocoons successfully nurtured on the mulberry leaves.

By 1869 two million trees had been planted in Los Angeles alone, but the opportunistic planting continued without coordination or care. The worms died, the trees wilted, and the experiment collapsed without a single silk factory ever going into production. The only known silk fabric woven within the Southland was used to make a flag for the capitol building; in round numbers, the sole shimmering banner cost a quarter-million dollars.

Coffee, cotton, and the castor (oil) bean were other Southern California crops exported in the belief that they, like the dried cowhides of yore, could stand thousands of miles of shipment. But each attempt was soon undone by the same forces that killed the silk industry: scarce, costly labor and exorbitant freight rates to far-distant markets.

Ultimately, it seemed best for the southern region to cease petitioning the well-endowed North for some reflected glow and instead begin selling the simple, isolated fact of itself. Thus, in the decade after Lee's surrender to Grant at Appomattox, the nation suddenly found itself entranced by two books: Charles Nordhoff's *California: For Health, Pleasure and Residence* (1872) and Benjamin Truman's inexactly titled treatise, *Semi-tropical California* (1874). The birth of systematic boosterism had occurred in 1873 with the founding of the first Los Angeles Chamber of Commerce. And though Los Angeles was especially vulnerable to the economic depression then ravaging California, the chamber printed and disseminated five thousand copies of *Condition, Progress, and Advantages of Los Angeles City and County, Southern California*.

This pamphlet, penned by native newsman A. T. Hawley, touted the virtues of the agrarian life in the Southland and urged the state's curious to cross through the Tehachapi Mountains by way of convenient new rail service and behold a magnificent basin where "the climate is essentially that of the northern part of the state but robbed of its cold winds and grown softer and milder."

The effect of the circular was significant, spurring others much further afield to rhapsodize about a marvelous Pacific meteorology capable of yielding such sun-polished jewels as the transplanted Portuguese lemon and Spanish orange. Introduced with the founding of the missions in the 1700s, the orange was one time-tested local product that had yet to be dispatched as a cash crop; it was not until 1877 that novice citrus grower William Wolfskill impulsively filled an entire freight car with the luminous fruit and pointed it toward Saint Louis as a publicity ploy. When Wolfskill's citrus consignment rolled into the midwestern depot a month later, it was still in impressively sound condition, the tangy refreshment becoming a sensation among the largely uninitiated Saint Louis citizenry.

Rheumatics were next targeted as candidates for western migration, and pamphlets were published asserting that Southern California's tart fruit, dry air, and absence of blustery winters were peerless agents to recovery. Health authorities, railroad flacks, and realty syndicates all proclaimed the Southland *the* foolproof tonic for tuberculosis and asthma victims, and sanitariums east of the Rockies were soon all but emptied in the hopeful rush to the coast.

It is not a canny thing, however, for human beings to invest their greatest hopes in climate; thin air and the things that ornament it are resources for a peculiar sort of dreamer. Yet these shining traits *were* the truest and most undeviating characteristics of Southern California, its cloudless expanses almost cunning in their constancy.

Though the physical landscape (an islandlike desert on the ocean) may be poor in resources, lacking minerals, rich soils, abundant rivers and lakes, or a sheltering coastline, Southern California is blanketed by a weather system that is an eerie wonderment of balanced grace. Thanks to the cooling benefits of the adjoining sea, the almost ceaseless sun is endurable.

When any moisture in the region is airborne, either from the zesty tides, the morning dew, or the rare sudden shower, the Southland's cruel ivory light is dramatically transformed. Filtering mists soften the ragged contours of the treeless hills that collar every vista and give their grainy brown and green hues a supple serenity of tone. The abidingly undulating wind, neither sticky with mosquitos nor mistral in its bite, melts the harsh edges of shadow and heat into a temperate salve too uniform to be termed either "tropical" or "Mediterranean." And when the truce between lustrous sky and stark terrain is in full, vaporous force, not even the Aegean in June can claim an ozone so rejuvenating—let alone one prevailing for all four seasons. So the Southland's sparkling Sahara by the sea was the type of place where the flat-out impossible became the merely difficult, the sweet sameness of every day taking the sting out of even maddening tasks.

Observers such as naturalist David Starr Jordan felt that the Pullman pioneers who journeyed into Los Angeles and environs on the Southern Pacific and Santa Fe lines during the late 1800s were destined to flourish in the clime, Jordan judging the ripening upper-middle-class females of the era to be perfect specimens for the dawning modern age. Clearly wishing that all young coeds could be from the Sunshine State, Jordan wrote that "California college girls, of the same age, are larger by almost every dimension than are the college girls of Massachusetts. They are taller, broader-shouldered, thicker-chested (with ten cubic inches more lung capacity), have larger biceps and calves, and a superiority of tested strength."

This sort of mythmaking was potent, and many Los Angeles boosters saw profit in the dissemination of it. Similarly, macho San Franciscan tale-spinner Jack London would touch the hearts of Southlanders in 1907 when he began chronicling his sensual sailing jaunts to Hawaii and the South Pacific, and in particular his experiences with the Hawaiian pastime of surfboarding, which he depicted in the October issue of *Woman's Home Companion* magazine. It was the surf- and sun-hungry readers of London's popular adventures that the Los Angeles city fathers and their salaried public relations essayists labored to hook.

The shockingly puny entry for the City of Angels in the 1910 edition of the *Standard Dictionary of Facts* put the city's predicament in plain view: "Los Angeles—on the Los Angeles River, 480 miles south of San Francisco." Even as late as 1915, popular enthrallment with California remained centered on the Bay Area, prompting newspapers as far away as central Kansas to grant front-page status to minor happenings (social notes, probate awards, lectures by current personalities) unfolding within proximity of the Golden Gate channel. Yet such Kansas papers as the *Hutchinson News* increasingly carried handsome advertisements for the Sunkist oranges of the Los Angeles–headquartered California Fruit Growers Exchange, as well as notices alerting land speculators, self-styled entrepreneurs, and ambitious small growers to business prospects in Southern California. The *Hutchinson News* was one of the state's best and most important dailies, being published from the site of a vital terminus of the Rock Island & Pacific, and Atchison, Topeka and Santa Fe railways, and its influence on the local populace was profound.

It was by means of such notices in the Hutchinson press that the family of plumbing contractor and sometime grape grower William Henry Wilson first became acquainted with Southern California. This progenitor of the Wilson clan believed passionately in those Sunkist ads, with their images of sunny prosperity and domestic idylls, as well as the various classified announcements extolling the charms of Southern California farm life and economic opportunity. Through trial and error, boom and bust, near-triumph and persistent tragedy, William Henry Wilson encouraged his descendants to pour their dreams and schemes into the impossible fulfillment of the California promise as emblazoned across the pages of his local paper.

This book is the saga of that struggling middle-class family, one among so many, that put their fiercest faith (as well as their strongest powers of pretending) into that promise.

Generations after the passing of William Henry Wilson, great-grandson Brian (who had never even heard of his ancestor) took it upon himself to tell in song his own story and, by extension, that of his entire heritage. As his fanciful forebear would have preferred, Brian's account was a doggedly idealized recasting of each heartbreak and disappointment. In this fashion the shy songwriter helped give America and the world a new leisure credendum and a determinedly youth-, romanticism-, and California-refracted lens through which to regard it.

The title of this book comes from an instrumental track on *20/20*, the Beach Boys' last album of the 1960s. While a strong effort in sum, *20/20* (a wry reference to hindsight) was largely a collection of recent singles, members' solo studio projects, and outtakes dating back to 1966. It was also the first Beach Boys album to feature group cover photos that did not include Brian Wilson. Instead, Bruce Arthur Johnston, the twenty-three-year-old L.A. surf-pop veteran who'd been serving since 1965 as the non-touring Brian's stand-in and supplemental studio contributor, was finally pictured as a full member. Johnston was an orphan (born Billy Baldwin in Chicago) who had been adopted and raised in Beverly Hills by a well-to-do executive of the Rexall drugstore chain. *20/20* contained Johnston's cowriting and production credits, and he would soon become the second most frequently mistaken Beach Boy (after Carl Wilson) for Brian. "It got to a point," he recalled of the group's late 1960s/early '70s artistic quandary, "where we were writing and I was vocal-arranging *in the style* of Brian Wilson because he really wasn't actively involved."

This was certainly true in the case of "The Nearest Faraway Place," a wistful two-and-a-half-minute piece composed, performed, and produced by Johnston. While Johnston says he took the instrumental's title from a *Life* magazine article by Shana Alexander, his melody and arrangement are strongly influenced by Brian's work on the Beach Boys 1966 *Pet Sounds* album, to which he contributed. ("Bruce did a very beautiful thing with 'The Nearest Faraway Place,' " Brian himself would later enthuse in the liner notes of the album's 1990 CD reissue.) To this day, as with Johnston's 1971 song "Disney Girls (1957)," many less astute Beach Boys fans assume this wonderfully delicate evocation of the California idyll is one of Brian's more nuanced efforts. That gentle ruse, of course, was precisely the point.

What follows is the tale of Southern California in the modern age, from the 1920s to the present day: a social history of how it was marketed and settled, how its very topography was transformed in a concerted effort to fortify a resolute reverie. Woven into the human chronicle are the novelties, products, ideas, and ideals that sprang from its participants, as well as the schemes and notions that went awry.

Dreams can come true, but never illusions; and fantasies are most pleasurable to those who encounter them at considerable distance from the source. Consequently, this rich and affecting epic of innocence and experience is told through the uncommon passage of the family and its associates who came to extol—but never quite embody—the most glorious visions of Southern California's secret potential.

2

● ● ● ●

The Nearest Faraway Place

He had an appointment the next morning at the probate court of Reno County, Kansas, and the errand made him feel as skittish as a felon: He was to pick up a marriage license.

William Coral "Buddy" Wilson, a twenty-four-year-old master plumber in Hutchinson, Kansas, had put this reckoning off for as long as he could. Unlike closest sibling Johnny Wilson, an outgoing fellow with a knack for ingratiating grandstanding, Buddy hated to take a fixed, public position on anything. It made him feel pinned down, diminished. But Buddy's frustrated fiancée and two sets of impatient parents had ganged up on him and forced a commitment.

Buddy Wilson quickened his step on the frosty and overcast Monday evening in central Kansas, tucking a copy of the March 2, 1914, edition of the *Hutchinson News* under his powerful right arm. He still had a final business call to make in the handsome new neighborhood rising beside the ramshackle local racetrack. Afterward he would drop his bulky black leather equipment case off at father William Henry Wilson's shop on

Second Street and then continue to 416 First Street West for a late supper and an early bedtime.

Big shifts and brittle transitions were in the offing, and both Buddy and his father were rattled by them. Having raised half a dozen boys to manhood (a daughter, Amelia, died at three), William Henry Wilson had elected several months earlier to end his brief plumbing proprietorship with John T. Hines, selling John the old Wilson & Hines service shop at 26 Second Avenue West and opening a new wholesale firm at the other end of the street: Wilson & Son, Plumbers, Steam and Gas Fitters. The senior Wilson's abrupt decision to pull Buddy into his practice (fed by modest municipal contracts) had only deepened the ambivalence his eldest son had about staying around Hutchinson after he was wed.

Sandy-haired and slim but solidly muscled, Buddy had his father's long, pointed nose, although it was slightly broader and rounder as a result of his mother's heritage. Indeed, he was less handsome than his smooth-faced and aristocratic-looking dad—a fact emphasized by similar short, sideswept haircuts—and the ruddy-featured son carried himself like a much older man: his shoulders slouched, the eyes downturned at the corners, the wide, thin mouth sagged to one side.

The young master plumber was a tense, hot-tempered personality, and his surly disposition was aggravated by severe chronic headaches that he had inherited from his father. Everyone had originally called him by his middle name, eventually twisting it into "Carl" with such casual disregard that he angrily insisted on "Bud" (his family soon softened it to Buddy). He was suspicious of his father's seeming generosity, wondering if the old man planned to push all the work off on him. And contrary to what his dad liked to boast—and the newspapers tended to embroider— the American frontier had engendered conformity more than rugged individualism: Immigrants and pioneers hewed to customs and lineal protocols as strict as those they emigrated to escape.

The Wilson clan was of mixed English, Irish, and Scottish extraction and had settled in Kansas after departing the poplar-canopied farming community of Longbottom, Ohio, which was situated on a curving bend of the Ohio River in Meigs County. William Henry's father, George Washington Wilson, had been born in nearby Pomeroy, Ohio, on January 1, 1820.

The product of New York stonemason stock (one of fifteen wayfaring children of Henry and Marilla Wilson), George was a wiry, broad-browed farmer with a wispy mustache who worked a sizable parcel of land on

Guyan Run in Meigs County. On March 13, 1857, seven days after the Supreme Court handed down the Civil War–precipitating Dred Scott Decision (in which a runaway Negro slave was ruled to have no rights as an American citizen), George purchased an additional seven acres and eighty rods' worth of property from adjoining neighbor Benjamin Watson.

The previous month, on February 26, 1857, George Wilson had married Mary Bailey, the pillowy, piercing-eyed daughter of prominent local farmer Joseph Bailey. Wilson had formerly been wed to Mary's sister Matilda, that ceremony having taken place in December 1852, but Matilda took sick after the birth of their second girl, Lois, and died suddenly. Conveniently, Wilson's second nuptials with a Bailey woman were performed by the same justice of the peace, Major Reed.

In July 1870, Wilson assumed control of more property in Longbottom and nearby Forked Run Farm after the death of Joseph Bailey. As a sentimental gesture to his motherless granddaughter, Grandpa Bailey had left his cropland to Lois Wilson, and since Lois was a minor, the local probate court appointed George Wilson the guardian of the inheritance until she could assume the responsibility of tending it.

George and Mary Wilson's union would produce five boys, the liveliest being the industrious third son, William Henry, born in the midst of the Civil War—April 27, 1863. It was some four months after Lincoln's Emancipation Proclamation and seven months before the president's Gettysburg Address. It was also the same year that Thanksgiving became a national holiday and James L. Plimpton invented the roller skate, the latter event prompting the much-remarked creation of roller rinks in California that rented skates to patrons.

Venturesome William Henry was excited by the upheavals and transitions of the times, a trait that had made him George's favorite, and they bonded to each other. After William Henry's marriage in the 1880s to comely Illinoisan Alta Lenora Chitwood, he began to pump his well-informed father about the railroad's inviting penetration of the plains states. The advent of local coal and salt mining had given the wage-earning children of Meigs County's dirt farmers a taste for the wider world in which such minerals were sold. Rail excursions to Kansas had recently come into vogue, and some young couples were turning them into one-way trips after finding the prairie's Arkansas River lowlands ripe for homesteading. Thus enticed, William Henry booked Alta and himself for tourist class on the next train to Chicago, and from there they caught the Santa Fe to the Sunflower State.

Father George Wilson followed, selling his Ohio land and using the money to purchase acreage in Kansas's Morton and Reno counties. He loaded four large wagons with farm equipment and household goods and left Ohio forever. Other relatives did likewise, and within fifty years Reno County was overrun with Wilsons, the surname seemingly everywhere as it was shouted from sod huts or painted in gold leaf on the display windows of jewelry and dry-goods stores.

Once resettled, William Henry decided the tough tableland of the Great Plains—the gigantic dried shoal bed of a prehistoric inland sea—was less receptive to tillage than Ohio sward. He declined to work the seventy-four acres of watermelon and squash his father planted beyond the sandhills on the northern outskirts of Hutchinson and instead aimed to hone both his salesmanship and Pomeroy-acquired pipefitting skills in the service of downtown Hutchinson. He opened a wholesale plumbing business that helped install the water and heating system in the Kansas State Reformatory during the years (1885–1900) required to construct the sprawling stone complex.

Contract plumbing on the prairie was a peaks and valleys enterprise, vulnerable to sharp rises in the local building market and sudden dips in a town's economic muscle. Success depended on a gambler's instincts and a boss's savvy to push his workers suddenly and hard—strategies suited to the restless head of a large family.

Buddy Wilson (born February 18, 1890) resented bosses, most of all his headstrong father, and so he found his mind wandering that winter evening in 1914, a plan of escape taking shape in his imagination until, almost without realizing it, his idea had become a secret resolve.

Gripping his newspaper, Buddy grinned unevenly and strode against the dusty gale driving through the elms of the tiny park between Thirteenth and Fourteenth Avenues. Monday's gazette was full of escapist reportage from California as well as the usual lavish advertisements for Sunkist oranges, the individually tissued fruit bursting from spotless packing cartons:

> Have this golden fruit for breakfast, dessert and "between meals." Cleanest of all fruits—never touched by bare hands. All the pickers and packers of Sunkist oranges and lemons wear clean, white cotton gloves. Tree-ripened, fiberless. Not a seed in Sunkist. Buy them by the box or half-box. They keep for weeks.

Without ever having to come out and say it, the pitch for the fruit was clearly intended as a simultaneous tout for the section of the state in which it was grown: clean, sunny, tree-filled Southern California. Here was a paradise untroubled by the cyclical droughts that beset a frontier plain, stuck in the epicenter of several opposing weather fronts, and it was unsullied by the dust storms that deposited Kansas grit between your teeth as you dozed off at night.

Buddy had already had a taste of the Southland and its luxuriant produce. A decade earlier, William Henry Wilson had impulsively sprung at the opportunity to buy ten acres of prime vineyard at the east end of Escondido, California. The Wilsons, including William Henry's then eighty-five-year-old dad George, hurriedly rented their Hutchinson house and left for Escondido, where the children were enrolled in local schools and Grandpa acquired a taste for local wine. The Wilsons had worked the grape ranch with greenhorn diligence, the younger boys happily trapping rattlesnakes in the adjacent Hog's Back Foothills while Buddy and his younger brother Johnny helped their dad tend the demanding vines. Come harvest, Buddy and Johnny filled an entire Santa Fe ice car with crates of the green table grapes, and they slept in the caboose as they accompanied the shipment back to Hutchinson for sale on the streets.

Although the vineyard had proven productive and Hutchinson bought all the grapes it could yield, William Henry was a dilettante grower at best and never came close to meeting his overhead. Three seasons later he sold out to a Mr. Fields and brought everyone (except Grandpa George, who died there in 1907) back to the stark shortgrasses of Kansas. The Wilson Wholesale Plumbing Co. took space in a bulky yellow building beside the Rock Island & Pacific railway tracks just south of town, and William Henry put his six sons (Buddy, Johnny, Ernest, Howard, Harold Dewey, and Charles) to work running it, the entire clan reluctantly returning to a life of steam-fitting supply, frigid Kansas winters, and the less lush uncertainties of what William called "the darn stubborn world."

Not that Kansas had any monopoly on bad weather or swift reversals in fortune. The *Hutchinson News* that Buddy clutched that night offered graphic accounts of the horrific blizzard back east (NEW YORK IS SNOW-BOUND; TEN INCHES OF SNOW FELL; FIVE LIVES ARE LOST) as well as grim southwestern vignettes of General Pancho Villa's menacing exploits in the Mexican civil war. The only lighthearted material on page one for this date was the bulletin on Christy Mathewson's contract renewal with the New York Giants, plus the column space accorded the quips of popular Kansas cartoon character Zimmie the Owl: "Yes, Lizzie," the wise bird assured his nesting mate, "there's a lot of men who won't buy a washing machine so long as they can marry one."

Wilson's fiancée, Edith Sthole, a robustly built seventeen-year-old who stood five feet eight inches in her coarse woolen hosiery, was no stranger to a scrub basin. Edith was the last of four children (two boys and two girls, but little Karl-Adolf was dead not long after his second birthday) from farmer Charles Sthole's first marriage to the late Maria Sofia Pettersson of Illinois. After Mr. Sthole remarried, to Maria Amalia Lindholm, Edith became her stepmother's strong right arm in their tiny white farmhouse on North Monroe Street.

It was tiny Edith who consoled Maria with her adoration after Maria lost her first child, Albert, at birth. And with Edith's siblings (pampered older sister Emelie, twenty; brother Karl, twenty-one; stepsisters Viola, thirteen, and Gladys, ten; stepbrother Garnet, nine) unable or unwilling to manage a full adult share of the chores, her broad back and bullish spunk would be missed after her marriage to Buddy.

The Stholes had come to Kansas from the southern Swedish province of Smaland in 1885. Edith's father, Charles (born October 10, 1867), arrived at the age of eighteen with his older brother Nils August, twenty. There were several dozen Smaland expatriates in Hutchinson to greet the Sthole brothers, all congregants of Emanuel Lutheran Church at Avenue C and Plum Street. It would be the family's house of worship for the next three generations.

Once settled in Hutchinson, Charles Sthole met and asked for the hand of a Swedish girl from Illinois, Maria Sofia Pettersson. The Reverend A. F. Irwin joined them in matrimony on a slate-gray Tuesday, December 17, 1889, while a stiff southwesterly wind rippled the Arkansas River.

Charles worked as a hireling in the brine pits of the Vincent Salt Company of Hutchinson and lived with his wife in a frame house at 807 Avenue B East. It took ten years for him to save enough from his wages to rent some fields for farming: a tract abreast the Hutchinson sandhills that he leased from wealthy local landowner James Rolands. Charles was barely breaking even on his initial gleanings of wheat, alfalfa, and corn when his first wife died, and he was promptly married to Mary Lindholm, the two making a go of their plantings and eventually able to add some cows for a small dairy.

The son of a poor retired soldier-turned–peasant farmer in Smaland, Charles Sthole felt fortunate. Father Adolf Fredrik Carlsson Stal had spent his own young manhood as a conscripted Swedish guardsman, something Charles had left Smaland to avoid. Crop failures, religious intolerance, rigid class structure, economic obstacles to the ballot box, and evasion of compulsory universal military service, coupled with emigration pamphleteering from flourishing Christian revivalist movements in the States, helped motivate large numbers of Scandinavians, particularly Swedes, to board ships to America.

In order to understand the excitement with American expansion and the appetite for liberated labor that brought Scandinavian immigrants to the plains, it's instructive to examine the circumstances of one pioneer family's forebears.

Charles Sthole's father Adolf was born on March 17, 1838, at Qvillemala, Mörlunda parish, Smaland, and entered the Swedish army at eighteen. He ultimately chose the army as a career, and since it was traditional for career soldiers to be given a home and some cultivable ground as part of their salary, Adolf was accorded a farm known as Skruvshult in the parish of Högsby. Many young Swedish men took more masculine-sounding names when beginning army lives, and the cocky "son of Carl" chose "Stal," meaning steel.

On April 7, 1860, Adolf Stal wed his parents' housemaid, thirty-year-old Christina Lovisa Adolfdotter of Lindas, Malilla parish, Smaland. They would have an unnamed stillborn daughter and four healthy sons: Carl Fredrik, Nils August, Karl Johan (or Charles John in its Americanized form), and Oskar Fredrik. Of Adolf's four boys, Charles and August were the most determined to leave Sweden.

Like the brothers Stal (originally misspelled Stohle on U.S. Immigration dockets, then further corrupted by Kansas census takers until it became Sthole), nearly all emigrants in the second surge of the fabled Swedish exodus—some 493,000 from 1879 to 1893—embarked by steamship from Gothenburg to the English port city of Hull. Transferred to trains, they were shuttled from Hull to Liverpool, then endured a layover of a few days before the voyage by American or British ship to Quebec, Boston, or New York.

On these steamships all but the well-to-do were consigned to communal living and sleeping areas, closed off from the passengers' quarters in the upper deck by large steel hatches. The demure Swedish commoners were less bothered by these cramped conditions than by forced proximity to the "rough and uncivilized creatures," the Irish. By the time the Sthole boys booked passage on their steamers to England and the States, the Gothenburg press advertisements contained boxed notices that assured the increasingly wary travelers that they "would not be thrown together with the Irish."

While the Swedes were assured physical segregation from Ireland's emigrants, they were not spared the steerage cooking of most ships' Celtic cooks. This fare consisted of a rotating trinity of one-meal-a-day menus: boiled cabbage, pork, and pea soup; beef, rice, and molasses; porridge and dried fruit. Each passenger below decks was also provided with five pounds of white rusk biscuits per week, with an equal measure of butter. Coffee was poured each morning and weak tea served at night. Each man also received a glass of schnapps every noontide.

Like most Swedish arrivals in the 1880s, the Stholes elected to disembark at New York City and were processed through the circular brick Castle Garden clearing station at the lower tip of Manhattan. (The famed Ellis Island facility had not yet come into use.) Afterward, a network of river steamers, canal boats, and special immigrant trains took the pilgrims as far as Chicago—a journey of, at minimum, four days. If they had no relatives to welcome them or if they failed to connect with Chicago immigrant community representatives who could untangle currency exchanges and boardinghouse rules, foreign entrants often surrendered their baggage receipts to carriages reined by con artists. Fleeced Swedes stranded in Chicago helped make it the world's third largest Swedish city.

If their funds held out, immigrants next made train connections to points deeper into the midwestern wilds and eventually crossed the last of the frontier scrub barrens by wagon. Upon reaching Hutchinson, many stragglers still clutched "The Emigrants Interpreter," a translation card of questions, phrases, and sample repartee regularly handed out by Swedish travelers' aides on all immigrant trains.

AT THE RAILROAD
Where are the emigrant cars?
Here sir. Step in.
Your railroads seen [sic] *not to be built so solid as that in Europe.*

This may be but our cars are much more convenient; you may walk about as you like, through th [sic] whole train during the passage, and you enjoy all of the conveniences as on a steamer.
Yes, that is true.

AT THE STATION
Passengers for the West change cars.
What shall we do?

Along the way, as Scandinavian transients solicited provisions and nightly shelter, they would sometimes find the courage to pose questions regarding the "Swedish Nightingale." World-renowned soprano Jenny Lind (1820–1887), onetime diva of the Stockholm Opera, had ignited "Lindomania"—as it was actually called—during her 1850–52 P. T. Barnum–sponsored tours of America.

The most successful and influential circuit of the States ever mounted by a single European musical celebrity, Jenny Lind's caravan ushered in a grand era of American music appreciation and throughout the nation stimulated explosive sales of pianos and other instruments, the building of music halls, and the formation of choral societies. The attendant merchandizing of Jenny Lind's performances, encompassing dolls, sausages, cigars, and fine china, easily eclipsed the rock-and-roll T-shirt franchising of a future epoch.

Besides possessing a beauty that beguiled Longfellow, Diamond Jim Brady, and Hans Christian Andersen, Lind proved a generous and skilled philanthropist: The beautiful young operatic, concert, and oratorio singer devoted much of her energies in the mid-1800s to the predicaments and goals of Swedish settlers—hence the immigrants' hungry questions.

In gratitude they named communities as far west as the Sierra foothills in Jenny's honor. But like so many myths concerning California that crept across the plains, the story that the Swedish Nightingale had once sung her theme song, "Greeting to America," near the mining town of Jenny Lind, Calaveras County, was entirely fictitious. The Stockholm superstar never set foot in the Golden State. Or in Kansas, for that matter. But her monumental impact in the United States imbued Lind's homesick countrymen with self-assurance and provided them with a pop culture identity figure without equal among their fellow immigrants.

The Stholes were initially drawn to the stable, cohesive Swedish set-tlements of central Kansas due to the potential for jobs, the land grants offered by the railroads, and a freer form of tenant farming.

The primary inducement was the bounty of the Homestead Act of 1862, which offered 160 acres of free land to any U.S. citizen or immigrant (who had filed citizenship intention papers), provided he or she was twenty-one years of age, the head of a family, or had served four-teen days in the U.S. Army or Navy. Military recruiting stations (initially for the Civil War, then for the subjugation of the western Indians) waited mere yards from the Castle Garden gateway, dispensing bonuses of several hundred dollars on enlistment and, by law, automatic citizenship on discharge. Those who worked and lived on their property for five years— free all the while to sell their produce or stock at market rates!—were awarded full ownership. (The five-year rule allowed for six-month annual grace periods during which homesteaders could earn money as miners, railroad gandy dancers, and lumberjacks without sacrificing their title to the soil; and the five-year regulation could be waived after six months' residence if the preemptor could swing the $1.25-an-acre fee.)

The prime Swedish advance to the Hutchinson area occurred in 1869 when the Osage Cession and the Cherokee Neutral Lands were opened for non–Native American use by dubious treaties negotiated earlier in the decade. And what sort of place was Hutchinson? The county seat of Reno County, Hutchinson was incorporated in 1871 by Santa Fe land agent Clinton C. Hutchinson, who conceived its basic street plan astride a rushing stream, just north of the Arkansas River. Rails were rapidly being laid through the broad Arkansas Valley, with all tracks across its trampled wheat fields bent in the direction of Colorado and the Pacific. As Mr. Hutchinson's portion of the railside development campaign heated up, the prolific land promoter rightly saw a certain fertile patch on either side of Cow Creek as his last opportunity to hang out a rail depot shingle with his own name on it.

In an age when the middleman, land syndicator, and propagandist could approximate the stature of a baggy pants statesman, C. C. Hutchin-son was a cut above the competition. Besides being a Baptist preacher, outspoken supporter of temperance, and part-time Indian agent, he was also a skilled public relations writer. In July 1871, the Kansas Bureau of Immigration allocated $2,500 for publishing and distributing ten thou-sand copies of *Resources of Kansas*, a 287-page illustrated promotional booklet that the clever Hutchinson had produced. The heavily illustrated text was brimming with immoderate travelogue prose ("luxuriant corn fields . . . the vigorous wild grasses of Eastern Kansas . . . vast herds of buffalo, as fat as stall-fed beef") and boisterous praise of the railroad lands still available.

Yet Hutchinson outdid all his contemporaries in calculating a bold tomorrow for the "Buffalo Grass Desert": "The effect of railroads and telegrams," he wrote, "is undoubtedly to cause more frequent showers, perhaps by promoting a more even distribution of the magnetic forces. . . ."

Soon numerous blond, husky, and sober Scandinavian settlers were in place on the former Indian hunting grounds of Reno County. The first Santa Fe engine steamed into Hutchinson on June 27, 1872, cheered by clusters of the town's 450 Scottish, Irish, English, German, and Swedish inhabitants as it snaked past a modest frontier labyrinth that included a bank, public school, two millineries, three bakeries, two hotels, five boardinghouses, three grocery stores, two land offices, five law offices, and a daguerreotype gallery. There were no bars, but hucksters vending beer and rye from under wagon tarps were not hard to locate.

Hutchinson was the fourth largest city in Kansas by 1914, its hallmarks of civic pride having long since sunk from temperance or railroads to the salt marshes. The mineral boon had been stumbled upon in 1880 during subsidized drilling for oil by a South Hutchinson scoundrel so notorious he had to depart disguised as a woman to avoid the tar bucket of a mob. Most of the mines used an evaporation process: Water was blasted into the shafts, and then the brine was suctioned out and sent to rotund, open evaporation pans. The refined sodium crystals were gunny-sacked and shipped. The local production of the Barton, Carey, and mighty Morton Salt companies would earn the municipality the appellation of "Salt Cellar of America."

Meanwhile, the social and cultural life of Hutchinson had moved beyond buffalo hunts (a voguish activity of the early 1870s) to include popular music. The town's first band made its inaugural public appearance in September 1875, with the repertoire including post–Civil War standards such as "John Brown's Body Lies Mouldering in the Grave" as well as the latest waltzes. And the durable legacy of Jenny Lind was manifested in the proliferation of singing classes and music and dancing schools. Operas presented at the courthouse became the rage, so much so that a fine two-story opera house, with seating for eight hundred, was erected in 1882 at the southwest corner of Avenue B and Main Street, and within two years it boasted its own resident orchestra.

By the late 1880s the phonograph, which Thomas Edison had patented in December 1877, could be heard with regularity in better homes within the Hutchinson town limits, its demure din derived mainly from Columbia cylinder recordings of John Philip Sousa's U.S. Marine Band. Even coin-operated phonographs had spread to the open range by the turn of the century. Conceived of in California, these "phonograph parlors" permitted patrons to order a five-cent selection by barking their request into a tube. They would then hear their request played back on a separate listening tube from the store basement, where a phonograph whirred away.

In the second decade of the twentieth century, Columbia's and Victor Records' double-sided wax discs brought the sound of Byron G. Harlan's "How Ya Gonna Keep 'Em Down on the Farm" and the Heidelberg Quintet's "By the Beautiful Sea" to landlocked Reno County. A. L. Wilson, a distant cousin of Buddy Wilson's and a leading Hutchinson jeweler, stocked the county's only complete inventory of Columbia records in his store on North Main Street.

The forces of nature thus harnessed and subdued on the Great Plains, residents looked once more to the railroad for novel avenues of conquest. Rate wars between the rival rail companies had fleetingly lowered the day-coach fare from Kansas City to Los Angeles to a piddling one dollar, and the Los Angeles Chamber of Commerce had recently celebrated its twenty-fifth anniversary, issuing a flood of new brochures to seduce the restive outlanders. The time was nearly ripe for another new beginning, a bid for a world in which the exotic enterprise of Jenny Lind and the pluck of the Kansas rounder could be merged to still greater pioneering effect. All that was required was a new generation of credulous seekers.

Bud Wilson sulked into the probate court office on Tuesday, March 3, 1914, to pick up marriage license blank number 15366. Four days later the document was completed, fit to be filed with the State Registrar of Vital Statistics at Topeka, with all the pertinent information stamped in or inscribed. To wit: William Coral Wilson had been joined in wedlock to Edith Sophia Sthole on a crisp and cloudless Saturday, March 7. The ceremony was conducted at the Stholes' farm by the Reverend William B. Stevens, esteemed Methodist-Episcopal parson of South Hutchinson. Besides being a zealous evangelist with a vast revival itinerary, Stevens was the first vicar in southwestern Kansas to use an automobile on his rounds. Charles Sthole gave his daughter away with glee, greatly pleased that Edith was marrying into a clan of tradesmen prosperous enough to advertise in the *Hutchinson News* yet sufficiently pious to attract the good graces of Mr. Stevens. The father of the bride signed with a flourish on the "witness" line of the marriage certificate. Probate judge Charles Stutton entered his name below that of the senior Mr. Sthole.

Sarsaparilla was served at a sedate house party after the nuptials, but several of the Wilson men huddled with Buddy for a whiskey toast. Normally music would have been provided—perhaps a Swedish hymn from Edith or a quick-strummed round of "Let Me Call You Sweetheart" with Johnny Wilson on guitar and Ernest Wilson on mandolin—but the Stholes wanted no undue revelry.

While the ladies chatted about church matters, conversation among the gentlemen was evenly divided between the upcoming boxing match in Paris between Jack Johnson and Frank Moran, and the Hutchinson High–Halstead High basketball game scheduled that evening, which was the last of the season for the Arkansas Valley League. Hutchinson was a sports-intent town, and the home team had not beaten Halstead in five years. As sundown approached, the men stepped outside to smoke Omar and Sweet Caporal cigarettes, their silhouettes angled against the unbounded horizon while the cow pasture turned an electric auburn.

It was just past twilight when the newlyweds gathered their gifts, bade everyone adieu, and took to their marriage bed. Several of the wedding guests went on to the basketball game, seeing the home team retain an early lead to win 44–29.

The next morning a number of the previous evening's celebrants made their way to Reverend Stevens's church. The central message of Stevens's sermon that Sunday, and for many more afterward, was: "Be satisfied with Kansas. Stay and build the territory. Any grand talk of seaside splendor in California is just idle gab of the grass-is-greener variety. Satisfaction waits in your own backyard."

It was a gospel echoed in the *Hutchinson News,* from the editorial pages to the personal columns, where those back from West Coast business trips were encouraged to contribute testimonials of the correct, affirmative tone. "I'm glad to get back to Hutchinson," one peripatetic native told a reporter. "Things look better here in every way than they do elsewhere." But Buddy Wilson did not believe a word of it.

While Buddy restrained his restless urges, his twenty-three-year-old brother Johnny, the shy, sensitive Wilson, was winning a measure of public acclaim. Of the six Wilson brothers, Buddy and Johnny embodied, respectively, the two distinct personality types most prevalent in the family pedigree: the unfulfilled hothead and the vulnerable but productive dreamer.

A locally beloved figure, Johnny was considered a true visionary and a precocious innovator by his friends, and in the summer of 1915 they were willing to pay twenty-five cents apiece for the privilege of a peek at his future. Inside a tent erected several miles outside neighboring Russell sat the impressive result of nearly two years of eccentric conceptualization: a steam-powered airplane.

Devouring every published scrap of technical information on the Wright brothers' flights at Kitty Hawk, North Carolina, while also drawing on the steam-fitting skills of his father, Johnny had devised a bantam boiler apparatus that fit snugly in the fuselage of a one-man biplane. Starting from scratch, the whiz kid of the Wilson clan had built the plane of laminated spruce and reinforced canvas, and had the boiler cast at a Hutchinson foundry. Johnny's firing mechanism was so effective that he was able to get superheated dry steam from the boiler in under three minutes.

The test flight for this sleek invention was scheduled for an afternoon shortly after Hutchinson's Central School had let out for the year, thus enabling fourteen-year-old Charlie, the littlest of the Wilson boys, to help Johnny tow the plane by horse cart from Hutchinson to its rustic proving grounds in Russell. Handbills were circulated two days prior, and several hundred curious locals passed through the wobbly white tent to gape at the first aircraft most of them had ever glimpsed. Unfortunately, a sudden cyclone swept out of the Southeast less than half an hour before the scheduled test flight, sending the pilot and the spectators scurrying into storm shelters. When the twister hit, the unprotected biplane instantly disintegrated, and its remains were strewn for three miles.

The irrepressible Johnny was markedly subdued in the weeks after the freakish mishap. Financing for a second plane proved difficult, and the work dragged. Months became years. By the time he was prepared to build the second, much-refined prototype, it was April 1917, and the United States had entered the Great War; the whole world was gripped by a far more sinister whirlwind as America joined its allies to stem Germany's imperialistic designs.

Buddy Wilson was exempt from the draft, being the sole support of a pregnant wife and two young children. Of the other five brothers, Johnny enlisted first, on October 12, 1917, in Chicago, becoming a private first class in the aviation reserves. The blue-eyed, caramel-haired, five-foot-four recruit was sent to the School of Naval Aeronautics in Berkeley, California. Confronted less than a month later with the fiercely determined but under-experienced aviator, his commanding officer, First Lieutenant Milton N. Williams, pronounced Johnny in "good" physical condition and of "excellent" character, but scrawled "service no longer required" on his honorable discharge papers and sent him back home with $146.28 from the paymaster. Undeterred, Johnny reenlisted back in Kansas on May 27, 1918, and was assigned to Company C of the 339th Machine Gun Battalion. Johnny's eligible siblings, Ernest, Howard, and Harold Dewey (the last of whom had been in the First Army Training Corps at Kansas's Central College), also answered the call, while sixteen-year-old Charlie Wilson fibbed his way into the Reno County National Guard.

That left Buddy Wilson the odd man out—just the way he always liked it.

3
• • • •

Leaving This Town

There are many ways to thank the local doctor for delivering one's second son. A firm handshake will usually do, but if prone to the grand gesture, the proud dad can also dip the smoking end of a fine cigar in aged brandy, set it in the M.D.'s mouth, and offer him a light. It's unlikely he would expect any greater show of gratitude, but if one is really convinced he is in the good doctor's debt, it is not unknown for the baby's middle name to be that of the physician.

In this way did Murry Gage Wilson greet the light at 3:00 P.M. on July 2, 1917, in a back bedroom of a chestnut- and maple-shaded bungalow at 726 Sixth Avenue East. Dr. G. P. Gage attended, and Edith Wilson and her husband were jubilant. Dr. Gage, in practice with one Dr. Hall, had been treating the Wilsons at the Gage-Hall Clinic on First Avenue West since their arrival from Ohio. In the mode of the protective Kansas pediatrician, Gage watched over the family members from prenatal travails to certifications of death. Hutchinson's Fairlawn and Memorial Park cemeteries were dotted with assorted tombstones of Wilsons whom the doctor had coaxed from the womb into their home on the range.

Since the birth of Edith's first child, Virginia Elenore, in December 1914, Buddy Wilson had been spending the bulk of his time away from Hutchinson, driving his Model T Ford back and forth to Escondido, California, in search of a grubstake that might allow him to cut his ties with his father's plumbing concern. Buddy had been present when first son Wendell Sthole Wilson was delivered but departed for work outside the state when the boy was four months old. Only rarely did Edith and the babies accompany him.

The family's financial pinch deepened over the next several years with the arrival of two more daughters, Emily Glee and Mary, the latter girl named for Edith's mother. A little stress went a long way in a man so piqued by his own inadequacies, and the pressure of feeding five young mouths, amplified by his fierce headaches, tormented Buddy.

Edith and Buddy's life at 726 Sixth Avenue East had never been leisurely, but when Buddy was home he would sometimes ask Johnny and Ernest over to pluck guitars and banjos while Edith played their secondhand upright piano and sang. For an encore, tone-deaf Charlie would do his stunt of walking down stairs on his hands. After a drink or two, Buddy would even contribute his coarse tenor to the domestic entertainments.

But the world war brought an end to such activities, and the birth of baby Murry was only a brief break in the somber mood of the household. President Woodrow Wilson had previously been a staunch isolationist, determined to keep the United States out of the global conflict, but now the frenzied pace of national rearmament pervaded even the Kansas countryside. Two days after Murry's birth, Buddy was informed by doughboy chums from Fort Riley, Kansas, that there was money to be made by installing running water in southwestern army camps then being readied to accept masses of recruits.

Buddy saw this opportunity as the means to fund his secret California dream. Convinced he could make a fortune as a journeyman plumber, Buddy took off on a base-to-base circuit that kept him busy—and away from home—for the next six months. When the Second Kansas Infantry marched into Eagle Pass, Texas, a Rio Grande boot camp about 120 miles from San Antonio, Buddy was there to lend his expertise, installing boilers and piping for its shower and drinking facilities.

Meanwhile, Edith occupied herself nursing little Murry and avoiding the *Hutchinson News,* whose pages were crammed with shrill stories of the war mobilization.

"At the present moment, we ask that America send us fighters in the greatest number possible and as soon as it can be done," begged British Prime Minister David Lloyd-George in a July 4 *News* dispatch printed below a garish four-column illustration of Lady Liberty embracing a doughboy, a sailor, and the Spirit of '76.

"For over two years," thundered Colonel Theodore Roosevelt in an adjacent article, "Germany has heaped insult upon insult on our people. Our supine inaction was partly due to the folly engendered in our people by the professional pacifists."

With the Wilson brothers soon packed off to bases in Kansas and Iowa, Buddy's loner pose lost its pungency, and he came home less and less frequently. When he did, the dominant talk around the Wilson hearths in Hutchinson was not of his own journeys but rather of the soldiering exploits of the family's fair-haired star, Johnny.

In July 1918, Company C of Johnny's 339th Machine Gun Battalion was sent to France. After a brief training period in the Côte d'Or, the company was assigned to engage Germany from the allies' position at Haute-Alsace in the Vosges Mountains. They set up their weapons in the trench sector at the extreme right end of the western front, within a few kilometers of the Swiss border.

The battle was pitched, the bombardment incessant, the area blanketed by a perpetual twilight of putrid smoke and ash. When night came, the fear of the young recruits was near paralyzing as they fumbled with their jam-prone machine guns. The easygoing Johnny, who was enormously proficient at repairing the guns, was constantly being called off his post to repair malfunctioning hardware. With no light permitted in the trenches, however, the difficulties with the guns were reaching desperate levels.

The mechanical whiz from Kansas had a practical remedy. Using blindfolds when necessary, he taught the men in his command a self-conceived system for disassembling, cleaning, and reassembling the troublesome arms in utter darkness. The procedure also gave the troops a nerves-steeling drill to perform when they were too pinned down by the oncoming fire to return it. Johnny's strategic gesture was appreciated by the troops, who had heard scuttlebutt that in the Argonne Forest the precious few veterans in Pershing's 308th Infantry were charging five dollars apiece to show petrified buck privates how to load their rifles.

For four years there had been no significant movement, only static slaughter, along the 466-mile slag strip of no-man's-land. On November 4, 1918, Company C, which had lost sixty-six men during the Haute-Alsace siege, was shifted to the Toul-Metz front for an offensive by the 88th Division against the German-held town of Metz. At the start of the drive, Johnny, who had been engrossed in his usual gunnery mainte-nance, was struck by a hail of shrapnel, the fragments of the Kaiser's exploding pellet bombs ripping deep into the fleshy parts of both legs but not hitting any bones. Ambulatory but in agony, Johnny could not be evacuated because of the constant shelling.

Company C had finally breached the German lines at the village of Lagney when the armistice was called; the conflict ended at the eleventh hour of the eleventh day of the eleventh month. Three men from the Hutchinson area died in the French campaign. Johnny and the survivors of his company were resting in the town of Gondrecourt when the peace treaty was signed. Promoted to corporal, Johnny was shipped home in the summer of 1919.

After three weeks in a Kansas hospital, Johnny came hobbling into the Wilson family's frame house at 416 First Avenue West in Hutchinson. He was undecorated save for one gold service chevron, and in the vague but cautioning phrase of his superior officers, he was "extremely shell-shocked."

Still an instinctive mechanic, Johnny found part-time work in several Wichita, Kansas, aircraft companies—the Swallow Airplane Company, where dashing young Kansas aviator Lloyd Stearman was the designer; and Walter Beech's and Clyde Cessna's Travel Air, where Stearman's brother Ivan was an executive. The Stearmans were Johnny's heroes: slim, square-jawed sons of the plains who simultaneously excelled in business, the emerging art of aerodynamics, and the skills of flying.

World War I had transformed the provocative novelty of powered flight into a technological necessity. The army had bought its first air-plane from the Wrights in 1908, but the outbreak of war triggered a military production explosion yielding fourteen thousand aircraft from 1917 to early 1919. With the armistice, the aviation industry saw its fledgling commercial wings clipped. Over $100 million in contracts were grounded, and production eventually sank, by 1922, to a paltry 263 craft.

Johnny told people that the commercial foundering of aviation in the early 1920s had "spoiled his taste" for airborne experiments, but the truth was that planes themselves had become associated in his war-clouded head with unwanted memories of death and carnage.

The industry gradually revived—Johnny didn't. He became a listless presence, indifferent to his postwar prospects in the hangars of Wichita where Beech and Cessna had their outfits. He wanted no job. He took long walks around Hutchinson and was often spotted talking to himself. He screamed in his sleep. The Wilson family was shattered by the deterioration of so vibrant a personality, and his parents even counseled him to reconsider his impending marriage to his eager wartime fianceé, Vale Humbert. But his sweetheart would not let him be swayed, and vows were ultimately exchanged.

Buddy Wilson was in the employ of a San Antonio plumbing contractor when Johnny had been discharged. Buddy's last trip home had been in April 1919 when he and Edith buried their second son, five-month-old Coral Manda Wilson, in a fifteen-minute ceremony at Fairlawn Cemetery. Dr. Gage attributed the death to congenital heart disease; the infant had died on April Fools' Day during a seizure occasioned by acute indigestion.

Buddy avoided the welcome-back celebrations thrown for his war-veteran brothers, so Johnny Wilson was out of the hospital and a husband when Buddy next saw him. The encounter was brittle: The disenchanted would-be aviator was ravaged by melancholia, and the insecure big brother was reduced to curt mutterings. Buddy shrank from Johnny's unsettling presence.

In the coming year Buddy's private wish to sever all Kansas ties became an obsession. By the autumn of 1920 he had fallen on especially hard times, money being so tight that Edith had to break up the family and send Emily and Murry to live temporarily with her second cousin. The forced economic separation of Edith from some of her offspring was a trauma that would leave her guilt-ridden for the rest of her days, but Buddy had insisted it be done.

In July 1921 he left once more for California but sent Edith a note a week after his arrival saying he was considering a search for work in Montana. That August he wired Edith from the road that he was en route to Encinitas to prepare interim quarters for her and all five children in a tiny oceanside hamlet called Cardiff-by-the-Sea, vowing they would never return to Hutchinson again. He forwarded $200 for the train fare.

Edith booked coach reservations for their family (Virginia, seven; Wendell, five; Murry, four; Emily Glee, two; Mary, eight months) on the Santa Fe Scout to Los Angeles with a separate train to Cardiff. The one-way excursion rate was $90 per person (no sleeping car privileges), with children five and under traveling free. It was 6:35 P.M. on a weekday at the end of August when Edith and her happily reunited children chugged out of Hutchinson. The Roaring Twenties were just beginning, but the era would be someone else's party.

The legendary Santa Fe Trail of the early 1880s had extended from Westport Landing (later renamed Kansas City, Missouri) to Santa Fe, New Mexico. By wagon the 750-mile journey to Los Angeles had taken some fifty days; by 1880 the Santa Fe Railroad tracks overran most of the old wagon ruts, and in 1885 the rails reached all the way to Los Angeles.

Traveled by train, the Santa Fe experience remained a memorable one. Edith and her offspring were part of a prelude to a slight 1922 recovery in passenger traffic on the predominantly freight-heavy railway, and their journey took roughly seventy hours.

The Santa Fe experience got underway even before the train left the station, beginning with the multigabled hotel-restaurant that graced the Hutchinson depot. The three-story Bisonte Hotel–Harvey House was a branch of the national Harvey Restaurant organization established in Topeka, Kansas, in 1876, itself a commercial improvement on the nation's urban lunchroom syndicates (Thompson's, Child's, Waldorf Lunch). While prices were reasonable, the Bisonte-Harvey's timbered rooms, silverplate and linen, and assiduous staff had a graciousness that put the town's recently erected Hotel Stamey on Fifth and Main to shame. John Philip Sousa, Theodore Roosevelt, and President William Howard Taft praised the Bisonte-Harvey's wide stairways and soothing fireplaces, and William Jennings Bryan lost his collar button beneath one of its beds.

On the day of their departure Edith treated herself and the children to tea, milk, and biscuits in the restaurant while waiting for the train, and the calming effect the inn had on her nervous little party was further proof of Frederick Henry Harvey's genius in standardizing the service in his forty-odd station-side dining rooms, which were staffed by primly uniformed "Harvey Girls." Throughout the franchise, from its alcove coffee shops to its capacious dining halls, there shone an understanding of the security and dependability a traveler craves.

While most of the riding population was simply enjoying the pleasures of peacetime "normalcy," the Santa Fe Railway had a specific objective in mind. The City of Los Angeles's population had swollen from 100,000 in 1900 to 500,000 in 1920 (with 900,000 in all of L.A. County), and the rail firm sought to entice as many more pilgrims to the palms as possible. "Ever see Los Angeles, Pasadena, Long Beach, Santa Monica, Catalina, or San Diego?" asked the Santa Fe Excursions placards posted in the coach sections. "Or Hollywood's movie studios? Ever hear the concerts in the new Hollywood Bowl or the mission bells at sunset?"

Edith Wilson had never before sat in the day coach of a steam locomotive (where she would have to remain, toddlers at hand, for the bulk of three days), nor had she broken bread at a table set by any other than blood relations. As the Santa Fe Scout exited Hutchinson with Edith and her offspring aboard, little Murry and the other children clustered around her tense form and watched new worlds whizzing by in a disorienting jumble. Edith cradled the infant Mary and explained the fleeting panorama as best she could.

But when her kids asked about their ultimate destination—and inquired if they would once again be split up to live in other households—a momentarily panic-stricken Edith could only shrug and repeat the few gruffly barked details her husband Buddy had provided. The most graphic advance information came from a treasured photograph that showed William Henry Wilson's old grape ranch, its neatly pruned groves fanned out before the eucalyptus-studded ridges of the Hog's Back Foothills. Tinted the dull brown of a sycamore branch, the picture had a look less tropical than biblical; it evoked the bulrushes and papyrus fields of Moses' time, resembling etchings in the new hymnals the Reverend Abel had obtained for the First Methodist-Episcopal choir.

Surveying the terrain as it sped by, Edith realized there would be no more choir practice with Reverend Abel, no more comforting "Kansas is best" sermons from Reverend Stevens. The other America she was entering was a harsh, competitive place, full of other people's ideas of right and wrong, quite different from the Eden of fatted steers and flowering pastures that Charles and August Sthole had once envisioned the New World to be. Edith's father had always steadfastly insisted that he had known just what he was getting into in America. "You can't surprise a poor man with hard work," he would mutter. But his brother Nils August would laugh low and wink.

The Santa Fe Scout slowed at Kinsey to cast off some mail sacks, and Edith considered the endless and vacant Kansas sod that rushed in from all sides. Southern California, she knew, was unlike anything thus far revealed in either Grandpa Wilson's photograph or the train windows. Edith was not a patient woman, but she sighed deeply, arranged her anxious brood around her, and prayed them all to sleep.

The alterations in the scenery were subtle as the train rumbled and swayed its way to Dodge City, Kansas, called "the wickedest little city in America" in 1875 but which Sheriff Wyatt Earp had helped clean up. Its failings were those of political corruption and rooming house ruffianism rather than the reckless gunslinging of popular fable. At its nefarious worst, Dodge City averaged only one and a half murders a year. Earp himself had left Dodge City by 1879; he was presently living in retirement in the Crenshaw section of Los Angeles, where he visited the movie sets of Western matinee idols Tom Mix and William S. Hart to lobby for bit parts.

As the train moved beyond Dodge City, the hackberry and black walnut trees common to the eastern end of the state blurred into stands of box elder and cottonwood. On the ground, sprays of Mead's milkweed, white-fringed orchids, and ivy-leaved morning glories dressed up the blank intervals of blue grama grass. And every so often there would be a windrow of locoweed, or "marijuana," as Kansas druggists and Mexican cattlemen called the steer-riling but somewhat medicinal plant the ranchers raised for hemp.

With the afterglow of sunset receding on the first day of Edith and company's train trip, the Colorado state line and the Arkansas River were crossed in succession, and keen-eyed spectators on the left side of the coach caught sight of jackrabbits and black-tailed prairie dogs scurrying across clustered mounds of gopher holes.

The next morning there were steep promontories coated with snarls of wild lilies and berry shrubs as the train traversed the lower corner of Colorado. Murry napped in his mother's broad lap as the train negotiated the highlands of northeastern New Mexico and passed through (without pausing in) Las Vegas, New Mexico, where Fred Harvey's La Castenada Hotel was teeming with much orderly ado.

As they barreled toward Santa Fe and Albuquerque, passengers saw a series of mesas shining in the sun, their copper immensity punctuated by tumbledown missions and the ruins of stagecoach junctions. Showing off the Spanish pronunciation, the coachmen were trained to tell riders that Santa Fe, the oldest city in the Southwest, was established in 1610 as *La Villa Real de la Santa Fe de San Francisco de Assisi.*

The sandy barrens were abruptly replaced by forest, and then the train sprang out again into blazing-red dried creek beds, signaling the startlingly steep drop through the Glorita Pass. Murry and Emily Glee squealed with amazement as they pressed their faces against the cool glass pane: Blooming turquoise sage and pink tamarisk framed the snow-capped miracle of the Sangre de Cristo Mountains.

Pueblo reservations burst from the brows of hills and multiplied, many of them ragged rows of blinding peach and yellow ramparts. Stone huts were crowded below the pottery fortresses, each boasting a domed clay *hornos* oven aglow with baking bread. Open adobe villages succeeded the stacked pueblo porches, their rusty-skinned inhabitants laying out baskets, earthenware, and jewelry as pale sightseers climbed out of their motorcars to inspect and barter the wares. This was Albuquerque, the 5:00 P.M. service stop. All passengers were encouraged to step off the train to stretch themselves and enjoy closer access to the painted desert.

Looking up, the sky stunned the midwesterners with its ponderous majesty. This was not the cozily nebulous ceiling that lent Kansas such a strange intimacy. The blue yonder in these parts was a sovereign phenomenon—depthful, unfinished, unexplorable. Hummocky clouds with dove-gray undersides performed a smooth, wily glide, the towered crest of one formation toppling subtly into another. As the thunderheads bowled and listed, they cast huge, fugitive shadows that crept across the desert floor.

An abbreviated stroll on the platform included timid brushes with Tiwa men from the village of Sandia, their braided sable hair as beguiling as the bright blankets they exhibited. Edith wanted to make a purchase, venture a comment, find some way to involve herself in the noble rituals of this community, but she lacked the nerve. The Wilsons were soon back inside the stifling coach, Edith fretting over her Swedish reserve as the train pulled away from Albuquerque.

Porters pointed out the ebony lava beds that were a prelude to Mount Taylor, an extinct volcano named to honor President Zachary Taylor, gallant general of the 1846–48 Mexican-American War. The cliffs below the mountain bore scarlet clay splotches. The land had been stained, according to Indian folk myth, by the hemorrhaging of a stupendous stag wounded in a prehistoric hunt by the Great Spirits.

With the Continental Divide imminent, the canyons deepened and the sun withdrew, and the Wilson group again succumbed to weariness —except for Edith. As crossing-gate bells stirred the post-midnight hush of Gallup, New Mexico, she lay wide awake, suspended in the tireless tremble of the full-tilt steam engine, wanting to assimilate today's sights and unable to picture tomorrow.

At seven-thirty on the second morning, the conductor shouted out the station stop of Winslow, Arizona. Some Navajo and Hopi traders arrived on the station platform, hoping to sell blankets to early risers, but only railway staff milled in the bleached dawn.

From breakfast time until late afternoon the journey lacked the previous day's capacity for fresh wonderments, the prismatic wasteland immutable in its craggy might. The children were bored and twitchy, Edith's erratic temper increased the tension, and yet the infant Mary, who had literally been crying all the way from Kansas, had been placid since noon. (For the rest of her life Mary would detest trains of any sort, blaming her aversion on the trip she endured as a newborn.)

A short 5:30 P.M. stop at the terminus of Needles signaled the crossing onto California soil. A raw wind raked the forked foliage of the Joshua trees as the Scout train entered the mazy rail yards of Barstow. The chilly gusts threw scratchy Mohave sand against the sides of the linked rail cars; animals yowled in the swirling gloom.

The Santa Fe rail system divided at Barstow, the upper leg connecting most major cities (Bakersfield, Fresno, Stockton) of the Great Central Valley before winding through the Bay Area to the northern tip of the state in Humboldt County. The lower rail leg extended into the Southland as far east as Mentone, reaching Los Angeles via San Bernardino and Pasadena before bending toward a seaboard route running through San Diego on the outer coastal plains to National City and the Mexican border.

It was this coastal stretch that would form the last leg of the trip, with the Wilsons spending another evening on the Scout before arriving in Los Angeles at 8:30 A.M. and then switching to an excursion train that entered Cardiff-by-the-Sea approximately at noon. The Wilsons were scheduled to be met by Buddy as they alighted at Cardiff, a remote beach town set between the flower-growing village of Encinitas and residential Del Mar, the traditional site of the annual San Diego County Fair.

With the long pilgrimage near its conclusion, innocent eyes searched Mama Wilson's for confidence and clues. Edith's mothering gaze returned devotion mingled with pity. These children barely knew their daddy since he had been home so little in the last few years. She wasn't sure if the family was starting over or finally getting started.

"Tomorrow will tell," she whispered, patting little Murry on the head. "Tomorrow, and your father."

4

● ● ● ●

Don't Go Near the Water

No fine house had been mentioned; a garden apartment would have been more than adequate, but never did Edith Wilson imagine her family would one day have to leave Hutchinson to go and live in . . . a tent.

Buddy Wilson slouched, eyes averted, and gestured toward the eight-foot-by-eight-foot bivouac pitched in the sand on the outskirts of the seaside squatters camp. It was an army field officer's flax-canvas tent with four poles in the corners, one pole in the middle, and a large flap opening in front. Buddy had bought the tent with wages earned doing steam-fitting work at the Standard Oil Company's drilling sites in Huntington Beach.

No one dared look at Edith, but Buddy and the children knew by seasoned instinct that there was a hellish fury in her gaze. As new arrivals, the six exhausted Wilsons were still covered with a fine layer of soot from their marathon train trek, and their disorientation was acute. An hour earlier, when the train had pulled up beside Cardiff-by-the-Sea's

fine new depot, its Moorish turrets and gold-domed tower redolent of a
storybook manor, the kids had squealed with glee, several asking their
mother if their new house was like the "castle." It was a fair question
since the broad, upwardly sloping eastward expanse they saw before
them as they alighted from the train contained only a handful of visible
dwellings of any sort—although vacant dirt thoroughfares had been laid
out by local land agents in an arid grid stretching past the horizon.

Buddy had seemed unusually gruff as he hastened his family into his
jalopy, but he hadn't made a sound since. Now, as the entire family stood
huddled together on the lonely stretch of the windswept state beach,
Buddy managed one barely audible mumble about the novelty of the
tent's wooden floor before Edith started shrieking.

Later that night Buddy and Edith hollered horrible things at each
other out past the reach of the campfire. The angry noise woke the kids
with a start beneath a dimmed kerosene lamp swaying on a hook from
the tent's center pole. They cowered in their cots, faintly hearing fragments of their protectors' ugly argument. Over the tumble and yawn of
the sea, they caught snatches of Mama's cries, her saying she had dis-
obeyed Papa Sthole to marry a man with no property and this was the
punishment, Daddy answering that the respect of any Swedish *dirtyneck*
(farmer) was worth less than ice water in Alaska.

When the wind smothered the feeble flame of the overhead lamp,
little Murry sobbed with his brothers and sisters. None of the children
wanted to venture out into the night to find their parents, their fear of
being alone overridden by their fear of becoming an annoyance to their
folks—and perhaps finding themselves again placed in separate foster
residences as punishment. So they clustered together to watch the lights
of passing freighters, Buddy and Edith's rantings drowned out by the
ocean and the wind that buffeted the sighing canvas walls of their new
home.

The Pacific Ocean." Those were the first words Mama spoke the next
morning as she stirred water and oatmeal in a tin pot over the wood fire
in the sand. She explained that the family would be "settlers" here, just
as her own parents had once been on the plains of Kansas, until their
father was able to find lodgings large enough for them.

The truth was that no one in the nearby beach communities had been
willing to rent at any price to an indigent Kansas family with five chil-

dren. The only possibilities appeared to lie farther inland, either in garden apartments that Buddy had heard of in lush Pasadena, a prosperous town in the foothills of the Sierra Madre Mountains, or nearer downtown Los Angeles, in a sparsely populated area called Inglewood that twenty years earlier had been subdivided from a portion of the old Spanish grants of the Aguaje de la Centinela and Sausal Redondo ranchos.

Buddy would need more money than he presently had to cover the advance rents increasingly demanded of newly arrived "boomers." Meanwhile, the business proposition that had drawn him to Cardiff— one of the city fathers offering seed money to several small service businesses willing to relocate on the commercial strip beside Highway 101— had bottomed out when Buddy and the town investor failed to get along. There were no other jobs to be had in Cardiff, a residential village whose only industry, a kelp processing plant, had shut down in 1915.

As she stirred the oatmeal, Edith informed her brood in her typically forthright fashion that they would be camping in Cardiff for several weeks, "maybe more," while their father worked laying pipe in the Huntington Beach oil fields, some seventy-five miles up the coast in Orange County. She explained that he would be coming back to Cardiff every weekend, and until then she wanted the children to—

None of the Wilson kids heard anything else, racing out of the tent in a tumbling dash toward the emerald surf. The sight astonished little Murry and his brothers and sisters with the gleaming marvel of itself. *Miles of water. Water that was alive.*

Mama seized Murry by the arm and drew him and his siblings back to the makeshift breakfast table, but the only other thing that penetrated their collective awe while they ate on that first brisk and tingling California day was the recurring musical phrase "Cardiff-by-the-Sea."

Cardiff had been christened for Cardiff, Wales, in June 1910 by land developer Frank Cullen according to the sentimental wishes of his Welsh wife, but the lyrical appendage to the town's title came from another local developer, German musician Victor Kremer, out of enthusiasm for the 1914 song hit by the Heidelberg Quintet vocal group, "By the Beautiful Sea." Kremer also named various Cardiff streets after beloved composers, including Mozart, Liszt, and Brahms. Indeed, if Buddy Wilson couldn't find a house by the beginning of the school year, Edith intended to enroll her older children in the elementary school located on the south side of the ravine known as Mozart Creek.

As it turned out, Edith would spend two solid months in Cardiff waiting for suitable lodgings while Buddy spent most of his time toiling up the coast in the Huntington Beach oil fields, customarily leaving his family on a Sunday night and returning on a Thursday evening. Strapped for gas money, Buddy often left his flivver with Edith (who drove only when she had to) and traveled back and forth by train.

Pacific City had been transformed into Huntington Beach in 1904 in homage to investor Henry Edwards Huntington, the owner (until 1910) of the Pacific Electric Railroad whose "Big Red Cars" currently ran from Los Angeles on one thousand miles of radial commuter and sightseeing routes in the coastal and mountain counties. (The nephew of Collis Huntington was also a key stockholder in the Southern Pacific Lines.)

Mr. Huntington pumped fresh capital into the area's original development group, the shaky West Coast Land and Water Co., and added a pier and a two-story Huntington Inn to a local bluff. The other backers exulted, giving him the local postmark in gratitude. Then, in 1907, Mr. Huntington brought George Freeth, a twenty-three-year-old of royal Hawaiian and Irish extraction, from Honolulu to demonstrate an "aquatic attraction" called "surfboard riding." Billed as "the man who can walk on water," Freeth rode an eight-foot, two-hundred-pound tapered plank of redwood while standing up; this publicity exploit bolstered the opening of the Redondo–Los Angeles spur line of the Pacific Electric.

Surf histrionics and antic socializing notwithstanding, Huntington Beach was a rural community, its citizens' cows grazing together on a central knoll, its tusked wild boars a delicacy for local Sunday supper tables. Despite rampant real estate hucksterism, enough marginal land could yet be found in its woods to satisfy the promotional needs of the Encyclopaedia Britannica, which acquired 420 gully and hillside parcels as free giveaways to those buying complete $126 sets of the home reference library.

But the discovery of oil at Huntington Beach (heralded by Standard Oil drillers detonating a gusher at a depth of 2,199 feet on the west side of Reservoir Hill on May 24, 1920) had blotted the serene tableau into oblivion. That August, Standard Oil had another strike at a depth of 2,381 feet that began delivering one hundred fifty barrels a day.

Then, in November, the Bolsa Chica drill crew's number one derrick on the rim of Huntington's "Gospel Swamps" peat bogs shivered atop a basso rumpus audible for a fifteen-mile radius. In a crackling howl it brought forth a ferocious fountain of crude. The resultant bounty broke down into a per diem draw of four million cubic feet of gas and 1,742 barrels of oil, the latter spouting so vehemently that five hundred extra hands were assembled to construct emergency dikes to collect the run-over.

This third Huntington Beach strike was in a class with the biggest fossil fuel finds ever recorded, and it was certainly one of the grandest wells within driving distance of any metropolis in the nation. An ocean of Huntington Beach's shimmering crude flowed beside an ocean of saline, and Los Angelenos on weekend outings drove forth in their Model T's to romp in these twin reservoirs of liquid cash.

In 1919 two-thirds of California's oil had come from the San Joaquin Valley, with San Francisco–area firms handling the refining. But the brea-smudged torch of oil drilling predominance would pass to Los Angeles in the 1920s, the basin fully equipped for all facets of the industry, and it became the largest oil port in the world. Within another five years, annual Los Angeles oil production would be valued at $369 million, the Northern California vegetable and fruit canning industry ranking second in total revenues. Combined with its citrus crop and its solar hospitality, Southern California had fallen keister over teacups into the big time.

As word of the bonanza circulated, Huntington Beach's population jumped from 1,500 to 7,000, doubling again as speculators hit the beach by the wagon- and busload. Anybody who could wrangle a city-lot's worth of drilling room appointed himself president of an oil company, issued stock, and counseled would-be millionaires into parting with their nest eggs. Publicity went national, and the California oil rush was on. The holders of the encyclopedia deeds did better than many a speculator, reaping dividends of a hundred dollars a month for many years.

Below the ranks of those who had bank accounts to risk, the beach line and its squatters caught the brunt of the obsidian boon. Nature's wholesome playground was put to rout, and a circus of debauchery was speedily contrived in its place. Confidence men and pettifoggers roamed freely in the tent towns; gin mills did elbow-to-elbow trade in public mockery of Prohibition, and gambling casinos were the only structures with an air of permanence.

By day, men lost their limbs dressing drill tools or lost their lives as surface-level dynamite charges were utilized in desperate attempts to stifle well fires. It took twenty-seven men to drill a single well, the teams operating in eight-hour shifts, and it took an average of six months to bring in a well. Most of the drilling was powered by steam engine, and it was Buddy Wilson's duty to serve as a maintenance man for the volatile boilers.

By night, the strains of work in the thicket of the derricks were dispelled by liquor, sex, or grudge fights with cudgels and rude cutlery. Scattered belongings, severed fingers, and worse were known to wash in on the morning tide. Like Buddy Wilson, many men on the rigs were disinclined to bring their families anywhere near the Sunbelt's version of Sodom and Gomorrah. Indeed, the young girls the Wilson kids had encountered while playing on Huntington Beach during several brief visits to see their father were prostitutes on their breaks.

During his weekly Huntington Beach forays, Buddy usually slept in flophouses. The flops rented beds on eight-hour tricks that corresponded with the work cycles; no mattress was empty for more than ten minutes. Amenities were subspartan: one toilet and sink for twenty-five or thirty men. No one washed clothes in the strict sense of the word. There was no time to be frittered away in such efforts.

Excepting his heaviest overalls, any work duds Buddy had brought from Kansas soon decomposed under the caustic slime of the rigs. From a dry-goods store he bought a new wardrobe consisting of two cotton burlap shirts and two pairs of stiff blue "genoese," or "jean" (the word comes from Genoa, Italy), pants—the double-seamed, rivet-pocketed breeches that Bavarian-born Levi Strauss had introduced in gold rush–era San Francisco. Strauss had gotten the idea of the rivets from Jacob Davis, a tailor in the Nevada silver mining fields of Carson City whom Strauss supplied with denim cloth. (California workmen adopted the garb after Strauss's son Simon exhibited reinforced navy work pants at San Francisco's 1915 Panama-Pacific Exposition.)

At the end of each shift, Buddy and his coworkers would strip to their shorts, douse their crude oil-caked clothes with kerosene to loosen the grime, and then throw them in a wood and tin receptacle referred to as the "blowout." The large lidded box was connected to a steam line, and Buddy would clean the clothing piled within by subjecting it to blasts of superheated boiler water so savage they would tear ordinary apparel to pieces.

Permanent relocation to Huntington Beach had been broached by the increasingly lonesome Edith since Buddy had been offered a better-paying position as a junior foreman, but he told his wife he wanted no men over him and none under him. He was "a hired gun," available to the highest bidder, even though Huntington Beach's skilled and semiskilled personnel were a work pool in which even the most adept of independent technicians was expendable. Drillers received seventeen dollars a day; the rest made twelve to fourteen dollars. If you overslept, there was a boomer ready to pull the bunk out from under you and another to fill your boots (often literally) on the derrick platform. Not even in the military camps during the war effort had Buddy seen wage "walkovers" so ruthless.

He told his wife he wanted to open his own plumbing shop in downtown Los Angeles, a proud storefront to rival that of his dad's back in Hutchinson. Besides, the hazards of domestic life on the Huntington Beach dunes were great enough that, if it had been solely a matter of simple hygiene, the area was no fit place to raise children. For instance, the odorous local drinking water was imbued with enough gas to mimic bicarbonate of soda, and it even spawned a local prank. A milk bottle would be filled to the mouth with tap water, stoppered with the palm to allow the bubbles to collect at the top, and then a lit match held to the opening invariably produced an alarming flash. When you can't trust a toddler alone with a glass of water, the local residents reasoned, you're in pretty hostile territory.

Nine weeks of scrimping and the boon of overtime work at Huntington Beach resulted in sufficient funds to enable the Wilsons to rent a small apartment in Pasadena. In less than twelve months they had moved to a bungalow on Stepney Street, half a dozen blocks from Centinela Park, which Edith said reminded her of Southside Park in Hutchinson, site of the old Reno County Fair.

Meanwhile, back in Kansas, Johnny Wilson was struggling to rejoin the land of the living. In November 1928, encouraged by his wife, Vale, Johnny took a job at the new Stearman Aircraft Company, which had relocated to Wichita after a trial year in Venice, California. Johnny began as one of the troubleshooting electrical mechanics in the Wichita factory on East Thirty-fifth Street, swarming over the one- and two-seater C3-B open cockpit training planes that were piling up on Stearman's own landing field at the rate of three a week.

When the wing-fuselage assembly for the popular training planes became bogged in knotty design snarls, Johnny invented what he called a "hexagonal universal joint," a device that also simplified any repair of the particular model. He got his brother Charlie a job helping him install them and then taught Charlie how to wire instrument panels. In the evenings they would go over to the company softball field for a pickup game with the other "greaseflies" from the hangars. Charlie was a solid hitter; Johnny was usually good for a couple of singles, but his mind had a disturbing tendency to wander while in the outfield. One night while fielding a grounder, Johnny hurried to the ball, halted, and let it roll between his legs; he removed his glove, dropped it on the base line near second, walked over to Charlie, and asked him to drive him home. He cried, without explanation, all the way to his front door. "Johnny can't forget the war," Charlie told his wife as they put him to bed.

As Stearman Aircraft's stock rose and production increased, so did Johnny's value to the assembly team. After Stearman became part of the giant United Aircraft and Transport Corporation, its Boeing and United Air Lines divisions came to Stearman with contracts for landing gear. The navy signed Stearman to a long-term agreement for an array of biplane trainers, and the army, the Philippines, China, Mexico, and twenty other countries placed orders. When representatives of the U.S.S.R. drove all the way from California to inspect the Stearman plant, the mayor of Wichita proclaimed what had long been the consensus: Thanks to Beech, Cessna, Boeing, and the rest of the resident firms, Wichita was the "Air City of the Nation," and Stearman was its centerpiece.

Johnny Wilson could have been among its star mechanical technicians, but his mental condition was too delicate; at the first hint of production pressures, he cracked, retreating into the dungeon-dark temperament of his postwar convalescence. Perhaps it was his grinding feeling of cowardice for never having climbed into the cockpit after the war to earn his wings as a fully certified civilian pilot. Regardless, he would experience month-long spells of depression during which he could barely function.

In the interval, the witness Buddy Wilson's children bore to their father's failure to forge a better life in the Southland cemented Buddy's own sense of shame. The throbbing headaches passed on from his father, William Henry Wilson, worsened. What pep Buddy possessed at the close of the workweek he often spent in cursing his fate and, on certain nasty occasions, cuffing his wife.

A proud, loyal, but not easily victimized woman, Edith Wilson fought back physically when necessary, but mostly she responded with a courageous and loving outlook. She told her husband she could contend with earning the household expenses and minding the children's wants if freedom from such stresses might help him find his place in the Southland. More babies would soon come (another boy and a girl), and she allowed that she could manage all seven offspring just as she had virtually run the children-filled Sthole house for both of her father's easily overwhelmed wives. Edith began taking in washing and piecemeal work, organizing chore schedules for her two older daughters as well as teenage Murry and his young brother Douglas. It was her own frontier upbringing being replayed, and the unselfishness of the exertion emboldened Buddy to inch forward.

In 1929, Buddy, Edith, and their three boys and four girls moved into a modest house at 605 West Ninety-ninth Street, a still unpaved avenue on the fringes of Inglewood, which had been the epicenter of a recent earthquake. It was an isolated neighborhood bordered by Hoover Street and the state highway of Figueroa, part of a lower-middle-class strip on former vegetable croplands that served as the buffer between the center of the city and the black ghetto of Watts (formerly called Mud Town).

Edith worked as a clothes presser for a garment manufacturer, while Virginia helped make the rent with a clerical job. Wendell and Murry concentrated on their schoolwork but took part-time jobs in neighborhood shops, and Emily Glee helped around the house. Confronted with this affectionate show of endorsement, Buddy played the stoic, keeping his own counsel.

Pulling on his overalls and catching an inner-city Yellow Car trolley at the corner of Ninety-seventh and Vermont, he would be whisked the short hop to the west- and southbound interurban Red Car stops on 116th and Figueroa. From there the oblong Red Cars, which were fast enough against frisky street traffic to warrant a crib-shaped cowcatcher, would carry him to freelance plumbing stints in Redondo, Culver City, Long Beach, or Santa Monica. En route, he would find himself among prosperous tourists and beaming residents with disposable incomes, the two groups using the Pacific Electric system for picnics, singing trolley parties, and moonlight spooning on the wicker chairs at the open end of the cars.

The commuter line offered three "day for a dollar" specials: the Triangle Trolley Trip, which traversed the Long Beach oil fields, the sugar beet furrows of Balboa, and Santa Ana's almond, lemon, and orange groves; the Balloon Trolley Trip, a balloon-shaped reconnaissance of beach and boom towns (Manhattan Beach, Hermosa Beach, Redondo, and Culver City) from Los Angeles to Santa Monica and back to L.A. via Venice; and the Old Mission Trip, a quasi-historical swing that included stops at Mission San Gabriel and the Ostrich Farm in South Pasadena for ganders at exotic bird life. Besides the cheap day-long jaunts, a swift round-trip to any seashore point was fifty cents.

Many were the evening rides home when Buddy was rousted from a catnap by young couples serenading the motorman with "Ain't We Got Fun?" and "I'm Always Chasing Rainbows." He would peer out at the poppies dotting the ravines in the moonlight and relive his Kansas youth: riding the roller coaster and miniature railway at Hutchinson's Riverside Park, playing poker and sneaking cigars with Johnny in the rear of his dad's plumbing shop, taking little Charlie along fishing to Carey Lake when he and Edith were courting, and the first time he kissed Edith, after borrowing two bicycles from landlord Jim Rolands's son Harry to ride along the dirt highway of the New Santa Fe Trail. How gentle her strong hand had felt when she periodically reached out and clasped his as they pedaled along parallel.

Buddy's reveries would inevitably end in silent rage as he recalled his parents cowing him, assuring that he would take over the plumbing shop whether he liked it or didn't. In retrospect, Buddy attributed William Henry Wilson's own pigheaded insistence on the issue to the fiasco his father had made of the grape ranch: Grandpa George had to supervise the tending and harvesting, showing that in spite of his severe arthritis he knew twice as much as William Henry about farming and improvised viniculture. Generation after generation it seemed the Wilson men would often find a way to humiliate each other.

Lifted from his brooding by the muffled clank of the high-speed train as it approached the Figueroa junction, Buddy's lined features would harden once again. He could have been mistaken for a fifty-year-old man although he was scarcely a year into his forties. As the Red Car shuddered to a halt, he'd step down absently and stride along Vermont Avenue in the darkness, contemplating the careless, unconventional path he had insisted on for himself, while in Southern California he knew he was watching all around him the maturation of a cultural playground in which he did not fit.

The Wilsons were part of the third wave (1920–30) of California migration sweepstakes—that is, the lower middle class. The second wave (1900–20) had occupied a higher rung on the economic ladder, and the first wave had been made up of the moneyed class.

Historian Charles Fletcher Lummus said of the first influx, "It was the least heroic migration in history." They were men who made their fortunes in the East, Canada, or San Francisco. Cushioned by damask and grounded in plutocracy as they entered Lotusland in the 1880s, there were no greater strangers to the steerage rat and the buffalo chip: Judge John Wesley North, cultured antislavery advocate, iron tycoon, and friend of President Abraham Lincoln, founded Riverside in 1870; educators Alfred Homans Smiley and brother Albert Keith Smiley, the wealthy aggrandizers of Redlands, gifted it with a ten-thousand-volume library and the botanical miracle of Canon Crest Park; George Chaffey established the Los Angeles Electric Company in 1884, which made the City of Angels the only metropolis of the age to be illuminated by the clean, efficient power; Yankee real estate syndicator Harry Chandler; foppish yachtsman, sugar, real estate, rail, and newspaper kingpin John Diedrich Spreckels (who "discovered" San Diego on an 1887 cruise); oil manipulator E. L. Doheny; and self-made, anti-union *Los Angeles Times* publisher Harrison Gray Otis.

The latter half of this roll call of nabobs (Chandler to Otis) were the powerbrokers who industrialized the sunny mecca. The personages at the top of the list (North to Chaffey) were social architects of a rarefied sort. Shipping and lighting millionaire George Chaffey saw the potential of irrigation science, hydroelectric power, and the collectivization of water rights in the aridity of the region, and his wisdom prevailed.

Chaffey and his colleagues also believed that the pietistic concord of the New England village could be transplanted *in toto* within the noble arboretum they saw the Southland to be. Thus, they designed whole communities, right down to the stained glass in the granite college hall, and strived to ensure that the right sort of people were installed in them. Pilgrims of all strata poured into the Southland, but the real estate boom did not endure. In four hurly-burly years (1884–88) realtors turned cartographic cartwheels to create more than one hundred fresh municipalities—sixty-two of which vanished by the next century.

Although busted in its expansion, the southern city could not sustain the swollen populace it held on to. The overpumped water levels in the Los Angeles basin aquifer were the most glaringly deficient resource, a predicament that led to the corrupt Owens Valley project. A two-hundred-mile aqueduct was built to deliver Owens Valley water to Los Angeles, with city fathers such as Harrison Otis profiting by secretly purchasing right-of-way land while Otis's *Times* concocted a drought scare. As water cascaded down the sluice of the completed aqueduct on November 5, 1913, the city's manipulators profited extravagantly, the Owens Valley's farmlands shriveled, and Los Angeles received four times the water it required. The flow from the aqueduct, which had been pushed on the citizens of the city by Water and Power Department czar William Mulholland as an urgent municipal project, was relegated in the main to outlying agricultural uses, as the once-desiccated San Fernando Valley took on a lush emerald mantle. Finally, municipal speculators who had purchased 108,000 acres of prime San Fernando property just prior to the arrival of irrigation now saw to it that the valley was annexed to the city. Land that had sold for five dollars an acre was resold at $1,000 per, deceptive investors making a killing of some $100 million over what had instantly become the largest city in the world in terms of geographic size.

With that compulsory annexation, the city's population quadrupled by the mid-1920s, but it gave the City of Los Angeles more communities to tax, more sprouting truck farms, vineyards, and citrus groves, more sprawling flatlands hopelessly dependent on the automobile, and more land mass to subdivide for the third wave of settlers who were now arriving largely by means of automobiles.

"Our forefathers in their immortal independence creed set forth 'the pursuit of happiness' as an inalienable right of mankind," stated a 1926 editorial in the *Los Angeles Times*. "And how can one pursue happiness by any swifter and surer means . . . than by the use of the automobile." The city fathers had expected 350,000 new citizens of Los Angeles by 1926; they got more than 1.2 million.

Otis, Chandler, and others who presided over the rape of Owens Valley and the acquisition of the San Fernando vale continued to reap ever-mounting real estate profits through further subdivided tracts of sunshine imperialism, which the Chamber of Commerce was ordered to populate.

Buddy Wilson was an honest man, but the profiteering so flagrant in the Southland in the 1920s was the sort of windfall he had supposed might filter down into his empty wallet. The Wilsons and the rest of the third wave were not establishing new roots to enhance their ripe years but rather to deliver themselves from a certain dead end.

It was a public rescue effort that provided Buddy with much of his best-paying work in the late 1920s as he and other skilled journeymen were recruited to repair the damage done to the Los Angeles aqueduct by sabotage from Owens Valley farmers. Seeing their orchards parched and their fields reduced to dust because the local water had been spirited away from them, the despairing farmers initiated a three-year (1924–27) guerilla war against the City of Los Angeles during which they blew up remote sections of the aqueduct, opened control gates, and wrecked engineering equipment.

Buddy spent long periods near Sequoia National Park and in the depths of the Mohave Desert fixing what the farmers' dynamite had destroyed. There was top pay for all hands willing to replace the ruptured twelve-foot syphons, particularly since frequent rifle ambushes meant the men had to work under armed guard. Buddy was on the wrong side of a moral issue, with Western film actor Tom Mix and even the *Los Angeles Times* (dictatorial owner Otis having been dead since 1917) expressing sympathy for the farmers, but that meant nothing to Buddy. As in the Huntington Beach oil fields, he knew there were many hungry immigrants who were only too eager to take his place.

Statistically, the third wave was the largest internal migration in American history. Gullwing-whiskered Frank Wiggins uttered the working charter for the Los Angeles Chamber of Commerce when he was its first director of promotions: "The Chamber sleeps not when it comes to keeping the country informed that Los Angeles occupies a most advantageous spot on the map of the United States." Advantageous not only for newcomers but also for those canny enough to serve their numbers' needs, whether they desired cool water from the public drinking fountain or a new cottage from which to enjoy the wonders of indoor plumbing.

Los Angeles was in the business of facilitation. Nobody wanted to be the source of sour notes confirming that everything was not possible in Southern California or that its own few exports to the rest of the nation were problematic or highly perishable. The Southland's bungalow style of architecture, for instance, was applauded and popularized by *Ladies' Home Journal* editor Edward Bok and imitated in such places as Hutchinson, Kansas, where Buddy Wilson had lived in a rented bungalow and where William Henry Wilson now had an enlarged version erected on a site on First Street West as a wedding present for son Charlie.

Praising both the magazine and the housing style, former President Theodore Roosevelt commented, "Bok is the only man I ever heard of who changed, for the better, the architecture of an entire nation, and he did it so quickly and so effectively that we didn't know it was begun before it was finished."

True. Nor did we know the half of what Roosevelt's favorite variety of domestic dwelling was actually about. The bungalow (from *Bangla*, meaning of or belonging to Bengal, by way of Rudyard Kipling) was distantly derived from the mud-and-thatch cottages of undivided Bengal on the Indian subcontinent. In the Southland, these sterile, shoebox-shaped suburban cabins had a water tank filling much of the upper half-story to absorb the broil of the sun. Kansas and California buyers of these often mass-produced lodgings saw them as an inexpensive way to access the airy simplicity of life in the tropics. And being unaware of the necessary option of the overhead water tanks, they believed the abridged top floor could serve as a dormer. These tenants discovered on the first air-less Hutchinson or Hawthorne night that the attic space of their bungalows was more terrarium than tenable boudoir.

Not that Southern California's other domestic innovations were any less dicey. With only a handful of cogent industries under way in the Southland by the 1920s, its work culture took on an improvised, service-intensive flavor in order to attract the patronage of its highly transient citizens. Agentry firms of every description, appliance-for-rent businesses, hobby marts, and swap outlets all assumed a legitimacy any Chicago ticket scalper would envy.

"Send us no more huddled asses, yearning to breathe glee!" pleaded the pundits, pointing with dismay to the advertising sections of the *Los Angeles Times;* its columns were crammed with notices for swamis, psychic healers, interstellar occultists, continental talent scouts, vegetarian cafeteria counselors, séances for starlets, and the supernaturally trite evangelist vaudeville of Aimee Semple McPherson.

Los Angeles's workforce remained, at bedrock, a rational and diligent crew of honest laborers, technicians, executives, and creative artists longing for credible transcendence. But as the 1930s approached, Buddy Wilson had to accept the fact that he would never surpass the modest strides of his parents. If anything, he was carrying on the rootless, wayfaring tradition of the Wilson ancestry, his plumbing talents making him seem, if only to himself, like an old-world street tinker. He grew bitter and more unpredictable.

Shortly after the move to the house on West Ninety-ninth Street, Buddy threatened his brother Charlie back in Hutchinson with physical reprisal if he should ever fall out of touch with him. "I'll kill you if you don't write," he vowed, "I swear I will." Yet in the many months that ensued, Buddy himself never responded to Charlie's affectionate three-page missives except to dash off another "Write me again!" postcard. In the summer of 1929 Charlie made elaborate plans to take off from his job as a salesman at Welch's Shoes on Main Street in Hutchinson and pay Buddy and family a visit. He wrote again, phoned ahead, let Edith know all the details of the trip; Buddy was always out or too busy to come to the phone.

Driving virtually nonstop, Charlie arrived an hour past sunup on the date of the long-awaited reunion, only to discover that Buddy had just left, bound for Texas on a spur-of-the-instant quest for work. Devastated, Charlie turned around and drove back home. Buddy never corresponded with him again.

Detesting his background, confounded by the torments of his directionless search for dignity, Buddy Wilson was certain only of the things he didn't want and couldn't stand. Chief among them was genuine intimacy with another human being, which might somehow require him to take stock of himself. Like the ochre plumber's grease that had invaded every pore of his person, Buddy found that the residue of these fears and revulsions would not wash off at day's end.

5

• • • •

God Only Knows

In the aftermath of the 1929 stock market crash, the Los Angeles Chamber of Commerce curtailed and then halted publication of its enticement literature. The basic maps and guidebooks that continued to be printed bore a cruel caveat: "WARNING! While the attractions for tourists are unlimited, please advise anyone seeking employment not to come to Southern California, as natural attractions have already drawn so many capable, experienced people that the present demand is more than satisfied."

In 1930, the Wilsons moved around the corner from their West Ninety-ninth Street house, taking a dark green former farmhouse at 9722 South Figueroa, next to the Ninety-seventh Street grammar school. The rent was twenty-four dollars a month. The move was unavoidable: There were now eight children under one roof, four boys and four girls, the newest member of the family being Charles Sthole Wilson. Mischievous Douglas (nicknamed Skeeter) was the terror of the adjacent elementary school, and three-year-old Jeanne Lind (named, of course, for

Jenny Lind, the Swedish Nightingale) was the current darling. The household budget was bolstered by daughter Mary, who was bringing in money as a telephone operator, and Emily Glee found a job packing bacon.

With entertainment such as movies being beyond the Wilsons' means, homespun distractions such as music had made a tentative comeback. Edith and Emily Glee sang together at a sagging secondhand upright purchased by the mother from some of her pressing and tailoring wages, with the now-teenage Murry joining in on a cheap guitar he was teaching himself to strum.

The 1932 Olympic Games unfolded less than five miles from the family's doorstep, in the Memorial Coliseum just off Figueroa Street, yet the events could have transpired in the Azores for all the adventure it afforded the overworked Wilsons. Sports was synonymous with leisure, which was in short supply in their household. Buddy was a moderate boxing buff, his praise reserved for brawling ladies' man Ace "Wildcat" Hudkins, a middleweight pug who made his name shaking off more pile drivers than he ever dealt. Buddy also admired the determination of "Homicide Hank" Armstrong, who later held the world featherweight, lightweight, and welterweight championships in the late 1930s, but he could never afford to attend either boxer's early matches.

Apart from family sings around the piano, most other recreation was either off-limits or out of reach, depending on the weekly pay packets Edith Wilson tallied at the kitchen table. A life conducted in the pursuit of pleasure and diversion was as foreign to her now as the day her parents recorded her birth in the ledger at Hutchinson's Emmanuel Lutheran Church. But Edith's children were fun-loving and free-spirited in a way she would never grasp; and their pleasures were simple ones. They adored the ocean, having been permanently entranced since that first day in Cardiff-by-the-Sea. On Saturdays, Wendell, Murry, Emily Glee, and Mary would ride the fourteen-odd miles from Inglewood to Hermosa Beach on borrowed bicycles to play volleyball and dive off the pier.

The Depression was a despised blemish on the complexion of Los Angeles's dogged self-assurance, but in their bland and secluded section of town, the Wilsons had few worries about economic pressures being exerted by the Joneses. In fact, it was considered nifty in the 1930s for students and show business folk to dress down in the bibbed overalls and pin-striped denim that were Buddy Wilson's daily wear. Still, everyone knew such attire remained the uniform of the oil field hacks and the citrus pickers and sorters who resided in the city's minority ghetto enclaves, or "jim-towns."

If it seemed acceptable for those well off to be making a costume of the lower classes' work clothes, it was mainly because a new social stratum had emerged in the West that was more despised and feared than the common poor. These untouchables were the homeless victims of the mammoth rural dust storms of the 1930s: Kansans, Arkies, Texies, and, as *Los Angeles Times* writer Ben Reddick coined the prevailing slur, "Okies," who were drifting to escape the soil depletion, drought, mechanized farming, and New Deal crop-abridgement dictums of the rural South and the plains states.

Popular wisdom had the Okies pointing their possessions-piled jalopies toward California because of the state's generous welfare policies. Part malicious myth, part patrician lie, it obscured the well-documented reality that Okies accepted government relief only during February when seasonally dormant farmland offered no labor opportunities. Nor did Okies affiliate with the labor movements among farm workers during the dust bowl diaspora; most were too impoverished to organize around concepts more lofty than survival.

With the high degree of economic and regionalist bigotry in the air, the Wilsons were not alone in harboring second thoughts about strong affiliations with their place of origin. Edith Wilson's pride resided in the fact that the Stholes had come from titled land; even though she couldn't correctly spell Skruvshult or explain the precise location of Högsby, her grandfather's parcel was part of a foundation of self-esteem upon which she laid any other small gains.

Sadly, the Stholes still in Kansas were stalled at the tenant farm level: Her brother Garnet leased his acreage from the second generation of the wealthy Roland family, longtime Hutchinson landlords. It was honorable work, but it was a form of borrowing, a livelihood largely pledged to another, a fate the steel-willed Adolf Stal would have been loath to countenance.

Of the 500,000 disfranchised tenant farmers and jobless agricultural laborers who worked their way west picking Arizona cotton at eighty-five cents a day or Idaho yams at eighteen cents an hour, more than 350,000 remained in California. In response, the California State Chamber of Commerce united with the Los Angeles contingent in stoking middle- and upper-class hostilities, while groups such as the California Citizens Association generated rumors and canards that cast the Okies as miscreants, sexual deviates, a subrace born of incest and vile transgression. But these were affronts that awaited those who actually made it across the border; L.A.P.D. chief James E. Davis formulated a policy called the Bum Blockade to prevent such trespass.

In gross abuse of the law, Los Angeles patrolmen deputized by local sheriffs interrogated transients at a network of checkpoints, barring those lacking bankbooks and proof of employment or unable to demonstrate "definite purpose in coming into the state." Violators were sent to penitentiaries on trumped-up vagrancy charges. The practice was abolished after the American Civil Liberties Union raised a well-publicized protest (and a prosperous former film director sued Chief Davis after being turned back from the Arizona border because his clothes were soiled; he had mining interests in the Grand Canyon State).

The degradation of present and former sharecroppers was sealed with the ecological blunder of the dust storms. Drought threatened from Maryland to Arkansas in the spring of 1930, and then the arid belt crept to the prairie. Kansans didn't fret at first over the drop in rainfall, dry spells being expected every quarter-century, with some parched pockets along the way. But sandy walls of wind-whipped loam, lifted into the airstream with such truculence that they blocked the sun in Buffalo and draped New York in a dull haze, revealed a coming debacle of biblical proportions.

Kansas cultivators should have known their tracts should not be overplowed. Yes, the plains were dry, and, yes, there was always a steady fifteen-mile-per-hour zephyr zigging from the South to the West— bringing notice of the belligerent braid of weather fronts ever-present in the region's upper atmosphere. But the windy dryness was tempered by the ancient fact of the grasses—sixty groups of 194 species dating back to the post–Mesozoic era—which brought a harmony of interreliance in the flush tracts of this yawning geography.

According to the natural system of allotment, there were bluestem for the foraging of cattle, cereal grasses to feed humankind, wire grass and alkali sacaton to keep the sandy ground where it belonged, and, when stretches were carelessly bared, the botanical first-aid of woolly plaintain and sneezeweed to damp the dirt down.

To prosper on the plains, one had to honor the absolute supremacy of the grasses, as did the buffalo, the pocket gopher, the white-tailed deer, the prairie chicken, and the burrowing badger. The Sioux nation of the Hunkpapa, the Minneconjou, the Sichangu, the Oglala, and the

Sishasapa also accepted this dependence, and the tribes of the Cheyenne and the Apache adapted in kind. President Thomas Jefferson's Louisiana Purchase of 1803 brought the future dust bowl lands into the United States, and sixty years later the Homestead Act delivered the grim peasant reapers who settled on the tableland. But the Enlarged Homestead Act of 1909, dangling 320-acre shares before each applicant, raked the face of the frontier to the bone.

Mechanization and the outbreak of World War I, which severed wheat imports from Russia, made novice farmers believe, as farmers *never* had in this nation, that the land might make them wealthy. Gasoline-powered harvester-threshers put two dozen wheat-scything bindle stiffs out of work per farm. The Reeves tractor was the Model T of the plains; and the shallow, pulverizing furrows that the newfangled disc plows carved in the soil guaranteed that a natural wheat factory of eleven million acres would be obliterated under a blizzard of black dust.

The spring of 1935 brought abject despoliation to the plains. Reports flew to Southern California and to the house on South Figueroa of the "Kansas dirt" that was fast sullying the country. Sudden dust storms engulfed children walking to school, leaving them asphyxiated in the drifts of silt. Trains were derailed by the downpours of dry soil. Indoors, a fog of dun-colored talc filled even rooms that had been meticulously sealed and shuttered. By noon many days the sun became a brown circle, edged in grizzled white, and then a premature evening of sooty pitch descended.

So thick was the static electricity created by the frictive showers of granular dirt that it shorted out the ignitions of automobiles. Squalls of sand scoured the paint off concrete buildings and the wooden outer walls of homes. If sleep came for the distressed, it was only with the assistance of a damp cloth draped on the bridge of the nose. In hospitals where respiratory cases were taken, nurses waved wet towels over beds in the wards to accumulate the fine silicon. Many patients perished from dust inhalation, vomiting mud before they expired.

Hutchinson was spared the brunt of the most sinister dust gales until the vicious erosion of 1935 and 1938, but that was scant comfort in a state strangled by the cataclysm. Associated Press reporter Robert Geiger, writing for the *Washington Evening Star*, baptized the growers' curse in a sentence of his April 15, 1935, story: "Three little words, achingly familiar on a western farmer's tongue, rule life in the dust bowl of the continent: 'if it rains.' " So "the dust bowl" it became. And when the rains finally arrived, the counties around Reno were so clogged with excess silt that Hutchinson saw much fiercely damaging flooding.

Massive misfortune was not a malleable commodity to be harnessed and bartered like water or oranges, so the mere fact of it was either ignored or rejected by the Southland. Even its own troubles were prey to pitiless dismissal. The Long Beach earthquake of March 10, 1933, represented the worst recent degradation of the Southern California wonderland, killing 120 and causing fifty million Depression-dollars' worth of ruin. But in 1938 when the Los Angeles Chamber of Commerce completed its latest edition of the *Know Los Angeles County* guidebook, there was no mention of the Long Beach earthquake, which had required the unprecedented deployment of every piece of materiel at the disposal of the Los Angeles Fire Department.

The Chamber could not relate the truth of the devastation because it had earlier lied in its literature about the stability of the L.A. basin: "Geologists say that the rock formation underlying the City of Los Angeles is of such a nature that it is as safe from any danger of earthquake as any locality in the United States."

Whether hosting the Olympics at Memorial Park or patronizing the high-seas gambling casinos that began popping up along the coastal waters from Long Beach to Santa Monica, Southern California's citizens resolved to deny the suffering of the Depression, the distant dust bowl, and any other upheavals in between. The sights of the Los Angeles basin's inhabitants were no longer set on health alone; increasingly, they sought the selfish pleasures of sensualism.

Edith Wilson was all too familiar with the trend, but solely from the vantage point of the overworked bystander. From 1936 onward, the local garment industry in which she toiled would increase production by nearly 500 percent. Most of the apparel draped across the steam presses during her ten-hour factory shifts was the lightweight, all-weather raiment *Esquire, Vogue,* and the Sunday supplement sections of the *Los Angeles Times* were hailing as "California sportswear."

The stuff of loose, functional tailoring, bright colors, Hawaiian floral patterns, and vaguely nautical reference details, the clothes were the rage from Connecticut verandas to Palm Springs putting greens. And then there were the form-fitted elastic "Lastex" and "Matlelex" swimsuits of the Los Angeles–based Pacific Knitting Mills and West Coast Knit-

ting Mills—better known as Catalina and Cole swimwear—that fleshed
out the photogenic wardrobes displayed in Miss America beauty pag-
eants and Hollywood films.

At the Wilson house on South Figueroa, an invisible but impervious
curtain was being drawn between the harsh world of the plains and the
hedonistic realm of the palms. Maybe it was the degradations of the dust
bowl refugees' reception in the Southland or a need to lay the more
personal pressures of their Kansas legacy to rest, but the Wilsons wanted
nothing more to do with their prairie roots.

Johnny Wilson was the last Wilson of his generation to immigrate to
California, and it was something sadder than the dust bowl climes that
motivated him to move. During the early years of the Depression, he
became little more than a drone bee within the expanding hive of the
aeronautics industry. Stearman Aircraft and California's Northrop Aircraft were consolidated in 1932 with United Aircraft and Transport.
Lloyd Stearman jumped to the temporary presidency of Lockheed and
designed the two-engined Elektra that would carry Amelia Earhart of
Atchison, Kansas, into oblivion during an around-the-world flight in
1937. The unsettled Wilson seemed to seek the same fate for himself.

Johnny could not keep up with the accelerating pace at the Stearman
plant. Navy training planes were pouring off Stearman's assembly lines
and being flown to the aviational school at Rockwell Field in San Diego.
Johnny's wife, Vale, thought a change of scenery might do him good, so
in 1938 she loaded their things into the trunk of Johnny's Buick Special
Victoria and drove them both to San Diego.

The sunny port city had little recuperative effect on the forty-seven-
year-old Wilson. San Diego was absorbed in dress rehearsals for another
war, while in Kansas the just-enlarged Stearman division of the Boeing
Airplane company was doing component work for the B17-E Flying Fortresses.

Scarred by the machinations of the Great War and now sidelined
amid the mobilization for its sequel, Johnny Wilson never bounced back.
All he would do, his wife told Edith Wilson, was sit and look out at the
ocean. Vale divorced him. The first and best hope of the Kansas generation of the pioneer Wilsons was a study in slow derangement: His mind
was racked by skeletons of biplanes and pieces of men, and the rolling,
fluid Pacific was his only avenue of psychic escape.

"I don't think Johnny should have married and been pushed to run on into his life after the war," said worshipful brother Charlie Wilson, making his halting remarks to a close friend at a Hutchinson family gathering shortly after Johnny left for the coast. "Maybe if he'd gone slow, maybe he could have gotten well. But no one let him go slow, and he's too sensitive. He was the hero of the family, full of ideas and dreams bigger than all the rest of us—especially Buddy.

"Buddy wasn't jealous. But when Johnny kinda caved in on himself and got so ill in the mind, everybody expected Buddy to be the strong one, the head of the family. Buddy wants no part of the arrangement—no part. Makes him so angry, worse than before. And that's how it's all kinda come apart."

In each family there are strengths and weaknesses, the obvious star and the apparent goat. The former sets forth the grand agenda, while the latter tries to avoid undermining it. The rest of the players in the blood matrix do their best to expand the atmosphere of expectation while keeping the whole tribe on course. A family needs to grow up in order to flourish and fulfill its promise. Given enough time, inherent fallacies and conceits are grappled with and dispelled, unforeseen individual merit is displayed, and each accepts the others' contributions.

With most families, bloodlines are the sole constant, renewal through new generations an abiding guarantee. As love and marriage supply new membership, the element of faith can be restored. But without trust and shared solace, the legacy of pain can be inherited—and felt—generation to generation, on and on, indefinitely.

Watching the torrid steam ooze from her presser in the garment mill, Edith Wilson's eyes often stung from the sizing chemicals that seethed from the colorful fabrics she would never wear, each outfit creased, wrapped, and shipped to consumers she lacked the energy to envy. The 1930s were culminating in fresh familial qualms and quandaries for the Wilsons, and as Edith pondered Buddy's brutality and self-torment, she asked herself if her own children would come to naught in America.

At the moment, eldest boy Wendell was even-tempered, reliable, and considerate—and forever fiddling with an old jalopy on blocks in the backyard, unable to get it running. Wendell had no zest for feats greater than happy self-absorption. Mary Wilson was the most outgoing of the younger children. In the streets of Inglewood she was known as a reckless roller skater who regularly hitched a tow by holding on to the backs of city buses. An amateur poet and a natural if nonchalant athlete, Mary

excelled at basketball, volleyball, and swimming. Her best friend at Bret
Harte Junior High was another promising swimmer named Esther Williams. "She taught me to swim properly, and I taught her to dive," Mary
would tell friends, laughing. Mary graduated from Bret Harte with more
athletic points than anyone in the previous history of the school.

Soon after entering George Washington High School at 180th and
Denker, Mary also revealed a gift for music, appearing in several operet-
tas with her sister Emily Glee. And while she never learned to play piano
as beautifully as her mother, Mary would sometimes perform "The
Moonlight Sonata" during family recitals. This was usually after Edith
Wilson had joined her coloratura with Buddy's tenor on the big 1922 hit
"I Dream of Jeannie with the Light Brown Hair," Buddy doing his best to
approximate the brassy concert tenor of Lambert Murphy, who had
made the song famous, while Edith accompanied him on the keyboard.

Yet, to Edith's mind, second son Murry held the most promise of her
brood. Like his brother Doug, he was good at sports, mainly football and
baseball, and he also had musical talent and the performing instincts of
an innate ham. But most of all, unlike the lighthearted Mary or the
poised and elegant Glee (as she was now called), he was driven. What he
lacked in personal dimension, he compensated for with an uncontain-
able will. Some saw it as an odd exaggeration in his otherwise agreeable
nature, but Edith respected it as the essential spark that Murry's father
lacked. To Edith, who had known her share of Wilsons, it seemed an
original, uninherited trait. Depending on her mood, that thought was
either a desperate hope or an admission of defeat.

As soon as Murry graduated from George Washington High School, the
strict Edith and the surly Buddy saw to it that he became a full-time
breadwinner. Murry had been an unexceptional student at George
Washington High, brimming with bias and bravado but bashful about
defining the goals underlying his impulses. Murry's mixed extraction had
produced a profile and bearing more solid than the man behind them:
The boxy Irish jaw and regal Scottish nose of the Wilson profile had fused
agreeably with the slender lips and husky build of his Sthole ancestry.
But he'd also inherited the same inferiorities.

For the last two years Murry had held a staff post with the Southern
California Gas Company, a subsidiary since 1890 of the Pacific Lighting
Corporation of San Francisco. The company had begun by selling gas

manufactured from resinous asphaltum, then switched to an oil deriva-
tive. The biggest users of what detractors termed the "noxious, offensive,
unwholesome, and discoloring gases" were saloons. When Thomas Edison's electric light was introduced in 1880, manufactured gas's prospects
as a domestic fuel appeared precarious. The detection of a tremendous
natural gas field beneath the Buena Vista hills beyond Bakersfield induced a conversion by Southern California Gas to the natural, odorless,
and colorless product, which boasted double the heating efficiency of
manufactured gas. Otherwise, that heating value would have spelled less
long-term profits for the company. But the intrepid conversion to the
new fuel was so expensive that Southern California Gas executives
risked their personal credit to get over the hump.

The gas distributor's field representatives were known in the 1920s
and 1930s for their rather disheveled look because the management was
unable to supply the harried staff with proper uniforms. The Long Beach
earthquake was the penultimate ordeal for the temporarily overextended
company—seventy-two hours of nonstop repairs for an already insolvent
clientele. As Murry assumed his clerk's post in 1936, the Depression had
so badly straitened customers that the service force was reduced to collecting only one dollar weekly from subscribers, rather than strike the
bulk of them from its rolls. It was not a plum position for a young fellow
in any kind of hurry.

Murry adored acceptance and affirmation, his critical faculties going
the way of his defective eyesight whenever in the company of a supporter. Sensing a receptive ear, he would push a palm across his Bryl-
creemed widow's peak, tap his gold wire-rimmed spectacles hard against
his bushy eyebrows, and begin gabbing with narrow-minded abandon.

His right eye had a nervous, boyish squint—not much removed from
a grimace—that surfaced when he was the object of a joke, affectionate
or otherwise. It was accompanied by a flinched cock of the head as if
alert to the possibility of a sudden swat. The mannerisms were owed to
the tyrannical teasing he received from his father. Buddy would sometimes punctuate his tart humor with a hasty slap, a "love tap," that
alcohol or general distemper could intensify.

Murry was sincere, and that was his key compensation. If Murry was
not a font of ideas, he was no slouch at appreciating the insights of
others. His blanket refusal to admit his own flagrant flaws bred a certain
obnoxiousness, however, because Murry was equally attuned to rejection.

Often those outside the household found these overweening urges of Murry's tiresome, but Audree Neva Korthof was not one of them. A bubbly young woman with wire-rimmed eyeglasses that matched Murry's, she saw virtue and a measure of gallantry in his garrulous manner. And she thought that he might be an antidote to the backward Netherlands conservatism by which she had been reared.

Audree was born September 28, 1917, at the family home on 3301 Grand Avenue in Minneapolis's Twelfth Ward, the second child of Carl Arie Korthof and the former Ruth "Betty" Finney. Audree was descended from Dutch immigrant farmer Aart Arie Korthof, who at the age of nineteen left Amsterdam aboard the liner S.S. *Anchoria* with one piece of luggage. Aart Korthof was one of eight hundred other third-class passengers on the three-masted, one-funnel, 4,168-ton vessel then entering its tenth year of transatlantic service, and he arrived in New York City on August 5, 1885. Aart wed the previously married Amalia Pregnitz Henning (she had outlived her first husband) in 1889 in Minnesota and renounced his allegiance to the king of Holland on October 25, 1894, to become an American citizen.

The professions of shopkeeper and retail salesman were dominant in both the Korthof and Henning families as they moved across the unbroken flatlands of Renville and Hennepin Counties establishing emporiums in the farming villages of Renville and Beaver Falls, where the father of Aart Korthof's wife had opened the town's first general store.

Audree's dad, Carl Arie Korthof, was born March 24, 1897, in Renville. He had a severe bout of rheumatic fever at the age of twelve, and the inflammatory heart disease nearly killed him. Carl hid his infirmities, and World War I accepted his service; afterward, he suffered the war-exacerbated disorders of the damaging ailment.

Like his father, Carl Korthof dabbled in a dozen different livelihoods (travel agent, night watchman, machinist, ad salesman for the *Minneapolis Tribune*, delivery man for the Purity Baking Co., clerk for the Gulf-Central-Canadian Construction Co., driver for the Phoenix Laundry), changing jobs and addresses thirteen times between Audree's birth and his decision in 1927 to take the family west. In the spring of 1928 the Korthofs rented at 1420½ West Fifty-second Street in Los Angeles, and Carl resumed employment as a salesman.

In the mid-1930s the family jumped to better quarters at 1829 West Eighty-fourth Street near the Inglewood town line. Carl's brother Chester, a baker, had also come to the California sun, getting a house in the Ladera Heights section of Los Angeles. By the late 1930s, Carl Sr., Carl Jr., and Uncle Chester Korthof had joined forces to run the Mary Jane Bakery in central Los Angeles. They often complained of having to run their ovens around the clock, but even during the Depression they held their own economically, a circumstance that reinforced their orthodox view of the world.

Audree expected no more from Murry than she had seen in her dad and brother; but less solemnity would have been a treat. She loved music, had been a member of the George Washington High dramatic society and glee club, and wanted a partner to share the gaiety and jocularity for which her solemn upbringing had bred a real hunger. Murry understood this, made common cause with her enthusiasms, and proposed marriage.

Saturday, March 26, 1938, was a typical twenty-four hours in Los Angeles, the temperature reaching a high of sixty-six degrees, the sea breeze a tangy northwest blow. Long Beach Harbor oil wells were bringing in 5,000 to 7,500 barrels on twin shifts. Former residents of Kansas announced plans for their state society's reunion picnic in Sycamore Grove. And Murry Gage Wilson and Audree Neva Korthof tied the nuptial knot, and then took up residence at 613½ West Eightieth Street in south Los Angeles near the downtown campus of newly founded Pepperdine College.

Murry had risen to a lower administrative slot at Southern California Gas when the Japanese attacked Pearl Harbor on December 7, 1941. Two weeks later a Japanese submarine surprised and sank the S.S. *Medio*, a cargo ship, off the northwestern seaport of Eureka, California. Outrage turned to panic and dismay when enemy subs slipped farther south to shell the Santa Barbara oil fields. The navy immediately drafted five Goodyear blimps, familiar sights above the 1932 Olympics and the annual Rose Bowl. The Los Angeles–based *Resolute* airship and others were armed and deployed for seaboard patrols.

Murry's sister Mary was aiding the war effort by working as a riveter, doing the machine work in the wind tunnel of North American Aviation's Inglewood plant for its P-51 Mustang, the nation's best-known fighter plane. Meanwhile, Mary's friend from Bret Harte Junior High, Esther Williams, had interrupted her studies at Los Angeles City College to join Billy Rose's Aquacade, where she had been spotted by an MGM scout and was about to make her film debut in *Andy Hardy's Double Life*.

Audree became pregnant in the autumn of 1941. While California feared for its coastal security, the Wilsons fretted over nursery space for their coming child. They moved a dozen blocks southwest of their Eightieth Street flat to a tiny clapboard cottage at 8012 South Harvard Boulevard. After nine hours of intermittent labor, Dr. E. G. Burrows brought Brian Douglas Wilson into the world at 3:45 A.M. on Saturday, June 20, 1942, at Centinela Hospital in Inglewood.

The Wilsons' first son emerged into a land that had become an increasingly desperate improvisation of an improvisation, a year-round vacation paradise that was on a war footing yet was determined not to break its stride as a realm of leisure and escape. Featured in the Home section of the *Los Angeles Times* on the first morning of Brian's life was a well-detailed hobbyist's tip—complete with carpenter's blueprints—on how to re-create the safety and security of the beach in the privacy of one's own household:

> Because of coast wartime restrictions and safety regulations, even the smallfry may have to forgo his occasional day at the beach this year. . . . You will find that a large, well-filled sandbox, such as the one designed here, will provide many happy, well-spent hours of play for children of all ages. . . . A huge box of sand holds more in store for eager hands and active imaginations than many elaborate, streamlined, and expensive pieces of playground equipment. . . . If you live close enough to the beach, sea sand can be had for your box, or it may be found in many of the washes here in Southern California. Children for years enjoy their sand boxes. . . . Later on, he enjoys making tracks and tunnels, a house or a cave, depending on his interests.

The next day was Father's Day, a moment for reaffirmation and prideful reflection. Murry made the most of his new status, handing out cigars, milking friends and acquaintances for congratulations—but giving his own father, Buddy, a wide berth.

Buddy, fifty-two, was now little more than a hard-drinking ex-handyman with no fond words for anyone in the family circle. He left the house in a huff each morning, lugging a bulky wooden toolbox and loudly announcing that the "damn kids" had somehow made him late for a job across town. At least half the time he was lying and would simply disappear into one of the blue-collar taverns in the nearby industrial community of Vernon. After six or eight hours spent on a bar stool, sipping short drafts and bitching along with various shifts of workers from the surrounding aluminum and glass-brick manufacturing plants, he would head home stinking of beer and bad cigars. Increasingly, Edith would castigate him as he ambled in the back door, shouting that the family would be on the streets if the children weren't contributing to the household by paying board. The length of her harangue depended on how far behind they were on the rent, with her harshest words saved for the days when Buddy had dared to dip into her grocery kitty for drinking money: "You're acting just like a Wilson."

But he wasn't. Buddy was something sadder than the rest of the Wilsons at their worst, and that's what really hurt. Not surprisingly, an occasion such as Father's Day was usually doomed to come off badly for all concerned, and Murry was eager to avoid a scene. His ties to his parent had been stretched to the snapping point in recent years by Buddy's chronic physical and verbal abuse of his kids.

The sorriest incident centered on Murry's little brother Charles, whom Buddy beat so sadistically for accidentally breaking his spectacles that the whole family temporarily turned against the father. Murry had to pull Buddy off the boy and then forcibly bar Buddy from the house until he regained his senses.

Like Buddy, Murry had grown up in hard-bitten precincts where poverty and other barriers to acceptance left no room for nonchalance regarding personal dignity. Browbeaters were not shrugged off, and an adult did not put his hands on another adult without expecting grave reprisals.

Buddy Wilson had become the very thing he most reviled—an unthinking tyrant—and Murry was increasingly forced to trade blows with him in order to prevent greater havoc in the household. For his second son, who loved him unconditionally, it was a ghastly task, and the depressive effects of it would linger long afterward, hindering Murry's own chances of charting an original path for himself.

The *Los Angeles Times* apportioned a generous number of pages to the observance of Father's Day, 1942. Film star Ronald Reagan, in a well-tailored army dress suit, was featured in a pipe-and-slippers-festooned photo spread of celebrities (Roy Rogers, Constance Bennett) and their youngsters. The Reagan caption read: "Ronald Reagan, a father in good standing and a Warner Bros. actor, bounces his daughter Maureen Elizabeth once more before he goes to serve in the cavalry."

The impression the photo spread gave of a stolen moment from pressing military duties was entirely deceptive since Reagan's regimental attire was little more than a costume. Ineligible for combat due to impaired vision, the B-movie actor had actually been first assigned to an Air Force desk job and then to the film propaganda office at Hal Roach Studios in Culver City, where civilian nonchalance ruled.

For ordinary working-class citizens such as Murry Wilson and family, the summarizing paragraph in a boxed essay in the City News section of the *Los Angeles Times* lent a more credible tone to the occasion.

> Today is Father's Day. Without argument he is head of the family today. His character and conduct should make him worthy of that position every day. When he does not have the admiration and love of his family, it is usually because he does not deserve it.

Shortly after Brian's birth, Murry departed the disarray of Southern California Gas for a junior supervisory position at Goodyear Tire & Rubber, whose block-long Central Los Angeles factory had been regarded as an industrial shrine when it rose during 1919–20 on property that had been cauliflower patches. Occupying a huge lot bounded by Slauson, Central, and Manchester Avenues and Avalon Boulevard, the building was another Chamber of Commerce success story. Goodyear was the first formidable eastern firm to construct a West Coast plant, and the *Los Angeles Times* showered accolades on the $11 million brick palace of rubber, capped with a floodlit clock tower, calling it "the greatest industrial advance the city has made and the first step toward industrial freedom." Handbills and posters placed around the city trumpeted actor Douglas Fairbanks's purchase of the first set of ribbed "Quick Detachable" cord tires manufactured on-site, which were delivered to him via the Goodyear blimp.

The fevered, can-do mood of the new Goodyear factory invested

Murry with a vitality he had never known, and escalating overtime demands were gladly shouldered. With Brian and the expenses of the slightly larger South Harvard Boulevard lodgings to consider, the bigger pay envelopes were a godsend. Yet the esprit de corps Goodyear elicited from Murry and his workmates was more than fondness for the paymaster. After experiencing considerable labor unrest in its Akron, Ohio, headquarters during the mid-1930s, Goodyear had resolved to bolster its regional plants by means of morale-minded perks.

There was *The Wingfoot Clan*, a homespun employee publication named for the company logo: the sandled, winged foot of Mercury, Roman messenger of the gods and patron of commerce. Goodyear also sponsored a comprehensive sports and activities program and fostered a policy of promoting from the ranks. And there was more: an intricate service awards association; scholarship fund; and the Goodyear Relief Association, a fund derived from employee contributions for sick and injured "Goodyearites."

On September, 21, 1942, the Los Angeles Health Department found itself fielding frightened citizens' complaints of eye and throat irritations. The problem went largely unaddressed until July 1943 when a spooky midday miasma fell on the Los Angeles basin. Blame for the acrid soup was directed at the Goodyear plant and a new synthetic-rubber factory in a former Southern California Gas facility on Aliso Street.

Between July 23 and 26 the acrid "gas attack" worsened; visibility was limited to three city blocks in any direction. Studies showed that a natural inversion layer of warm air, hemmed in by the San Gabriel Mountains, had prevented dispersal of the smoke stack–originating industrial fog—"smog"—fouling the air. Los Angeles's renowned rainlessness was another factor since the air went unwashed for months upon months. The breezes of the summer were too soft to edge the smog out to sea, and the sun wreaked more biological havoc as it cooked the cauldron of dreggy troposphere. No one, least of all Goodyear, cared to point the finger at the highway-infatuated region's prime polluter—automobiles—yet the handwriting was on the wall: The Southland would no longer be synonymous with health.

The smog inversions had been causing Murry's always sensitive eyes to water and redden so badly, he sometimes found his assistant-supervisor duties in the tire shop difficult to perform, yet he defended the many airborne irritants and hazards in the plant as necessary evils.

All around the basin, citizens' groups began pressing for solutions to the filthy air, but corporate opponents of expensive smog-retarding measures insisted that defeating Hitler and Tojo took priority.

Radios in the barbershops and soda fountains of Los Angeles were synchronized on Monday, December 4, 1944, to the hourly *Times* news reports on KMPC radio, which told of decisive victories in the European and Pacific theaters of the war. Boeing's Flying Fortresses were blitzing Tokyo for the fourth time in nearly a week. On that same day, Audree gave birth in Centinela Hospital to golden-haired Dennis Carl Wilson.

The South Harvard Boulevard house was insufficient for two children; word around the Goodyear plant was that easy mortgages were available in the flatland municipalities five to six miles from Santa Monica Bay. Lying between the bluffs of Playa del Rey and the hills of Palos Verdes Peninsula, this erratically settled urban outcropping was called the South Bay. Its pleasant coastal cities of El Segundo, Manhattan Beach, Hermosa Beach, Redondo Beach, and Torrance offered smog-reduced respite from the Los Angeles snarl, but housing was far cheaper in its more chaste inland townships, such as Lawndale, Gardena, and Hawthorne. After several weekend drives scouting the area, the Wilsons put a $2,300 down payment on a five-room cottage at 3701 West 119th Street in the South Bay town of Hawthorne.

Murry was promoted early in 1945 to another secondary management slot at Goodyear; he was charged with instructing new trainees on the cramped and stifling main assembly line. The increased wages were welcome, but the sultry working conditions were not and the hot-tempered Murry was a poor candidate for teaching duties.

One afternoon Murry was demonstrating the procedure for finishing freshly molded tires, and the perceived timidity of a young novice was trying Murry's patience. Before the two sweating men was a wheel-like rack on which the tires were rapidly rotating. Trainees were supposed to swab the sides of the tires with an acid-dipped pole, the harsh solution acting as a hardening agent. The chore took a steady hand and an alert eye, but Murry's pupil was careless and diffident; as a result the pole he was holding against the spinning tire was slipping threateningly, flinging acid to and fro.

Cursing the new kid, Murry hastily cut the power on the revolving tire pedestal. As he did, the pole jammed in the mechanism and was whipped out of the trainee's unsteady grasp. Flying free of the wheel rack, the stick hurtled like a harpoon straight into Murry's left eye. The pole shattered the lens of Murry's glasses as it plunged into his eye socket. The awful jolt of the projectile knocked Murry back on his heels for an instant, and then he crumpled to the concrete floor in shock, the stick slipping away as blood poured from the pulverized eye.

Murry was rushed across the street to Avalon Hospital where intravenous Pentothal was administered as a general anesthesia. The surgeon on duty examined the eye and the traumatized encircling tissue and saw that the eyelid was unharmed. He decided to enucleate the ruined eyeball (remove it from its membranous setting in such a way that it comes out clean and whole, like a nut from a shell).

As Murry slept, the surgeon performed the enucleation, severing all the connective tissues by means of a pair of curved-blade Stevens scissors. The surgeon knew that the tighter the muscles around the membrane remained, the better the ocular prosthesis (synthetic simulated eyeball) would ultimately behave. A two-metric-inch crystal implant ball was inserted to prevent retraction of the upper lid, and then a clear plastic conformer (a molded insert to retain the size of the socket and maintain pressure to prevent orbital bleeding) was set in place under the lids.

After several weeks of primary healing, Murry was referred to Centinela Hospital for further scrutiny and was fitted with a swiveling plastic base implant for a glass prosthesis; all of the medical expenses were paid by Goodyear. The surgery left Murry badly shaken; since his own birth, he had been in the hospital only twice in his life, having his tonsils removed at age five and receiving minor elbow surgery from a sports spill he had suffered while a sophomore at Washington High. Now he feared the world would view him as a cripple or a freak.

He returned to work at Goodyear in mid-1945, often wearing an eye patch instead of his glass prosthesis because of residual soreness in the socket. Determined to prove himself, he adopted an ultra-aggressive tack. "When I was twenty-five, I thought the world owed me," he fibbed to friends, inverting his true outlook. "Since I lost the eye, I try harder, drive harder." But never hard enough to get the respect he now felt he deserved. He felt he was stuck in his present position at Goodyear, a sympathy case without further chance for advancement.

Murry grew obsessed with overriding the fact of the operation, of the handicap. (Yet he was also unnerved by the complete lack of acknowledgment of the injury by his father.) Impulsively, Murry quit Goodyear and was hired at AiResearch, the manufacturing arm of the Garrett Aeronautics Corporation, located on a former bean field on Sepulveda Boulevard.

Murry remembered how, during his adolescence, his father would sometimes brag to others about how Uncle Johnny Wilson had "done all right" in aviation manufacturing at Stearman Aircraft back in Kansas. Well, AiResearch made parts for Boeing's Stearman division, and AiR even had a snappy logo similar to Goodyear's—a flying "A."

Besides, Murry told Audree, who was soon expecting their third child, it was the wave of the future.

6

····

Shut Down

Murry Wilson had been employed as a foreman at AiResearch for less than a year when the troops began returning home from World War II. Most were ex-grunts looking for a fresh start and some career-spawning education, courtesy the GI Bill, but many of the California boys were skilled auto mechanics who returned with hands-on flying and maintenance knowledge of the most sophisticated turbine and prop aircraft of the age.

Fit, cocksure personalities applied in droves at the personnel offices of AiResearch, Northrop, Douglas, Lockheed, Boeing, North American Aviation, Hughes Aircraft, Western Airlines, Continental Airlines, and Garrett. They were survivors of a necessary nightmare and had the scars and the camaraderie to confirm it. They felt entitled to ignore any changes that had taken place in their absence, reclaiming old haunts and the habits that went with them.

Once hired at the aeronautics plants, the new talent was equally unrestrainable, taking orders from none but their own. Murry had fought his battles and had his wounds, obvious and otherwise, but these young men saw him as a white-collar floor walker who had gotten by in safety while they had skinned their hindquarters holding beachheads. If they had to have an overseer while they installed superchargers or cabin pressure devices in the Lockheed Constellation (the first postwar luxury air transport), they preferred a veteran from the flight deck of an aircraft carrier or the bowels of a B-52—anybody, even an ex-staff sergeant, before a "civvie."

When the closing whistle blew at AiResearch and other nearby aerofirms, Sepulveda Boulevard became the main artery for hot rods when euphoric "tinkerers" with butch haircuts turned gas stations neglected during the war's fuel rationing into peacetime motorpools. Roadsters made the best hot rods, a roadster being an open automobile with a single seat for two or more people, often with a rumble seat or luggage compartment in the rear. A hot rod, that is, a fast roadster, was an automobile of dilapidated vintage, stripped to the rods (chassis) of all nonessential items and with its engine and drivetrain adjusted, modified, rebuilt, or "swapped" (replaced).

Henry Ford's revolutionary 1932 V-8 was the most popular raw material for a hot rod. It had been produced in fourteen different body styles, and its eight-cylinder monoblock powerhouse, combined with the model 40 chassis, made it a highly reliable package that featured low fuel consumption and an unmodified cruising speed of eighty miles per hour. Its favor among the young and restless was assured after Henry Ford made public a congratulatory letter he received from Tulsa, Oklahoma, on April 10, 1934:

> Dear Sir:
> While I still got breath in my lungs I will tell you what a dandy car you make. I have drove Fords exclusively when I could get away with one. For sustained speed and freedom from trouble the Ford has got every other car skinned, and even if my business hasn't been strictly legal it don't hurt anything to tell you what a fine car you got in the V-8.
> Yours truly,
> Clyde Barrow

If it was good enough for such getaway experts as Bonnie and Clyde, the nonbankrobbing portion of the youth population assumed that postwar castoffs of the cars could be coaxed to new peaks of maverick velocity. From the late 1930s until Pearl Harbor, outlying Los Angeles was turned into clandestine speed-testing sites. The tinkerers took the most titillatingly unstructured aspects of speed, privacy, and license and had a field day. Los Angeles was still a scattered collection of satellite suburbs, orange groves, and pinched plateaus, connected by broad, straight roads that were sparsely patrolled by motorcycle cops. But it was in a certain Mohave Desert expanse that the prewar hot rod came of age: Muroc Lake, a remote dry-bed pool beside jumbled rock mesas.

The setting was quite a sight: stark and vivid in its primary colors, vintage California in its spare layering of purple-shaded hills and vast desert sky. Indeed, it could have been a vision from one of the celebrated orange crate label illustrators in the golden era (1925–45) of Los Angeles's famed Western Lithograph Company. Lying 48.7 miles west of Barstow, in the Kern County jurisdiction of the Mohave, Muroc was forty-four square miles of tabular alkali clay. Originally known as Rodriguez, the flats became "Rogers Dry Lake" on the cracked lips of the wagon tramps who drove the twenty-mule teams hauling borax across Death Valley on the 165-mile trip from the Harmony Borax Works to the Santa Fe shipping town of Mohave.

Oil drillers from Huntington Beach heard about the excellent consistency of the mud that formed in the Muroc bed during rainy season and took away thousands of tons to prime their rotary drills. In the mid-1930s, the Army Air Corps employed the lake's east shore as a bombing ground for aerial dreadnoughts.

And then the Southern California Timing Association (SCTA), formed in 1937, made Muroc one of the prime proving grounds for the clocking and speed-regulating of hot rods. Being the agency of record, the tinkerers flocked to where the timing association was gathering the official stats of history in the making. Leaving Los Angeles on a Friday night in their roadsters, the tinks would make the ninety-mile trek to Muroc, camp until daybreak, and then climb into the drivers' seats and "run what you brung" for fun, profit, and spare parts.

From the east, across a perfect saucerlike depression in the wasteland, trailing a fat plume of desert talc, would come the scantest jots of two vehicles, bulleting along with not a trace of an impediment in their paths. Roofless cars, each with the proportions of a brick, one a stripped '29 Model A, the other a '32 coupe, their windshields, fenders, and headlights removed, a tarp tied over the open seats, with a square space left for the goggled drivers. They ripped past at eighty-five miles per hour, the boys behind the wheels grinning mindlessly, a last lunatic touch added by the scalloped "flames" limned from the radiator casing to the brim of the hood. Sublime despoilers of the ancient desert silence, they were raising hell in Hell itself.

Back in Los Angeles by Saturday evening, their hot machines twinkling with a veneer of alkali crystals, the rodders would cruise proudly on Sepulveda and Colorado boulevards, hold timed quarter-mile drag runs on La Puente Boulevard, or converge on the parking lot of the Palomar Ballroom to race their "souped-up" engines while inside Count Basie and His Orchestra launched into "Sent for You Yesterday and Here You Come Today."

Dry runs at Muroc became so crowded that the weekend action spread to the adjoining Mohave lake beds of Rosamond, El Mirage, and Harper. Speed soon slipped over into the public thoroughfares, where style had previously mattered most. As many as four hundred cars would convene at the predawn "shut down" street races of the tinkerers, scheduled at a lonely crossroads beneath a wire-suspended traffic light. Rods were chopped (the top of the car lowered to the hood line), channeled (the body dropped between the wheels), and then dragged (raced on a straightaway from a dead start, usually at the first green glow of the traffic signal).

World War II had trimmed the ranks of the original tinkerers, who took their copies of Vida Orr's *SCTA Scrapbook* from Berlin to Bataan. Their GI buddies from towns far from the Pacific Rim couldn't believe anyone would dare treat an appliance as expensive and important as an automobile with such frivolous abandon.

That reaction, coming largely from regions where hidebound religion, tradition, and power sapped personal fantasy, really infuriated the California boys. Fantasies acted on become social realities, they argued, explaining that Californians inhale this fact with the air they breathe. Their barracks mates, inexperienced but keen to live and learn, were converted, as were the young families who entered Southern California in 1941 to work in the defense plants. Rosie the Riveter couldn't help noticing that the planes she was assembling were sensational-looking pieces of aluminum.

When the war ended, Detroit reverted from the business of amphibious transports, jeeps, and plane engines to midsize sedans and sports sedans, and Raymond Loewy's aerodynamic design for the 1947 Studebaker set the pace with its bullet nose, thrusting fenders, and wrap-around windshield. Thanks to Loewy, the line of demarcation between prewar, wartime, and postwar car models was accentuated, so yesterday's bodies became the plentiful province of the returned rodder, who raised dust anew on all the dry lakes.

Thousands of spectators—muscled gung-ho tinkerers with tattooed arms around their pregnant wives—rode out to the Mohave Desert to watch Don Blair's "Goin' Goat," a supercharged, twenty-one-stud flat-head-powered sprint car, cut the crystals at 134 m.p.h.

During the war, Muroc Lake had become Muroc Field, test site of the Air Force's latest aviation technology, where America's first jet—the Bell XP-59A Airacomet—was flown on October 2, 1942. Northrop Aircraft, Inc., which had moved in February 1940 from the Hotel Hawthorne to a 122,000-square-foot plant on Broadway in the South Bay town, tested the MX-334 Rocket Wing at Muroc on July 5, 1944. Three years later, on October 14, 1947, Captain Charles "Chuck" Yeager lifted off from Muroc Field behind the controls of the Bell X-1 and broke the sound barrier, his cabin pressure equipment supplied by AiResearch.

Yet Murry wouldn't, couldn't last at AiResearch. Despite its strong esprit (the company had an Employees Flying Club) and intensely paternalistic personnel relations program (emphasizing the hiring and rapid promotion of the physically impaired/handicapped, including disabled war veterans), AiResearch was an extension of a clubbish military-industrial subculture to which Murry had no direct entree. He had ignored the war's preliminaries, been absent from the main event, and then miscalculated the peace, being as uncomfortable with the ex-GI talent at AiResearch as it was with him. Moreover, he lacked the seasoned technical skills essential for ascendance in aeronautics hierarchies.

Murry resigned from AiResearch on the same day that he received his five-year service pin, telling Audree that he just couldn't stand to work for anyone else; he was determined to be self-employed and make his own way.

The Wilsons were still bystanders at the big parade, Murry unable to contrive a shortcut into the mainstream, and embittered father Buddy Wilson repeating a familiar pattern by gradually reassigning all blame to his second son. The Buddy-inflicted batterings that Murry had endured as an older boy, the accidental occupational impairment he had suffered during his first adult stride toward independence, and the intimations that he was letting down both his immediate family and his ancestry were all tough to bear.

The two-bedroom house on West 119th Street became redoubt and stronghold for thirty-year-old Murry, and Buddy Wilson was welcome only on rare occasions. Murry concentrated on his own kids and began telling himself his day employment was actually secondary to the secret ambition he had retained from his teen years: to succeed as a popular songwriter.

Unlike Buddy, Murry was eager to include his immediate family in his dreams and desires, initially as a captive audience and then as a captive resource. The degree to which Murry fleshed out his goals through his infant children was in fact peculiar. He tried to transform every quaint babble and snatch of gurgling from his baby boys into songs, pounding a Hammond piano beside Brian's playpen for hours and giving his son the kind of playful pep talks that betray, at best, a budding stage father: "That's my new song! Did you like it? Of course you did! You loved it! Now I'm gonna teach you the words! Someday you're gonna sing your father's songs and make us both famous! Okay, here we go."

An affection for homemade music had always been prevalent in the Wilson clan, but as an outlet rather than an imperative. Audree liked exposing her children to music's pleasures, but in a manner more passive, as when she sang nursery rhymes in their presence or took the boys to Grandma Korthof's house and played her tiny collection of classical and popular albums. Glenn Miller's 1943 hit rendition of George Gershwin's "Rhapsody in Blue," which featured horn solos by Bobby Hackett and Tex Beneke, seemed to fascinate Brian. At the age of three he was requesting the Victor 78 be replayed.

But Murry's often-strident display at the keyboards, which grew into his principal way of relating to the youngster, made Audree nervous. Her husband could not help himself. Ultimately, he had to understand the potential of what Audree and he were creating together, however he chose to cast it in his own mind. On Saturday, December 21, 1946, Audree had her third child, Carl Dean Wilson. That same night an interview with President Harry S. Truman was broadcast on the radio. Friends at work sometimes wryly compared Murry to Truman, a slushy, anxious midwesterner whom few had expected to shine after replacing the fallen F.D.R. in the closing days of the war. Truman had foundered at business and been an unassuming, economy-minded vice president, but the top job brought out a latent sternness. It was "Give 'em Hell" Harry who told the Pentagon to drop the A-bomb. Does a soft man get tough when he's taken lightly, or when he's forced to face his own failings?

"The nation's security depends not only on its military strength," Truman told radio listeners, "but also the physical, spiritual, religious, and moral fiber of its young men.

"Great republics of the past," the president added, using the slightly peppery tone he reserved for pet urgencies, "have always passed out when their peoples became prosperous and fat and lazy and were not willing to assume their responsibilities!"

None of those things had yet happened to Murry Wilson, not a one. It wasn't a point of pride.

The Wilsons had not been without well-wishers and family ties when they moved to Hawthorne. Indeed, the area was leavened with cousins: Burns Luzere Wilson, brother of William Henry Wilson (who died in Kansas on March 30, 1948), had several granddaughters and great-granddaughters in the area. Emma Wilson wed Earl Wiltse, who ran a plumbing shop in Hawthorne; later, Betty Wilson married Ralph Bent, teacher and author of textbooks for Northrop Aeronautical Institute, the company's school for training aircraft mechanics.

Hawthorne had been founded as a land development in 1905 by partners H. D. Lombard and B. L. Harding, whose daughter Laurine named the Hawthorne Improvement Company after author Nathaniel Hawthorne, whose birthday she shared. The land was advertised as a budding community "Between City and Sea," the Los Angeles city limits being three miles away and Manhattan Beach and the Pacific lying approximately five miles to the west. Thousands of flyers were distributed along the coast advertising the sale of lots for as little as eighty-five dollars. The interurban steam train service of the Los Angeles–Redondo Electric Railway was prominently mentioned, but the lack of electricity elsewhere in the area—it did not arrive until 1910—was not.

The town was incorporated in 1922 and hired its first police force; the qualification for the four officers was ownership of a motorcycle. A town council motion was carried for the haphazard tract development to rechristen itself the "City of Good Neighbors," and among their number

were fledgling actress Jeanne Crain; Leonard Slye, better known as Roy
Rogers; wrestler Gorgeous George, who lived at 126th and York Avenue;
and Norma Jean Baker, aka Marilyn Monroe, who boarded with her
grandmother on 134th Street.

Hawthorne Hall (later the Hawthorne Club) off 126th Street was the
scene of notorious marathon dances in the late 1920s; future singing star
Frankie "Mule Train" Laine held his partner up for six days to win a
grand prize. World heavyweight boxing champ Max Baer refereed exhibition matches at the club in the early 1940s.

Forty-five percent of the population had been on relief in 1935–36,
with only minor improvement until the Northrop Aircraft Company rescued the near-bankrupt town from default in 1939 by breaking ground
for a major plant that provided twenty thousand new jobs.

After leaving AiResearch, Murry became a junior partner in a profitable heavy machinery–leasing business that his brother Doug ran, but
with all the light industry moving into Hawthorne for subcontract work
from Northrop, Murry thought he could do better on his own. Borrowing $20,000 against his mortgage, he started the A.B.L.E. Machinery
Company (Always Better Lasting Equipment) in a vacant building at
4969 East Firestone Boulevard in the warehouse and auto assembly district of neighboring Southgate, so-named because it formed the south
gate to Los Angeles from the Los Angeles–Long Beach harbor area.

A.B.L.E. was installed in the two-room storefront; the display area
was filled with new Binns & Berry Bros. high-speed engine gap lathes of
British manufacture that were visible to passersby in the floor-to-ceiling
windows on either side of the doorway. In the rear was a repair-leasing
shop where lathes could also be rented by the hour for on-site tool-and-
die work.

Murry circulated thousands of flyers and brochures throughout the
aeronautics community, and his emphatic sales style was apparent in
every assertion:

> If you have need for a large swing lathe for Production
> Runs, Prototype, Missile, Experimental, Maintenance Work,
> or General Job Shop machining, the 25-inch swing Binns &
> Berry Bros. Ltd. lathe lends itself easily to all of these different
> types of work. We believe that no other machine offers so
> many outstanding features, with such a large amount of tool-

ing, at anywhere near the price, and we invite you to come into our showrooms to inspect personally our machines on display.

Murry G. Wilson, President
A.B.L.E. MACHINERY COMPANY

As Brian, Dennis, and Carl reached school age, they were enrolled two blocks from home at York Elementary School on Prairie Avenue and 118th Street and taken each week to the Sunday School at Inglewood Covenant Church. Audree and Murry were not avid churchgoers but wanted their sons to be reared, as they had been, in a Christian atmosphere.

It was at these classes that Brian's bell-like soprano was initially noted and nurtured, and he was invited to participate in various church choirs. One Christmas, Brian was the featured singer for "We Three Kings" during the Inglewood Covenant holiday service, and his family marveled at his composure as the full choir soared behind him.

His sure sense of pitch was doubly impressive in light of Brian's near-total deafness in his right ear, an impairment detected at the time of the Christmas choir program because of his tendency to direct his left ear to others when concentrating on their comments. A family doctor diagnosed the swelling as a nerve impingement and felt the problem would be corrected by a needed tonsillectomy, but he was wrong. Additional theories, held in the main by Audree, included "congenital nerve deafness" and a scuffle she had witnessed Brian having with another child on 119th Street when he was a tot.

Brian himself believed it was the possible result of a blow Murry had dealt him, a sharp slap to the ear for an instance of cranky disobedience shortly before his third birthday. Brian's two earliest and most vivid childhood memories were that incident (which left a ringing in his ears that occasionally grew piercing when he was overtired) and his own plaintive request as a toddler to have "Blue," meaning "Rhapsody in Blue," replayed at his grandmother's house.

Brian would continue to play and replay recordings of "Rhapsody in Blue" throughout his formative years, but he didn't press the issue of the deafness in his ear. Murry reacted so menacingly the one time Brian had brought up the subject during an impromptu family discussion of his hearing that Brian never again spoke of the handicap with his father.

Come what may, Audree loved Murry—that was the premise under which the Wilsons proceeded. It was the means by which he persisted in the A.B.L.E. venture, which in its best times earned him an annual after-tax profit of $15,000 from rentals of lathes, small cranes, and other hardware. Audree's reflex love was also Murry's backstop when domestic friction he had engendered threatened to undermine his authority.

Although the boys were still in their preteens, they had learned to form a coalition with their mother when protesting the dictatorial rants of their father. "Audree, if you love me, you will see my point and don't give in" is how Murry often pleaded his shaky cases. He maintained there was a master plan behind his every outburst and overreach, and whenever this pronouncement wasn't immediately accepted, he hammered it home with truculence: an object-tossing tantrum, a wringing grip, a hard shove, a punishing spanking, or some combination of these.

Murry showed his love for his boys through music, flattering every warble while footing the bill for instruction, instruments, and records. Brian took lessons on a toy accordion; Carl received brief guitar guidance. Murry bought a Hammond organ, and Audree accompanied the boys in adenoidal harmonies on "When You Wish Upon a Star."

These sing-alongs assumed a formality when Murry's sister, the former Emily Glee Wilson, and her husband, nominal cellist Milton Love, brought their five children together with the Wilsons for holiday parties. The Loves lived in a substantial three-story home on the corner of Mount Vernon and Fairway in the upscale View Park section of West Los Angeles, near exclusive old Baldwin Hills.

Glee (named for actress Glee Starr) had met Milton through his brother Stanley while they were all students at Washington High. They dated for four years after Milton's graduation in 1934, often dancing to Benny Goodman at the Palomar Ballroom, and were wed in 1938.

The Loves were of English-Irish lineage. Milton's father, Edward, settled in Los Angeles, circa 1912, after a boyhood spent in Plain Dealing, Louisiana, a small town midway between Shreveport and the Arkansas-Louisiana border. Edward had lived first in a small house near Eighteenth and Flower and found work at a sheet metal shop on Twenty-third Street near Santa Fe Avenue. He soon broke away and opened his own sheet metal business in a shop at Washington and Normandie.

While living on Thirty-first Street in downtown Los Angeles, Edward met and, on January 4, 1917, married the former Edith R. Clardy, who had been reared on an orange farm in Glendora, California, located in the eastern quarter of the San Gabriel Valley.

Milton was born in 1918 when the family was living on Catalina Street, and he was five years old and attending Hyde Park Elementary School when his father, who was thriving due to restaurant supply work, built a fine new house for his family on Seventy-fourth Street between Third and Fourth Avenues. The house was so far out in the "boonies"— there were only five homes in the vicinity—that Milton would recall being awakened on Sunday morning to the rifle reports of locals hunting rabbits.

The prewar years were a profitable era for the sheet metal business, with U.S. Army camps and recruitment centers in the Los Angeles area in need of large-scale kitchen facilities and custom appliances. Sensing an opportunity for entrepreneurial pluck, Edward Love broke off a nine-year association with the Cass Manufacturing Company in 1938 and started the Love Sheet Metal Service at 1882 West Washington Boulevard in Central Los Angeles. Although the senior Love's education had never gone beyond the fifth grade, he suddenly became the employer of approximately one hundred skilled laborers. Sons Stanley and Milton (who flunked out of UCLA) joined him in the business.

Love Sheet Metal's work for the army led to jobs installing hotel and cafeteria kitchen hardware: steam tables, dishwashing facilities, sinks, ranges, and the stainless-steel facing that enclosed them. Edward Love moved Love Sheet Metal to new quarters at 2438 South Grand Avenue in the mid-1940s, and he expanded into wood cabinetry. Contacts that Edward had built up in the L.A. municipal construction network enabled him to bid on the creation of custom items such as laboratory tables for the junior colleges proliferating to accommodate the influx of students supported by the GI Bill.

Overnight, Milton (who handled the sheet metal angle, while Stanley supervised the woodworking) had become wealthy—and audacious about it—and built his elegant three-story Mediterranean manse in View Park. Yet even as the quietly awed Wilsons filed into the Loves' fourteen-room hillside house, admiring the fine furniture, Steinway piano, Hammond organ, and exquisite concert harp, as well as the gourmet Christmas dinners that Glee prepared as a prelude to their family recitals, there was trouble at Love Sheet Metal. The business was growing too fast, lawsuits and countersuits were erupting between the company and disgruntled clients, and the building upsurge was leveling off after only a few years of galloping growth.

Sitting opposite each other in the vast sweep of the Loves' living room with its spectacularly plush red pile carpeting and rear sundeck overlooking the twinkling View Heights vista, the two families were contrasting examples of the offspring the Southland's third-wave settlers had produced. Since the start of A.B.L.E., Murry and Audree had acquired the pillowy proportions of nervous eaters. Their boys, with their high Swedish foreheads and sharp Celtic noses, reflected the lines drawn within their household. Polite, reticent Brian, the eldest, was tall and gracefully handsome, his wavy brown hair, dark blue eyes, and squeaky voice conveying an authentically engrossed integrity; he least resembled his mother and father. Carl, olive-skinned, pudgy, and pliable, with a sincere stare and a solicitous giggle, was Audree's child. Dennis, sandy-haired, pink-skinned, and freckled, eyes fixed in suspicious slits, his lean physique rigid with apprehension, was Murry's son from top to bottom, a canny amplification of the father's unfinished self.

The Loves had none of the muttlike mien of the Wilsons. Glee was beautiful in a pert, unceremonious way, the right angles of the Wilson visage more relaxed, the lips less thin, the jaw unjutting. Milt Love was a princely complement, his elegant nose and sculpted cheekbones contributing mightily to the comely aspect of all their kids.

Sons Michael, Stanley, and Stephen Love had the rangy frames and reddish blond thatches of the homegrown California WASP; sisters Maureen (a gifted harpist), Marjorie, and Stephanie shared their smoothly planed features and poised carriage. But all six lacked the typically tranquil gaze of the contented Californian. Their eyes, cornflower blue in the main, were disconcertingly cold.

While the Wilson children were browbeaten into demonstrating personal direction, the Love kids were more methodically prodded to fertilize their artistic temperaments. Charm was the ideal, guile the subtext; Glee encouraged the former, Milton inspired the latter. The after-dinner Wilson-Love music performances were a closed competition, one in which each family's musical assets were tempered by comparison with each other, iron sharpening iron. The louder the laughter around the room, the higher the anxiety.

Each of the kids was acquiring his or her favorite pop music role models, Brian's and Mike's being the most influential because they were the oldest boys (Mike was born March 15, 1941). Brian admired the Four Freshmen, a jazz-influenced pop vocal quartet from the Arthur Jordan Conservatory of Music at Indianapolis's Butler University. The group had scored a national hit for Capitol Records in August 1952 with "It's a Blue World," their tight, five-note chordal harmonies making them the Ivy League equivalent of the Modernaires or Mel Tormé's Mel-Tones.

Mike was much taken with black singing groups such as the Drifters, who clicked out of New York in 1953 with the farcical Atlantic Records single "Money Honey." On nights when Brian would sleep over in the extra bed of the trim knotty pine bunks built into Mike's bedroom wall, Mike would hide a transistor radio under the covers so they could dial into the late-night rhythm and blues on KGFJ and KDAY. Love's pop and R&B leanings were reflected in the chorales he led, whether the song was "That Old Black Magic" or the hymn "Come Down from Your Ivory Tower."

Back home in Hawthorne, Murry's own songs had found a few receptive ears. In 1951 he established a relationship with Guild Music, a modest recording and publishing business on Melrose Avenue in Hollywood. The publishing interests of Guild's owners, husband and wife Hite and Dorinda Morgan, were an offshoot of the no-frills demonstration (or "demo") recording facilities they oversaw. Through liaisons with people such as the Morgans, Murry found his material accepted by little labels regularly sifting the Los Angeles studio slush piles.

Palace Records, a tiny Los Angeles label whose talent roster included such minor-league acts as singer Jimmy Haskell and a Washington, D.C., vocal group called the Bachelors that recorded briefly for L.A.'s Aladdin Records, was one such outfit. Haskell recorded two of Murry's composition's, "Hide My Tears" and "Fiesta Day Polka," and the Bachelors did a rendition of Murry's hoedown-style novelty piece "Two-Step Side-Step," which Lawrence Welk and His Orchestra performed during a live radio hookup from the Aragon Ballroom in Santa Monica.

In 1953, Glee graciously organized a private concert in which a hired instrumental trio played selections from Murry's songwriting catalog, the "tribute" culminating in a performance by Brian of a song Mike wrote at age nine about a World War II casualty, entitled "The Old Soldier." Murry had revised the lyrics of the maudlin ditty, his shattered uncle Johnny an unavoidable influence as he recast it as an inspirational poem to a bygone trooper's bravery, titling it "By His Side—When Jesus Calls His Soldiers."

Both versions were sung, and, as Murry saw it, Brian "brought the house down." It was the last time the Loves and the Wilsons paid each other that amount of familial homage. As the Loves' financial predicament deepened and Murry struggled with A.B.L.E., their short-lived closeness subsided. Several of the children stayed in touch, but that association and the individual personal development that informed it somehow remained beyond the purview of both sets of parents.

7
• • • •

Gettin' Hungry

D ennis liked to dawdle by the front door, peering out at nothing for hours on end. It was a habit acquired in infancy, a bid for isolation in an environment dominated by low-level hysteria and irrational regimentation. Long after he had grown to manhood, Dennis would remember the salty metallic smell of the door's metal screen as he idly pressed his nose up against it, gazing outward, watching, eager for any agreeable distraction. He surveyed the light traffic on West 119th Street, spied on his friends and fellow students, cast a careful eye on every female who passed by the stoop, and dared the world to show him something new.

But mostly he waited—for his heart to stop pounding. Long before he had a word to describe it, Dennis was a chronic victim of acute nervous tension, free-floating anxiety that seized him with a force verging on violence. Since the age of three he had woken in clammy sweats, shaking off dreams of pursuit, of dropping helplessly from a high place, of dying, but mostly of the sluggish passage of time. How, he wondered, does anybody fill time? Its sheer abundance struck him as a scourge.

Carl, on the other hand, was customarily glued to the television in the living room, content to forget himself in its flickering scenarios of bliss, sorrow, and adventure. Dennis was his tormentor, envious of his gift for serene detachment, calling his brother "Porky," "Fatso," and "Mama's Boy." Since the three boys shared the master bedroom of the house (their parents having taken another bedroom), they craved their own space. Carl often found distance from Dennis's teasing in a favorite Saturday night TV program called *Hoffman Hayride,* a variety show broadcast from the Santa Monica Ballroom and hosted by "your fiddlin' friend and mine," Spade Cooley, leader of a western swing band. A pastiche of skits, comedy, and music, *Hayride* was bankrolled by the Hoffman Television Company, which furnished TVs "made in the West for western folks."

Donnell Clyde "Spade" Cooley was an Oklahoman who went to Modesto, California, in the dust bowl days, later gaining fame in Los Angeles by fronting ballroom orchestras in the country swing mold of Bob Wills and his Texas Playboys. In 1945 he notched a number 1 country hit with "Shame on You." A year after Paramount Pictures' Experimental Station W6-XYZ (later KTLA-TV) debuted at 8:30 P.M. on January 22, 1947, Cooley's down-home debonair style made him the local station's star, and *Hayride* would remain in the top ten of the local ratings until 1952. Cooley soon returned in *The Spade Cooley Show,* and Carl was hooked anew by Spade's aw-shucks virtuosity on his instrument plus his cute all-girl orchestra, the Cooley Chicks. The normally bashful Carl would plant one foot on a stool to mimic Cooley's fiddling stance, and he could often be heard singing snatches of the star's repertoire ("Ain't She Sweet," "Limehouse Blues") as he poked through the pink kitchen cabinets in search of snacks.

Brian was the most assertive of the Wilson boys, willing to exert himself in the service of any passion. He took six weeks of accordion lessons as a toddler, quickly outgrowing his bantam model of the instrument. Unfortunately, his parents could not afford an intermediate accordion or the more sophisticated instruction he craved, so he compensated by spending more time at the piano.

Plunging into choral singing at school, he boasted an exquisite alto tone and had no vocal insecurities until his classmates began taunting him as a "sissy," at which point he hurried home in tears and declined for years to show his falsetto range in public. Yet he practiced it extensively in private, playing and singing high notes along with an instructional record called *The Instruments of the Orchestra*.

He was a top tetherball player at York Elementary and proved to be a pint-size authority on the syndicated *Hopalong Cassidy* TV series, acting out each exploit of actor William Boyd's Western hero who dressed in black and rode a snow-white stallion. Brian also adored Sheriff John's daily local children's show.

On his own, Brian joined the Little League "Seven Up" squad and found he was a natural athlete, with steady hitting skills and the reflexes of a budding infielder. But when Murry learned of this involvement and began frequenting the games to coach and criticize his son, Brian switched to left field to escape his father's sideline hectoring.

In time Brian became a secret assimilator, absorbing input from radio, television, and phonograph records and then distilling it in the privacy of his room. Television continued to have a profound impact on him, one markedly influential program being *Time for Beany*, a daily puppet show that ran from 1949 to 1955 on KTLA. The ongoing sketches centered on the unlikely bond between Beany, a guileless little boy with a propeller hat, and Cecil, the world's only seasick serpent. In the hands of writer-puppeteers Bob Clampett and Stan Freberg, the story lines were laden with winking wit, double entendres, and parodistic send-ups—all of which the mischievous Brian liked to parrot—as Beany and Cecil rode the seas with Captain Horatio Huffenpuff of the good ship *Leakin' Lena*, battling archvillain Dishonest John. The Emmy-winning *Time for Beany* was droll enough to earn a devoted adult audience that included actress Lana Turner and, in the last years of his life, physicist Albert Einstein. It also helped spark Brian's own sense of humor, shaping the sight gags and ironic spoofs that enhanced his popularity in elementary and secondary school.

Murry's sons had a diffident approach to life, and such behavior regularly incurred their boisterous father's wrath. Living several blocks from Northrop Aircraft and Hawthorne Municipal Airport, their conversations often drowned out by the drone of corporate planes and experimental military prototypes, the Wilsons—at least in their dad's estimation—were in the path of great events, and he demanded they prepare to take an active role in them.

No matter that Hawthorne was still a half-zoned "cow town" without adequate sidewalks and storm drains. In Murry's view, Hawthorne was now a flourishing industrial satellite of jet-age Los Angeles, an emerging technological mecca where a real man could get a head start on all things modern and lucrative. The dawning 1950s were characterized everywhere—in glossy magazines, in video pitches for appliances, in the commercial architecture of the Hawthorne Boulevard shopping district—as a masculine, assertive decade in which postwar American ingenuity would remake civilization.

One Christmas after Brian had confessed a mild fondness for Tinkertoys, Murry responded by bestowing the most elaborate Erector set on the market. The hefty box contained hundreds of assorted miniature steel girders, each dimpled with rows of recessed holes for easy nuts-and-bolts adjoinment into skeletal superstructures. They appeared under the yule tree the same year that Carl and Dennis were given a Lionel train set complete with scenery and miniature houses and station. As the younger boys were regaled with stories of the early Santa Fe Railway that brought their relatives to California, Brian was goaded into building a model for a new airport like the one in Los Angeles from which grandfather Carl Arie Korthof did his private flying. "Build your dreams!" Murry would bellow. "Go on! Do it!"

During 1948 six-year-old Brian had been taken by Audree's father for a series of four coastal and inland flights in his small one-engine prop airplane. Grandpa Carl was extremely fond of Brian, and as he showed the boy the aerial splendors of Santa Barbara, the Channel Islands, and San Juan Capistrano from five thousand feet, he gave the boy his first taste of freedom. Those trips aloft, just Brian and his grandfather at peace in the sun-rimmed clouds, were for Brian times of unprecedented trust and excitement. Brian had quietly marveled at the fifty-one-year-old pilot's confidence as he indicated landmarks below, made amusing observations about the landscape, and swooped down to give a closer look. This was a man in charge of himself and his life, his strong hands steady and his judgments prudent as he maneuvered the craft.

When Grandpa Korthof died at 8:00 P.M. on December 12, 1949, a casualty of congestive heart failure, it also meant the forfeiture of a fleeting anchor and exemplar in Brian's life, never to be replaced or forgotten. Brian constructed his Erector set airports out of respect for his grandparent, and whenever his classmates discussed the latest exotic Northrop test craft being publicized in the *Hawthorne Citizen*, Brian thought of Carl Arie Korthof, picturing him in the cockpit of the magnificent Flying Wing jet bombers undergoing trial flights between Hawthorne and Muroc Field (renamed Edwards Air Force Base in 1950 to honor crashed Flying Wing pilot Captain Glen W. Edwards).

Murry Wilson was a far less inspiring role model: He was too busy during the week to relate to his sons, and on weekends he badgered them into endless menial chores while he lounged in bed with his pipe and his newspapers. He would order Dennis to stock the record player with 78s of Murry's own music, cueing Jimmy Haskell renditions of oily Murry ballads while their composer scanned the *Los Angeles Times* business section for get-rich-quick schemes, most of them related to show business.

Meanwhile, Brian would sit in his bedroom doing his homework, often adapting his music class assignments to suit his current pop preoccupations, as when he employed the 1952 Four Freshmen hit "It's a Blue World" for a lesson in which he had to write out the notation of a given song and then plot out its lyric structure according to singing breaths and pauses.

Murry had the vague notion that his kids could be child stars, and he especially encouraged their enthusiasm for singing cowboys such as Hawthorne's own Roy Rogers. In 1952 during the second season of *The Roy Rogers Show,* Murry presented Brian with a complete Roy Rogers play outfit: cowboy hat, six-guns and holster, vest, and red calico kerchief, as well as a few pointers on the star himself. Rogers's popular half-hour NBC-TV series was set in the present, not the Old West, and after each Sunday afternoon broadcast Murry liked to debrief Brian regarding the significance of Roy's exploits.

As Murry saw it, Roy was a man of genuine ability and enterprise; he was a crack shot, an expert horseman (astride the well-trained Trigger), and a successful rancher whose wife, Dale Evans, owned her own restaurant business. He had a successful singing group (the Sons of the Pioneers) and, as the credits disclosed, he also produced his program! By the time the last notes of the "Happy Trails to You" theme song left Roy's and Dale's lips, Brian was expected to have absorbed some practical lessons in rugged individualism and the star-making machinery.

Brian had a small boy's sense of romance about the Old West but was most interested in that reckless period as it had actually been lived. He was fascinated by tales heard in York Elementary classes of the placer miners of the gold rush of 1849, a statehood-spawning influx of ninety thousand prospectors. Indeed, one of Brian's first attempts at songwriting was a gold rush–inspired rewrite of Stephen Foster's "Oh! Susannah," which nine-year-old Brian wrote in longhand on two pieces of plain school paper, carefully dating the effort May 3, 1952. He titled it "Song of the Gold Diggers."

> I came from placers country with
> My washboard on my knee
> I'm going to California
> The gold dust for to see. . . .

Three years later the Wilsons took a drive up to Anaheim to visit Walt Disney's celebrated new theme park, Disneyland, and the prospect of seeing its much-publicized Frontierland section thrilled Brian. In Murry's care, even an innocent family outing to Disneyland could be turned into a junior achievement seminar as he lavished praise on Disney's power as promoter and showman. Built on an initial parcel of one hundred and sixty acres of former orange groves, Walter Elias Disney's extravagant "leisure park"—as he preferred to call it—had opened to the public on July 18, 1955; its rides and amusements were based on the animation and film characters he had been creating or adapting for the screen since 1928.

Critics of Disneyland condemned its attractions as reductions of romance, science, adventure, and fantasy into soulless promotional devices for Disney film and TV projects—among them a seven-year deal for a Disneyland-centered TV series with the American Broadcasting Company/Paramount Theaters, Inc., the financing from which helped fund the construction of Disneyland itself. But the Wilsons joined millions in adoring this slick mega-modification of the classic carney sideshow.

The Wilsons began taking Carl, Dennis, and Brian to Disneyland twice a year, the pilgrimages in Murry's lumbering 1950 Henry J automobile being a high point in their childhood. Mouseketeer caps bought on the initial visit were worn for the return trips. Carl liked the submarine ride in Tomorrowland, with its porthole perspective on the "polar ice cap" and the audio-animatronic struggle between a giant squid and an octopus. Dennis was partial to Tom Sawyer's Island. Brian was won over by the Matterhorn bobsled ride, Disneyland's dizzying update (unveiled on June 24, 1959) of a roller coaster. The artificial mountain that the bobsled ride girdled was two acres of metal lathe embellished with a three-inch covering of cement, topped with twenty-five hundred gallons of white acrylic resin to simulate snow. Hidden speakers sent a tape loop of wind sounds through the caverns, augmenting the *whoosh* of the sled as it sped toward a concluding splash beside a computer-regulated waterfall. The ride seemed daring, but the Disney organization took pains to reassure patrons that each attraction was perfectly safe for children of all ages. Brian particularly loved the idea of "safe danger" and a controlled experience.

Audree admired Disneyland's extreme tidiness, its fairways and paths kept broom-clean by an unobtrusive militia of sanitation personnel. Murry most appreciated the McKinley-era architecture of the park's Main Street. The Victorian Second Empire styling and Italianate facades of the three-quarters life-size buildings, painted in pleasing pastels, were designed by Walt Disney as an idealization of his hometown of Marceline, Missouri, although for Murry they evoked the chief business artery of Hutchinson. (Disney's father had lived in Ellis, Kansas, as a young man and worked laying railroad tracks across the plains.)

In this homogenized model of the past, Murry could reflect on his roots without the messy difficulties of the actual trek, while envying Disney's sentimental genius for merchandizing.

B rian carried his own Tomorrowland in his head, and it was dominated, like his dad's, by the magnetism of popular music. In January 1955, Brian was smitten by the boisterous "One-two-three-o'clock, four o'clock-rock!" countdown of former Chester, Pennsylvania, country and western singer Bill Haley's single "Rock Around the Clock," which KFWB radio beamed out to Brian and the rest of greater Los Angeles.

KFWB's Channel 98 signal was the city rage from the late 1950s to the mid-1960s and featured such "Top 40 Color Radio" personalities as B. Mitchell Reed, Gary Owens, Wink Martindale, Bill Ballance, and Gene Weed pumping out a steady playlist of more Bill Haley ("See You Later, Alligator," "Rip It Up") and much Elvis Presley ("Heartbreak Hotel," "I Want You, I Need You, I Love You," "Don't Be Cruel," "Hound Dog," "Love Me Tender").

Each afternoon in 1956 after Brian's classes at Hawthorne High, the fourteen-year-old freshman would head to the Gunga Din, a town-sponsored recreational center located on Grevillea Avenue behind City Hall. Open from 3:00 to 5:00 P.M., the Gunga Din held yo-yo tournaments and baton-twirling classes while its big jukebox blared. Admission was free once you had bought a one-dollar membership card. On Saturday nights there were sock hops in its large L-shaped hall for seventh and eighth graders from Hawthorne Intermediate School, with high school students taking over on Tuesday and Friday nights.

The Gunga Din existed for a reason. Hawthorne's biggest woes besides mob infiltration of public works were burglaries by transients and juvenile delinquency—social ills common to factory communities where overlapping production shifts left homes and adolescents unsupervised for extended intervals. Merchandise disappearing from garages, closets, and cupboards was usually the sort easily pawned or fenced or valuables that had hot rod relevance.

Dismayed by the outlaw image being imposed on most reasonably law-abiding hot-rodders, *Hot Rod* (founded in 1947) and its editor Wally Parks formed the National Hot Rod Association (NHRA) in 1950, and the California Highway Patrol sponsored the first legal drag race in July of that year at the Orange County Airport in Santa Ana.

Hot-rodders were strictly persona non grata within the Hawthorne city limits before the Centinela Valley Car Club Association (CVCCA) was founded, circa 1954, to subdue some of the midnight-to-dawn escapades of the "lakesters," as the speed demons who shuttled between the South Bay and the Mohave dry lakes were locally dubbed. Members of the Hawthorne Benders car club were known to engage in illegal races under cover of darkness, but they and the rest of the young engine heads of the CVCCA (the Wanderers, Hi-Winders, Mad Hatters, Rambling Rods) were soon sucked into the disciplined custom car subculture, which favored organized rallies and exhibitions over high-stakes road racing.

Thus, the back streets of Hawthorne became the turf of high school rovers and dropout gear gypsies, and the petty criminals who catered to them. Mounting local alarm with hot rod delinquency intensified in 1956 when the police reported that teenage marijuana use was now epidemic. Most youths were nabbed in garages, smoking what were believed to be "narcotic cigarettes" smuggled in from Mexico. These theories were dispelled as cops discovered more and more plants thriving in backyards. One neighbor of the Wilsons on nearby West 123rd Street was among those taken into custody on charges of cultivating and selling hemp stalks.

Juvenile gang violence overtook Hawthorne and adjoining towns such as Lawndale and Lennox during the same year, with arrests of sixteen- and seventeen-year-old students at Hawthorne and Leuzinger high schools increasing sharply as aggressions assumed a town-versus-town character. Hawthorne kids were reputed to be the "toughest," according to police surveys published in the *Hawthorne Citizen.*

"All these kids know when we arrest them on a charge that we can't hold them," said Lieutenant R. H. Harrison of the sheriff's office in a typical public statement after finding knives, pipes, boards, blackjacks, and an assortment of lewd literature on the persons of five underage Hawthorne youths cruising in a '49 roadster. "They ought to be put in the county jail for two or three days and then let their parents bail them out. It's the humiliation of the parents that could discourage these kids from committing more crimes."

Murry used these incidents as a pretext for a re-creation of the boyhood purgatory he had known. The slightest hint of disobedience from his sons could draw his impulsive pummeling or perverse torments. Dennis disliked raw tomatoes, so Murry would compel him to eat them on every possible occasion, slapping him on the back of the head as he swallowed. Dennis grew so petrified with such methodic debasement that for years he would retch at the sight of tomatoes.

But the issue of teenage misbehavior was pressed most relentlessly with the eldest boy. Aware that Brian was as repelled by his father's glass eye as Dennis was transfixed, Murry would repay Brian's mild insubordinations by removing his artificial eyeball, grabbing a sobbing Brian by the scruff of the neck, and forcing him to peer at the mangled interior of his father's empty socket.

Sadly, much of the hooliganism and youth crime in Hawthorne could be traced to twin policies of repression and disregard that increasingly characterized portions of the thriving community. Indeed, most citizens seemed to care less and less about the actions and opinions of those whose lawns and driveways bordered their own. Overnight, Southern California had been able to revamp its blue-collar war machine into a vigorous consumer economy. The Northrop company called press conferences to announce periodic pay hikes for its rank and file. Nationally, wage earners in the $4,000 to $7,000 middle-income range had increased from 5.5 million in 1929 to 17.9 million in 1953. Food, rent, and utilities were dirt-cheap; the dollar had enormous buying power. Suburbanites like the people of Hawthorne were now 35 percent of the nation's population and drew 42 percent of its salary revenue.

And when Hawthorne plant workers punched the clock at closing time, they weren't necessarily headed home to their trellised cottages. Tattooed bachelors drove to the seven-nights-a-week burlesque shows at The Irish World on Imperial Highway. Good husbands gravitated to the gleaming auto showrooms on La Brea Boulevard to price the new Ford Thunderbird. Wives would be engrossed until early evening in the advertised "Shopportunities!" at the spiffy new South Bay Shopping Center. Once home, it took only twenty minutes to heat and serve the family a dinner of meatloaf surprise and Birdseye succotash—and then everyone piled into the new T-bird to catch a 9:00 P.M. showing of *Godzilla, King of the Monsters* in Inglewood.

Teens imitated their elders' rampant spending. Brian got a job sweeping and stocking shelves at a jeweler's on Crenshaw, but all his wages wound up in the cash registers of Melody Music on South Hawthorne Boulevard and Lishon's Record Store off Imperial. Lishon's featured prepurchase "demonstration booths" for record listening, and Brian killed a week's worth of afternoons auditioning the Four Freshmen's *Freshmen Favorites* album before deciding to purchase it. He had never listened to an album-length menu of pop music before, and the experience was a genuine epiphany. Once he brought the album home, he did all his ninth-grade homework to the nasal drone of "Graduation Day."

The buffed sheen of the Four Freshmen's unique five-part jazz harmony style (one voice would sing the shift notes) was fully realized as far back as the late forties. The original quartet (called Hal's Harmonizers, for original member Hal Kratzsch, when they sang barbershop quartet–style, or the Toppers when doing jazz vocals) had come together while at college in Indianapolis. Signed to Capitol Records in 1950 on a recommendation from bandleader Stan Kenton, they scored a series of hit singles in the early fifties: "It Happened Once Before," "Day by Day," and "Charmaine." When "Graduation Day" reached the *Billboard* Top 20 late in the spring of 1956, the group consisted of founder Ross Barbour, his brother Don, cousin Bob Flanagan, and newcomer Ken Albers.

When the Four Freshmen were booked for a concert at the Crescendo Ballroom, the Wilsons could not afford to attend en masse, but Audree convinced Murry to take Brian, who afterward sang the entire set list in the Wilsons' living room. Carl was less lucky when Spade Cooley headlined Hawthorne Night at the Casino Gardens; the price for even two tickets was more than Murry could spare.

Early in 1957, Los Angeles deejay Art Laboe formed an independent record label called Original Sound, his music publishing being coordinated by Guild Music. Frankie Lymon and the Teenagers were currently a sensation on the national charts with "Why Do Fools Fall in Love" and "I'm Not a Juvenile Delinquent," and Laboe sought a local Lymon soundalike for a song he had penned, "Chapel of Love" (unrelated to the 1964 hit by New Orleans's Dixie Cups, a female vocal trio, on Red Bird Records). Murry arranged an audition for Brian through Guild co-owner Dorinda Morgan, and at home portrayed the appointment as a make-or-break opportunity for Brian and exerted enormous pressure on him to prepare himself. When Laboe decided against the boy's formidable falsetto, Brian was flustered and depressed, later telling Dennis he had to be more wary of their dad's urgent schemes.

As the summer of 1957 approached, the talk among Brian, Carl, Dennis, and their schoolmates centered on polio immunization shots, the "bitchin' " Snark SM-62 intercontinental guided missiles under construction at Northrop, and the "rat packs" of Lawndale kids who were bushwhacking Hawthorne boys. Adults gossiped about Mrs. George Venaris, whose son James—popularly known as the "Turncoat GI"—had apparently decided to defect after being captured by Chinese communists during the 1950–53 Korean War. Parents had mixed feelings about Robert Paul Smith's best-seller *"Where Did You Go?" "Out." "What Did You Do?" "Nothing,"* which twitted those who meddled in adolescents' pursuits or tried to contain them through Scouting or the PTA. And everyone, young and old, was tracking the progress of the notorious "Pantie Slasher," who in the last dozen weeks had been ripping and stealing women's underthings that were hanging on Hawthorne's clotheslines.

But nothing compared with "the day that had two afternoons," as awestruck local TV newscasters described it. On Friday, July 5, 1957, a tremendous multisecond flash obscured the full moon in the Hawthorne-Lawndale area as the largest A-bomb ever exploded in the United States was detonated at the official atomic test site in Nevada. The next morning Joe Roggy, who lived around the corner from the Wilsons on Kornblum Avenue, showed Murry a photo he had taken of the mighty silhouette that the neighborhood's trees, homes, and backyard swings had cast against the nuclear light.

"Kinda makes you feel like a kid again," said Murry, thrilled as he examined the amazing shot of the phenomenon. Several days later he bought Brian a 200-power telescope, and Brian, keeping a nighttime vigil in hopes of glimpsing another atomic flash, instead located the rings of Saturn. He vowed to write a song one day about the solar system.

Meanwhile, something appeared to lure thirteen-year-old Dennis off the front stoop. One October morning in 1957 a furiously puttering vehicle built from a simple tubular frame suddenly materialized on his street. It was a motorized go-cart ridden by a kid who lived over on Doty Avenue. A Southern California revision of the old soapbox racer, the go-cart could reach a speed of nearly thirty miles an hour by means of its chain-driven lawn mower engine.

Since 1955 the go-cart craze had been steadily acquiring the cachet of a national sport, with special cart tracks, a governing association, and thousands of supervised meets taking place, leading up to a one-hundred-lap Memorial Day stampede at Dean Moon's "Moonza" track in Santa Fe Springs, California. Race regulations kept costs within range of its teenage enthusiasts: no bodywork allowed; no fancy suspension or steering systems; tires must be heavy-treaded or race slick (treadless) in the five- to twelve-inch bracket; optional disc brakes; forty-five-inch wheelbase; only chain-driven engines ranging from five-cubic-inch two-stroke mills to the national club engine displacement limit at 16.5 cubic inches (thus permitting some small motorcycle power boxes into the field).

Of the approximately forty makes of carts (among them Dart-Kart, Comet-Kart, Gar-Bro Wheel, Drag 'n' Fly, Acer Racer, Cool-Cart, Go-Boy, Putt-Nik, Berkeley Scrambler, Gooney Cart, and Spinster) being produced between the Midwest and California, the seminal Go Kart Manufacturing Company of Azuza, California, was the foremost producer of vehicles. Inglewood Tire Service's "Pos-A-Traction" slicks were the prime tires for extra grab on the straightaway.

Murry took Dennis and Carl to an authorized Go Kart outlet and bought them the 400B Go Kart kit for $129.50. It took about eight hours to assemble the vehicle, Murry cursing a blue streak as he grappled with the brakes and floor pan. The next day they took it to a go-cart track on Crenshaw, north of Hawthorne, to give it a workout. Carl was giddy as he leaned back on the padded bucket seat, but he seemed intimidated by the sensation of tearing along, three inches above the tar, in the quivering conveyance. Dennis had no qualms about the cart or its horsepower, zipping into the tight curves with an open throttle. He loved to make the cart fishtail on the turns and to roar past Murry whenever his parent scolded him for his recklessness, pretending he couldn't decipher Murry's screams over the engine's rumpus.

Known throughout the neighborhood as "Dennis the Menace," Denny had a well-earned reputation as a screwup and prankster. There was no malice in his stunts, though they became his way of responding to authoritarianism and blatant unfairness. With Brian the brightest light among the brothers and Carl the blameless babe, it was inevitable that Murry would vent his biggest frustrations on Dennis.

Murry would never take the time to explain a task or chore to Dennis, so most of them usually blew up in Dennis's freckled face. (The deep scar under his chin was from three separate early-childhood tumbles—in the tub, off his tricycle, and down the steps.) Murry strapped Dennis so regularly with his heaviest leather belt that the boy grew unruffled by the rite, so Murry resorted to harsher treatment: flogging Dennis with a plank in front of his friends for school truancy or thrusting him into the bath stall and running scalding water on him as retribution for absconding with Murry's glass eye for use in a school presentation.

Besides acquiring a seeming indifference to physical abuse, Dennis gained a relative disregard for the property and feelings of others. He was arrested for starting sizable neighborhood brush fires and cut down a neighbor's prize tree, which Murry had to pay five hundred dollars to have replaced. Dennis was nabbed for shattering the passenger windows of moving automobiles with BB shot from a Daisy air rifle and charged with multiple juvenile counts of illegal entry and petty theft.

Nonetheless, all Murry needed to do to secure several weeks of good conduct from Dennis was take him seriously, speak to him in a civil tone, and treat him with grudging respect. But Murry usually couldn't bring himself to do it. Dennis was his most convenient punching bag, and he was reluctant to "coddle" him. In time, Dennis's only ambition was to be as different from his father as possible. That proved difficult. Murry's hair-trigger anger had temporarily infected him: Dennis would fight any kid on the merest pretense, barking out a Murry-like "Oh yeah?" before pounding his opponents.

One place where the testy Dennis did not behave like Murry was at the dinner table. Audree spared no amenity in the fattening of her flock, and Murry loved her banal but filling cookery, which consisted largely of heavy breads, big roasts, and baked or fried potatoes. Since she realized the table was the only place she could express sympathy for the boys, she crammed each course with as much rich fare as possible, smothering the staples in cream sauces and dense gravies. Anything resembling fast food or so-called convenience meals was banned from the house, particularly the Swanson TV dinners that had become so well liked by teenagers, although Audree would permit an occasional Sara Lee cake to share space with her own baking.

Murry was the first to exhibit the rounded bearing of the Korthof diet. Brian required conscientious stuffing, due to his height and fast metabolism, while Carl was, well, a piece of cake. Dennis declined to bulge. On select Saturdays, Audree would whip up a huge batch of Aunt Jemima pancakes as a main supper course, heaping each helping with piles of butter and double drafts of maple syrup. The sweet tooth that all her Wilson men had was transported by this "treat"—except Dennis's. Surrounded at the kitchen's Formica dinette table by the frenetic forks of his kin, Dennis would squirm and slip away.

A more unifying factor on Wednesday evenings was CBS-TV's popular half-hour sitcom, *The Adventures of Ozzie and Harriet*. On April 10, 1957, the series featured an unprecedented episode in which seventeen-year-old Ricky Nelson sang Fats Domino's "I'm Walkin'." If Elvis Presley was the king of white rock and roll, Ricky instantly became the student prince, and the youth of America looked up from its D.C. Comics to egg him on. Brian was no different. He began stomping around the room in time to Ricky's courteous R&B, thrilled that TV's quintessential American family gave their son free rein to rock. And because the Nelsons' middle-class credentials were impeccable, even Murry Wilson could admire this upstart. At the very least, Brian Wilson understood the primary impulse behind Ricky Nelson's TV performance. Shy Ricky had let father Ozzie Nelson (who created, wrote, and directed the series) talk him into doing the song on the air since Ricky longed to impress a girlfriend. Ozzie himself had no love for rock and roll, but since he had met his wife, Harriet Hilliard, when she was a singer in his 1930s dance band, his son's hopes made sense to him.

That Ricky would become one of rock and roll's biggest stars because of his television exposure could not have been more incidental to his initial, almost guileless gesture. Since both rock and roll and television were in their innocence, it was the awkward ordinariness of his adolescent desires that electrified the moment and gripped the imaginations of viewers like Brian. Brian, too, had known stardom in his own living room, exciting family and friends as he sketched the faint outline of his future in their admiring faces. Maybe, with the consent of his parents, Brian could turn his bungalow realities into a rock-and-roll dream.

Murry Wilson had closed off the family garage and turned it into a music chamber where he could peck out melodies on the piano (he couldn't play an instrument) or ask Audree to play the Hammond organ while she harmonized with the boys. Now it was Brian who took over that chamber, playing records by the Four Freshmen, the Everly Brothers, Ricky Nelson, the Four Preps, and the Hi-Lo's, studying each layer of their vocal blends, fashioning counter-harmonies, and constructing supplementary melody lines. For his sixteenth birthday he was given a sophisticated Wollensak two-track tape recorder, and he began writing his own odes to adolescent crushes, staring through the wallpaper into the better world that awaited only his powers of invention.

Coincident with Ricky Nelson's maturation as rock minstrel was mass acceptance of stereophonic sound. Two-channel stereo sound experiments had been under way at Bell Laboratories since the 1930s, the two simultaneous channels perfected in 1948—just in time for implanting in Dr. Peter Goldmark's microgroove long-playing records for CBS. Boasting 224 to 300 grooves per inch on a vinylite ten-inch or twelve-inch disc, they delivered twenty-three minutes of prerecorded music per side, bursting from a stereo turntable at $33^1/_3$ revolutions per minute.

RCA Records introduced the 45, which it claimed was ideal for sound reproduction of both popular hits and symphonic works, though the company later conceded that CBS's LP was best suited to classical music, allowing listeners to enjoy a Bach concerto without record-changer interruptions in the middle of a phrase. But the 45 bore up masterfully under the two-minute demands of Gene Vincent's "Be-Bop-A-Lula" or Ricky Nelson's million seller of 1957, "Be-Bop Baby."

As the record collections of audiophiles were updated with vinyl LPs (replacing boxed albums of heavy, brittle shellac 78s), the realism and spacious precision of stereo also accelerated the acceptance of portable tape recorders. Primitive wire-spool, paper-disc, and tape recorders of the 1940s were supplanted in the marketplace by the innovative, Bing Crosby–financed concepts of John T. Mullen's for Ampex, whose studio-quality taping system enabled der Bingle to eliminate stressful live radio broadcasts from his schedule. When the 3M Company's Scotch high-fidelity red oxide, acetate-backed magnetic plastic tape first reached consumers in 1948, home recording was a colorful novelty. By 1957 it was a national hobby.

Terms such as "hi-fi," "woofers, "tweeters," "amplifiers," and "diamond cartridges" found common usage among stereo buffs during the late 1950s. Across the country, devotees subscribed to audio publications, joined mail-order record clubs, and rigged their rec rooms with loudspeakers for demonstrations of sound effects that LPs could deliver—the rumblings of the rail yard or the drag strip.

Brian was adept at combining the gimmicky side of home taping with the audio excellence that his Wollensak afforded, dubbing instrumental and falsetto vocal lines on top of each other until his demos sounded like the effort of a pop quartet. He would also assign various vocal parts to family members—Murry taught to carry a few basic bass notes, Carl taking the low alto, and Audree trilling little filigrees. Played back, Brian's carefully arranged components took on a captivating charm.

But sports were the shortest route to recognition at Hawthorne High. Brian went out for football in the fall of 1957 and as number 51 landed the backup quarterback position on the B team—the entry-level squad of the B, C, junior varsity, and varsity rankings. The B's wound up undefeated, taking the Pioneer League title for the second straight year. The high scorer on the team was Rich Sloan, a short, stern-faced boy with whom Brian had become close friends since they met in their Little League days; Rich had taken notice when Brian, rattled by Murry's imperious prompting from the bleachers, would choke at the plate, unable to screen out Murry's useless static. Another important friendship reaffirmed during the season was with teammate Keith Lent, Brian's partner in pranks.

Brian's other buddies included honor student Steve Andersen, a varsity football player and member of the prestigious Scholarship Society and Knights Club; Robin Hood, another honor roll member, hot rod enthusiast, and Science Club member of the non-nerd variety, even though he took a lot of ribbing from Brian for his name and his epileptic condition, which required Dilantin to prevent seizures; and outgoing Ted Sprague, a superb athlete who lived on Rossburn Avenue.

It was a formidable clique, boasting good looks, high grades, broad shoulders, and prowess on the playing field. But an agile sense of humor and a thick hide were the true prerequisites for inclusion in the group because all six could dish it out with zeal. Of the bunch, Brian was the least popular schoolwide; by his own admission he was "well liked mostly by association," although his skewed jibes and pealing *haw-haw-haw* of a laugh endeared him to those outside his enviable social circle.

Brian's forte was the put-on, exploiting the general perception of him as a square-toed tagalong, forthright to a fault. In a moment of self-disclosure, Robin Hood might state he had seen a psychiatrist to help him adjust to his epilepsy. Brian would nod pensively, put a comforting hand on Robin's shoulder, and make a deadpan speech to the rest of the guys: "I told Rob to pull his pants down the next time he has to see his shrink and crawl in the doctor's office backward, saying, 'I have a complex, sir! I like the way my ass looks much better than my face!' " If not for the unerringly modulated delivery, the crack would have been outrageously cruel. Instead, the element of surprise wrapped Hood's difficult admission in a blanket of uproarious laughter, all of the boys sharing his relief at disclosing an uncomfortable fact.

Other shenanigans centered on weakness, emasculation and indefensibility, as when Brian would pretend to be insensate after a slip in the gymnasium showers or when—in an elaborate, recurrent sight gag—he would hang his head out the passenger side of a car at a traffic light and rattle onlookers by pouring a concealed milk carton of wet oatmeal onto the pavement in a simulated fit of vomiting.

Cited for cutting a half-day of school with sidekick Keith Lent, a sublimely straight-faced Brian stood before the class and told the teacher, "Well, what happened, sir, was that I went to the bathroom to relieve myself in the urinal. It got all over my pants, darn it, so I had to go home."

"Wilson," the instructor replied, "that's the best one I've ever heard. I can't punish you."

Not every scatological stunt of Brian's was benign. Once, in reprisal for a furious thrashing by Murry, Brian defecated on a plate and left the excrement under an overturned soup bowl on his father's dinner plate. Discovering the reeking appetizer, Murry chased his son out of the house and up the street. Unrepentant, Brian stayed at a friend's house until the furor died down.

Among Brian's more insolent capers at Hawthorne High was a cherry bomb incident freshman year, the fireworks tossed by a Brian-led group into biology class. The students' ears rang for days afterward, and expensive lab equipment was ruined in the uproar. Brian never conceded guilt, but neither did he contest the final "D" he received as a penalty.

Brian was also party to the usual locker-room larks (streakings, snapped jockstraps, golden-shower ambushes) as he ascended to the varsity ranks in football, track, and baseball, in which he was a fine center fielder. Baseball fever gripped the metropolitan area's imagination following the Dodgers' relocation to the Los Angeles Coliseum from Brooklyn's decaying Ebbets Field in 1958. It was a prime era in the Southland to be a promising young ball player, especially after the Dodgers beat the White Sox in the 1959 World Series, and scouts turned up at many local high school diamonds. But this would not be Brian's route to renown: His best hitting for Hawthorne never rose above .169.

Brian's gridiron stint as third-string quarterback was hampered by his fear of collisions and tackling. On one occasion a bad pitchout by Brian caused a pileup that fractured the leg of starting fullback Al Jardine, who also happened to be a vocalist with a Hawthorne folk group, the Islanders. Because of Brian's wholehearted apology, the two became cordial but lost touch when Brian's football career came to an abrupt end. During a game in the middle of the 1959 season, Brian was knocked unconscious in a vicious sacking. Revived after thirty seconds, he got to his feet, said "I'll see you, coach!" and quit on the spot, despite the protestations of teammates, who knew the season wouldn't be the same on or off the field without him.

While on the varsity cross-country team his senior year, Brian entered a long-distance race against Dorsey High, Mike Love's alma mater. Brian and Keith Lent took off with the sizable pack (which included Mike) as it hurried into the wooded cross-country trail. They slowly allowed themselves to be passed and then dropped behind until out of sight. Brian and Keith stole away to a diner, had a bite, then slipped in beside the stragglers before the last leg of the race, Brian coming from behind to take the trophy. No official ever learned of the ruse.

Of all the games Brian engaged in, his favorite was an artless 119th Street trifle called Hit the Bat, which he played on the asphalt in front of his house. Only two players were needed. A bat was laid in the middle of the road where the tarmac was smoothest. The pitcher rolled the ball toward the bat with the intention of making it pop up when it struck the wood. The opponent tried to catch the ball and tag the bat before the pitcher could. If the catcher succeeded, the pitcher had a point. If the pitcher tagged up first, he got one. For Brian, the appeal of Hit the Bat was in its intimacy: He and Rich Sloan or Keith Lent could while away entire days playing it while joking, free-associating, discussing girls and social pressures, or dramatizing great games from baseball annals, without any of the corporal horseplay Brian had come to loathe.

"I could play this game forever!" Brian liked to exult, and he meant it.

The 1958 and 1959 school terms were a time when the City of Good Neighbors seemed uncomfortable with itself. A program for putting a recoverable manned space lab into orbit within three years was announced by Northrop in a festive and well-attended public ceremony on Tuesday, April 29, 1958, while within a mile of the plant, three hundred bored, loitering students clashed in a gang-agitated near-riot at 111th Street and Inglewood Avenue.

For Northrop's part, it sent company lecturers into Hawthorne's elementary and high schools to combat delinquency by motivating and then recruiting graduates into its aerospace programs. Most of the students were receptive: The offspring of plant workers had long traded and collected publicity stills of rockets and jets as if they were baseball cards. Now they annoyed the corporate classroom spokesmen with the kinds of questions raised by Inglewood UFO investigator Riley Crabb, who gave speeches in Hawthorne auditoriums about "Flying Saucers and the New Consciousness," describing the alleged landing of alien craft at a West Coast military base in 1954.

Drug and antisuicide counseling were also stepped up in municipal classrooms due to abundant drug busts and police interventions in self-destructive teen incidents. Contributing to a public awareness of the problem was an April 1958 incident in which actress Mary Pickford's adopted son, twenty-one-year-old Hawthorne aircraft apprentice machinist Ronald Charles Rogers, had tried to take his own life with an overdose of drugs.

The Hawthorne Department of Motor Vehicles declared a crackdown on unlicensed go-carts, while school boards debated an 8:00 P.M. curfew for the latest rage: skateboards. Students at Hawthorne, Morningside, and Dorsey high schools were using their shop periods and private hours to construct skateboards from a length of plank or two-by-four and two sets of wooden-wheeled roller skates. "I tried it once and it's hard to conquer," said Morningside High principal Eldon Boyd of the skateboards, "but it's a lot of fun."

Shortly before the 1958 summer vacation recess, pamphlets containing testimony by a Dr. Fred C. Schwarz before the United States House of Representatives Committee on Un-American Activities concerning the "communism menace" were distributed to all high school students in the Centinela Valley Union High School District. Dr. Schwarz, a former math and science professor at Australia's Queensland Teachers' College, was a self-described "international debater against communism," and his talks at South Bay garden clubs drew big crowds. But nothing engaged the attention of the community more completely than another transplanted Australian preoccupation: the Hula Hoop. Several official Hula Hoop Days were announced at city halls in the valley, and twelve-year-old Carl Wilson was one of the more smitten fans of the fad.

First surfacing in California toy departments in January 1958, the stateside Hula Hoop was a product of the Wham-O Manufacturing Company, a sporting goods firm begun a decade earlier in a South Pasadena garage. Wham-O was a mail-order business formed around its fancifully named wooden slingshot. Also in its catalog were a fencing foil, throwing knife, water skis, a safety heater for camping, and another import from Down Under, a boomerang. The company, owned by Richard Knerr and Arthur Melin, was convinced it had found its fortune in 1955 with the rights to the Pluto Platter, a disc toss sold at the Los Angeles County Fair by inventor Fred Morrison.

Melin would take the Pluto Platter to the beach and throw it around to illustrate its soaring and hovering qualities. People stared, but nobody bought. "What's wrong with you people?" he would whine. "Don't you want one of these?"

Platter sales were still hovering in limbo when a pal of Melin's returned from an Australian trip with a bamboo exercise ring. Melin's wife Suzie and his business associate Richard Gillespie realized the ring could be spun at the waist and then held there with the proper hulalike jerk of the midsection. This time Melin took his own children to the park and beach to demonstrate the toy. Crowds accumulated, and kids clamored for their own. Thousands were given away free, each owner becoming a walking promotion.

Next, Wham-O became one of television's pioneering national toy advertisers, their commercials showing children wriggling within the brightly hued plastic rings. From March 1958 onward it was the most renowned toy in America. Over the next twelve months, eighty million hoops were sold globally (the Wilson boys among the takers), making it the best-selling toy in history. Wham-O's Pluto Platter was still stalled in midair, however, and the company's partners contemplated a new campaign using the name Frisbee—which is what Yale undergraduates called the Frisbie (*sic*) Pie Company tins they scaled aloft on campus.

The mammoth reception for the Hula Hoop raised anew the national consciousness for Southern California's whimsical outdoor esthetic, with its numerous new games, pastimes, and leisure products. As before, the Los Angeles Chamber of Commerce circulated reams of publicity shots of barefoot Southland children skipping and shimmying with their hoops, living emblems of the insouciant Empire of the Sun.

Unemployment reached nearly 8 percent (5.5 million) nationally in May 1958, and the cost of mailing a first-class letter rose from three cents (the rate since 1932) to four. But business at A.B.L.E. (now spelled Able on company stationery) couldn't have been better for Murry Wilson. Brian remarked to his mother one morning, "Gosh, I've never seen the old man smile so much."

Machinists were flocking into the South Bay to take advantage of manufacturing assignments and a steady spillover of component work from Northrop, AiResearch, and North American Aviation, where the dark and shiny X-15 "Space Flight Airplane" was displayed on October 15, 1958, before flight trials from Edwards Air Force Base.

The lathes of Binns & Berry Bros. that Murry imported were integral to the needs of the subcontracted component makers, and rentals were brisk. Noting how the current home-handyman passion was raising the circulations of magazines such as *Popular Mechanics* and *Popular Science*, Murry also briefly considered recapitalizing Able so it might begin handling heavier jigsaws and shop tools. But as one of Able's steady customers accurately predicted, "It's just another of the things Murry launches into whenever he's packing his pipe."

A more successful local entrepreneur who had earned Murry Wilson's admiration was L.A. inventor Earl "Mad Man" Muntz. Muntz was a middleman like Murry who had the motivation—but also the cool-headed audacity—to turn inferiority into superiority by becoming an alternative source for goods and services. Muntz made tidy sums in the early fifties marketing his own televisions and automobile model, the Jet. Lightweight (3,000 pounds) and frisky (it featured the innovation of seat belts, if only to underscore its 165-horsepower Lincoln flathead V-8), the Jet was a canny American sports car that predated Chevrolet's Corvette by two years.

Murry fixated on a new Muntz invention announced in 1958: the four-track car stereo tape player. The cartridges were conceived for use in providing background music for Southland offices and factories, but Muntz's $249 auto player hooked Hollywood's gadget hounds, Sammy Davis, Jr., being the first to install one in his town car. Southern California's leading record companies agreed to furnish tapes, and Reprise, Dot, ABC-Paramount, Westminster, and the Tops budget label were among those that added to the library of master recordings—which is when Murry really began to bubble about the device. "Sheer genius! We've absolutely gotta get one of those auto stereos!" he told the family, foreseeing a time when the songs Brian taped on his Wollensak could be offered directly to any music enthusiast. But Murry never got around to purchasing the Muntz Stereo-Pak. A soft touch, he repeatedly took funds earmarked for the splurge and spent them on some other contraption for which the boys had been pleading.

The requests by Brian, Carl, and Dennis were more difficult to fulfill than in former years when Mickey Mouse Club Mouseketeer merchandise could be had for nominal fees from Mattel, Inc., the licensed toy concern based in three Hawthorne buildings at 5432 West 102nd Street. Besides being the official manufacturers for Walt Disney Productions, Mattel also had King Features Syndicate's Popeye account. Sales of their own battery-powered Tommy-Burp toy submachine guns had been large enough to justify the construction in 1958 of a $500,000, seventy-thousand-square-foot painting and shipping plant at Rosecrans and Anza Streets; the groundbreaking was punctuated with piercing salutes from a dozen Tommy-Burps.

The new factory space was necessary for a revolutionary 11 1/2-inch fashion doll that the company was testing. Barbie was named after the daughter of Ruth Handler, the doll's creator, who was married to one of Mattel's founders, president Elliot Handler. While the Barbie figurine would not debut officially until the March 1959 Toy Fair in New York City, it could be found in the hands of Hawthorne ingenues late in 1958.

The initial reaction to Barbie from national department store representatives was not enthusiastic since large, life-size but physically neutral dolls were currently in vogue. Also sparking much dissension was Barbie's adult anatomy: sylphidine measurements (if magnified to human scale) of 39–21–33; gloriously long and shapely gams; and breasts that jutted out at a consternatingly rigid forty-five-degree angle. Sears, Roebuck and Co. initially balked at placing a single order.

Just before Christmas, fourteen-year-old Dennis was sauntering home from a schoolyard basketball game with a buddy when they ran into the buddy's two sisters who were toting Barbies given them by their father, a Mattel employee.

"That's a doll for little girls?" Dennis remarked with blunt surprise, snatching away the buxom, ponytailed pixie in striped bathing suit and pump heels. "Whoa! I'd rather have this in my room than a stag magazine!"

As it turned out, Dennis would never have to settle for plastic companions, and his awakening to the pleasures and paroxysms of sex would lead, by a direct but unexpected route, to a development that would forever alter his family's destiny.

8
• • • •

Please Let Me Wonder

O n Christmas morning Audree ushered Brian out of the house
and led him half a block down West 119th Street before pausing
to point at an automobile parked alongside the opposite curb. "Brian,"
she said quietly, a grin growing on her round face, "there's your new
car."

It was a 1957 Ford Fairlane 500, light pink and beige, its hefty air-
planelike grillwork, fat whitewalls, and chunky chrome hubcaps glowing
in the hazy sunlight.

"Oh, my God!" Brian yelled, crossing the street in three running
strides and leaping into the front seat of the two-tone sedan. The car was
a bold improvement over the clunky bluish maroon '51 Mercury stick
shift he had been driving since passing his driver's test in August. ("I'm
gonna buy you a car, son," Murry had said pensively—as if talking to
himself—en route to the used car lot, " 'cause I want you to be able to
drive to school like everybody else. All the parents buy their kids cars,
so why shouldn't I buy you one?") At the time, Brian had been surprised

and touched by the gesture, but once its novelty had faded, the Merc's true status as a tired heap was hard to overlook.

Brian turned the Ford's ignition key to hear the engine hum and switched on the dashboard radio, half-listening as the pop hits of the season poured out: "It's All in the Game" by Tommy Edwards, Conway Twitty's "It's Only Make Believe," the Kingston Trio's mournful "Tom Dooley," and "To Know Him Is to Love Him" by the Teddy Bears.

Tooling to Hawthorne High in these handsome wheels would indeed put him in sync with his status-conscious classmates, although the prime showplace for such a flashy possession remained Foster's Freeze at 533 North Hawthorne Boulevard, where he and Rich Sloan customarily hung out after school, gulping a cherry slush (aka sludge) and joking with the rest of the juniors—including Carol Mountain, a winsome blond cheerleader on whom Brian had an unrequited crush.

Opened in March 1957, Foster's Freeze was a franchise store run by local couples Willa and Victor Oliverra and Walter and Donna MacArthur. Known to the parent firm as outlet number 18, the Hawthorne milkshake-and-burger stand was one of a flowering statewide network of roadside stops begun by native Californian George Foster in 1947. Originally a mobile fleet of freezer trucks hawking twenty-cent sundaes in shallow paper cups, Foster's Freeze liked to boast that it had pioneered the "soft-serve" cone at its permanent retail sites throughout the Southland. More dramatical, these informal Foster's snack bars, with their walk-up outdoor counter service, patiolike eating areas furnished with picnic tables, and spacious parking lots, frequently became the most popular local gathering places for teens eager to flee the stifling confines of the tract-house sprawls beside which Foster's liked to situate its stands.

For Brian, Foster's Freeze was principally a weekday rallying point; on weekend nights he and his friends went to the Studio Drive-In movie theater on Sepulveda Boulevard. Outdoor drive-ins were a novel attraction currently peaking nationwide, but their popularity was unwavering in Southern California where the marquees of such theaters were crammed with youth-oriented B movies from Columbia Pictures producer Sam Katzman, Samuel Z. Arkoff and James Nicholson's American International Pictures, as well as MGM, Republic, Twentieth Century-Fox, Warner Bros., Universal-International, and Allied Artists. The 1958 release schedule was a roundup of every paranoid parental fantasy or adolescent dream then titillating the citizens of the region: *Dragstrip Riot, The Cool and the Crazy, Joy Ride, Juvenile Jungle, Life Begins at 17, The Nar-*

cotic Story, The Party Crashers, The Restless Years, Senior Prom, Stakeout on Dope Street, Summer Love, Teenage Caveman, Teenage Thunder, Unwed Mother, Young and Wild, Live Fast, Die Young, and *Sing, Boy, Sing,* most of which circulated on double or triple bills.

The filmgoing tastes of Brian and his chums were indiscriminate, particularly since drive-ins represented a weekly opportunity for clandestine drinking. Just before reaching the Studio Drive-In, Brian would pull into the parking lot of a nearby liquor store, politely stop an older patron about to enter the store, and ask, "Could you please buy us some six-packs of Miller High Life?" After enduring a half-hour of brushoffs, a serviceman or trucker would usually oblige, and the beer (or an occasional bottle of vodka and several quarts of orange juice) would be stowed in the trunk until they were safely in the theater lot. There, Brian and his buddies would get drunk as they mocked the bad movies.

Cruising and carousing in his handsome Ford, Brian was encircled daily by the raw material (youth, puppy love, mobility, pop music, franchised ambition, and entrepreneurial guile) that would characterize his generation's vision of the California dream. In time Brian would come to know the dominant contemporary catalyst to be music, and the man he perceived as the preeminent visionary was the author of "To Know Him Is to Love Him"—Phil Spector, born December 26, 1940.

Son of a suicidal father who asphyxiated himself with carbon monoxide when his Bronx-bred boy was nine, Harvey Philip Spector subsequently moved with his mother, Bertha, and sister Shirley to the Fairfax section of Los Angeles in search of a fresh start. Given a guitar at thirteen for his bar mitzvah, Spector was writing folk songs by seventeen and started a short-lived combo called the Sleepwalkers with friends Bruce Johnston and Sandy Nelson. His next group, formed while he was still attending Fairfax High School, was the Teddy Bears, consisting of Marshall Leib and Harvey Goldstein. Goldstein left and was quickly replaced by Annette Kleinbard, an attractive, sweet-voiced student at Louis Pasteur Junior High School.

The Teddy Bears rehearsed at the home of Spector's girlfriend Donna Kass, where practice sessions were often conducted in the garage. A post–World War I innovation in domestic architecture, the garage (from the Middle French *garer*, to protect) grew from a fashionable mid-1920s selling point for home buyers to an indispensable 1950s fixture in car-savvy Southern California. Besides being a haven for hot-rod tinkerers and home handymen, the garages of the Southland were gaining popularity as the headquarters of ham radio operators and amateur deejays. In the exploding post-Elvis world of neighborhood rock and roll, the customarily cement-floored enclosures became the echoey rehearsal halls and makeshift recording studios for a generation of pop hopefuls. After all, Elvis had been inducted into the army in March 1958 and posted overseas, so the field was wide open . . .

At roughly the same moment the Teddy Bears were organizing in Donna Kass's car barn, University High students Jan Berry, Dean Torrence, and Arnie Ginsburg were in Berry's Bel Air garage taping a demo of a song they had written, inspired by the show of a local stripper named Jennie Lee. Torrence was serving a six-month hitch in the army reserve when "Jennie Lee" was picked up by Arwin Records, a small label owned by actress Doris Day and her husband Marty Melcher, and after being bolstered by instrumental overdubs, the finished record leaped to number 8 on *Billboard*'s Top 100 (retitled three months later the "Hot 100").

When Torrence returned from the service, Arnie departed for the navy, and the newly christened duo of Jan & Dean jumped to Dore Records, a subsidiary of Herb Newman's and Lew Bidell's Era label. Fairfax High graduate Herb Alpert (himself just two years out of the army) and his buddy Lou Adler were producer-songwriters for Dore, which had recently signed another act to its tiny teen roster: the Teddy Bears.

Most of these people either knew or knew of one another, and in any event they all shared the same rampant California pop ambitions, exemplified by Hollywood High's own Ricky Nelson. In 1958, Nelson was the top-selling rock-and-roll star in the nation with five consecutive hits that year: "Believe What You Say," written by Compton residents Dorsey and Johnny Burnette; a rendition of Sonny Burgess's "My Bucket's Got a Hole in It"; "Poor Little Fool," written by a fan from Newport Beach named Sharon Sheeley; and Baker Knight's "Lonesome Town" and "I Got a Feeling."

Like most of the young pop aspirants, Ricky passed afternoons in Wallichs' Music City in Hollywood, grazing through the record racks for obscure R&B and country singles worth reviewing in the store's listening booths as cover possibilities or repositories of lyric and production ideas. A great many of the resultant songs came to control-room fruition either at Bunny Robyn's Master Recorders on Fairfax Avenue, a studio popular with local R&B producers (as well as Ricky Nelson, who cut "I'm

Walkin' " there), or Gold Star Recording Studios at Santa Monica and Vine in Hollywood.

Gold Star was founded in 1950 by partners Dave Gold and Stan Ross; it expanded in 1957 into adjacent commercial space vacated by the defunct Malibu Hosiery Company. Ross was on duty as engineer the day Phil Spector, Marshall Leib, and Annette Kleinbard entered to cut "To Know Him Is to Love Him."

The trio had previously recorded a dismal song titled "Don't You Worry My Little Pet," but Annette's plaintive vocal quality moved Spector to tell her, "I want to write a song for your voice." He adapted the lyric for the latest attempt from the epitaph on Ben Spector's gravestone ("To have known him was to have loved him"), and the track for the composition was done at Gold Star in approximately twenty minutes. Stan Ross engineered, Sandy Nelson played drums, Annette sang lead, and Marshall and Phil split the backup vocals, Phil handling the "voh, doh, doh" punctuation. It took two takes: one to get a sound balance, the second as a keeper. Studio fees totaled $40.

"To Know Him Is to Love Him" was released by Dore just as the 1958 school year was getting under way; it swiftly became the most requested record on local radio stations in the Southland, the calls pouring in from junior high and high school supporters. Debuting on the *Billboard* Hot 100 on September 22, it hit number 1 and stayed there for three weeks, a classic teen pop home run complete with the obligatory appearance by the Teddy Bears on Dick Clark's *American Bandstand*. The Teddy Bears would not repeat their success as Spector shuttled them between Gold Star and Master Recorders in search of the follow-up formula, but Phil became acquainted with Lester Sill of Gregmark and Trey Records, who would sign him to a publishing and production contract.

Suddenly the producer-writer was as sought after a personality as the recording idols he composed for and counseled. Southern California upstarts were changing the rules in the music business. Brian Wilson, hunched before his dashboard radio as he rode through Hawthorne, wanted to be an upstart, too, but the only contacts he had in the music business were in his own family.

Mike Love graduated from Dorsey High in 1958, a "D" student and often-suspended disciplinary problem whose worthy reputation as a school athlete was somewhat tarnished in the process. Once he received

his diploma, the attention he had earned running cross-country or playing football for the Dorsey Dons vanished, his green-and-white varsity
sweaters and jackets making him a conspicuous has-been when he reported for part-time work at Love Sheet Metal or the Standard Oil station
at Washington and LaBrea, where he pulled night duty pumping gas.
Mike lived at home—the Loves' magnificent Baldwin Hills residence—
from whose rear deck one could see the snow-covered San Gabriel
Mountains and the Los Angeles Coliseum. The Loves often threw a
Fourth of July party because the view of the fireworks at the coliseum
was matchless, but Mike was beginning to find the atmosphere of his
father's house stifling.

Milton Love tried in his own way to be the all-around dad. Before
work each morning he would drive younger boys Stanley and Stephen
around in his pickup truck so they could cover their joint paper route by
tossing the rolled-up early edition off the back of the vehicle; then he
would take them the five miles to handsome Windsor Hills Elementary,
the brand-new grade school he and wife Glee preferred they attend. At
home Milton regaled the family with tales of his California youth and the
experiences he had accumulated tooling around town with pals in their
Model A's, congregating at roadside outlets of the Chili Bowl chain, playing high school football (he was a left end), and earning extra money
picking beans in fields that would become the runways of Los Angeles
International Airport. His first summer after high school, he reminded
Mike, was spent in the Civilian Conservation Corps, in a fire-suppression
work crew in the dry-brush hills above Pasadena.

It was continually implied that Mike should do as Milton and grandfather Edward Love had done: turn a marketable technical skill into a
business that could gain work farmed out from the numerous municipal-
and government-subsidized industries of the region. Such affiliations
were an unbeatable hedge against hard times, enabling Milton to court
the former Glee Wilson in the depths of the Depression and take her to
Clark Gable or Robert Young movies at the Mesa and Seville theaters in
addition to regular dances at the Lick Ballroom. For an industrious
young man, Milton liked to say, "California is the ultimate."

Yet the dark side of this prideful pragmatism was the lot of Glee Love's
mother, Edith, still shackled to Buddy Wilson, whom his daughter detested. Even in front of her children, Glee made no secret of her hatred
for her father, whom she described as "a no-good alcoholic" who continued to raise his hand to her mom. When visiting Edith, Glee could not

tolerate being in the same room with her dad, except to remind him of his unspeakable cruelty in beating her beloved brother Murry with a baseball bat for perceived "disrespect" when Murry tried to shield their mother from Buddy's drunken wrath.

Issues of child-rearing and delinquency were persistent in the greater Hawthorne area, and much discussion was generated in April 1959 by the well-attended series of free lectures on "Family Living" by educator Dr. Barney Katz: "Popular Misconceptions of Child Training," "Faulty Personality Patterns of Parents," "Modern Methods of Child Discipline," and "Helping Your Child Develop Successfully," the last of which focused, according to the *Hawthorne Citizen*, "on television, radio, comics, allowances, household duties, manners, and music lessons." Further disseminated by word of mouth in ensuing weeks, the lectures were the type that conservative households like the Loves' took to heart. The signals Mike received from his parents gradually sifted down to a simple rubric: Behave like Grandpa Love and Milton, or you might end up like Grandpa Wilson and Murry.

But given a choice between his own prim household and the Wilsons', Mike decided he would prefer to end up wherever Murry's kids landed since they shared his deep affection for rock and roll and a happy-go-lucky attitude toward anything else. When Brian visited Mike's house to listen to records, Milton Love would rail against the disagreeable racket, so Brian and Mike would retire to Mike's Nash Rambler in the driveway and play the car radio softly as they sang along—sometimes until daybreak.

Brian was spending increasing amounts of time pounding out the rudiments of the latest *Billboard* hits on the piano, an activity whose boogie-woogie– and Chuck Berry–flavored rhythm and blues applications had great appeal for Mike. And Brian had begun taping more of his voice and piano interpretations of pop songs on his Wollensak home recorder as part of an eleventh-grade music writing course in which he received a "B."

In his senior year Brian enrolled in instructor Fred Morgan's piano and harmony course, and in the fall of 1959, Brian saw his chance to garner increased acceptance within elite Hawthorne High circles by writing a campaign theme song for classmate Carol Hess, who was running for student body president. The song, the melody for which was borrowed from the Olympics' "(Baby) Hully Gully," was sung by Brian and some pals at a rally. It led to a request for Brian to lead a combo at a special student-activities ceremony on a weekday evening. Carl Wilson and Mike Love rehearsed with a singer from Brian's earlier combo for the Carol Hess campaign, but Carl threatened to chicken out, so Brian bolstered his brother's ego by saying that he would call the quartet Carl and the Passions.

With the ultrapopular Carol Hess on the committee of assemblies (she was also a candidate for the townwide Hawthorne Community Fair Queen), more school appearances followed, but the personnel around Brian was interchangeable. Brian enlisted Keith Lent, Varsity Club member Ben Barrows, and crony Bruce Griffin in a student government rally that sealed his repute on campus as senior year was cresting.

Al Jardine, the folk music buff and champion Hawthorne Cougars fullback whom Brian had accidentally injured years earlier, encouraged Brian's intrigue with the folk scene. The Kingston Trio, a San Francisco singing act consisting of guitarists Bob Shane and Nick Reynolds and banjo player Dave Guard, hit number 1 nationally in November 1958 with their Capitol Records release of "Tom Dooley," a rendering of the venerable 1866 "Tom Dula" folk dirge. Bassist Jardine's own local Islanders group played the song, and Brian and Al would get together to toy with it and other tunes from the Kingston Trio repertoire.

Folk music had been drawing fans locally as a relaxed "beatnik" counterbalance to the bohemian West Coast jazz scene of the 1950s, whose nerve center was the Pacific Jazz Records offices, located over Roy Hart's Drum Shop on Santa Monica Boulevard in Hollywood. Pacific Jazz had been formed in the fall of 1952 by businessman Richard Bock, Roy Hart, and accountant Phil Turetsky, with brilliant L.A. jazz photographer William Claxton joining as art director and full partner. Among its roster of stars and discoveries were Gerry Mulligan, Chet Baker, Russ Freeman, Chico Hamilton, Art Pepper, Les McCann, and Bud Shank, who also provided the sound track in 1958 to *Slippery When Wet,* a documentary about the rising sport of surfing directed by young filmmaker Bruce Brown. Pacific Jazz also released albums by folk blues artists Sonny Terry and Brownie McGhee, hipster monologist Lord Buckley, and sitar master Ravi Shankar.

Latter-day L.A. jazz clubs supplementing the storied 1930–40s Central Avenue nexus of the Club Alabam and the Downbeat—clubs such as the Tiffany, The Haig, the Oasis, the California Club, and Howard Rumsey's Lighthouse in Hermosa Beach—soon had some coffeehouse folk counterparts. The Ash Grove was opened in July 1958 at 8162 Melrose Ave-

nue by twenty-two-year-old guitarist Edward Pearl (whose guitar
teacher at UCLA had been Bess Lomax Hawes, daughter of folk musicol-
ogist John Lomax), and was followed in 1959 by poet-painter Eric Nord's
Gas House, an art and performance gallery and beat hangout on Venice's
Ocean Front Walk just south of Market Street.

Music-minded hot-rodders shuttling between these two popular
spheres of influence might pause at Oscar Crozier's and Ed Roth's car
customizing parlor in a former realty storefront on Atlantic Boulevard in
South Gate (not far from Murry Wilson's Able shop) for a pinstriping job
on their hood, dash, and doors. Then they would audition it over chili
burgers in the bustling car lot of the Wich Stand on Slauson at Overhill.

Also gaining popularity in 1959 was Bayonne, New Jersey–born
movie actress Alexandra Zuck, aka Sandra Dee. Her roles in *A Summer
Place*, the Sloane Wilson tale of teenage ardor and adultery in a summer
resort, and *Gidget*, based on the Malibu beach experiences of novelist
Frederick Kohner's daughter Kathryn, transformed her into the nation's
reigning nymphet. Although it would go on to spawn five inane sequels
and two TV series (none of which featured Dee), the original *Gidget* was
most notable at the time for its international exposure of Southern California's Hawaii-spawned surfing scene. Culled from the recounted
meanderings of five-foot-tall Kathy Kohner's adolescent heyday among
Malibu surfriders as mascot and harmless pest, it had its beginnings on a
June day in 1956. Terry "Tubesteak" Tracey, Mickey Dora, and Mickey
Munoz were clustered on the incline overlooking the Malibu break
when a short, skinny kid in a blue parka slid out of a parked Buick
convertible and hoisted a Velzy/Jacobs board and headed down the steep
path to the beach.

"Hey!" yelled Dora in a threatening tone. Joining in, Munoz added,
"Go back to the valley, you kook." Intimidated by the harangues, the
little surfer tripped, and the board bounced down onto the rocks.
Tubesteak rushed to lend assistance, and as he got closer, he exclaimed in
shocked surprise that the kid was a *girl* as well as a midget—a "gidget"!

The much-embroidered film that evolved from this typical Malibu
turf skirmish was presented to the unwary as possessing a faint patina of
authenticity since top surfers such as Munoz, Dora, Johnny Fain, Diane
Kivlin, Pete Peterson, and Phil Edwards served as extras or stand-ins for
the non-hotdogging Dee and costar James Darren. Actor Cliff Robertson,
who also appeared in the film, dabbled in wave riding and later opened a
small custom-board business in Venice, but the preferred product—con-

taining polyurethane foam cores instead of balsa—came from sources closer to the spray and the competitive fray.

Like cohort Joe Quigg, famed Malibu surfer Bob Simmons had sought a lighter substitute for balsa in his Pasadena workshop as early as 1950, trying polystyrene, while Capistrano Beach designer Loren Harrison and Santa Monica's Dave Sweet did separate analyses of polyurethane foam in 1955–56, shaping plausible models just as balsa felt a steep fall from favor in 1957. The accepted new standards in polyurethane foam boards emerged from Hobie Alter's latest shop, opened in 1958 in Dana Point, and Floyd Smith's San Diego garage, where he and partner Larry Gordon (whose father ran Gordon Plastics) made molds in 1959 to blow foam surfboard "blanks" for their Gordon & Smith line.

The effect of *Gidget*'s popular embrace was immediate: The double features at the Studio Drive-In on Sepulveda diverted within the next eighteen months to silly beach comedies and surf melodramas. The young people of America were becoming aware of their sheer numerical might—plus their power to appall parental figures while captivating the media—and anything that amplified this generation's view of life as the pursuit of fun was championed.

Northrop was advertising late in 1959 in *Hot Rod* magazine for aviation mechanics; if readers filled out an application to join the National Hot Rod Association, they were eligible to compete with other members for a full three-year tuition at the Northrop Aeronautical Institute, its own technical training school. ("For several years," said the ad copy, "the Institute staff has noted that hot-rod enthusiasts make excellent students.")

John Severson, a boyish board rider and former high school art teacher who made independent surf documentaries for a tightly knit network of serious enthusiasts on the Southern California 16-millimeter lecture circuit, had been quietly amassing a small catalog of genuine surfing chronicles (the Hawaii-minded *Surf*, 1957; *Surf Safari*, 1958, whose opening shot was a twelve-foot over-the-walls wipeout at the Redondo breakwater; and the Hawaii- and California-celebrating *Surf Fever*, 1960). The booklet of photos and text he intended for use as prerelease promotion for *Surf Fever* became a thirty-six-page magazine, its affable writing style a reflection of Severson's reverence for John "Doc" Ball's pioneering 1946 pictoral book *California Surfriders*. Severson called his magazine *The Surfer*, subtitling it "John Severson's First Annual Surf Photo Book," and sent flyers to the surf shops that said, *"The Surfer* is coming!" Initial bundles of the ten-thousand-copy press run (cost: $3,000) were dropped off by van at Hermosa Beach in 1960 and sold for $1.50 per copy. The first five thousand went quickly; the second five thousand moved steadily on back orders, and the sport's first publication was under way.

Hawthorne High was graced with a touch of West Coast pop's seaside glamor when the Four Preps, a vocal combo modeled after the Four Freshmen, the Four Aces, and the Four Lads, came to sing at a school assembly. Formed in 1956 at Hollywood High, the Preps (lead tenor Bruce Belland, high tenor Marvin Inabnett—replaced in 1958 by Don Clarke—baritone Glen Larson, and bass Ed Cobb) were a livelier and more whimsical edition of their forebears, and they had seven *Billboard* chart successes to their credit, most notably "26 Miles (Santa Catalina)," which was number 2 nationally for three weeks in 1958, and "Big Man," which reached number 3 the same year. The group had also made a half-dozen appearances acting and singing on *Ozzie and Harriet,* toured with Ricky Nelson, and sang "Cinderella" onscreen in *Gidget.*

Dressed in dark blazers, tan slacks, and white bucks for the Hawthorne High program, they gave a witty, offhanded show backed only by piano accompaniment, which lent a charge of inspiration to the material that Brian was developing in Fred Morgan's music class.

Though a familiar attraction at local high schools, the Preps were perceived as a hip college act, and the college-bound Brian envied the reputation their concerts enjoyed on Southern California campuses. Brian applied himself academically in his senior year but also made a final push for social acceptance, gaining membership in the Varsity Club while on the baseball and cross-country teams. He and Keith Lent doubled for the Backwards Dance on April Fool's Day and got their pictures in *El Molino,* the class yearbook, for their clowning.

After graduation in June 1960, Brian Wilson decided to attend El Camino Community College, a local tuition-free institution founded in 1947 to serve the Centinela–South Bay portion of southwest Los Angeles County. Brian took both psychology and music courses but soon found his teachers in the latter were contemptuous of rock and roll. Being told what his musical tastes should be irked him, mirroring as it did the annoying prodding he faced at home to learn his father's stilted romantic ballads. He needed what the lofty speeches at his high school commencement had promised but not yet produced: a clean break from the past.

Brian grew restive and stubborn in his desire to play Chuck Berry rather than chamber music, but he had no campus compatriots.

Al Jardine, who was also a student in the two-year school, re-encountered Brian one afternoon on the grounds of the 116-acre El Camino complex. Born in Lima, Ohio, on September 3, 1942, Al was the second child of Lima Locomotive Company staff photographer Charles Jardine and the former Virginia Louise Loxley. Alan came to California as a boy when his father handled blueprinting for the Scott Railroad Company and the Air Force. Al grew up on 117th Street in Hawthorne.

The kick of seeing Brian again moved Al to cajole him into folkish jam sessions in the college's music room and the nurse's activity room of the college medical center, where they sang Four Freshmen and Kingston Trio hits. On one occasion Al brought along a swarthy football buddy who had a basso voice to flesh out the harmonies, but the bruiser couldn't stay on key.

Others were moving more aggressively toward their teenage goals. Phil Spector, now graduated from Fairfax High but still a legend around the school, was recruiting recording talent from its current enrollment for his deal with Lester Sill's and Lee Hazelwood's Trey Records. Guitarist-vocalist Russ Titelman, a Fairfax student whom Spector would use on "I Love How You Love Me" and other Paris Sisters productions, was taken into Gold Star to help Phil cut the first of two 45s in 1959–60 ("I Really Do"/"I Know Why" and "My Heart Stood Still"/"Mr. Robin") under the name the Spectors Three.

Born August 16, 1944, in Los Angeles to clothier Herbert Titelman and the former Leonore Greenberg, Russ Titelman was a descendant of the Puritan sportswear founders who created Ban-Lon shirts, and he was a versatile musical resource for Spector, in this case helping him to create the appearance of a successor to the Teddy Bears or a soft-pop rival to Dolton/Liberty Records' Fleetwoods. Spector also convinced two of Titelman's schoolmates, Warren Entner and Annette Merar—soon to be Spector's first wife—to embody Spectors Three for the sake of publicity stills and TV lip-synch spots. (The actual singing was done by Titelman, Spector, and a local girl named Rickie Page.)

The quickie Spectors Three singles earned only local notice, but the photogenic trio's burst of TV and print press helped build Spector's reputation in trendy teen and industry circles, which had been the point.

When Al Jardine pushed Brian Wilson harder with the idea of forming their own group, Brian suggested they bring his guitar-strumming baby brother Carl into the fold, noting that Carl had a high, smooth voice comparable to his own. Brian also recommended his cousin Mike, a frequent informal singing partner, praising his instincts for song lyrics.

In truth, Brian was concerned about Michael, who had gotten his cheerleader girlfriend, Frances St. Martin, pregnant in the autumn of 1960. With his meager pay from his two small jobs, Michael and Franny barely had enough income to set up a household, let alone raise a child. Mrs. St. Martin got wind of Mike's plan of taking her daughter to Tijuana for an abortion and went to his parents, demanding that a wedding date be set. It was: January 4, 1961.

Milton took the news badly but Glee took it worse, banishing Mike from the house. His younger brother Stephen, thirteen, watched in tears as his mother ran upstairs to Mike's room, emptied all his closets and drawers, and tossed Mike's clothes through a stained-glass door that opened on a second-floor balcony overlooking the front of the house. As suits, shirts, and green-and-white Dorsey High varsity apparel rained down on the winding flagstone entryway, Mike stood outside in a stupor, his little brother sobbing.

"That night traumatized Mike forever," Stephen would tell friends. "He never quite got over that sudden loss of his home and family."

A year later the Loves themselves lost their fine Baldwin Hills house when Milton Love's sheet metal business went bankrupt. The Loves were forced to relocate to a dingy three-bedroom house at 10212 Sixth Avenue in Inglewood, a tough, crime-plagued neighborhood in the path of Los Angeles Airport. The sounds overhead of planes landing and lifting off at three-minute intervals was often deafening, making it difficult for Stephen and little brother Stan, eleven, to study. One night a depressed Glee Wilson lost her composure and drank too much, screaming, "I don't want to live like this!"

Milton Love remained stoic, toiling six days a week to settle his debts and legal fees with small-contract jobs, and he eventually went to work for Anthony Chulich Sheet Metal in South Gate, supplying food service equipment for schools, factories, and the Pup 'N Taco fast-food chain. In a twinkling the Love family's position as paragons of Southland prosperity had been whisked away. Now it was the Wilsons who were looked to as the hope of the extended clan. Obviously, as even Murry knew, that really meant Brian.

And Brian was surprising even himself as he laid out plans with Al

Jardine for what sounded like a formal musical outlet but also a family enterprise. Brian spoke highly of Mike Love's voice and Carl's guitar capabilities, but he didn't mention Dennis as a member of the new group since Denny didn't sing too well or play anything beyond halting piano. But a role for his younger brother was inevitable because Audree would insist on it and because Denny had become a strong source of themes for Brian's recent attempts at songwriting.

On weekend mornings Denny and Mike would go fishing on the Redondo Beach breakwater, leaving at 5:00 A.M. and not returning until just before dusk. Dennis would then fill Brian in on the day's exciting events: how he and Michael had talked about girls, about each other's difficulties with their hard-nosed dads, about the uncertain future, and about the other intriguing predawn habitués who always kept him and Mike company around the breakwater: the surfers.

9

• • • •

The Warmth of the Sun

A few months past her eighteenth birthday, she was one of the cutest of the crop of young coeds who had appeared at Manhattan Beach Pier over the seasonal school recess to watch the surfers catching the winter's peaky south swells. When Dennis bumped into her in the parking lot overlooking the surfing area, he had been honestly distracted, admiring several of the deft late-afternoon nose rides for which Manhattan veterans were justifiably known. When Dennis asked her, with an appealing meekness, to watch his blue nine-foot board (which Murry had bought for him) while he ran to get himself a hamburger, he thought he could sense a strong susceptibility in her chiming assent, which is why he also bought her a burger and fries.

While she ate on his blanket and kept an eye on his wallet and uneaten burger, he took the board out as the tide rose, the waves breaking evenly at a height of four feet. He snagged one sluggish but impressively lengthy ride from a string of hasty attempts, fade-turning and hopping off just as one of the older hotdoggers shot the pier, slicing

122

through the treacherous corridor of pilings with finesse. By yelling to her and pointing, Dennis made himself an accessory to the daring deed, and as he ate his cold burger, she was full of excited chatter about the spectacular sport.

As the last slivers of sun hung behind the Santa Monica Mountains, they strolled along the water's fringes toward the lights of Redondo Harbor. She chatted about her delight with college; he talked bluntly about cutting high school classes. Somehow he managed to make his aptitude for goofing off seem more venturesome than her tidy plans for the future. By any logic she should have brushed off the attentions of this smoothly muscled blond brat, but he had the offhanded poise absent in most of the mature Adonises who daily crowded the shoreline.

Within two hours she was back on Dennis's blanket, furled snugly in its folds, his solid frame shuddering with the same dark energy that had drawn her in the first place. He was a sixteen-year-old boy but exuded the compressed fury of an adult. Dennis was a little scary, but the tender hunger at the core of his demeanor melted her reservations. Then she mentioned coyly that her father was a local cop.

"I deserve that," said Dennis with a nonchalance no one could fake, and they laughed together for a few moments before resuming their affections.

"I'm not like Dennis, I'm not a real cocksman," an openly bewildered Brian would tell his buddies, marveling at how easily Dennis could attract females. "I'm a subtler kind of guy. I do it all on the conversation level." But Dennis was not a fan of the banter-heavy Foster's Freeze or drive-in circuits. Now in the full reckless flush of adolescence, he liked the more earthy, nonverbal social components of the beach, those free of physical inhibitions and heedless of physical jeopardy. For Dennis, the sand and surf meant sex, and sex meant a momentary suspension of his free-floating fears.

That these activities overlapped with the acceptance in the Santa Monica Bay of the ancient Hawaiian sport of *he'enalu* (literally, wave sliding) was serendipity of the most casual sort.

Hawaiians had held surfing in sacred esteem since before the fifteenth century, *kahunas* (sorcerers) offering chants named for the beach *pohuenue,* or morning glory vine, to entreat the spirits for auspicious breakers. Before the ancient people of the South Pacific surfed their seas, they spoke to them, chanting quests for advice. Because the ocean always responded to their words, it was given the status of a god. In Hawaii he was Kanaloa the just, to whom the making of all surfboards was dedicated.

Indifference at any stage of the rite of cutting and carving a board was considered sacrilegious. The wise man remained as focused during the final refinements as he was when first approaching and hugging the *wili wili* (Hawaiian balsa), *ulu* (breadfruit), or *koa* (Hawaiian mahogany) trees that would yield the boards. *Wili wili* was a material reserved for chiefs and their favored representatives, the plentiful *koa* was for everyone, and *ulu* was a matter of taste. Each log was trimmed to a width of some two feet and a length determined by the craftsman's standing in Hawaii's ancestral caste: sixteen feet was the thick *olo* span for the *alii,* or nobility, and ten to twelve feet the proper *alaia* size for the thin board of the peasant class.

When English explorer Captain James Cook sailed the *Endeavor* into Hawaii's western Kealakekua Bay in 1779, it was these exquisite blade-like floats he saw the islanders riding. But when nonswimming evangelists and Protestant missionaries landed in Hawaii in the nineteenth century, they curtailed what they considered the hedonistic pagan observance of surf riding and decried surf bathing as a source of illness and disease. Mark Twain was nonetheless brazen enough to buck missionary scorn in the vicinity of Hawaii's Kona coast while recording the travel experiences he published in his 1872 volume *Roughing It:*

> I tried surf-bathing once, subsequently, but made a failure of
> it. I got the board placed right, and at the right moment, too;
> but missed the connection myself. The board struck the shore
> in three-quarters of a second, without any cargo, and I struck
> the bottom about the same time, with a couple of barrels of
> water in me.

By 1900 the decimation of the Hawaiian populace (from 300,000 at Cook's first landfall to 40,000 in 1893) due to epidemics imported by foreign visitors, plus the repressive atmosphere of mainlander clergy, had made surf riding almost extinct in Hawaii.

The Waikiki Swimming Club was using short, thin boards of approximately six feet in length for their club activities between 1903 and 1908, but the outside world took no notice. In 1908 a group of prominent gentlemen athletes, enlivened by the fashionable "physical culture" movement gaining disciples in Europe and America, decided to resurrect the Hawaiian sport, whose vestiges had dwindled to the three huge antique *olo* boards hanging in Honolulu's Bishop Museum. Led by journalist and gadabout Alexander Hume Ford and native surfer Duke Paoa Kahanamoku, son of a Hawaiian police captain, they organized the Outrigger Canoe and Surfboard Club, whose entrepreneurial charter read:

> We wish to have a place where surfboard riding may be revived . . . to spread abroad the attractions of Hawaii, the only islands in the world where men and boys ride upright upon the crests of the waves.

This healthful stab at boosterism found a disciple in author Jack London, illegitimate son of an astrologist and a spiritualist, who turned from writing best-selling novels about man against nature *(The Call of the Wild,* 1903; *The Sea Wolf,* 1904) to author *A Royal Sport: Surfing at Waikiki,* a 1907 tract about the wave riding of a twenty-three-year-old Irish-Hawaiian beach boy named George Freeth. The essay, published in October of that year in *Women's Home Companion,* was based on a summer of personal experimentation while sailing the South Seas with wife Charmian aboard their forty-three-foot yacht, the *Snark.* London's chronicle of Freeth's masterful shaving of the Waikiki billows made George famous.

Industrialist Henry Huntington turned that fame to practical advantage when Freeth became a paid promotional barker in 1907 for the Redondo–Los Angeles Railway and, inadvertently, the Father of California Surfing.

W hile Dennis was never enough of a gremmie (overeager teenage novice) to worship the waves, he saw the relief from stress that surf-related sex provided as an answered prayer. Indeed, Dennis's discovery of sex was akin to Brian's dawning diagnosis of music as an identity element and guiding principle.

While Brian spent Wednesday evenings with cousins Mike and Maureen Love at the Angeles Mesa Presbyterian Church Youth Nights, playing Ping-Pong while they did three-part harmonies on Everly Brothers hits, Dennis was often holed up back home in the bathroom of the master bedroom, intent on issues of *Playboy* and the seamier skin magazines.

Brian soon took his vocal talent public, his tapings of Four Preps approximations and family covers (with Carl on guitar) of Cole Porter's "Night and Day" quickly leading to high school assembly performances. Dennis, still lacking a substantial singing voice, was shunted aside. Without realizing it, he veered away so deliberately from the aspiration-heavy atmosphere of his musical household that his habits became those of a West Coast strain of postwar misfit: the jock drifter, that is, the beach bum.

Hitchhiking out of town—initially on weekends to escape Murry's Saturday morning lathe-cleaning detail at Able, but eventually most weekday afternoons, bumming rides as soon as the final bell sounded at Hawthorne High—Dennis disappeared down El Segundo Boulevard, bound for "the Strand," the shoreline of the South Bay. Out there, role models and heroes awaited.

Greg Noll, an outspoken lifeguard of well-knit physique who had excelled in the surfing runs at the 1956 Olympic Surf Carnival in Australia, opened a board shop in his native Manhattan Beach. Manhattanite Dale Velzy and Hermosa's Harold "Hap" Jacobs were Noll's cordial competitors, custom-building surfboards since 1953 out of a shanty-sized outlet just up the asphalt from Hermosa Pier. These were dedicated surfers, catering to their cohorts, but their attitude and their products attracted a huge younger following. The avuncular Velzy decided to shape smaller versions of both his ten-foot-two-inch "Squaretail" Ecuadorian balsa board and the hot Velzy-Jacobs ten-foot-six-inch polyurethane foam "Pig" model for the adolescent gremmies who roamed between Twenty-second and Second streets, trimming the prices accordingly.

Huddled on the twenty-two-odd surf beaches between Hubbyland and Haggerty's were conclaves of bedraggled young strays of a breed unlike any since the hot-rod tinkerers. Many of the older male rovers were navy hobos who had acquired the surfing bug in Hawaii between Pearl Harbor and VJ day, or shaken Korean War veterans who wanted nothing more of society's dirty work. But mainly the guys were recent high school dropouts, semipermanent truants, or coddled Beverly Hills discipline cases for whom a diploma meant little.

Strapping specimens with crew cuts, military butches, or close-cropped duck's-ass hairdos with dangling forelocks, they loitered and slept in their army-surplus sweat clothes, hand-sewn canvas trunks, or silk Hawaiian print shirts. Beach shelter consisted of palm and plywood *palapas* huts that were frequently dismantled and hidden piecemeal behind the dunes' retaining fences until nightfall. Some also had the luxury of homes or apartments to retreat to when the weather turned foul, but more than a few slept in their rattletrap 1946 Mercury wood-paneled station wagons ("woodies") and frayed convertible sedans. If you were a "mooncalf," a true tramp beachcomber, you scavenged after the day's sunbathers had withdrawn for mislaid wallets, loose change, clothing, shoes, and cigarettes, selling or pawning the surplus items.

The best board riders among the men tended to have swimmers' bodies, striated in sinew, with flat pectorals, angular haunches, and broad hands for paddling. Most also boasted naturally splayed toes for balance on the board, enabling sure step-over acceleration into nose rides without "pearling" (poking into the bottom of the wave), and quick kickouts, pullouts, and whitewater recoveries.

The women were big in the bones and bold in the gaze, wearing their sun-bleached hair in backswept "boycuts" or pushed into knit swabbie caps. Dressed in clam diggers, rolled-up chinos, and flowered short-shorts with bikinis underneath, they gave off a saline-tinged scent of stale Shalimar that mingled with the aroma of the roast rock crabs that were the pinnacle of cuisine in their boyfriends' shacks.

Everyone smiled easily and often because they rarely did anything they didn't care to do. And Dennis smiled back. He was witty in the way a worldly adolescent with good timing can be; honest, as any fazed kid is when he wants to minimize further hurt; and direct, out of the simple desire for companionship. So he was accepted.

Within a year Dennis's transformation from anonymous Hawthorne teen into truant was total. Increasingly being ordered out of his classes for incidents of fighting and other insubordination, Dennis lost all or most interest in school except that aspect the guidance counselor would call "interpersonal relationships." His pals at Manhattan Beach had taught him, more by example than by preachment, to take not a grain of guff from anyone, especially his persecuting father. Since Murry's every outburst held the promise of a flashpoint, and Dennis loved him despite the worst aspects of his temper, he avoided his dad. But his evasions had their consequences, too.

Drinking was the second vice Dennis acquired at the beach, where vodka and orange juice was the pet refreshment. As another antidote to anxiety, Dennis found screwdrivers had much to recommend them (although no one ever got a hangover from sex). Alcohol also removed the angry edge of Dennis's instinctive boldness, supplanting it with a buzz of absurd well-being. It was in such an inebriated frame of mind that he borrowed Murry's new 1959 Ford one weekend morning while his father slept, intending to make a run out to the beach for a swim (he found he liked the sensation of cold water against his liquor-benumbed body). His foggy head crowded with these constructs, Dennis stripped the Ford's gears.

Murry threw a fit when he found out, mercilessly beating Dennis for his harmful stunt but not guessing the role that drinking had played in the mishap. That Christmas, during a holiday party at the Loves' house, Murry actually caught Dennis syphoning Smirnoff from the cocktail caddy and threw his son against the dining room wall, knocking several framed pictures to the floor as other guests gasped. Dennis sobered up in a hurry when Murry launched into a diatribe in which he warned Dennis that he would find himself in a certain military boarding academy— or possibly a reform school—if he was ever found sneaking spirits again.

Milton Love leaped in to support Murry in his chastisements. Love's boy Mike, like Dennis, had long been a target of Milton's own ruffian style of reproachment. But Mike was too old to ship to a reformatory, and, like Murry, Milton really couldn't afford the freight. Dennis didn't pause to consider these fine points; aghast at the prospect of being barred from the beach, he pleaded with his parent for a reprieve.

Being increasingly exiled from their families, Mike's and Dennis's early-morning fishing trips to Redondo Pier became more frequent. When Jan & Dean scored a Top 10 hit in September 1959 with "Baby Talk," Mike told Dennis (and Brian) that he heard the song had been produced in Jan Berry's garage, and he pushed Brian to cut their own home demo of the Everly Brothers' "Wake Up Little Susie." Back at the pier, Mike asked Dennis to urge Brian to get serious about a recording career.

Mike would also tell Dennis about the good times he had at Dorsey High, how much he enjoyed singing in the showers with the African-American students after practice, standing amid the sea of tile to harmonize on Danny & the Juniors' "At the Hop" or the Platters' "Twilight Time." With his balding head and brusque demeanor, Mike seemed older than his years and was readily accepted by his black teammates for his knowledge of R&B.

Mike had also proven himself in one of the painful macho rites of Dorsey High, the "penny stomp," in which the toughest students would throw loose change on the floor and challenge others to pick it up without getting their hands stomped on. Mike eventually withdrew from this ritual after more than once having his fingers bloodied and sprained, but because he never flinched or complained, he was considered cool.

Shunning booze for his probational period, Dennis learned instead to do something equally cool for the era: smoke dope. He concealed the nagging odor of the practice by scrubbing himself down afterward in public toilets and rinsing his mouth with a squirt from the toothpaste tube he carried in his back pocket.

When the surprisingly infrequent pitfalls of intimacy (crab lice or gonorrhea) snagged Dennis, the older guys at the beach were cool about advice and health care, whether an out-of-pocket loan for drugstore supplies of Pyrinate A200 (although shaving was always counseled as the first resort) or cash for penicillin shots. Such sexual mishaps held no stigma among the beach crowd; far more objectionable was selfishness with rides, gas money, or marijuana.

Living in such close quarters with Brian and Carl, Dennis devoted considerable energy to keeping the better part of his beach habits and their drawbacks to himself. The main thing Brian noticed was that Dennis could no longer pass a garbage can without lifting the lid for a leisurely gander. "He gets up in the morning, not liking to wait around for the family to get up," a mystified Brian told his cohorts, "and he goes out searching for trash cans, looking in trash cans, just for stuff to find." Brian would shrug. "I guess he's gone from being a sports guy to a nature boy."

If Dennis saw something of interest in the refuse piles—say, a piece of furniture that one of his friends in the shacks on the Strand could use— he took the salvaged artifact along with him, squirreling it in bushes at school or tucking it in some cul-de-sac until he could lug it to the beach. Dennis the Menace became Dennis the Moocher. As long as Dennis kept his alibis untangled for Murry, ate much of what Audree set before him, changed his clothes each day to preserve appearances, and did not confide in his brothers, he was truly home free.

Dennis's distaste for high school sports was confirmed in his sophomore year when his wrestling coach caught him smoking a cigarette. The coach put Dennis in his car, drove him back to Hawthorne High, and made him run ten laps on the athletic field. For the rest of the year the coach made him repeat those laps each day, saying, "If you're gonna smoke, you're gonna run!" Dennis refused to stop smoking, however, and went on to do well in a championship meet, quitting the team in triumph. "The running paid off, I guess," he told a teammate afterward, "but I'll never quit smoking."

A "D" to "D-minus" student, Dennis regularly failed math and did terribly in English, largely because, in his words, "I was a dreamer; I'd lay in school in my dreams." Quoted in its entirety, a 1961 English paper, "Sports Car Racing," illustrates the problem:

> Sports car racing is very dangerous. Just think, you are going about 120 miles per hour down a curved mountain road, then you have to make a hard right or left. The main thing is you have to keep your eyes on the road, not in the deep blue sky.

The beach extended an uncritical *aloha* (welcome) to this unfettered dreamer, his similarly disengaged friends making others who had spread the word to more passels of freedom-lured nomads. Some were certified runaways, others petty criminals and drug dealers; the rest just wanted to slide on water and follow the sun. A black market in hijacked hot rod parts often overlapped with the scene, attracting the "safari" freaks willing to drive great distances to stalk the tubes (perfect, enclosing waves) and skip the mush (crestless rollers, characterless surf).

Hot rod spills were nearly as frequent as the wave-riding variety, and with grimmer consequences, but the beach culture dictated that mourning be minimal and casual. When eighteen-year-old Jerrie Whitener, a Hawthorne chum of Dennis's, was killed in a summer car wreck on the Golden State Freeway at the Newell turnoff, Dennis sneaked into the Pierce Bros. Mortuary in Inglewood on a dare to peer at the embalmed body. Leaning over for a closer look, Dennis lost his balance in the semi-darkness and fell against the head, accidentally squashing the reconstructed nose of the corpse.

Various surfing-safari hot rod caravans traced the Southland action from Point Conception, Goleta, Santa Barbara–Carpinteria, and Ventura County on down along the North and South Bays, Palos Verdes, and Orange County. Crossing into San Diego County, the drivers sought the Oceanside, Encinitas, and Del Mar heavies as well as the La Jolla, Sunset Cliffs, and Coronado–Imperial Beach waves that were a prelude to connoisseurs' finds in the Channel Islands (San Miguel's Cardwell Point being a must-surf) and the stingray- and scorpion-beset expanses of Baja California.

The majority of the South Bay regulars hung out on the Strand whenever the surf was cooperative and the ambience correct, hairballs (big breakers) pumping in succession, hondos and valley goobs (inlanders and rule breakers) minimal, and spectating women plentiful. The ocean took them all in, ceaseless in its own liberties, indiscriminate in its welcome. Standout surfers ruling the Strand's soup (the milky foam of the breakline) were Mike Bright, Mickey Munoz, Dewey Weber, Phil Edwards, Mickey Dora, Bob Cooper, and George Rice.

The South Bay surf was normally chopped by a westerly sea breeze, but south blows could reduce the sets (sequences of waves) to glass. Righteous beach breaks came alive on any respectable swell, the surf supreme just after daybreak before the wind rose. Southwest swells stoked by storms in the South Pacific or by *chubascos* (hurricanes) off Baja could generate July and August waves as high as twelve to fifteen feet. North Pacific storms in autumn produced west swells between four and twenty feet. Gales from winter to spring close to the bay yielded bunched-up sets in heights up to ten feet. But all offshore blows regularly generated tubes of gremmie-gobbling force, and the riptide kept cluttersome wanna-bes (neophytes) and soakers (surfers who decline every wave) out of the line of fire.

Although there were no coastal campgrounds in the South Bay, the entire sector was public land. The Los Angeles County lifeguards were hipper and better trained than the North Bay's Los Angeles City guards, and the cops weren't Nazis like those in Orange County. While Manhattan, Hermosa, and Redondo nixed surfing on summer weekdays between noon and 4:00 P.M. (and on weekends and holidays from 11:00 A.M. to 5:00 P.M.), all-day slides were available in the snug surfing lanes of Ballona Creek, Toes Over, D&W's, and Redondo Breakwater as well as the larger corridors of El Segundo and Torrance Beach.

Water temperatures varied from a nippy January fifty-five to a tepid sixty-seven off Muscle Beach in August. On a bread-and-butter board day in the depths of summer, the oyster-white morning would begin without any breeze, but the sky's pothered film usually disappeared by noon. The air temperature would rise to a feathery seventy-four, and the ocean-chop would establish a ruffling wind flaw that endured until two hours before sunset when the sea achieved a glazy polish and the waves uncoiled like iced velvet.

Whenever Dennis dared surf during the summer, it was usually in the smaller swells a quarter-mile north of the Redondo jetty or at First Street between Manhattan Pier and the hotdogger's showcase that was Twenty-second Street—and usually just prior to sunset. With the horizon a sooty auburn, he would drag his stocky blue "stick" into the drink, pushing it before him across the whorls of soup until the water was waist-high. Hopping on top with a sideward slap, he would rest his thick chest on the wax-and-sand stubble of its surface, cup both hands as they sliced into the emerald plash, and arch his long, bowed arms, paddling hard. Grazing the shallow boa and rock weed beds that sometimes cause un-calculated wipeouts, he would ease into the darker, chillier water, a quarter-mile beyond which elk and bladder kelp help reduce the wind-chop.

The southerly rip at Manhattan would take control about eighteen to twenty feet out, so Dennis would dig in with his ropy forearms, stroking north on an acute diagonal until the current relaxed and he was strad-dling the lineup of a dozen or more surfers.

He would let a set pass as his neck muscles tightened, keeping track of what the pack thought of the day's peaks. Sitting up, dropping his legs over the sides of the board, he would try to empty his head of distrac-tions and concentrate on the bowl and list of the water, measuring the backs of the waves with his shanks as small fish tickled them. Aiming his board with a twist of his trunk muscles, Dennis would drop forward onto its rigid polyurethane rind and paddle like mad. Usually he stopped stroking too early, got stranded on the top of the curl, and was pitched out into its blossoming boil, free-falling behind his lost board as he was sucked and streamrollered to the basement of the sandbar.

On certain choice occasions, however, Dennis could judge the flash of a break line. Staying low, crouching, and then whipping his feet up under him, he would stabilize with his lead foot and shimmy his trail foot into a perpendicular steering stance. Cutting the face of a wave with sufficient angle to feel the bumpy *clamp* sensation that meant he had cleaved into the safe low line of the waterwall, he would blast out along-side the fluttery spray, slouching tall in the sunlight.

If you were young, virile, and accepted like Dennis Wilson, with a cute coed often witnessing every fleeting moment of mobile poise, there was little reason to doubt that surfing was the sport of kings and funky sorcerers.

10

. . . .

Add Some Music to Your Day

On July 15, 1961, Frances Love, Mike's eighteen-year-old wife, gave birth to daughter Melinda, their first child. The proud father, who had just dropped out of Los Angeles City College, was desperate to provide a comfortable home for his new family—and bitterly determined to outshine his folks, whose deepening financial troubles and coincident banishment of him engendered a rage within Mike to reclaim the fine lifestyle they had just forfeited.

Mike believed a recording career was the surest avenue to instant affluence, and late spring singing sessions at the Wilsons' house with Carl, Brian, Al Jardine, and Mike's sister Maureen convinced him that the talent for the enterprise was within his immediate circle.

While Phil Spector had recently cowritten Ben E. King's "Spanish Harlem" and produced 1961's "Be My Boy" and Barry Mann's and Larry Kolber's "I Love How You Love Me" for San Francisco's Paris Sisters, the notion of turning homespun teen idylls into pop hits had first taken shape in Love's mind as news of Jan & Dean's garage-derived hits spread around the South Bay.

Dore Records producers Herb Alpert and Lou Adler had insisted on two months of rehearsals before the vocal duo formally recorded the Melvin Schwartz song "Baby Talk." Between trips to the beach and nights cruising the local Goody-Goody's drive-in, Jan and Dean learned the lyrics and harmonies in four-bar segments, with the inventive Alpert (born March 31, 1935, in L.A.) doing the arrangements. When they finally got into the studio, the vocals and instrumentation were cut separately and grafted together. These well-pared pop tutorials paid off, with Jan and Dean appearing on Dick Clark's *American Bandstand* television show. Dore Records included "Baby Talk" on a 1960 debut album, *Jan and Dean,* whose bonus glossy photo insert was plastered on the inside of many a South Bay schoolgirl's locker.

Three more nationally charting singles had since emerged from the twin-tape-recorder echo chamber in Berry's Bel Air garage ("There's a Girl," "Clementine," and "We Go Together") before Jan and Dean entered Western Recorders for more professional sessions for "Gee" and "Heart and Soul" (the latter a number 25 hit in June 1961), and by then the pair had also supplied uncredited vocal backing on Dante and the Evergreens' "Alley-Oop."

Like Wilson and Jardine, L.A. natives William Jan Berry (born April 3, 1941) and Dean Ormsby Torrence (born March 10, 1940) were still in college, Jan in premed at UCLA and Dean studying to be an architect at USC. Pop music was strictly a part-time lark, yet in the autumn of 1961, Jan and Dean bypassed Dore and the other mom-and-pop labels (Arwin, Challenge, Ripple) for which either one had sung, and signed a deal with Simon Waronker's Liberty Records. Housed in a smart, low-slung brick building in Hollywood, Liberty had a hip but idiosyncratic catalog that included the Fleetwoods, the Ventures, Gene McDaniels, and the late Eddie Cochran, who had perished the previous year in a car crash. Liberty's leading sellers were steamy lounge singer Julie London, a former actress found via London's songwriter and fiancé Bobby Troup (author of the Four Freshmen's "Their Hearts Were Full of Spring"), and novelty act David Seville and the Chipmunks, who had a new CBS-TV cartoon series.

Simon Waronker (born 1915) was a classically trained violinist who started Liberty in 1955 after twenty years as film composer Alfred Newman's orchestra assistant during the making of every Newman-scored movie from *The Song of Bernadette* (1943) to *Love Is a Many-Splendored Thing* (1955). Three years later Simon became the namesake of a singing chipmunk, the brainchild of discovery Ross Bagdasarian, a songwriter whom Waronker renamed David Seville.

Seville's first number 1 for Liberty was "Witch Doctor," but his tape-speed falsetto concept for the Chipmunks (Simon, Alvin, and Theodore were the unofficial alter egos of Waronker, Liberty vice president of A&R Al Bennett, and label engineer Ted Keep) delivered Liberty's second chart-cresting success, "The Chipmunk Song," all but bankrolling the label until Jan and Dean arrived.

Waronker believed the duo could be bigger than all his previous signings combined and assigned them to top house producer Tommy "Snuff" Garrett, for whom Waronker's son Lenny was an apprentice.

Al Jardine's itch for pop stardom was even more severe than Mike's or Brian's, and when Murry Wilson overheard Al's aspirations, he suggested that Jardine see Hite and Dorinda Morgan, whose tiny Guild Music publishing and studio cottage on Melrose Avenue had been the setting for Brian's first demo session.

Jardine auditioned with two other friends in the Morgans' Stereo Masters/Guild Music control room, Al on guitar, his buddies on banjos, vigorously attacking assorted Kingston Trio songs. "They had been very good," Dorinda later reflected, "but they were imitators, not innovators. It is hard enough to get a new group off the ground, impossible if they don't have something different to set them apart."

Undeterred, Jardine, who lived two streets over in Hawthorne, asked Brian to sketch out the vocal harmonies on a song the Morgans' son Bruce had written called "Rio Grande." A friend of Jardine's named Gary Winfrey joined Al, Brian, and Brian's Hawthorne High sidekick Keith Lent for a few harmony sittings, but the chemistry was off.

Next, Jardine requested Love, Brian, and the other Wilsons accompany him to Stereo Masters to try out the pop vocal mesh they had contrived in the music room of the Wilsons' Hawthorne home. On an overcast day in late August 1961, the singers presented themselves at the Melrose office. Clustered around the desk in the front room were over-eager Al, his smile as wide as a Studebaker grille; blond, charismatic

Dennis; tan and child-faced Carl; cocky and edgy Michael, his adult worries etched on his taut face; and, finally, the tallest member of the delegation, who spoke first, his treble tone and near-exaggerated courtliness making Dorinda Morgan grin.

"Mrs. Morgan," began the nineteen-year-old leader, "you don't remember me. I am Brian Wilson, Murry Wilson's son." Brian was correct —she didn't—but after recounting his earlier, unsuccessful stab at "Chapel of Love," he hastily explained that he had recently left college after one semester to concentrate on songwriting.

When the group ran through their cleverly arranged vocal repertoire, however, none of the material was original, and Mrs. Morgan expressed disappointment. Wasn't there something new around which they could build a song?

"All the kids listen to the surfing reports on the radio!" Dennis suddenly exclaimed, the assertion perplexing Morgan and rattling his associates. "It's new," said Dennis of the sport, backing up to face both the studio owner and his companions, "but it's bigger than *you* might think!"

Seeing the intrigued looks on Hite and Dorinda Morgan's faces, Dennis grew bolder. "Actually," he bragged, "Brian already has a song called 'Surfin'.' We could practice that for you!"

Brian froze at the statement, too stunned by the notion to endorse or denounce it. Mike leaped in, swapping Redondo Beach surf lingo with Dennis and suggesting there was grist in the slang for some more lyrics. As Mike jotted a few terms down on a piece of paper, Dennis hurriedly described "The Stomp," the hip new dance his friends at the beach were doing, and noted that numerous bands were gaining renown with surf singles.

The Frogmen had clicked locally on the Astra label in 1960 with the surf novelty "Underwater"—complete with frog sounds—which was picked up by the Candix label in March 1961 and became a national favorite. The Seattle and Tacoma, Washington–based Ventures had seen a string of hits on the Liberty Records–distributed Dolton label that were popular with surf bums during 1960–61, including "Walk Don't Run," "Perfidia," "Ram-Bunk-Shush," and "Lullaby of the Leaves."

But the avatar of surf rock and roll was Dick Dale (aka Richard Monsour), a native of Beirut, Lebanon, who had come to California in 1954 after growing up in Quincy, Massachusetts. The Monsours settled in El Segundo during Dick's senior year in high school, and Dick worked for

Hughes Aircraft after his graduation. Time spent woodshedding on guitar in country bars led to a name change urged by rotund country deejay T. Texas Tiny.

Deejay and promoter Art Laboe added Dale to rock and roll concert bills with Johnny Otis and Sonny Knight at the El Monte Legion Stadium, and Dick landed a bit part in Marilyn Monroe's 1960 movie *Let's Make Love*. After recording various pop ballads for his father's Del-Tone label, Dale moved down the coast to Costa Mesa to be closer to the Balboa Peninsula, where he jammed at the Rinky Dink club with fellow Fender Stratocaster guitarist Nick O'Malley, pianist Billy Barber, and drummer Jack Lake.

Dale opened a record shop opposite the Rendezvous Ballroom and repaired phonographs and gave guitar lessons on the side. His shop quickly filled with surfboard-shouldering teens looking to purchase the Safaris' "Image of a Girl" on the tiny Eldo label or Capitol Records' "Brontosaurus Stomp" by the Piltdown Men (led by the Four Preps' Ed Cobb). The surfers bartered wave-riding tips for guitar pointers, and Dale was soon enticed into shuttering his shop each day until 3:00 P.M. to catch the morning swells at Huntington Beach, Dana Point, or the Wedge in Newport.

Afternoons at the shop segued easily into Friday and Saturday night performances by Dale and his Del-Tones band at the Rendezvous Ballroom, and his loyal following of fellow surfers began requesting more stark, rumblesome instrumentals akin to the Tune Rockers' "The Green Mosquito" or "Tequila" by the Champs, an L.A. combo. Dale obliged, adding heavy staccato picking to his Strat on vibrato vamps—calculated to evoke "the feeling of white water caving around your head in a tube ride"—that would evolve into crowd pleasers such as "Surf Beat," "Surfin' Drums," and "Shake N' Stomp."

Brian Wilson and his Hawthorne High pals drove to the Rendezvous Ballroom to investigate Dale's tumultuous gigs and were awed by the intensity of the kids. Dale's heavier and louder numbers also drew the notice of Clarence Leo Fender, owner of the Fender Electric Instrument Co. in Fullerton.

Born in 1909 in a barn near the border of Anaheim and Fullerton, Fender was an ambitious ex–farm boy keen to overcome a handicap (Fender had lost his right eye in a childhood accident on his father's wagon). In admiration of his uncle who ran an auto/electric parts shop in

Santa Maria, Fender rebuilt radios after his graduation from high school in 1928, and this business expanded into custom-built public address amplifiers. After dabbling in accounting, Fender met inventor Clayton "Doc" Kauffman, an associate of Adolf Rickenbacher (later founder of Rickenbacker guitars), and together they explored electric guitar and amplifier design and devised an improved record changer.

In 1943, Fender's concept of a "direct string pickup unit" for guitar electrification became a prototype that was rented to musicians. Two years later Fender and Kauffman manufactured six K&F Hawaiian guitars in a tin shed behind Fender's radio store. In 1946, Fender introduced the Fender Fine Line Electric Instruments, and noted Los Angeles steel player Noel Biggs told bandleaders Spade Cooley and Bob Wills about the excellence of the amps and guitars. Spade Cooley's band members used Fender steel guitars and equipment on Cooley's KTLA television program.

Dale, who had appeared on Cooley's show, was a devotee of the Fender Stratocaster and was a perfect candidate to test Leo Fender's new Showman amp, which was intended for exactly the kind of high-volume rock-and-roll punishment Dale was benignly inflicting on his "Shake N' Stomp" fans. Leo let Dale experiment with an array of amps—Dale blowing the speakers in approximately forty of them—prior to the introduction of the heavy-duty Showman model. Dale received the virgin cream-colored cabinetry that soon became a collectors' item. Fender also allowed Dale to subject to concert trials the prototype of the portable outboard reverb unit, a stumpy little monster the size of an electrician's toolbox that lent chords and piercing double-picked solo guitar lines the deliriously drenched sensation that became surf rock's distinguishing attribute.

In gratitude for Dale's utilization of the Rendezvous as a product-proving ground, Fender presented the left-handed guitarist with a custom left-handed instrument that had a left-handed headpiece on a right-handed neck—the ideal adaptation for a player accustomed to riffing with an upside-down axe.

Average nightly attendance at Rendezvous surf dances during August was 327 patrons. As Dale dispensed with "Sugar Blues" and "The Sunny Side of the Street" and increased the content of surf music in his shows, he found himself pulling crowds of thirty-five hundred, and women bent the padded restraining bar at the edge of the ballroom's checkerboard stage to touch the edge of his madras blazer. Within weeks he was drawing four thousand on Thursdays, Fridays, and Saturdays, and four thousand–plus at the State Theatre.

On August 23, 1961, Dale entered a tiny Hollywood studio to record a cantering instrumental named for a playful call-and-response exchange that Dick had with the surf stompers each time he plucked its opening guitar line: "Let's Go Trippin'." L.A. radio stations initially ignored the song, but record retailers found it impossible to keep the single in stock. Shrewd competition crept in. Joe Saraceno, an L.A. producer who had cut minor acts such as Tony and Jo for Era/Dore Records, quickly assembled a group of black studio musicians, including gifted R&B drummer Earl Palmer, and recorded them under the name the Marketts in November 1961 for a surf single on the small Union label: "Surfer's Stomp"/ "Start." Liberty Records licensed the record for national release in December, and its Top 40 success led to a *Surfer's Stomp* album completed by a different (and white) complement of session players, which also did well. Surf rock was nearing the mountaintop, and the lean, bronze twenty-two-year-old Dale was the undisputed King of Surf Guitar.

Dale played his last Rendezvous Ballroom show on December 23, 1961, the weekend box office thereafter plummeting to two hundred, while his month-long January 1962 stand at the Pasadena Civic Auditorium attracted capacity crowds of three thousand every weekend, the overflow throng often exceeding four thousand. Pasadena police were dumbfounded, telling reporters they had no idea the area contained that many teenagers.

When Dale issued his *Surfer's Choice* album on his father Jim Monsour's Del-Tone label, there were advance local orders of 80,000 units. *Surfer's Choice* was one of the first albums ever to depict surfing on its cover; the photos were taken by *The Surfer* magazine founder John Severson (who also designed the record jacket) while Dale busted a few spilling breakers on a perfect day at Dana Point. Dale rode a nine-foot six-inch Hobie gun shaped expressly for him from a Gordon "Grubby" Clark foam blank at Hobie Alter's custom shop at 34195 Pacific Coast Highway in Dana Point.

Thus had the surf beat gone from a natural turn-of-the-century phenomenon to a certified adult profession. No longer simply an athletic or poetic sensibility, it had become a recognized sport and the basis for a marketable lifestyle as well as a new esthetic.

In 1960, Walter Katin and his wife, Nancy, opened a canvas boat cover business next to a tiny surf shop. One day a surfer asked for some trunks made of canvas. Just to get rid of him, Walter stitched up a pair. The surfer returned a week later with three friends, and within two weeks the Katins had twenty-five orders. "Kanvas by Katin" surf trunks, the only handmade canvas trunks, became the world standard, and the company sponsored a prestigious annual award at the U.S. National Surfing Championships.

Founded in 1957, the Ferus Gallery on La Cienega Boulevard in Los Angeles had blossomed by 1960 as the fine-arts equivalent of a beach shack for an important school of West Coast abstract expressionists, including the Kansan transplanted from Sweden, Billy Al Bengston (whose nickname as a fifteen-year-old L.A. surfer was Moondog), and former Dorsey High graduate and hot rod buff Robert Irwin. These were artists weaned on car customizing and beach culture, whether living the late-'50s beatnik life in San Francisco's North Beach or running their 'rods between Baldwin Hills and the all-girls sorority weekends at Balboa. Making extra money doing fancy lacquering jobs on dashboards and motorcycle gas tanks, sleeping off summer hangovers in the same skinny patch of Leimert Park where Milton Love and son Michael had each hung with their respective teenage buddies, Robert Irwin and his fellow beach and car bum painters became the cutting edge of Los Angeles's postwar abstract school. Jules Langsner, premier L.A. art critic of the period, summarized the dawning attitude of these hotdogging young daubers in his June 1959 *Art News* review of Irwin's initial Ferus show: "Irwin paints with a sense of exhilaration in the way color and texture can be sprung into an independent mode of existence."

Champion surfer Joey Cabell founded The Chart House restaurant company in 1961, urging former surf rat John Creed to take a dishwashing job in one because he felt sorry for him (Creed later became president of Chart House). While most outlets were in Southern California, the first opened at the base of the famed "Little Nel" ski run in Aspen, Colorado. Its decor was nautical and was largely hand-built by the owners. Each rough-hewn dining room table was trimmed with teak and had authentic nautical charts laminated across the top. Covering the walls of the restaurants were personal photos of surfing and skiing, the overall effect intended to express, in the words of the owners, "enthusiasm for individual excellence while challenged by nature, or by the need to be involved in the intensity of competition." And a job waiting tables at a

Chart House became customary first employment for teen surfers at locations from San Diego to Sausalito.

This independent mode of existence, this zeal to challenge nature, had embraced most of the points between art and commerce, even spawning instrumental music that mirrored surfing's propulsive will. Why not a theme song?

Fourteen-year-old Carl Wilson had been taking guitar lessons from Hawthorne instructor Johnny Moss, whose other pupil was a neighbor of the Wilsons', David Lee Marks, the Pennsylvania-born son of Jo Ann and Elmer Marks, who brought David to California when he was seven. Because of his lessons with Carl and his friendship with Dennis, David had become part of the developmental sessions taking place in the Wilsons' home music room. No one had yet mentioned the fact of a "group" being formed, but when the boys came back from their meeting with the Morgans, energized by the need to cook up some surfing songs, David thought he might be included. And when he saw how intent Carl suddenly became on improvement, asking Johnny Moss to help decipher the chord patterns to Dick Dale's "Let's Go Trippin' " as he had Chuck Berry's "Johnny B. Goode," Marks caught an infectious glimpse of the *frisson* of pop motivation.

Carl had also received instruction in saxophone at Hawthorne High from music teacher Fred Morgan, who told Carl's father the boy was "squirmy but very talented." Dennis Wilson's short-lived drum lessons from Fred Morgan earned a similar assessment: "A beater, not a drummer. A fast learner when he wanted to learn."

Above all, eldest brother Brian wanted to learn: about surfing lore, about songwriting, and about pleasing the Morgans—and as rapidly as possible. Prior to the tryout at Stereo Masters/Guild Music, Brian had been down on surf music, deeming it a tepid knockoff of the utterly predictable Ventures. Dick Dale was a fantastic live act, Brian felt, but personally he wanted to aim higher with his own music, locating a new plateau midway between Gershwin and the best Four Freshmen material.

Yet something in the automatic enthusiasm the Morgans had expressed for Dennis's ideas compelled Brian to reconsider the entire proposition. Plotting out the surfing song with cousin Mike, Brian restructured the surf lyrics he had fashioned for Fred Morgan, making them into a straightforward, boosterish anthem and embellishing with references to morning surf reports, the Stomp, and surf "knots" (friction-generated calcium deposits on surfers' knees and insteps). For the vocal arrangement he lifted the corny "bop" vocal exertions and "di-di-dip" rhythmic chants featured on Jan & Dean's early singles.

Murry and Audree Wilson had planned to spend the Labor Day weekend in Mexico City with business friend Barry Haven and his wife. The boys would stay behind, adult neighbors agreeing to look in on them. Audree had shopped for breakfast cereal, sandwich meat, and various other foods that could be eaten cold so that her sons didn't go hungry in their absence or "burn the house down" while cooking, as their father feared. Murry gave Brian nearly two hundred dollars in cash, ordering it to be reserved for emergencies, and good-byes were exchanged.

The Wilson parents were gone less than half a day when Al Jardine and Brian hatched a plan to rent musical equipment for the weekend in order to properly polish their new version of "Surfin'." They drove to Wallichs' Music City in Hollywood and picked up carbon microphones, guitars, drums, amplifiers, a saxophone for Carl, and a stand-up bass for Al that they tied to the roof of his 1957 Ford. The one hundred and fifty dollars they had set aside for the rental didn't cover the costs, so Virginia Jardine agreed to cover the rest of the fee, arriving in time to sign the guarantor's slip. The boys spent most of the next three days playing endless variations of "Surfin'," Brian sometimes taping the best takes on his Wollensak tape console. Dave Marks, who was just thirteen and couldn't get his parents' permission to stay up rehearsing, was shouldered to the sidelines.

By the time Audree and Murry returned from Mexico, the spell of the home session and its accomplishments had so consumed the boys that their first impulse was to share it with their parents. Thus, no one was prepared for Murry's reaction when he saw the clutter of expensive instruments and heard the explanation of how they had been obtained: He threw Brian against the living room wall for "disobedience," shouting that the money had been *"strictly* for emergencies" and insisting it be paid back "within one week."

It was over an hour before Audree calmed her husband, soothed her boys and their friends, and urged them to play something on the instruments before—at Murry's shrill insistence—they were returned to Music City.

Out came "Surfin'," and Murry became very quiet. As the last notes faded, he cleared his throat and, with the exaggerated cool of a would-be impresario, stated that the song, though hardly professional, should be recorded.

Brian nodded but said nothing; as usual, he was way ahead of his dad.

The new group had chosen the name Pendletones, its wordplay an alloy of Dick Dale's Del-Tones and the woolen plaid Pendleton shirts (from the family-owned sportswear firm of Pendleton, Oregon) so popular with beach rats. Their song was demoed in a three-track session by Hite Morgan on his Ampex 200 deck at Guild Music on September 15, 1961, a week after *Life* magazine featured a seven-page photo spread on surfing at Malibu and Doheny, headlined THE MAD HAPPY SURFERS, A WAY OF LIFE ON THE WAVETOPS. The outside world was closing in on the alluring subculture, hungry to witness a defining moment.

Dennis had been so unruly in the days prior to the session—he was currently on probation from Hawthorne High for hurling a screwdriver at the skull of a fellow student in his wood shop course—that Brian had brought in a substitute drummer. A rimshot-prone showoff from a hill-billy band based at a local country and western haunt called the Shed House, the drummer chewed tobacco during warmups, insisted on a solo break in "Surfin'," and overplayed to such an extent that the Morgans intervened, calling a recess while they paid him union scale on the spot and requested he go.

The boys performed two ballads created in the Four Freshmen mode —"Luau," written by Bruce Morgan, and an a capella ode to twilight by Dorinda Morgan called "Lavender." Brian cautioned his cohorts on the latter track: "Hey, go *slower*, you guys. Make it slow."

The sole percussion was casual finger snaps. The studio wasn't acoustically insulated, and passing traffic on Melrose was faintly audible.

"Keep rolling, Hite," said Brian, catching his breath before the first and only take of "Surfin'."

"Here we go," he whispered to the group. "Let's do it."

Mike handled the "bop-bop-dip-di-dip-di-dip" and sang lead on the verses, with Brian, Carl, and Al lending harmonies as Carl strummed solo acoustic guitar. Two minutes and twenty-six seconds later, the track ended with a stray "bop" by Mike.

While the group filed into the tiny control room to hear the playback, Hite Morgan wrote "Pendletones Surfing Song" on the log sheet of the tape box.

Did Morgan like the sound? He looked up and answered that he intended to book formal studio time as soon as possible at World-Pacific Studios at 8175 West Third Street in Hollywood.

On October 3, 1961, two days after the New York Yankees' Roger Maris broke Babe Ruth's 1927 record by hitting his sixty-first homer in the last game of the season, the Wilsons, Love, and Jardine recorded twelve takes of "Surfin' " and ten takes of "Luau" at the World-Pacific facilities. Hite Morgan chose take seven of "Surfin'," editing out the mumbled prelude in which a nervous Mike Love coughed and haltingly asked Brian, "This is a complete take? From the beginning?"

A small quantity was pressed on Robert and Richard Dix's X Records label under catalog number X-301. Hite sent several to Herb Newman of Era Records, which had released both Phil Spector's Teddy Bears and Jan & Dean on its Dore Records subsidiary.

Newman liked "Surfin' " and wanted to issue it on the Dix brothers' fledgling Candix subsidiary label, which had scored a number 44 national surf hit in the spring with the Frogmen's "Underwater," but he hated the Pendletones' name. Newman gave the tape to Joe Saraceno, now an A&R man for Candix, who dialed Russ Regan, an agent for Buckeye Record Distributors, which handled Candix's product locally. Saraceno played "Surfin' " over the telephone.

"Wow," said Regan. "It sounds like a Jan and Dean record!"

Asked who the band was, Saraceno said they were currently calling themselves the Surfers (an alternative Hite Morgan had just negotiated with the group). Regan reminded Saraceno there was a Hawaiian act on Hi-Fi Records called the Surfers and suggested he consider something like . . . the Beach Boys.

It was not until the initial run of Candix singles had been pressed and released on December 8, 1961, that the group discovered their new name. By that time Herb Newman had sent a copy to Bill Angel, the record librarian at KFWB radio.

Brian, who had never surfed or thought to, heard the song pouring out of the radio in his 1957 Ford as he drove away from Foster's Freeze with his brothers and Dave Marks. "Surfin' " had just won an on-air contest, getting the most listener requests after a showcase spin, and it was added to the station's regular playlist. On December 29, 1961, "Surfin' " would enter the KFWB Top 40 survey at number 33.

Brian, a cherry slush in his free hand, suddenly realized his dashboard daydream of three years ago had actually come to pass.

. . . Surfin' is the only life, the only way for me. . . .

Struggling with his composure as his passengers began gagging on their refreshments, hollering to neighbors and pounding on him in spasmodic glee, Brian stopped the Ford and swallowed hard. He felt as if he was going to be sick.

11

Don't Worry, Baby

Nothing was turning out as he had planned. Brian always imagined he would become a songsmith at the top end of the popular idiom, composing in a vague nether zone somewhere between Broadway, the Hit Parade, and Hollywood; between George and Ira Gershwin's "Summertime," the Four Freshmen's *Voices in Modern,* and the Shirelles singing Burt Bacharach and Hal David's "Baby It's You."

The only paid employment Brian had ever known prior to the success of "Surfin' " was the after-school job he had held at fifteen, sweeping up in a Hawthorne jewelry store on Crenshaw and 114th Street—and that lasted only four months.

Now, as a result of the cocky outbursts of his brother Dennis, he was something called a Beach Boy. But Brian wasn't into surfing, didn't care about the sport, didn't know a thing about it. He was scared, and *really* scared of the ocean. Even when his father insisted he at least try surfing to help the group's image, he wouldn't go out. Instead, Dennis told him stories and Brian made up songs.

Dennis insisted all the kids at school would like the surfing songs, and on that level Brian felt reassured, speaking with gratitude when he told his little brother, "Hey, that's great!" But then this Beach Boys thing, this suggested side trip of a pose, predicted on an anything-for-local-popularity caprice, had chanced to spawn a hit record. The musical gifts he revered and held as refuge had transported him to the right place but for what seemed the wrong reasons, with his closest friends and family—including his imperious father, who had immediately appointed himself the Beach Boys' manager—pleading with him for more songs on subjects he could scarcely fathom.

Unlike the whirlwind that seized and smashed his uncle Johnny's homemade airplane back in Kansas, these unforeseen forces lifted Brian's dreams into full flight. For the first time in two generations a member of the Wilson clan was in sight of his heart's desire. Yet the strange direction and lack of freedom this endeavor suddenly assumed brought a secret degree of disappointment.

Brian knew he had to devise a way to make the effort honest, render it worthy, regain control. Grandpa Carl Korthof, the unflustered amateur pilot who once took Brian flying over Southern California in his single-engine prop plane, would have been an ideal source of advice and counsel. But Grandpa Korthof had been dead for more than a decade, and there was no blood relative possessed of the temperament and wisdom to guide Brian. He would have to find his way alone.

Public appearances were necessary to sustain the local interest that "Surfin' " was generating, which meant serious rehearsals so the Beach Boys could adequately play their hit and a wardrobe to complete their image. The group's first live show had been a pre-Christmas booking for the intermission slot before Dick Dale's set at the Rendezvous Ballroom. Before the show, the guys visited haberdasher Gene Ronald's fashionably conservative shop on North Main Street in Santa Ana, the only truly Ivy League clothing outlet in Orange County. Ronald, who also had a shop on the USC campus, was a serious fan of West Coast jazz and dressed clients such as Cary Grant in the natural-shoulder Ivy look—the pinnacle of California cool for hipsters from jazz saxophonist Gerry Mulligan to Santa Ana's own stylish Chantays of "Pipeline" instrumental surf-roar renown.

Ronald spied the Wilsons hanging around the tie rack in the shirt department and learned they wanted "something Ivy League" for the Rendezvous show. He sold them matching navy blue Gant "pop-over" short-sleeved dress shirts—smart and sporty accents to their tight white chino pants.

The gig itself was just a two-song shakedown date and more trouble than it was worth, since Murry refused to carry any rented instruments in his car for fear they would mar the upholstery—so they were stuffed into Brian's and Mike's automobiles. The set lasted barely ten minutes, with Al on rhythm guitar, Brian on bass, Carl on lead guitar, and Dennis on drums, and was distinguished only by Brian's and Dennis's stage fright. Their stultified performance and the hostility of Dale's highly ter-ritorial Orange County partisans left Brian feeling the *stokaboka* (super-stoked) crowd would never accept the Beach Boys as real emissaries of the post-"instro" surf sound.

The Beach Boys' second concert was the Richie Valens Memorial dance on New Year's Eve, 1961, at Long Beach Municipal Auditorium; the Beach Boys were immediately preceded on the bills by the Ike and Tina Turner Revue. Their earnings of three hundred dollars for their three-song segment left Mike Love slightly dazed by the "trip" of getting paid for playing music. Brian told Murry his good ear was hurting him from the amplifier volume.

On January 9, Murry sent television personality Soupy Sales a West-ern Union telegram in care of KABC-TV: "Bless your heart for playing our song 'Surfin'.' We appreciate it very much. The Beach Boys, all five of us."

Later that month, while "Surfin' " (with "Luau" as the seldom-spun B-side) was still bubbling under *Billboard*'s Hot 100 at number 118, twenty-four-year-old Gary Usher, a bank teller at City National Bank in Beverly Hills, was visiting his uncle Benjamin Jones at his home on 119th Street in Hawthorne. Usher, who lived nearby with his grand-mother, was a night student at El Camino Junior College and a fledgling recording artist with several independent single releases to his credit. Hearing the Wilsons practicing in their garage music room across the street, he strolled over at the urging of his uncle and introduced himself to Brian, who nonchalantly handed him a guitar and bade him play while Brian noodled accompaniment on the family organ.

Both were huge fans of Phil Spector and began tinkering with what Usher called "Teddy Bears–type chord patterns" as Gary tossed in frag-ments of a lyric he had started earlier. So mutual were Gary's and Brian's worldly shortcomings and musical enthusiasms that within twenty minutes the bank teller and the bashful teenage Walter Mitty of the South Bay surf scene composed an exquisitely melancholy hymn to the world they could portray but never occupy, entitled "Lonely Sea."

On February 8, 1962, the same day the U.S. Army organized five thousand American troops in Vietnam into a "Military Assistance Command" to train South Vietnamese to fight the Vietcong, the Beach Boys returned to World-Pacific Studios to cut some potential follow-up singles to "Surfin'." For Brian, whose draft deferment was due to his deaf ear and chronic bed-wetting, the full-scale war looming for the United States in Southeast Asia was of no concern, although GIs returning on leave from the region would soon spread tales in *Surfer* magazine of South Vietnam's excellent coastal surfing conditions.

A few days before the second World-Pacific session, Murry broke out his wallet—maintaining as always that it was merely a loan—and bought Brian a dark sunburst Fender Precision Bass from the guitar firm's 1961–62 catalog. Carl was given an Olympic white model of the new Jaguar electric guitar, its flick-up mute switch supplying the *tick-tick* staccato attack indispensable for the turbulent special-effects touches of surf music.

Hite Morgan was again in charge in the World-Pacific control room for the four songs the Beach Boys wanted to tape ("Surfin' Safari"; "Little Surfin' Girl," aka "Surfer Girl"; "Judy"; and "Beach Boy Stomp," aka "Karate"), and Dino Lappis was once more serving as engineer with session guitarist Val Poliuto assisting.

"Surfin' Safari," a Chuck Berry–inspired Wilson-Love song, was a C-F-G chord progression celebrating an early-morning getaway in a woodie crammed with a quiver of boards. The lyrics noted many of the prime point breaks (Malibu, Rincon), reef breaks (Channel Islands), and beach breaks (Huntington, Sunset Beach) in a Southland arc of public surf spots. The sites and terms were provided to Brian and Mike by surfer Jimmy Bowles, brother of Brian's new flame Judy Bowles, a blue-eyed blond beauty he had met one afternoon while helping a buddy coach Little League.

"Surfer Girl" was a rapt sonnet of post-adolescent longing with a melody line that loosely telescoped the structure of the Four Freshmen's 1952 single "It's a Blue World" and a Bobby Troup–penned Freshmen hit from 1953, "It Happened Once Before." Brian had conceived the ode to the unattainable surf siren—his first full-fledged composition—while tooling around Hawthorne in his latest car, a cardinal red 1960 Chevy Impala with chrome wheels.

"Judy" paid tribute to Judy Bowles, plain and simple, with a warm if wavery lead vocal by Brian. Carl stretched out in the middle of the track with a Chuck Berry and Dick Dale–tinged lead. "Beach Boy Stomp," with its shouted "Karate!" coda, was a quintessential set filler, the sort of jaunty, rambling send-off riff that dozens of surf bands plowed into at dances before each hourly pause for refreshments.

"Surfin' Safari" was the obvious grabber in the material, and by the fifth take the group had a keeper, although Brian had to keep telling a daydreaming Dennis to stay in tempo on the lingering refrain that led to the fade-out.

The first take of "Surfer Girl" began with nervous chatter about burping on microphone, Mike counting off into a horrible flat drone that made Brian holler, "Stop the whole thing!" Before the second take, Brian yelled to Hite Morgan in the control room, asking, "Can I do this without the bass this time? And dub the bass with our voices next time?"

"No!" said Morgan.

"Huh?"

"No!"

"He says no," Mike repeated cautiously.

While the second take had an empty, uneven mood owing to the mixing board's faltering echo and sloppy faders, the vocals were strong, and Morgan pronounced it a master take. No one noticed that Dennis's brush strokes on his snare drum were continually behind the beat.

After the session was wrapped, Dennis's brothers, cousin, and neighbor scattered, and the Morgans were left to drive him home. To cheer Denny up, they stopped for a snack at Tiny Naylor's coffee shop on La Cienega Boulevard near Wilshire, the drive-in moderne spectacle with a futuristic diamond-mosaic design by architects Louis Armét and Eldon Davis, rendering the restaurant a reverse-chic curbside landmark and hot rod way station since it was erected in 1957.

Dennis slipped into a booth amid the airy geometry of glass, stone pillars, and angular aerospace light fixtures, and began to pour his heart out, telling the Morgans his role in the band was hopeless and fraudulent, as pathetic a fit as his position in the Wilson family. "I'm a duck who was born with two chickens," he sobbed in reference to Brian and Carl, and then he confessed he really wanted to be a writer, perhaps an author of novels or possibly a screen and stage actor like James Dean. Anything but a musician.

On March 8, 1962, Hite Morgan summoned the Beach Boys back for additional recording, but only Brian, Carl, and Al were available, so Audree Wilson fleshed out the harmonies with her nasal trills. This quirky Beach Boys quorum cut two tracks written by Bruce and Dorinda Morgan, "What Is a Young Girl Made Of" and "Barbie," the second track written to capitalize on the mammoth international sales of Mattel Toys' sylphidlike doll, which had spawned a male counterpart in 1961 called Ken (named for creator Ruth Handler's son Kenneth).

Morgan was hoping to assemble enough material for a full-length Beach Boys album on Candix and was confident "Surfin' Safari" could succeed "Surfin'" on the *Billboard* singles chart, where the latter tune was in the 90s and rising. Al Jardine did not agree. Although the prime mover behind the group's catapult into prominence, Jardine decided after prolonged discussion with his parents that the prudent next step for him was to exit rock and roll for academia. He bowed out and went to attend pharmacy school at Ferris University in Big Rapids, Michigan, his ultimate aim to become a dentist or a doctor.

The sudden loss of Jardine was a crisis for the Beach Boys, whose need for continued public exposure was acute. "Surfin'" was in regular hourly rotation on KFWB (whose morning forecasts of surf conditions made it the "surfer's choice"), and rivals KRLA and KFI had followed suit to keep pace with an obvious pop craze. Meanwhile, Love and the Wilsons were asking friends of friends in the South Bay and the San Fernando Valley to phone each station during request times to boost the song's playlist rankings.

"Surfin'" topped out at number 2 locally, but by March 24 it had climbed to 75 in *Billboard*'s Hot 100. Candix estimated unit sales at 50,000, but manufacturing demands for the release had pushed the feebly financed label into a grave cash-flow crunch. Hite Morgan stepped in, attempting to induce Herb Newman's Era Records to assume Candix's obligations and distribution. Although the ink was hardly dry on Murry's March 29, 1962, contractual letter of intent with the Morgans, Murry interpreted Morgan's action as a breach of their understanding. Moreover, the first Candix royalty check had come through, and Murry was livid to see it was approximately nine hundred dollars. He ponied up enough pocket cash to pay the Boys an even two hundred dollars apiece.

With numerous shipments of "Surfin' " unpaid for, Candix owners Robert and Richard Dix were compelled to file bankruptcy; all hope of issuing the "Surfin' Safari" single as a stopgap collapsed since there were no funds to press it.

Murry castigated Joe Saraceno for not informing him that Candix was on the brink of failure. And after several labels such as Dot had rejected the Boys' demos, Murry told Hite Morgan that the role he and Dorinda had played in the Boys' music was done, notwithstanding the publishing rights the Morgans still retained for the band's studio output. Murry then proclaimed his intention to start the group's career all over again. He believed he knew a way to get the Beach Boys a bigger, better deal at Capitol Records, home of the Four Freshmen, whose biggest recent hit was the previous winter's "Their Hearts Were Full of Spring," a song he maintained the Boys could sing every bit as well as the Freshmen had.

Desperate to replace Jardine, the Beach Boys approached guitarist-leader Paul Johnson of the popular Redondo Beach band the Belairs to see if he was interested. The Belairs were riding high with the local chart surge of "Mr. Moto" on Arvee Records, which had been cut at Liberty Studios. They had headlined several stomp mixers that the Beach Boys had played at in the Monica Hotel and Newport High School stadium. Johnson first talked with the Boys when they shared a ride home (Hawthorne being just a few miles inland of Redondo Beach) following a joint guest shot on *The Wink Martindale Dance Party*, a Los Angeles TV show. "Mr. Moto" had just slipped on the city surveys, so the offer was appealing, but while Johnson began hanging out regularly with Dennis and Carl, he ultimately turned the group down.

Thus it was that Brian, Dennis, and Carl Wilson and Mike Love assembled in the living room of David Marks's house at 11901 Almertens Place on a Saturday night as he sat cross-legged watching an episode of NBC-TV's *Bonanza*. They told the gaping rhythm guitarist, now nearing fourteen, that they wanted him to be a Beach Boy.

David's father, Elmer, shook his head; his mother Jo Ann's intrigued smile betrayed a definite maybe. David himself spun away from the Ponderosa teleplay and squealed, his voice cracking in an emphatic "yes!"

When Brian stepped out into the chilly spring night again, he was scowling. First his group was singing about surfing and then about a girl's dress-up figurine known as Barbie; now they had a *kid* in the lineup. Was popular music about perfecting a craft or just playing with toys?

12

• • • •

Custom Machine

Gary Usher, Brian's newfound songwriting partner, was also an avid hot rod buff who ached to own a 409 (a Chevy with a 409-cubic-inch engine). In the early spring of 1962, Usher and Wilson were driving down Western Avenue into Los Angeles searching auto parts stores for hardware for Usher's current street rod when Gary suggested they write a song called "409," the lyric erected around a "giddy-up, giddy-up" entreaty for increased horsepower. Returning to Hawthorne, the friends finished the rough draft of the three-chord song in fifteen minutes.

Usher's hunger for such a muscle machine was fueled by the performance-car power struggle between Ford and Chevrolet ("Fords for gow, Chevys for plow," as the drawled jibe went) that was ignited in 1955 when Chevy's spirited small-block 265-cubic-inch V-8 debuted in its Power Pack option, bringing horsepower to 180 and ending Ford's dominance of hot-rodding. As asserted in a famous December 16, 1953, corporate memo by Chevy's Special Vehicles Development designer Zora

Arkus-Duntov (architect of the Corvette innards): "Since we cannot pre-vent the hot-rodders from racing Corvettes or Chevys, maybe it's better to help them do a good job at it."

By 1961, Chevy was offering a single four-barrel 409 that handled Ford's modest 390 with ease. "Dyno" Don Nicholson won the stock eliminator drag competition at the 1961 Winter Nationals with a 409 Impala doing 105.88 miles per hour on the quarter-mile. Ford upped the ante to 406 in 1962, but Chevy thrilled street rodders and racers that year by countering with an improved 425-horsepower dual four-barrel 409 truck motor. In late 1962 came the Factory Experimental (FX) race cars, with Chevy's awesome Z11 package for 1963: a stroked 409 sport-ing 427 cubic inches to take advantage of the National Hot Rod Associa-tion's seven-liter displacement limit.

Despite GM's official "no racing" ban on its modified Impalas, such monster 409s became dream machines among muscle rodders. Ousted from the Muroc dry bed to make room for full-time aircraft testing by U.S. military authorities, Southern California rodders had wandered dur-ing the late '50s between the Rosamond and Evans dry lake surfaces in the midsection of the Mohave Desert before settling on the 120-degree daytime comfort of El Mirage—where a Chevy engine bolted into a '29 Model A roadster from Milton Love's era had no trouble hitting 189.05 miles per hour under the empty azure sky.

The Colton airfield dragstrip sixty miles east of Los Angeles was an-other racer's haunt, and stripped and modified Model A Fords could also be found roving the two-hundred-foot dunes of Pismo Beach. Autono-mous movement at a fast clip was now an urgency as well as an indul-gence in the L.A. basin since the last Red Cars on the high-speed interurban lines between Long Beach and downtown Los Angeles were closed in 1961, with all city trolleys bound for scrap by 1963.

And so unblinking motorcades of street rods wound through night-time Los Angeles, inevitably converging at Inglewood's Wich Stand on Slauson and Overhill, whose Armét and Davis–designed glass loggia of slanted angles, pinioned by a giant glowing spire, prefigured the inter-planetary lunch counters on ABC-TV's *The Jetsons* cartoon series, which premiered that fall. If surfing was the new culture of youth, cars were the cult mode of transport to "surf city," otherwise known as Huntington Beach but symbolic of all the gothams of grinders and good times avail-able on safari.

When Murry took the Beach Boys (including Dave Marks) into

United-Western Recorders on Sunset Boulevard in April 1962 to recut "Judy" and remaster "Surfin' Safari" for a new demo for Capitol Records, he chose "Their Hearts Were Full of Spring," "Lonely Sea," and "Four-Oh-Nine" (as spelled on the studio lead sheet) as supplemental material. Engineer Chuck Britz was on duty in the control room, and the instant rapport between the thoughtful technician and the sensitive songwriter proved a fertile buffer between Brian's fragile ideas and Murry's obtuse blandishments. (Brian did accede to Murry's idea of speeding up the "Safari" tape by one whole tone to put the song in a younger-sounding key.)

Both Decca and Liberty had rejected the Morgans' latest session tapes, and Murry wanted to make sure the Beach Boys' pop harmonies and rock-and-roll trend-spotting were well represented for this last stab at being signed by a major West Coast label. Murry nervously added a spoken tag line to the four tracks, directly addressing the Capitol A&R man he had targeted: "That was a sample of the Beach Boys, Nick . . . Venet."

Of the three A&R operatives at Capitol in the early '60s, Ken Nelson was the country-rooted elder who had signed Sonny James but also discovered Gene Vincent and the Blue Caps. Voyle Gilmore was the general pop practitioner from the big band era who produced the Kingston Trio and lured the Four Preps away from Ricky Nelson's employ. Nick Venet was the sly young junior executive who eclipsed the Preps in 1961 by signing the Lettermen. (He smuggled them into Capitol's studios during unused Prep studio time to cut the initial Lettermen hit "The Way You Look Tonight.")

When Murry met with Venet, he spent most of the meeting boring the A&R offficer with blarney about the wonder of his band's abilities. But the moment Venet heard the opening eight bars of "Surf and Safari" (as titled on Murry's tape box), he knew he was in the presence of a hit. The other tracks had their strengths—though "Judy" and "Hearts" belonged to a Four Freshmen formula rapidly growing passé—and "409" was electrifying. Usher had insisted on recording revved engine noises and whooshing drive-by sound effects for the track, taping the automotive hubbub outside the Wilsons' house by hooking Brian's Wollensak to a one-hundred-foot extension cord. Usher made four strident passes up and down West 119th Street in his Chevy before the entire neighborhood's porch lights sprang on and sirens were heard approaching from the distance. The curbside taping session was swiftly halted, but the

Beach Boys had the authentic din they needed to give the song a terrific aural hook.

Venet could scarcely wait to get Murry out of his office, minus the tape, so he could play it for his boss Gilmore. As the last refrain of "She's real fine/My 409" drifted away, Gilmore ratified Venet's excitement. With "Safari" and "409" encompassing twin aspects of an exploding teen adventurism, the two A&R executives recognized how the heretofore rock-and-roll–poor Capitol label could now change the course of California pop.

Murry wanted a three-hundred-dollar advance per song master, a respectable fee for the period, and Venet had to prevail upon Gilmore's superior to get the check clearance. Venet also wanted the publishing rights, but Murry had earlier clashed with Usher on that subject, insisting that everything had to go through Murry's own Sea of Tunes company, newly created to "protect" his underage sons and their group. The pie for Usher's work with Brian would be carved between Brian, Gary, and Murry.

The Beach Boys signed with Capitol Records on July 16, 1962, their contract covering an initial period of one year while granting Capitol six additional consecutive option periods of one year each. During the first period the group was to deliver a minimum of six different song masters, with the masters of "409," "Surfin' Safari," and "Lonely Sea" being purchased concurrently from Murry to be applied at Capitol's discretion as partial satisfaction of the minimum number of masters. The second one-year option period called for a minimum of six masters; the third required eight; the fourth, ten; and the fifth and sixth, twelve. Total royalties for each period were set at 5 percent, with the sums to be evenly split among the members.

In a rider attached to the contract, the Beach Boys agreed "to indemnify and hold Capitol harmless from any claims made and/or damages and expenses (including reasonable attorneys' fees) incurred and/or litigation brought by Hite Morgan, his successors and assigns and/or Candix Records and its successors and assigns" because of Capitol's use of the group's name.

The Boys also agreed that any vocalists, musicians, arrangers, or copyists (who write out the instrumental parts of each arrangement on sheet music for each musician) who might be selected by Capitol to help record or complete a master to the company's satisfaction would be paid out of the group's royalties. This aspect of the deal took on added importance when Capitol added the stipulation that it would "have the sole right to approve the arrangements of the selections to be recorded hereunder," besides requiring the Beach Boys to "agree to perform such approved arrangements."

Moreover, Brian, Dennis, Carl, Mike, and Dave were contracted not as a band of players who sang but as "vocalists" (notwithstanding Brian's private insistence that guitarist Dave never be permitted to open his mouth on any Beach Boys records—a ruling that was adhered to). Capitol wanted as much supervisory oversight as possible regarding the Beach Boys' sound on record, while ensuring that the relatively untried group foot the expenses for much of its studio education.

Because the Wilsons and Dave Marks were minors, they had to appear with their parents in California Superior Court at 9:00A.M. on November 8, 1962, when Capitol petitioned for approval of their contract. The court allowed the deal, while ordering Capitol to impound 25 percent of each underage member's royalties for trusteeship savings accounts administered by Audree Wilson for her sons and Elmer Marks for his. No withdrawals from the accounts could be made without a court order.

All legal obstacles removed, "409" and "Surfin' Safari" were issued on June 4, 1962, on the 45 RPM single Capitol 4777, the label's promotion people pushing "409" as the A-side because of its perceived appeal in the nonregional world of stock car racing. "Surfin' Safari" was the instant favorite, however, breaking first in Phoenix, Arizona, and New York City, sites rarely included on the average surf expedition. The song debuted on the *Billboard* chart on August 11, while "409" did not appear in the Hot 100 until October 13. "Safari" climbed to number 14 over the course of seventeen weeks, while "409" stalled at number 76 after one week. Interestingly, once it vanished from current airplay surveys, "409" proved the more durable radio perennial as the public beyond California grasped the hot car's recreational connection to cool-water sports.

With two major-label chart singles to their credit, it was time for the Beach Boys to begin fulfilling their contract with formal recording dates, and they entered the studios at the Capitol Tower for sessions on August 8 and September 5–6, 1962.

Frank Sinatra, Nat King Cole, and the Kingston Trio were the label's heaviest hitters at the time, and Judy Garland's 1961 *Judy at Carnegie Hall* album had lingered at number 1 nationally for thirteen weeks, gaining Capitol four Grammy awards at the 1962 ceremonies, including Album of the Year. But in 1962, Capitol cofounder Glenn Wallichs gave a keynote speech at the Miami Beach convention of the National Association of Recording Merchandisers in which he exhorted national rack jobbers (who stocked and maintained racks of just the top-charted albums and singles in syndicated, variety, drug, self-service food, supermarket, department, and discount stores) to do more to assist in developing new artists and their long-term potential.

Wallichs might just as easily have confined his remarks to the Beach Boys because as Capitol's first rock-and-roll stars they would create a marketplace and a milieu all their own and spawn several lifestyle-related subgenres of music. As Capitol launched the Beach Boys, so the Boys relaunched Capitol into a vast ocean of buoyant possibilities.

Capitol Records was conceived over lunch at Lucey's restaurant in Hollywood in 1941 by Johnny Mercer, Buddy DeSylva, and Glenn Wallichs. Mercer was the renowned composer and recording artist who sang duets with Bing Crosby for Decca Records on such 1938–40 hits as "Mr. Gallagher and Mr. Shean," "Small Fry," and "Mister Meadowlark." Songs he wrote on the 1942 Hit Parade included "Tangerine," "Blues in the Night," "Skylark," and "I Remember You." Buddy DeSylva, a former Broadway lyricist with the team of DeSylva, Brown, and Henderson, now served as executive producer at Paramount Pictures.

Wallichs was an innovative L.A. retailer who in 1940 sold his five local radio repair shops and used the capital to create Wallichs' Music City, the "supershop" situated across from NBC on the northwest corner of Sunset and Vine. The store stocked records, sheet music, radios, record players, and musical instruments, and also featured a custom on-site recording service for radio spots, audition discs, and the personal recordings for separated loved ones that were so popular during World War II.

Mercer and Wallichs first met in one of Wallichs's radio shops, and often fretted in the five years that followed about the poor arranging, sound quality, and merchandising of commercial recordings. DeSylva would come to share their gripes, and for prospective recording artists he suggested venerable bandleader Paul Whiteman, who had just left Decca, and rising actress Betty Hutton. He also volunteered to put $25,000 seed money in the bank for the venture.

Mercer's wife Ginger recommended calling the label Liberty (the name under which the partnership was hastily incorporated), and when that gaffe became obvious—Sy Waronker's local Liberty Records being one of the top twenty-five national labels—Ginger rebounded by offering Capitol as a consolation. All parties liked the second choice's official War Office ring, and Glenn Wallichs added the quasi-military touch of the four stars crested over the logo of a capitol dome.

Since both Mercer and Wallichs had other enterprises to juggle during the company's first shaky year, DeSylva became the president and corporate coordinator, with Mercer taking charge of recording and song selection, and Wallichs assuming production and distribution details. Capitol's first release was a 78 RPM shellac platter, pressed in cooperation with the MacGregor electrical-transcription firm, of Paul Whiteman's New Yorker Hotel Orchestra unwinding on "The General Jumped at Dawn" backed with "I Found a New Baby."

Reception for the debut was subdued, but a clamor soon arose for two other early releases, Johnny Mercer's "Strip Polka" and eighteen-year-old Texas songbird Ella Mae Morse's "Cow Cow Boogie." Written and orchestrated by Wisconsin pianist Freddie Slack, the cute brunette and the suave bandleader helped promote the jazz-pop tune by performing it in the Columbia film *Reveille with Beverly*.

Capitol managed to endure both wartime shellac shortages and a protracted ban on all recording that commenced August 1, 1942, instituted by the American Federation of Musicians, which feared the record industry was destroying the livelihoods of its union membership. Capitol shrewdly rushed to stockpile recordings in the one-month grace period prior to the shutdown and managed to ride out the year-long, studio-emptying strike with a crop of completed releases or purchased acetates —among them a master scrounged from a combo Wallichs knew from the bowling alley cocktail lounge next to Music City. The band was Nat King Cole's trio, and the song was "All for You," which became a Top 20 Capitol hit for 1943. When the strike ended that November, Capitol signed Nat King Cole to an exclusive contract.

The label's stars and successes in its first decade included Pee Wee Hunt's "Twelfth Street Rag," Peggy Lee's "Mañana (Is Soon Enough for Me)," Les Paul and Mary Ford's "How High the Moon," Kay Starr's "Wheel of Fortune," and Nat King Cole's many smashes: "Too Young,"

"Mona Lisa," and "Nature Boy" among them. Capitol also cornered the postwar baby boom audience with kiddie releases such as Bozo the Clown's debut, *Bozo at the Circus*.

Besides finding unique new faces who could deliver hits, Capitol had a shrewdly noncombative distribution, marketing, and promotion mind in Wallichs, who was the first to give free advance copies of releases to deejays. Labels had previously made the radio outlets pay to discourage them from the "free play" that they presumed undermined sales volume! Wallichs engendered a fondness and loyalty among broadcasters that translated into untold, unhyped promotional airplay (a new concept) for his artists.

In 1948, Capitol abandoned the cumbersome acetate-disc mode of recording in favor of the versatile new magnetic tape. In 1949, while other major labels were locked in format wars over the 78, 45, and 33⅓ RPM disc speeds, Capitol began pressing records in all three configurations, a move applauded in a *Billboard* editorial headlined THREE SPEEDS AHEAD!

DeSylva died in July 1950, and when Mercer withdrew from the everyday corporate fray to concentrate on songwriting, Wallichs became president. After Capitol landed the post-Columbia Frank Sinatra in 1953, it became a world-class company, and British Electric & Musical Industries, Ltd. (EMI), purchased a controlling interest for $8.5 million.

The buyout left Wallichs in command and gave him huge cash reserves for domestic and international expansion. Wishing to fix the audacious young company in the minds of a symbol-susceptible public, Wallichs approached Welton David Becket, a University of Washington architect whose joint designs with W. Wurdeman had produced some of the most striking streamline moderne buildings in 1940s Los Angeles: the Pan-Pacific Auditorium, Bullock's Pasadena department store, the Prudential Insurance headquarters on Wilshire Boulevard, and—after Wurdeman's death—the Beverly Hilton Hotel.

Becket's commission to design the Capitol building and studios gave him free rein to expand his "total design" philosophy of economical space planning and integrated decor. His concept for "the world's first circular office building" evoked nothing so much as a shifting stack of long-playing records astride a portable phonograph case. Wallichs backed off when he saw the renderings of the proposed structure—until Becket showed his patron how much money would be saved by means of circular design principles: 14 percent used for service areas instead of the 20 percent that was usual in a square edifice; fewer and shorter corridors; more efficient heating and air-conditioning (it would be Los Angeles's first completely air-cooled office complex); smaller outer surface area. Each aspect was ingenious, and to Wallichs the monetary savings were just as disarming.

Practicalities were forgotten, however, as Capitol gave consideration to the structure's crowning touch. The eighty-two-foot trilon spire was solely for space-age embellishment—as if in intuitive homage to the Wich Stand and Tiny Naylor's emporiums that within a year would cater to Capitol Tower's most famous clients.

At the grand opening of Capitol Tower on April 6, 1956, Leila Morse, granddaughter of telegraph inventor Samuel Morse, pulled the switch that lit the beacon atop the spire, which thereafter blinked red as it spelled out H-O-L-L-Y-W-O-O-D in Morse code.

From a business standpoint, the tower's foremost features were the three superb recording studios on the ground floor, the first ever designed for the primary purpose of making high-fidelity records. Each studio was constructed to rest on a pliant underbed of asphalt-impregnated cork to protect it from the unwanted hum and whine of external traffic vibration. The studios' wall panels were reversible, with birchwood surfaces to capture a hard sound and fiberglass sides to soften the acoustics. The most uncommon features were the four shock-mounted concrete reverberation chambers sunk twenty-five feet below the Capitol parking lot for the luxury of creating sophisticated echo effects. Frank Sinatra had christened the facilities in February 1956 while leading a fifty-six-piece orchestra in a session of Nelson Riddle's instrumental compositions called "Tone Poems of Color." Like many strange instrumental works destined to originate from Capitol's lavish studios, it proved an instant obscurity.

Nonetheless, the label's best and brightest (Sinatra, Nat King Cole, Judy Garland, Peggy Lee) used the rooms to mold their hits. Expected to emerge with masters suitable for an album to be titled "Surfin' Safari," the Beach Boys entered the tower's recording sanctum in the autumn of 1962 to record one (shelved) Brian song ("Land Ahoy"), five of Brian's collaborations with Gary Usher ("County Fair," "Ten Little Indians," "Chug-A-Lug," "Heads You Win, Tails I Lose," and "Cuckoo Clock"); a cover of Eddie Cochran's "Summertime Blues"; "The Shift," a tune about women's beach dresses by Brian and Mike Love; a cover of "Moon Dawg," the 1961 World-Pacific Records surf single by the Gamblers, whose personnel on the original track included keyboardist Bruce Johnston; and "Little Girl (You're My Miss America)," a ballad cowritten by Jan & Dean producer Herb Alpert on which Dennis was to sing his first vocal lead.

Each song and its affiliation carried a facet of the shadows and light converging around the Beach Boys, a million-mile journey of self-revelation commencing with the singular reverberations beneath an L.A. parking lot.

13
• • • •
Fun, Fun, Fun

Whether perceived as rowdy "instro" bands, bleached-blond collegiate pop stars, or chino rockers proud of their pealing vocal arrangements, the surf musicians themselves were waking to their curious footing as an emerging artistic community, much as the small Southland towns that fed their ranks were catching up to the performers' mounting cachet as a social force.

The Beach Boys were recruited in 1962 for a high school public service film clip narrated by KFWB deejay Roger Christian called *One Man's Challenge*, which documented the solemn drive by the city of Azuza's recreation director to create a local teen canteen: "It calls for the complete teamwork of public officials on every level and is designed to provide an acceptable social recreation program for teenagers" to keep Los Angeles County's after-school idlers off the streets.

The Beach Boys' appearance at the Azuza canteen, which had a suspiciously staged air, showed the band arrayed before a palm-draped photo scrim of the rolling Pacific; Dave Marks, Brian, and Carl were in a tight phalanx on the right, a skeleton-thin Mike Love slouched at the microphone bleating "Surfin' Safari," and Dennis hammering surely on his sparkle-finished Gretsch drum kit.

In such instances surf pop was portrayed as a cure for delinquency, although an equal number of national TV news spots attributed the rise of the music to the incipient decay of a "kicks"-obsessed new generation that moved in packs and posses. Temporary road manager Elmer Marks saw both sides of this in 1962, writing Audree Wilson from Wichita, Kansas: "I kept two hundred and seventy-five dollars [from box office receipts] because the Boys want to go to the Doc to get penicillin shots" to cure their gonorrhea. Soon after, twenty-year-old Brian, pondering the piano keys in Capitol Studios during the preproduction stage of his combo's first album, would have relished the fellowship of a posse of compeers as he quietly cultivated the stick-to-itiveness necessary to finish writing his vulnerable songs.

Brian had watched with a queer sense of isolation as Hite Morgan tried unsuccessfully to garner additional return on his Beach Boys investment by coupling the "Barbie" and "What Is a Young Girl Made Of" tracks he had cut with Audree Wilson, Al Jardine, Carl, and himself, releasing them on the Randy label under the pseudonym Kenny and the Cadets. Bothered by Morgan's brazenness and yet intrigued by such entrepreneurial bluffs, Brian started a label of his own called Safari (stamping his 3701 West 119th Street, Hawthorne, California, address below the simple logo's sans serif Metro-medium typeface) and released two tracks by Bob & Sheri, a singing duo the Beach Boys had met when they appeared together at a USC frat bash. Bob was Bob Norberg, a semiprofessional musician and swimming instructor who planned a career in commercial aviation. Sheri was Sheryl Pomeroy, his girlfriend. The sides Brian produced for them on Safari were his own "The Surfer Moon" and Norberg and Pomeroy's "Humpty Dumpty," and although neither made the charts, they served as calling cards for the duo when securing bookings on local TV dance shows such as *Shiveree*.

An impromptu talent search by Brian and Gary Usher for a West Coast equivalent of the Goffin-King discovery Little "The Loco-Motion" Eva aka Eva Boyd (their Belhaven, North Carolina–born babysitter) resulted in a session with one Betty Willis, who sang the Wilson-Usher songs "The Revolution" and "Number One" on a Dot Records 45, albeit to scant commercial effect. The cashbox kismet that came so steadily to Phil Spector continued to elude journeyman producer Brian Wilson.

As for the *Surfin' Safari* album now in progress, Brian was most proud of "Ten Little Indians," an idea he and Gary Usher had borrowed from "Running Bear," Texas singer Johnny Preston's 1960 number 1 hit about adolescent ardor between the title character and an Indian girl. The original song, written by J. P. "The Big Bopper" Richardson and featuring Indian calls by him and country crooner George Jones, had a casual, scampering tempo that Brian and Gary wanted to duplicate. But the structure of their knockoff attempt was greatly speeded up in the recording process, Brian instructing Mike to give a near-martial reading of the nursery rhyme lyrics about the "squaw who loved the tenth little Indian boy." Brian also wrote Mike a bass part for the chorus and suggested collective "woo-woos" and war-whoops to enhance the Native American theme.

Conceptually, the preproduction effort for *Surfin' Safari* was ultimately a solitary one, but Brian was thrilled with the mechanics of rehearsals, teaching his often elaborate but usually logical notions of each track's final format to his band. Nick Venet would receive a producer credit on *Surfin' Safari*, but Venet's contribution was primarily as a corporate liaison, advising Brian when it came time to whittle his songs into a form compatible with Capitol's marketing plan for the Beach Boys.

Given Brian's ignorance of the technical side of studio work, it was engineer Chuck Britz of Western Studios who would translate Brian's torrent of ideas into studio voicings and working mixes, monitoring pitch and microphone placement as Brian psyched the group members into mastering the increasingly intricate catechism of distinctive instrumental and vocal parts. A fairer reflection of the division of labor on subsequent Beach Boys albums might have been a producer credit for Brian, and coproducer designations for Britz and Venet. But the recording industry was still a corporate organism rooted in the big band era wherein the company produced the record while the bandleader and his duly appointed arranger supplied and conducted the music. Since most rock-and-roll bands had no organic hierarchies that resembled this balance of power, the musicians were regarded as juvenile guests in an adult enterprise, permitted to cast about for lucrative pop ephemera on valuable company time.

The sounds Brian chose sometimes sprang from coffee shop think tanks with Gary Usher, whose mutual excitement with 1962's spring-to-fall crop of national pop pith (the Four Seasons' "Sherry," Dee Dee Sharp's "Mashed Potato Time," and Bobby Bare's "Shame on Me") pushed the two impressionable novice writers toward story-telling songs with picturesque control-room touches. It was Phil Spector's production on the Crystals' rendition of Gene Pitney's "He's a Rebel," however, that hit Brian hardest.

Cut in Los Angeles for Spector's new Philles Records label (financed with partners Lester Sill and Harry Finfer), the record was Phil's third singles success with the Crystals and his first number 1 for Philles. Fresh from a staff apprenticeship at Atlantic Records, Spector had recently accepted an offer by Snuff Garrett to become Liberty Records' East Coast head of A&R when he heard Pitney's demo version of "Rebel" (intended for singer Vikki Carr) in Liberty's New York office. Telling Garrett he was contemplating a European sabbatical, Phil instead hopped a flight to Los Angeles and recorded "Rebel" in Gold Star Studios with the Blossoms' Darlene Love substituting for Crystals lead vocalist Barbara Alston.

"Rebel" also was arranger Jack Nitzsche's first association with Spector. At Phil's behest, Nitzsche (whom Spector met through Lester Sill) had hurriedly assembled a roomful of freelance musicians that included keyboardist Leon Russell, guitarist Glen Campbell, and drummer Hal Blaine, the last of whom played on Jan & Dean's "Baby Talk."

Spector wanted Pitney's song cut in an R&B pop vein, so Phil told Nitzsche he wanted the sax parts by baritone Jay Migliori and tenor Steve Douglas to cop the declamatory horn feel used earlier in 1962 on Vee-Jay star Gene Chandler's chart-topping "Duke of Earl."

When Brian heard the sexy shuffle tempo that opened "Rebel," its plinking piano cadence and heavy tom-toms aping the unsettled heart of a teenager in heat, he gawked in shock. This was a production with an almost preternatural sensory impact, the stop-time vocal chorus and hand-clap effects that lead from the horn break creating a tangible tremor of amorous exultation. Drawing from his own experiences with Usher, Brian tried to create the same picturesque immediacy, if not the sensuous charge, of such songwriting. "County Fair" was the product of a daily writing interval with Usher during which they recalled the tawdry charm of a San Bernardino carnival at which the Beach Boys had appeared months before, evoking the midway's colorful rides and comely girls. "Chug-A-Lug," the ode to root beer that Brian saw as the follow-up to "Surfin' Safari," was conceived as a coy recasting of his friend's behind-the-wheel drinking bashes at the Studio Drive-In on Sepulveda Boulevard, but instead it captured the anxious camaraderie of his ripening band. "Heads You Win, Tails I Lose" was the preferred end product of a two-song burst of composing that also yielded a hackneyed country and western honker called "Timber, I'm Falling in Love with You." The last of *Safari's* joint Wilson-Usher tunes, "Cuckoo Clock," was a send-up of a frustrated teen tryst (as well as a swipe at Murry Wilson's pet mynah bird) and showed a rompish humor foreign to a songsmith like Spector, who had few qualms about addressing the visceral side of emotional release.

At this same moment in the autumn of 1962, Randy Newman, a rising singer-songwriter at Liberty Records who was exploring a pop approach midway between Spector's lush carnality and Brian's colorful reserve, had become a staff writer for Liberty's Metric Music division. Newman's boyhood friend Lenny Waronker brought him to his father Simon's attention, and the fact that Randy (born November 28, 1943) was the nephew of film composer Alfred Newman, Sy Waronker's mentor, gave Randy an added edge.

Randy had just seen his song "They Tell Me It's Summer" become the flip side of the Fleetwoods' new hit "Lovers by Night, Strangers by Day"; had placed "Somebody's Waiting" as the B-side of Gene McDaniels's "Spanish Lace"; and issued his own unsuccessful "Golden Gridiron Boy" (coproduced by singer Pat Boone) on Dot Records. Newman's bittersweet-to-sardonic songs were the shaky but promising vision of an outsider who didn't mind announcing that fact, making him a Southern Californian antiromantic slightly ahead of himself as well as his era.

Spector, Wilson, and Newman drew studio support from the same pool of session players and admired the Brill Building genius of the New York–bred writing teams of Gerry Goffin and Carole King, and Barry Mann and Cynthia Weil. But only Spector was actually turning out hits that Goffin-King ("Every Breath I Take" for Gene Pitney) or Mann-Weil ("He's Sure the Boy I Love" for the Crystals) had written.

As *Surfin' Safari* neared completion, Brian felt the need to communicate creatively with other artists outside his immediate sphere—people he could sing with, write with, and also produce himself. In the back of his mind Brian wanted to build a body of production credits at a pace comparable to Spector's, but he also needed to establish working alliances beyond his bond with Gary Usher, who was resisting the three-way publishing split Murry had demanded per the policies of his Sea of Tunes publishing company.

Murry had formed Sea of Tunes early in 1962 to administer Brian's copyrights, father and son orally agreeing they would be equal partners in Sea of Tunes but that Brian would retain all of the copyrights. Murry had coerced his son into the move after learning Brian had been approached by Aldon Music, the prestigious song publishing firm started by Don Kirshner and Al Nevins whose roster of writers included Barry Mann, Cynthia Weil, Carole King, Gerry Goffin, Howard Greenfield, Neil Sedaka, and Neil Diamond.

"Aldon Music wants to sign me up!" Brian yelped one afternoon as he arrived home, bubbling about the good luck of having stopped by the Screen Gems/Aldon office of Lou Adler, who worked with Jan & Dean.

Murry flew into a rage. "Don't ever sign *anything* they tell you to sign!" he seethed. He called his son an idiot and an ingrate for even considering such a step, and said he would instead establish Brian's *own* publishing company. To show his appreciation for the added workload that Murry was willing to take on as a manager and publishing administrator, Murry told Brian he should make Murry his partner—and keep interlopers such as Aldon Music and Gary Usher away from the family businesses.

Brian allowed his father to void the Aldon deal; he admired Aldon's writers but didn't know them well, as Murry sternly admonished. But Brian found it harder to disregard the tension that was growing between Usher and Murry, who hated the idea that a former bank teller could stroll into his home and collaborate with Brian while he, the doting parent who bankrolled and managed the Beach Boys, remained persona non grata when much of the gratifying and lucrative songwriting took place. After "409" became a piggyback hit on the flip side of "Surfin' Safari," generating a fat Sea of Tunes royalty check for Usher besides establishing him in Los Angeles as a credible writer-producer, Murry's jealousy presaged an unraveling of the B. Wilson–G. Usher link. When "Ten Little Indians" made a poor showing in the Hot 100, stalling at number 76, Murry began to openly bad-mouth Usher.

While Brian still liked and admired Usher—and would not give his father the immediate satisfaction of forcibly severing the collaboration— he nonetheless reached out to the next acquaintances who might amplify his muse: singing duo Jan Berry and Dean Torrence, aviation student and surf guitarist Dave Nowlen, Hawthorne High drummer Mark Groseclose, and KFWB disc jockey Roger Christian.

Roger Christian was a native of Buffalo, New York, born July 3, 1924, and an avid hot rod buff who hitchhiked to Los Angeles at age fourteen in search of a job that would help earn him the cash for a 1932 Ford—a deuce coupe. Christian found employment washing dishes at a Chinese eatery in Long Beach and boarded in a room behind the restaurant; he scanned the classified ads in the *Los Angeles Times* for the preferred chassis as he amassed $400 in savings. Late in August he saw what he wanted, selling for $375 in the old Southern Pacific railway town of Lancaster. He thumbed a ride from a passing semi-truck, paid cash on the spot, and drove the coupe straight to Buffalo, the unlicensed, underage adolescent unmolested by state troopers.

Christian had the car he longed for but it was hard to keep a year-round hot-rodder in Buffalo after he had seen the blacktop idyll of Southern California. Christian later returned to Los Angeles, finding work in broadcasting, and he became a popular late-night deejay on KFWB. He was at his microphone one evening during his regular 9:00 P.M.-to-midnight shift, illuminating listeners about the automotive subtleties of the 409 on which the Beach Boys had based their latest single, when the night switchboard received a call from a man named Murry Wilson who claimed to be the parent and manager of the Beach Boys. Christian took the phone and listened as Murry praised his knowledge of car culture and inquired whether he had ever written any songs on the subject.

Christian said he had a whole diary of torsion-bar jottings and drag-strut stanzas, and Murry arranged for Brian and Roger to meet at Christian's earliest convenience. Getting acquainted over hot fudge sundaes at a cafe called Otto's following Christian's midnight sign-off at KFWB, Brian asked to see Christian's notebook and came upon the lyrics for a song called "Shut Down." Stirred by its dense dragster terminology regarding a quarter-mile street test between a 413 Dodge and a fuel-injected Corvette Sting-Ray, Brian set to work contriving a melody to accompany the words. The results became one of four tracks (including "Farmer's Daughter," "Surfin' U.S.A.," and "Lana") Brian recorded with the Beach Boys when he returned to Hollywood's Western Studios in late January and early February 1963 to work with engineer Chuck Britz on the sequel to *Surfin' Safari*.

Indeed, "Shut Down" would be the B-side of the single featuring

"Surfin' U.S.A."—which essentially was a rewrite of Chuck Berry's "Sweet Little Sixteen"—on which Judy Bowles's surfer brother Jimmy once again helped Brian by providing a litany of hip surfing spots for him to name-drop in the lyrics. "Surfin' U.S.A"/"Shut Down" was issued by Capitol on March 4, 1963, and the featured side rose to number 3 in *Billboard*'s Hot 100, while "Shut Down" hit number 23. When the *Surfin' U.S.A.* album hit the stores on March 27, it already had two songs with national reputations, and Roger Christian found himself spinning his own collaborative Beach Boys sensation for night owls tuned to KFWB.

Besides cutting Dick Dale's "Let's Go Trippin' " and his '62 hit "Misirlou" for their *Surfin' U.S.A.* release, the Beach Boys also recorded four tunes for the album on which Brian claimed sole writer's credit: "Farmer's Daughter" (which boasted heart-stealing singing by Brian), "Noble Surfer," "Finder's Keepers," and the instrumental "Stoked." Mike Love sang lead on roughly half of *Surfin' U.S.A.*'s songs including the title track and "Shut Down," and showed dramatic strides in vocal confidence. Carl contributed his first solo composing effort, "Surf Jam." The group also covered the mid-fifties' Bill Doggett standard "Honky Tonk," and Brian and Gary Usher's doleful "Lonely Sea" finally landed on a Beach Boys record.

As Usher's collaborative access to Brian started to dwindle, Gary spent more time with Dennis, with whom he enjoyed a mutual loathing of Murry. Since both longed to stay as far away from the Wilson patriarch as possible, Dennis briefly shared an apartment with Gary on Eucalyptus Avenue near the Hawthorne-Inglewood line. The two took Benzedrine one day and drove to Tijuana in quest of "local action." En route they wrote two car songs, "R.P.M." and "My Sting Ray," the latter lyric evincing Dennis's great desire to own a Corvette. The two sides were cut for the Warner Bros.–distributed Challenge label under the pseudonym the Four Speeds, with Dennis playing drums, and did well locally.

Sadly, the two-sided single led to Dennis's settling for a custom metallic-blue Corvair that he quickly smashed in a drunken accident. A former go-carting companion of Dennis's and Carl's named Mark Groseclose was hired to replace a badly shaken Dennis for four Beach Boys gigs, beginning with a Valentine's Day dance at Hawthorne High. Groseclose had known Carl since seventh grade when they sneaked cigarettes after school and taped dirty bongos-and-acoustic-guitar renditions of folk ballads on Brian's Wollensak, and Dennis had been in Mark's sophomore woodshop class. Groseclose learned the band's material quickly, playing well enough that Dave Marks openly expressed the hope that Mark could stay on despite Dennis's recovery—a notion Murry quickly nixed. However, Brian admired Groseclose's playing enough to invite him to sit in on outside sessions he was producing. One was a date at Gold Star studios with a side group called the Survivors that Brian had formed with guitarist Dave Nowlen.

Born on February 19, 1944, in Grand Rapids, Michigan, Nowlen was an assured picker of the Stratocaster persuasion, teaching himself by copying the entire Ventures catalog, *ping* for vibrato *ping*. Graduating from high school in 1962, he received a 1960 Chevrolet Biscayne as a gift from his grandfather and loaded it with clothes, a tape recorder, guitar, and amp, and pointed himself toward Los Angeles, where he enrolled at the Northrop Institute of Technology to study aviation engineering.

Nowlen was well aware of the Beach Boys and was surprised to find their leader living in the modest Crenshaw Park Apartments complex in Inglewood. Brian and buddy Bob Norberg's quarters consisted of two beds, a couple of lamp tables, and a four-button phone on which Brian fielded business calls. Nowlen attended classes during the day and pickup gigs at night with a local act called the Pharoahs, but when he and Brian were free they rode around in Brian's red 1960 Chevy Impala, singing along with the car radio.

"Bet you can't make this note," Brian would boast, his falsetto soaring. Nowlen would match him, pitch and timbre, on any treble peak, while Brian gave him strange sidelong glances.

They frequented the car circuit that flowed nightly from the A&W stand on Hawthorne Boulevard to the Wich Stand on Slauson, whose one-hundred-auto parking lot would be filled to capacity with 'rods swarming with either crew-cut surf bohemians and bubble-haired *wahines,* or broody "hodad" greasers and their snug sweater-cum-capri-pants molls. The Wich Stand was truly the agora of the Southland's golden teenage city-state, part peerless trading post, body and fender bazaar, and great mosque of the misbegotten, luring a fleet new generation with vanilla Cokes the purchasers could spike, french fries infused with exhaust fumes, and flirts willing to follow through on their winked affirmations.

So Brian wrote a song for the Survivors called "The Wich Stand," in which he described cruising the strip in a "metal-flake blue Grand Prix";

reaching the Wich Stand, he and his three buddies find "honeys all over the lot," and decide to pursue a promising foursome, since they "can get eight in this car."

Brian cut the track at Gold Star in 1963 with Dave Nowlen singing lead, Brian on bass and piano, Bob Norberg and Nowlen on guitars, and Hal Blaine drumming. Capitol nixed the track, and Brian wrote a substitute song overnight: "A Joyride Cruise" ("We'll grab a bite to eat and then we'll jump in my car"). Unable to arrange immediate studio time, he impatiently wrote yet another tune, "Pamela Jean," and summoned all the talent at his disposal. Brian, Groseclose, Nowlen, singer Rich Peterson, and Norberg met at Gold Star Studios where they recorded the Dion and the Belmonts–flavored ditty with a "wop, a-wop, a-what I do" vocal bed. Brian and Norbert later added a B-side instrumental called "After the Game."

Professing excitement with the tracks but actually only eager to corral Brian's extracurricular recording activities, Capitol postponed release of the Survivors' one-minute-and-fifty-seven-second "Pamela Jean" single until January 6, 1964. Despite prominent label copy that noted it was "arranged and conducted by Brian Wilson," Capitol allowed the 45 to languish. Capitol also sanctioned Brian's involvement with a young singer on its roster, Sharon Marie Esparza, but two Sharon Marie singles that Brian produced in 1963–64, "Runaround Lover" by Wilson-Love/ "Summertime" by Gershwin and "Thinkin' 'Bout You, Baby"/"Story of My Life," both by Wilson-Love, soon vanished.

Brian's other freelance production involving Nowlen and Groseclose was organized for a new discovery, a girl group called the Honeys that Brian had arranged to be signed by Capitol. Brian had met the group late in 1962 when the Beach Boys were playing a seven-day stand at Pandora's Box, a trendy L.A. coffee bar on Sunset Strip. Gary Usher had brought the three young women along to see the band for which he had been generating material. At the time, Usher was dating one of the Honeys, fifteen-year-old singer Ginger Blake, aka Saundra Glantz, a Chicago native whose family had moved to California in 1955 along with that of her cousins, the Rovell sisters (Diane, sixteen; Marilyn, fourteen; and Barbara, thirteen). Glantz had been featured on Usher's 1961 Titan Records single "You're the Girl"/"Driven Insane," and cut a 45, "Love Me the Way That I Love You"/"Truly," on the tiny Tore label under the name Ginger and the Snaps.

Usher's party sat at a table at the edge of the small stage, and Brian made steady eye contact with fourteen-year-old Marilyn Rovell (who had initially flirted with Carl). The daughter of Lockheed metal worker Irving Rovell and his wife, Mae, Marilyn had her dad's sincerity and her mom's perky charm. Between songs Brian requested a sip from Marilyn's cup of hot chocolate, and he spilled the rest of it on her legs when he floundered handing it back. Usher and his guests returned repeatedly during the week-long engagement, and while Brian was attracted to Diane and Marilyn (who still had eyes for Carl), there was an unaffected grit to the girl's garrulous glow that made him phone her. A series of conversations at all hours led to steady companionship, her concern with his private demons dovetailing with his interest in her singing career.

Within weeks he wrote several songs ("Surfin' Down the Swanee River," "[Oly Oxen Free Free Free] Hide Go Seek," and "The One You Can't Have") for the female trio, which chose its name from the opening couplet of "Surfin' Safari" that stated "some honeys" were certain to be coming along on the early-morning caravan. Groseclose and Nowell played on "Seek," Jack Nitzsche arranged other tracks, and Brian and Nick Venet coproduced the batch.

The Beach Boys, Honeys, and Usher's Four Speeds with Dennis Wilson on drums soon shared a triple bill for shows such as the KSEE radio–sponsored "Surfing Spectacular" in July at Veterans Memorial Stadium in Santa Maria. That fall, Usher and Dennis issued another overlooked Four Speeds single on Challenge, "Cheater Slicks"/"Four on the Floor." As for the Honeys, although "Swanee" did well in Sweden and Denmark, none of the trio's Capitol singles sold domestically during 1963, including ones they wrote themselves such as "Pray for Surf," whose strong Jan & Dean influence was owed to the Honeys' presence as backup singers on several of that duo's hits.

Jan & Dean's initial professional meeting with the Beach Boys occurred at a teen hop run by a local promoter at a high school in one of the South Bay beach communities. Jan & Dean were the headliners on the bill the promoter had packaged, but the vocal duo lacked a steady band, so the Beach Boys were induced to rehearse a half-dozen songs with Jan & Dean and serve as their backing band. Being fans of the pair (as their emulative vocals on "Surfin' " indicated), the Boys were thrilled to share the stage with the stars, who had had eleven singles charted nationally since 1958. After the Beach Boys' own thirty-minute opening set, the group supported Jan & Dean for their short program that included a Mann-Weil tune they had just recorded for Liberty called "My Favorite Dream."

The show was a breath shy of an hour when Jan & Dean completed their prepared material, but the crowd hollered for more. A flustered Dean Torrence turned to the Beach Boys and said, "Well, why don't we play *your* songs?" The group was stunned by the compliment and launched into a two-song Beach Boys encore, Brian joining Jan & Dean on harmonies.

Afterward, as the musicians packed their grip, handshakes and phone numbers were exchanged. On March 4, 1963, the Beach Boys were invited to visit Jan and Dean at Conway Recorders, where they were asked to play and sing the backing parts on Jan & Dean's own renditions of "Surfin' " and "Surfin' Safari," with Jan Berry and Brian producing.

Jan & Dean had just entered the *Billboard* charts with "Linda," which had previously been both a number 1 and a number 5 hit in 1947 for, respectively, British bandleader Ray Noble with vocalist Buddy Clark and for Charlie Spivak and His Orchestra. The song was written in 1947 by songwriter Jack Lawrence in payment for legal fees by show business attorney Lee Eastman, its title a tribute to Eastman's five-year-old daughter Linda. (Sixteen years later, when Jan & Dean re-recorded it, Linda Eastman was twenty-one and a former student of the University of Arizona, as well as a fan of the Beach Boys, whom she had met when they roomed in the apartment next to hers while gigging at a University of Arizona fraternity house.)

With "Linda" headed toward *Billboard*'s Top 30, Jan and Dean elected to merge their hit single and Beach Boys–kindled interest in surf pop into a nominal concept album for Liberty called *Jan and Dean Take Linda Surfing*. After they prevailed on Brian for more prospective songs, Brian sat down at the piano and sang several verses of "Surfin' U.S.A.," which Jan and Dean promptly requested permission to cover. Brian shyly declined, explaining it was already slated to be a Beach Boys single, but proffered two other songs: "(When Summer Comes) Gonna Hustle You," a piece about an adolescent suitor (later cut by Jan & Dean as "The New Girl in School"), and a ditty originally called "Goody Connie Won't You Come Back Home" but now named "Two Girls for Every Boy." Jan loved the latter tune's latest working title and exclaimed, "We'll take it!"

With alterations plus the addition of an uncredited verse Jan borrowed from a Roger Christian tune that Jan had commissioned about the

'34 Ford wagon, called "Surfin' Woodie," the song was finished and renamed "Surf City." Jan and Dean were heartened by the surf-pop credibility that Brian Wilson's name afforded them, achieving their first number 1 hit with "Surf City" in the summer of 1963.

Capitol Records proved less enthusiastic. Capitol promo men instinctively phoned radio stations in anger when the single was first aired, assuming jocks had somehow gotten a test pressing of the newest Beach Boys release. When they learned the harmony-rich beach anthem was a Jan & Dean song on Liberty in which Brian had played a pivotal role, there was blood on the walls. Nick Venet tried to dissuade Brian from involvement with Jan & Dean and non-Capitol artists, but such projects were the essence of Brian's Phil Spector–inspired vision of his career. Such restraints were unthinkable—as well as a legal quagmire due to the Beach Boys' ambiguous boilerplate contract. Although Murry detested Jan and Dean for absconding with Brian's stand-by hits, he threw his support behind his son, battling to keep Brian as independent of Venet's wiles and dictums as possible. Since Capitol found Murry an intolerable pest, Voyle Gilmore allowed him to prevail, and the group suddenly found itself allowed to record outside the precincts of Capitol Studios—a major political and logistical concession in a period of strict corporate controls.

More significant for Brian was the artistic freedom that the physical distance from Capitol's executive minders afforded. Now he could experiment further with the vocal double-tracking he had utilized on "Surfin' U.S.A.," a technique of synchronized vocal layering—taping singing parts two or more times on top of each other—that enabled him to "strengthen" and "brighten" the Boys' vocal harmonies without dependence on Capitol's own prized echo chambers, whose effect was too artificial for Brian's tastes.

In Liberty sessions throughout 1963, he and Dean Torrence perfected Brian's double-tracking method on other Jan & Dean songs Brian coauthored such as "She's My Summer Girl" (a B-side cut at the "Surf City" taping) and "Drag City." When Brian didn't assist in the writing of Jan & Dean material, he sang backing or doubled segments on their tracks. And Roger Christian likewise became a casually shared resource, as illustrated by the "Honolulu Lulu" single that followed "Surf City."

"Honolulu Lulu" was completed during a July 12, 1963, recording date that followed a wee hours' stint of writing between Roger Christian and Jan Berry over a bowl of tapioca pudding at Los Angeles's Copper

Penny all-night diner. Producer Lou Adler had suggested the title, and a bleary-eyed Christian scrawled the lyrics on a napkin, which he neglected to retrieve when the waitress cleared the dishes. Realizing his carelessness, Christian asked Berry to help him scour the diner's back-alley dumpster in search of the rough draft of the song; he finally found the precious napkin at 4:00 A.M.

"Honolulu Lulu" hit number 11 on *Billboard*'s Hot 100, while "Drag City," the Berry-Christian-Wilson–crafted hot rod reply to their earlier smash, would reach number 10. Jan & Dean sounded almost pious in their praise of a blue coral wax job that "sure looked pretty" and how they were gonna get their chicks and make it out to Drag City. Like "Surfin' U.S.A." and "Shut Down," these were songs around which the youth of America were constructing their daydream idylls. But they proved tough for their exponents to live up to: On March 4, 1963, Frances Love filed for divorce from Mike Love in Los Angeles County Superior Court, charging "extreme cruelty."

14

• • • •

I Get Around

It had been two years and two months since Mike and Frances Love's wedding, and the couple had been living in a rented two-bedroom home at 5642½ Aldama Street in the Highland Park section of Los Angeles's Thirteenth District with their daughters Melinda, one, and Teresa, three months.

Community property consisted of their residence's furniture, furnishings, and appliances, a checking account at the Highland Park Bank of America containing $226, a savings account at the same bank with $40 on deposit, one $75 U.S. Savings Bond, three life insurance policies for Michael totaling $17,500, and a 1961 Jaguar E-type sports coupe with a 3.8-liter engine. Outstanding medical and family debts totaled $1,457.

In court papers twenty-year-old Frances charged that Michael, twenty-two, had struck her on the arm and ripped her clothes on February 19, 1963, and threatened to injure her on other occasions. She added

that she was "in fear of severe bodily harm" if Michael "was not restrained from molesting, annoying, harassing, or bothering" her in any
manner whatsoever.

Frances, a college student whose sole income was the $90 she re-
ceived as a part-time clerk at the UCLA library, sought custody of the
children as well as support payments. She maintained that Mike had
collected $1,400 in Beach Boys royalty payments in January 1963 and
would collect $4,000 more in March, and that from that money he had
earlier agreed to settle a $1,400 debt owed to Frances's relatives.

On May 10, 1963, Judge Jesse J. Frampton awarded custody of Melinda and Teresa Love to their mother, with reasonable visitation rights
accorded their father. Mike was ordered to pay $250 on the first day of
each month, as of June 1, for maintenance of the minor children until
further court notice. Alimony payments were awarded to Frances of
$150 per month until March 1968, and she retained their former home's
furniture and appliances. Mike was ordered to settle all common debts
(including those to Frances's family) by April 15, 1963, and pay attorney
fees of $300 plus court costs, besides agreeing to purchase an automobile
for his wife for not more than $300. Both Frances and Mike waived the
right to inherit the estate of the other.

Mike, now living in Hermosa Beach, was allowed to keep the Jaguar,
bank accounts in his name, and life insurance policies, but in the event of
Mike's death the children would be irrevocable beneficiaries until they
reached their majority. The court ruled the divorce would become final a
year hence, on May 22, 1964.

Mike's initial fondness for Frances occurred at the very frontier of
their adulthood, a time when choices and limitations were the furthest
things from their minds. Prior to learning of Frances's pregnancy, neither
partner had seriously considered the prospect of what became a shotgun
marriage leavened with public shame, thus ensuring that the newlyweds' fundamental tensions would never abate. A sense of humiliation,
rancor, and mistrust permeated the relationship, enforced by the cynical
sides-taking of their elders. And Mike, whose cockiness was the banner
of his insecurities, was forever on trial, the surest focus of all disparage-
ment—just as he had been while under his parents' roof.

No one in California liked to have his or her longings unfulfilled, and
those who faltered in their adaptability to fate often fell hard in the eyes
of their fellow seekers. The Love men were of a magisterial breed—
dutiful, ambitious, and detached—and the women they bonded with

tended to match them in their competitive drive and sharp critical expectations. Mike had never known a woman whose neediness was balanced by a nurturing instinct; one penalty of his adolescent sexual misadventure was an inability to perceive any such qualities amid the strains and judgments his sudden new circumstances with Frances imposed.

One female in Mike Love's background who showed him unconditional approval and support was Edith Sthole Wilson, his maternal grandmother. From boyhood Mike was Edith's favorite. She liked his individuality, spirit, and decisiveness, and she let her daughter Glee and the rest of the Love and Wilson clans know it. Mike Love lost a wife in a breakup that was half his fault, but he also lost a blood ally that same year when Edith died at the age of sixty-six. In her grief, Glee Love took little notice of her own son's loss, instead mixing mourning for her beloved mother with venomous rage toward her father, Buddy Wilson, whom she blamed for sending Edith to an early grave. Now that the matriarch who had safely brought the Wilson children to the West was gone, Glee felt she had no further call to accommodate, humor, or even acknowledge the existence of Buddy Wilson. Although most of his brothers maintained some contact with Buddy, he was effectively expelled from the other wings of the Wilson tribe for the remainder of his long, acutely lonesome life.

Mike Love had no great fondness for his grandfather, but he, like Buddy, knew what it felt like to be scorned and dismissed. And all these actions and reactions, hurts and harbored grudges, would be stored in the souls and psyches of the Loves, the Wilsons, and their offspring, building on one another, exerting an insidious sway on the shapes and structures of the lives of those who retained and inherited them. They would enforce old cycles of behavior, wheels grinding within wheels, as their reservoirs of dark energy seeped and sputtered and sometimes exploded into the tidal currents of each descendant's destiny.

Meanwhile, the sphere in which the newly divorced Mike Love excelled was the stage, where his utter confidence in his own tastes, opinions, and outlooks served him well. But this was hardly a place where his former wife and young children could have supported or complemented him. In fact, their public presence would have been awkward and encumbering because Mike and his cousins and cohorts in the band had to exemplify the flaming youth of the era, prime stewards at the feast of the sun: uncomplicated, unentangled, and undivided in their attention to regaling audiences with their California creed.

Looking less like a Beach Boy than a beach bachelor—lanky and bantering in demeanor, but balding and carefully poised in carriage—Love's sportive attitude and knowing nasal vocals lent roguish adult accreditation to his group's most sentimental visions. And of all Brian's collaborators, he was already the most important and least appreciated—or credited. A good ad-libber in the studio, Love had the glib tendency to offer memorable tag lines like "she's real fine, my 409" to fill out the spaces behind each scripted chorus. During the summer and early fall of 1963, as Brian assembled material to feed a hungry public and a ravenous Capitol product stream, it was Mike (himself a game, if ungifted, neophyte surfer) who was able to supply Brian with crucial lyrics for songs such as "Hawaii," an utterly convincing fugue of the South Seas surfing matrix, and "Catch a Wave," a canticle to the crest-riding that Brian was loath to attempt.

And when Brian sat at Murry's piano to play Bob Norberg and Dave Nowlen a fervent new psalm to school spirit entitled "Be True to Your School," it was Love who supplied the suitably vainglorious opening gambit: "When some loud braggart tries to put you down . . ."

In 1963 the Beach Boys' *Surfin' U.S.A.* album spent two weeks at number 2 in *Billboard,* and their high tide of popular success lifted every vessel of the surf-music ethos on the horizon. The Chantays, a Santa Ana quintet, enjoyed a number 4 *Billboard* Hot 100 chart success in May (and a number 16 hit in England in June) with an instrumental called "Pipeline." First demoed in popular surf-instro mill Pal Studios in Cucamonga (but recut in stereo in Downey Records' Downey, California, control room), the song was named for the famed tube curl of waves off Ehukai beach on the north shore of Oahu, Hawaii.

The previous November, an instrumental act from Glendora called the Surfaris cut a gimmick instrumental at Pal's facilities that opened with the simulation of a wave-swamped surfer tumbling off his disintegrating board. Opening effects for this "Wipe Out" included an old shingle splintered on the mike to echo a snapped surfboard and a wicked-witch cackle courtesy of Glendora record producer Dale Smallin. The drum solo redolent of the pounding wave collapse was a cadence that Surfaris drummer Ron Wilson borrowed from the repertoire of the Charter Oak High School marching band, adding breaks akin to those on Oakland bongo player Preston Epps's 1959 Original Sound Records hit "Bongo Rock." After pressing two thousand copies on his own DFS label, Smallin interested the Princess label in a deal that led to radio response in Santa Barbara and Fresno and a licensing deal in April 1963 with Dot Records, which took the single to number 2 nationwide.

It was an interval of innocence and cynicism, faith and folly. President Kennedy's Commission on Drug Abuse declared war on narcotics importers. The Telstar 2 communications satellite was launched into orbit, followed a week later by the Faith 7 manned Mercury space capsule that carried astronaut Gordon Cooper, Jr., around the planet twenty-two times. But in Birmingham, Alabama, police were ambushing black civil rights marchers with attack dogs and fire hoses.

By May 1963, Brian Wilson was calling in sick for Beach Boys concerts; sporadic spells of stage fright were exacerbated by the toll the volume at live shows took on his good ear. He was also enervated from the tug of his affection for Marilyn Rovell of the Honeys and its overlap with the mixed emotional signals he was getting from Judy Bowles, his oldest flame, the girl with whom he had lost his virginity and the woman to whom he had nearly become engaged (she turned him down).

It seemed an apt time for Brian to pull back from all external stresses and concentrate on further studio refinement of the Beach Boys oeuvre, and the centerpiece of this effort was Brian's unreleased song from his February 1962 sessions with Hite Morgan, "Surfer Girl." The spontaneous outcome of a moment of concentration while driving, he had refined it all—the bridge, the lyrics—in one day's effort at the family piano. Even his own brothers assumed Brian had written the Four Freshmen–flavored song in homage to Judy Bowles, but the actual spark for the ballad of idealized ardor was Leigh Harline and Ned Washington's "When You Wish Upon a Star," the Oscar-winning song sung by Jiminy Cricket in the animated 1940 Walt Disney film classic *Pinocchio*.

In the story's original magazine serialization by nineteenth-century Italian writer Carlo Collodi, the cricket was a nameless companion whose resolve to serve as Pinocchio's conscience ends with the bug being crushed under the indifferent puppet's wooden foot. The Disney version transformed the hapless insect into a self-reliant sidekick whose moral admonishments were valued and heeded, leading to the grasshopper's reward of a special blessing from the ineffable lovely oracle with whom he had become smitten: the Blue Fairy.

For Brian, the object of desire in "Surfer Girl" was as idealized as Disney's comely Blue Fairy. Drawn from a solitary stream-of-consciousness whim conceived en route to a Hawthorne hot dog stand one day in late 1961, Brian's Disney-inspired theme depicted an out-of-reach goddess whose charms eclipsed those of Judy Bowles, Carol Mountain, Carol Hess, and every other unfulfilling high school infatuation. Arriving home, he composed the bridge, devised the harmony structure, and marveled at the two-minute grandeur of his handiwork: the first song he ever wrote.

Vocally, Brian's biggest stylistic beacon on the "Surfer Girl" track he re-recorded at Western Studios was the real-life source of Jiminy Cricket's silky warbling, Cliff Edwards. Known in the 1920s as Ukelele Ike, Edwards had an oboelike tenor voice whose inflection verged on being pretty while remaining inarguably virile. Edwards's vast rota of hit recordings from Broadway shows and over fifty early film musicals included "It Had to Be You," "Who Takes Care of the Caretaker's Daughter?", "Paddlin' Madelin' Home," "I Can't Give You Anything but Love," "Singin' in the Rain," and "It's Only a Paper Moon," as well as his other Jiminy Cricket–conveyed smash from *Pinocchio*, "Give a Little Whistle."

The strongest tonal purity of Brian's voice also resided in the falsetto register. Although he loved testing his high-pitched articulation in the privacy of his room, Brian would confide to Judy, Marilyn, and mother Audree Wilson that its unmanly aspects were one of the biggest "hang-ups" of his life. Yet somehow the sound and image of Cliff Edward's Jiminy Cricket bravely intoning "When You Wish Upon a Star" emboldened Brian to step beyond his inhibitions and sing his falsetto heart out. In *Pinocchio*'s "Wish" sequence, Jiminy urged the puppet to foster the credo that he could become a flesh-and-blood little boy, much as the noble cricket himself might hope for rebirth as a fit suitor for the Blue Fairy. Brian made himself believe a woman as supreme as the phantasmal surfer girl would respond to the courtly love of his pop poetry.

From such impossible visions are uncommon deeds ordained. On June 12, 1963, the day after Governor George Wallace stepped aside and allowed National Guard troops to enforce enrollment of two black students at the University of Alabama, Brian Wilson and the Beach Boys began recording their *Surfer Girl* album.

That day NAACP field director Medgar Evers was murdered by a sniper while leading a voter registration drive in Jackson, Mississippi. His older brother Charles immediately took Medgar's place in the ultimately triumphant effort. "The only way to change the system," said Charles, "is to become the system."

In his own milieu, on his own terms, Brian Wilson sought to subvert the system by which his music was funneled to the outside world. Bucking the corporate methodology by which Nat King Cole cut *The Christmas Song*, Al Martino made *I Love You Because*, and the country's leading folk-pop act created *The Kingston Trio #16* (each a Top 10 LP in '63), Brian demanded total production authority on the third Beach Boys album. He wanted no staff A&R men vetoing songs, hiring sidemen, and meddling with arrangements; no go-betweens of any kind except Western Studios' chief engineer Chuck Britz, who would toil for *him*.

Capitol bristled. Murry was sent in to make his manic, overweening points on behalf of his boy wonder—and Brian won. For the first time in the history of rock and roll the artist himself had absolute studio authority over his album-length output. To fix the mettle of his autonomy in the minds of label and band alike, Brian carefully chose the musicians he wanted to assist him in the definitive version of "Surfer Girl."

Still, Brian intended the project to be an inclusive one. Mike Love now had a Ford deuce coupe, and he advised Brian to pen a song about the hottest rod in the Southland. Brian remembered that months before he had glimpsed some stanzas topped with that very title in Roger Christian's motor-minded notebook, and he hastened to ask the disc jockey if he still had them. Brian took the words, added a line about the pink slip that denoted California car ownership papers, and built a demo around them on the same day he cut "Surfer Girl." Mike sang lead, and Dennis supplied some drums.

But Dennis's rhythm was too unruly. Brian asked Hal Blaine, the Spector/Jan & Dean session percussionist who had played on "Surfin' U.S.A." and had just done the "Surfer Girl" takes, to help lay a new backbeat-heavy line over Denny's inadequate part, emphasizing the low snare and up-pitch floor tom-tom that Brian preferred.

Returning to the studio on July 16, Brian recorded his own rendition of Bob & Sheri's "Surfer Moon," double-tracking his own harmonies, as he also did on "Your Summer Dream." The boogie-woogie tempos he often pounded out for the benefit of schoolmate Rich Sloan's tape recorder were resurrected with a classical-safari twist on "Boogie Woodie," its melody tracing Rimsky-Korsakov's "Flight of the Bumble-Bee."

"South Bay Surfer" and the instrumental "The Rocking Surfer" (the latter originally called "Good Humor Man") had the bare-feet-on-cold-linoleum brio of the early after-school hops young Brian attended at the Gunga Din recreation center.

And Brian decided the moment had come to put "In My Room," the haunting song he had penned with Gary Usher, on a Beach Boys album. Bringing Dennis, Carl, and himself before the tube U-47 microphone in Western Studio 3, he taped an opening harmony verse that mirrored the three-part chordal vocals he had taught them when they were kids and shared the same bedroom in the house on West 119th Street.

Mike's sister Maureen was invited to play her harp on "In My Room" as well as "Catch a Wave," the latter song featuring her sibling on lead vocal.

Mike shared vocals with Brian on "Hawaii," Brian soaring on a falsetto break so impeccable it made onlookers' eyes well up in admiration. Brian and Mike teamed again for the main vocals of "Our Car Club," an intricate arrangement influenced by Mongo Santamaria's hit of the previous spring, "Watermelon Man." Originally titled "Rabbit's Foot," the track was done at Gold Star Studios, Phil Spector's headquarters, with co-owner Stan Ross and staff technician Larry Levine engineering. Hal Blaine substituted for Denny on drums.

Since Dennis was the most active board rider in the band, he became lead singer on "Surfer's Rule," which examined the rivalry between surfers and the switchblade-and-sideburns ranks of the hodads. It was a beach-versus-asphalt antipathy that Brian personalized as a West Coast–versus–East Coast pop rumble by slyly singing a snatch of the New Jersey–bred Four Seasons' number 1 hit of the past winter, "Walk Like a Man."

Other tensions and rivalries seethed into an uncertain stew once *Surfer Girl* was completed. In the Beach Boys' camp, Brian was refusing to accompany the group on its current tour commitments. Al Jardine, who had returned to El Camino Junior College, was summoned back to the fold to replace Brian on the road. Thus, for a few months the Beach Boys became six: Al on bass, Carl on lead guitar, Mike on vocals, Dennis on drums, Dave Marks on rhythm guitar, and Brian as writer, producer, and studio vocalist.

However, Murry, who was traveling with the band as its manager, began needling Dave Marks over minor failings and stage infractions such as not smiling enough. The nitpicking escalated after Jo Ann Marks challenged Murry on the low pay scale and subsidiary status her son was accorded. Marks and Murry were in the same car on the Beach Boys' way from New York to Philadelphia when the two had their most dyspeptic quarrel and Dave quit (though he agreed to complete the band's remaining road dates).

Marks signed a formal Capitol Records amendment to the Beach Boys' July 1962 recording contract, which stated that "Capitol has been advised that on August 30, 1963, David L. Marks ceased to be a member of the group performing as 'The Beach Boys,' " adding that "David L. Marks is hereby released and discharged by the signatories hereto"— Brian, Dennis, Carl, Mike, and Capitol vice president F. M. Scott III— "from any and all obligations and/or liabilities for or in connection with masters unrecorded as of August 30, 1963." This meant that tracks from the July 16 *Surfer Girl* sessions, among them "Little Deuce Coupe," would be the last to contain Marks's playing.

All future sessions, including the one slated for September 2 to cut additional tracks for an impending hot rod collection of old and new Beach Boys car songs, would feature the rhythm guitar of Al Jardine or others. The front of the jacket art for the October 7 release of the album to be titled *Little Deuce Coupe* was a photo of a mighty chrome coupe courtesy of *Hot Rod* magazine, but the already completed back cover imagery included Dave in group pictures around a Corvette Sting Ray; Capitol opted to retain the misleading band portrait rather than go to the time and expense of redoing it. Brian was also under pressure to generate enough car material to supplement the recycled "Deuce Coupe," "Shut Down," "409," and "Our Car Club" on the Boys' car corpus.

The Survivors' "Pamela Jean," still not due for single release by Capitol until January 1964, was quickly rewritten by Brian as "Car Crazy Cutie." His old "Land Ahoy" piece from 1962 was recast as "Cherry, Cherry Coupe," and Bobby Troup's "Their Hearts Were Full of Spring" was revamped as a post–car crash eulogy for martyred screen idol James Dean.

"Spirit of America" was a Brian Wilson and Roger Christian tribute to speed racer Craig Breedlove, whose jet-powered "Spirit of America" three-wheeler rocket car had set a land-speed record of 407 miles per hour that August on Utah's Bonneville Salt Flats. The Wilson-Christian "Ballad of Ole Betsy" and "No-Go Showboat" joined Brian's "Custom Machine" to round out the engine-head raveups on the record.

By this time, Brian and Bob Norberg had moved to a large, furnitureless house on 102nd Street in Inglewood that the whole band was using as a flop pad, and guitarist-friend Dave Nowlen of the Survivors had an apartment two blocks away on 104th Street. Brian was driving a brand-new 1964 Grand Prix, cruising the Wich Stand with Dave, as the group was putting the final touches on *Little Deuce Coupe*.

In their off-hours, Murry insisted that the Boys and their friends help renovate the Wilsons' Hawthorne home, remodeling Carl's room and the living room. Bob Norberg and Dave Nowlen (for whom it was a paying gig) were painting the living room a light pink on the afternoon Brian rushed in to explain his concept for *Little Deuce Coupe*'s crowning track, "Be True to Your School," on which the Honeys would act as cheerleaders for the rah-rah-rah chorus of the track. Nowlen and Norberg were present for the "School" session at Western Studios, in which a complement of Spector session musicians participated, including Hal Blaine on drums.

On September 26, 1963, exactly ten days after the release of *Surfer Girl*, Brian was invited to attend a 12:00 P.M. to 3:00 A.M. taping at Gold Star Studios for Phil Spector's forthcoming *A Christmas Gift for You* album featuring holiday selections by Darlene Love, the Ronettes, the Crystals, Bob B. Soxx & the Blue Jeans, and assorted others in Spector's stable. The task at hand when Brian entered the room was a run-through of the Crystals' reinterpretation of a holiday favorite first popularized by Bing Crosby and the Andrews Sisters, "Santa Claus Is Comin' to Town."

Approaching Brian expectantly, Phil motioned him over to the piano and suggested he take a pass at the melody line. Startled by the nonchalant entreaty of his hero, Brian froze and demurred. Spector glowered, shocked by the refusal. As the other thirteen musicians who were gathered for the session (among them bandleader Stephen Douglas Kreisman, bassist Ray Pohlman, guitarist Tommy Tedesco, horn player Jay Migliori, and Hal Blaine) stared nervously, Brian was again urged to sit down at the keyboards. He sheepishly complied, riding with the existing instrumental track for several takes before Spector curtly relieved him. A month later, just before Halloween, Brian received a check from Philles Records for his services on the Christmas album date, made out in the amount of American Federation of Musicians scale as approved by Union Local 47: $56.

Back in New York City, Lenny Waronker (born October 3, 1941) was working as a promotion man for his father Simon's Liberty Records. It was the summer of such films as *Bye Bye Birdie*, *Irma La Douce*, and *Beach Party*, starring Frankie Avalon and Annette Funicello (with brief appearances by Roger Christian, Gary Usher, and Brian Wilson), and the season that saw the introduction of ZIP codes, the Trimline phone, and the Instamatic camera.

Waronker heard an odd vocal harmony on WINS radio one morning.

It seemed strange to encounter such lush and sophisticated vocal harmonies sung to a romantic rock-and-roll melody—but he instantly recognized "Surfer Girl" as a Beach Boys record. Being from Southern California *and* the beach, Lenny wasn't particularly interested in the surfing angle, but the odd hybrid of Brian's harmonies and the rock sensibility seemed weird and wonderful.

"Boy," said Lenny Waronker to his coworkers at Liberty, "somebody in that band must *know* something."

15
• • • •

Our Car Club

When faced with the challenge of fashioning another enhancement of Southern California's hot rod fantasies, the artist always began with a clean, dry surface, made a few easily erasable sketches, and conversed freely with associates as he imagined the flowing diagram of his heartfelt ideas. The entire procedure consisted solely of a seamless series of lyrical lines, so choices of color and curvature were crucial to suggest a sense of substance, as were the contours utilized to manifest speed, grace, and the confidence of forward movement.

Since the effort was really an exercise in controlled daydreaming, physical comfort during the undertaking was essential. Therefore he never worked within the path of direct sunlight, wind, rain, or other unsettling elements. The influence of Mother Nature was integral but passive and reflective—because relaxed concentration was the key to the casual purity of the finished work.

He loved to experiment and try wacky new notions of composition and balance, dropping in some touches for effect, yanking others without apology, frequently wiping smudges and smears of impetuosity into oblivion and starting over again.

Having people watch used to bug him, make him extremely paranoid, but he learned to behave as if they weren't there. Taking a deep breath at regular intervals to steady his thoughts and his hands, he would literally walk the line in the service of his art, exhaling slowly in a Zen-like attunement of his attention span. Whenever possible, he tried to follow existing impressions and markings to find his bearings before devising apt or playful points of departure. And when his handiwork was done, he waited with childlike expectancy for a reaction, needing to know if bystanders approved of every little stroke and spiral.

That's how Ed "Big Daddy" Roth assessed his highly temperamental technique as one of the country's top custom automobile pinstripers toiling in the South Bay towns of South Gate and Maywood during the mid-1960s. But it could just as easily have been Brian Wilson's recounting of the methods he used to create the finest car-culture hymns ever written, particularly "Don't Worry Baby."

Cued by a less solemn modification of the dum-dum-dum-whap! bass drum and snare pattern that begat Phil Spector's 1963 "Be My Baby" production for the Ronettes, "Don't Worry Baby" was written later that same year by Brian Wilson and Roger Christian as a virtual sequel to the Ronettes' number 2 chart skyrocket. Brian upped the vocal ceiling in his emulative arrangement to accommodate the Wagnerian Minnie Mouse yodel that was Ronette lead singer Ronnie Bennett's standard sonic slope.

Brian's gesture was the sincere reflex of an ingenuous fan, and he passed the word through the L.A. studio pipeline that "Worry" was Phil's for the asking. Spector declined, having no yen for material he couldn't own.

While seeking, perhaps unconsciously, to construct a ladder to scale Spector's castle wall, Brian instead rendered something much more pliant, impressionistic, and unpretentious.

Instinctively avoiding the darker chill of Spector's "Baby"—a joint work with Jeff Barry and Ellie Greenwich in which a proud lover craves a partner for the envy it will inspire—Wilson composed a hapless love token that showed its strength in its sudden, surpassing humility. "Don't Worry Baby" is the rock rosary of a young braggart so enamored of his street rod that he pushes the other guys in his clique into a potentially lethal shut down. Gripped on the eve of the race by a premonition of his own demise, he peers through the panicky spell of his self-pity to see that the only worldly possession not worth losing is the unconditional love of his girl. He confesses his shame, and she restores his courage with the loving counsel that comes as second nature: "Don't worry baby."

Brian wrote this and many of his best songs at home in Hawthorne, in the neutral comfort of his music room, a grateful distance from the squealing rubber slicks and man-against-time anxieties of an actual drag race. Brian's chief pressure in concocting "Don't Worry Baby" was also his primary satisfaction: the sight of someone potentially transported by the musical flights of his imagination, as he took half-written lyric ideas into the near-religious realm of a melodic absolute.

The word pictures for "Don't Worry Baby" never quite jelled beyond the force of their prayerfulness, but Brian sang them with celestial zeal. Although fated to be one of his last cooperative bursts with Roger Christian, it was also among the most uplifting, Wilson's reverence for Spector's rakish gifts putting him in a frame of mind where he could thrill Christian and himself with his knack for upgrading the pop impulse.

As Ed Roth well understood, such natural talents were easy prey for cynics. His generation's "motor mania" made auto shop a standard course in most Southland high schools, and now Brian's car music ennobled its blue-collar devotionalism. Snobbish skeptics missed the sense of joy such practical skills conveyed, as well as their catchy capacity for valuing the artistry of small moments.

Brian was happiest bent over the grinning ivories of his Hawthorne upright, bringing the car culture scene unfolding around him into tuneful concord. Roth was most content poised over a '39 Chevy with a split manifold, tracing impeccable curlicues around door handles and wheel wells with a Stabilo pencil before applying $1/64$-inch striations of primrose yellow paint along its body lines with the tapered squirrel hairs of a West German MAC or Dagger brush.

In either case the automatic comments of "Co-o-ol, man" that such keen displays drew from Roger Christian or Ed Roth's adolescent clients were the very soul of the reward that the car culture bestowed on all comers in the shining moment that was 1964, when the promise and ingenuity of the prewar tinkerers bore fruit that turned the world's heads.

Roth called himself and his jumbled colleagues "teen carneys"— unashamed carnival barkers, shills, and touts for an insurgent society on wheels, once so marginal, now so magnificent in its open celebration. Appearing at the Pomona Fair or in the Los Angeles Civic Arena in elaborate weekend congregations, Jan & Dean and the Beach Boys would sing their current releases while loopy draftsman George Barris would exhibit outlandish lead sled dream cars such as the "world of tomorrow" Golden Sahara and the flying saucer–shaped XPAC 400 Hovercraft, each swathed in whorls of angel hair.

At the nucleus of it all stooped Ed Roth, indicating the chrome undercarriages of the prizewinning custom rods he had built for himself, such as the Outlaw (featuring a fiberglass body and a 1955 Cadillac V-8) and the bubble-topped Beatnik Bandit and Road Agent. Unlike those of most show car designers, Roth's autos were not commissioned works or prop prototypes; each was a fully functional vehicle, made from stock parts, that sprang from his private enthusiasms. He sold off his fleet gewgaws only after he had genuinely tired of cavorting in them.

Hurrying around signing autographs and letting infants tug at his goatee, Roth sold trademark Rat Fink T-shirts and pin-striped anything mobile, whether a child's red Radio Flyer wagon, a wheezing Volkswagen bug, or a tractor trailer. All fees were modest, all souvenirs homemade and vended with loving grace.

The first quantum flick forward in the delicate science of pin-striping was the doing of a Compton sign painter and motorcycle/car refinisher known as Von Dutch. In 1955, Von Dutch began using his half-moon Grumbacher "flats" (flat-ended signage brushes) to daub hairline piping and scalloped caricatures over the "grinder marks" (leaded seams in metal bodywork) exposed after the bodies of rods and street machines had been stripped of their old door handles and similar hardware. When the highly polished surfaces of the resultant customized rigs revealed further body blemishes and flaws, Von Dutch's stylized "chickenscratch" camouflage assumed its own design urgency as symmetrical patterns were invented to conceal the irregular paths of the imperfections. Von Dutch's fondest solutions included a set of flying eyeballs that attained logo status. Pin-striping itself became an attraction in every usedcar dealership on Firestone Boulevard, and Wall's Custom Cars was among the local lots that offered it as a regular option.

Roth, a close associate of Von Dutch, found his own pictorial signature circa 1959 when he was arguing over the origins of Disney's Mickey Mouse at a lunch counter in Maywood called the Apollo. He drew Mickey in his earliest "Steamboat Willie" incarnation as a stick figure

and then limned a derisive picture of one of Mickey's primordial forebears: a potbellied rat in overalls. For good symbolic measure, Roth
added the initials R.F. to the rat's droopy chest—shorthand for "Rat
Fink." (In racing terms, a fink was a confirmed cheater who flagrantly
ignored the rules.) The next day Roth's assistant asked Ed to airbrush his
rat fink on a T-shirt. Within months Roth was silk-screening them by the
thousands and selling a generous portion of each batch via mail order in
Hot Rod and *Car Craft.*

In 1960 in Linden, Texas, avid teenage fan Don Henley pushed the gas
pedal of his mail-order Go-Kart to the metal and scattered tumblebrush
as he ripped down Farm Road 1399, a two-lane blacktop leading from
Linden to Marietta, Texas. Henley, the son of a National Auto Parts Association (NAPA) dealer, was a trophy-winning cart racer in the $2^{1}/_{2}$ horsepower class, and he wore the Rat Fink T-shirt he had just obtained by
answering an ad in *Car Craft* magazine.

In 1961 the Venice, California, branch of Revell Toys phoned Roth in
the midst of his morning shave and asked Roth if he would allow Revell
to add scale models of his show cars, Rat Fink spinoffs, and hot rod
ghouls (Tweedy Pie, Angel Fink, Fink Eliminator, Mr. Gasser, Mother's
Worry) to their line of model kits for kids and hobbyists. Roth consented,
earning a two-cent royalty on every kit sold. The children of America
were enchanted, and its mischievous adolescents made Rat Fink an icon
and a treasured antidote to Mickey Mouse.

But Revell publicist Henry Blankfort found Roth's name too bland for
the company promotional campaign. Informed that Roth's high school
nickname had been "Big Ed" and aware of a revival of beatnik-hipster
argot where young Hollywood intersected with car and beach boho
types, Blankfort suggested Roth become "Big Daddy." "Cool!" Roth replied, and the alias and likeness of Ed "Big Daddy" Roth was added to
box illustrations for the Mysterion and other roadster kits, as well as the
Drag Nut and Surfink figurines that Revell billed as Ed's Custom Monster
Parade.

In 1962, Revell titillated the industry's annual toy fair when, amid
new H-O train sets and kits for the S.S. *Hope,* it introduced retailers to its
$^{1}/_{25}$-scale model of Ed "Big Daddy" Roth's Outlaw, offering it at a suggested retail price of $1.98. By 1963, Roth was on the art staff of *Car-
Toons,* Petersen Publications' answer to *Mad.*

The capstone of Roth's 1963–64 automotive vaudeville was the
Surfite, a squat, one-passenger fiberglass beach buggy sporting a duckbill

hood and a wide-paned driver's booth, with a Gordon & Smith surfboard held in an easel-type rack on its right side. The droll coach was fabricated upon the frame of a junkyard-salvaged Mini-Cooper, enlisting several South Bay board shapers to help smooth the Surfite's rails and hull. The contraption seemed to spoof the goofiest woodie wagons in Rick Griffin's comic drawings in *Surfer* magazine, yet its sidewinder four-cylinder engine ran faultlessly on safaris. Like Roth himself, his wildest passions were always road tested and proven to be practical.

Born March 4, 1932, in Beverly Hills to cabinetmaker Henry Roth and wife Marie, Ed was descended from a long line of German-Polish tradesmen (tinsmiths, tailors, joiners, broom masters) of Christian and Jewish heritage. Ed and his younger brother Gordon were reared in a reserved German-American home with models of zeppelins on the mantel and books on military history in the parlor. As a lad he felt discomfited by what he called the "mechanical language" and "precise thought" of his stiff relatives who were inclined to make statements like "This is how it should be done, Edward." He found the Madison Avenue version of English more persuasive, adoring the hectic pitches and euphonious jargon that streamed from radio and television broadcasts. Entering Bell High School, Ed divided his time between drawing war scenes in class and making after-school forays to local junkyards, where he and his friends bartered car parts that they carried back to their garages.

New cars hadn't been available since the outbreak of the war. Between the gas rationing and the scarity of even secondhand '42 autos, there was nothing running you could get cheap. Since California law allowed one a driver's license on one's fourteenth birthday, the principal pastime of Ed Roth's eager generation was to build a heap from the ground up, simultaneously turning every garage in the Southland into clubhouse sanctuaries that were off-limits to adults.

When a scavenged engine turned over for the first time, the teenage tinkerers and "toolies" ran their raspy jalopies out to Slauson Avenue after dusk to drag for pink slips, seizing ownership of losing rods driven by opponents from rival Huntington Park High.

The pocket book–size hamlet of Maywood was a great site on which to drag since long and bare Slauson bisected it like the center crease in an open pulp novel. You could tear unimpeded down the mammoth fold of the thoroughfare, your car's tailwind wafting the sandy rises on either side, and since Maywood had only two patrolmen (who seldom made a show for the chief), civil apprehension was unlikely.

If pursued, however, one could swerve into the orange groves on the south side of the straightaway beyond the Los Angeles River or lurch into the Molokan Orthodox Russian Cemetery on the north side of the street, hiding out until it was safe to regroup at Stan's Drive-In at Firestone Boulevard and Atlantic Avenue in Bell. The fuel economy of the quarter-mile sprints was a help in petroleum-pinched 1945, but gas was more plentiful when Roth got his driver's permit a year later, so he never learned restraint.

Attending East Los Angeles Junior College, Roth obtained an associate degree in mechanical engineering. He joined the Air Force in 1951, got married in 1952, read his first copy of Petersen Publishing's *Honk!* customizing magazine in May 1953, and was hooked by the time it changed its name to *Car Craft* that December. Discharged in 1955, Roth held down a day job in the display department at Sears while moonlighting as a journeyman pinstriper and pathfinding fiberglass shaper. Roth helped pioneer the use of the meltable/moldable silica cloth and resin, which had formerly been a plumbing and insulation material, as a versatile body-and-fender alternative to costly metal.

Roth made his first diagrams of the Outlaw (initially dubbed the Excalibur) while in the service, but it wasn't until 1959 that he built the car and took it to Disneyland for one of its earliest public showings. Comprised of a Cadillac V-8, a '48 Ford rear end, '58 Chevy taillights, a '27 Dodge windshield, '59 Rambler headlights, molded interior, and custom motorcycle wheels in front, the Outlaw combined the look of a hot rod and the attitude of a custom street racer—and it was an immediate national sensation, the archetypal mean machine.

At Capitol, Dot, Liberty, Decca, Columbia, Tower, RCA, Warner Bros., Mercury, and dozens of smaller labels there was a feeding frenzy afoot for anything that smelled of sea air, surf wax, and West Coast fuel exhaust, all hands riding the emblematic shirttails of a certain Hawthorne group still learning to fill its own mufti.

"Surfer Girl" climbed to number 7 in *Billboard*'s Hot 100 as Labor Day 1963 sunburns and celebrations faded and back-to-school consumer campaigns ensued around the country. The single's "Little Deuce Coupe" flip side jumped to number 15 on its own propulsive merits as hot cars took seasonal precedence over the nine-foot-six-inch Phil Edwards–model guns (big wave boards) that Hobie Surfboards had recently introduced.

But there was more cross-merchandising to come. Capitol Records

The Wilson grape ranch, in the Hog's Back Foothills, Escondido, California, 1904 *(Courtesy Charles Wilson)*

Pomeroy, Ohio, farmer and land owner George Washington Wilson was the patriarch of the Wilson clan, and the local family of his wife, Mary Bailey, were dear friends. George signed this July 1870 guardianship deed to the Forked Run Farm, near Longbottom, Ohio, which his young daughter Lois inherited from her beloved Grandpa Bailey.

To the Probate Court of Meigs County, Ohio:

The undersigned represents that *Lois Wilson* was born on the 31st day of *November, 1854* that

that she is Minor Children of, *George W. Wilson* and that the said Minor is a resident of the said County of Meigs: And the undersigned further represents that the said Minor

THE STATE OF OHIO, MEIGS COUNTY, SS.

George W. Wilson

George W. Wilson

Signed in my presence by *George W. Wilson* and sworn to by him before me, this 25th day of *July A.D. 1870*

Probate Judge.

Main Street, Hutchinson, Kansas, 1920s *(Courtesy Kansas State Historical Society)*

Alta Chitwood Wilson and her husband, William Henry Wilson, Ohio, 1880s, just prior to their move to Kansas

Hutchinson News advertisement for Wilson & Hines plumbing business, 1913

DURABLE PLUMBING

The length of service is the true test of plumbing cost. Our work is done in accordance with the best methods, and we install "Standard" plumbing fixtures which are guaranteed, so you need have no fear of the durability of your plumbing when we do the work.

Our methods, experience, and ability for handling your contract form the basis upon which we solicit your order.

WILSON & HINES
19 2nd East.

Birthplace of Murry Wilson: 726 Sixth Avenue East, Hutchinson, Kansas *(Photo by Larry Caldwell)*

William Coral "Buddy" Wilson *(Etching by Mark Summers)*

Coach of a Santa Fe Scout railway car, 1920s *(Courtesy Kansas State Historical Society)*

TOP LEFT: Homesteaders' land catalog; Hawthorne, California, 1907

TOP RIGHT: Audree Korthof Wilson and Murry Gage Wilson as newlyweds, late 1930s

ABOVE: Wilson cottage at 8012 South Harvard Boulevard, Los Angeles; Brian's first home *(Photo by Lester Cohen)*

LEFT: Brian Wilson, pupil; York Elementary School, early 1950s

TOP: Foster's Freeze outlet number 18, 533 North Hawthorne Boulevard, early 1960s: the inspiration for the Beach Boys' song "Fun, Fun, Fun" *(Courtesy Foster's Freeze Archives)*

ABOVE LEFT: "Their Hearts Were Full of Spring": Brian Wilson, Carl Wilson, and David Lee Marks in Four Freshmen–styled stage attire

ABOVE RIGHT: Brian Wilson, Hawthorne High varsity baseball practice, late 1950s

RIGHT: Alan Jardine, starting fullback, Hawthorne High Cougars, late 1950s

Murry Wilson, parent, publisher, and manager of the Beach Boys, early 1960s

The Pendleton shirt–clad Beach Boys in a 1962 Capitol publicity shot *(clockwise from top left)*: Mike Love, Carl Wilson, Brian Wilson, David Lee Marks, and Dennis Wilson

The Wilson home on West 119th Street in Hawthorne, as it appeared several years after Murry's mid-1960s remodeling. The house has since been demolished. *(Photo by Suzan Murphy)*

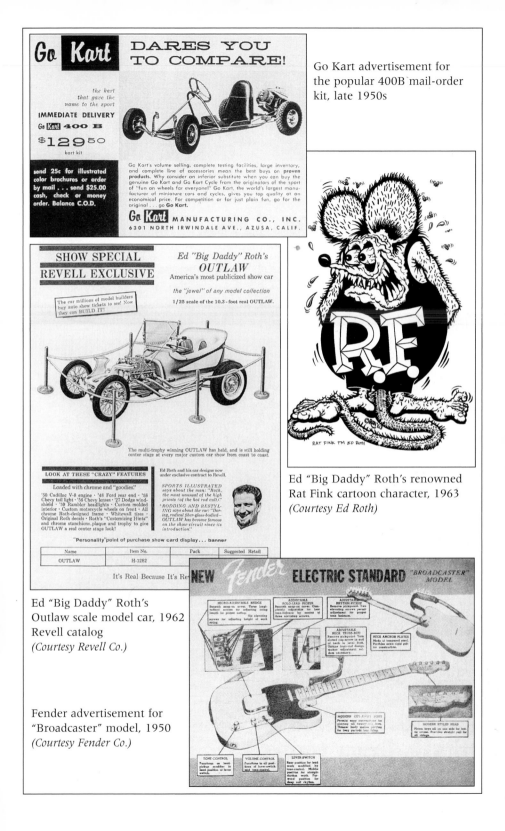

Go Kart advertisement for the popular 400B mail-order kit, late 1950s

Ed "Big Daddy" Roth's renowned Rat Fink cartoon character, 1963
(Courtesy Ed Roth)

Ed "Big Daddy" Roth's Outlaw scale model car, 1962 Revell catalog
(Courtesy Revell Co.)

Fender advertisement for "Broadcaster" model, 1950
(Courtesy Fender Co.)

Simon Waronker, founder of Liberty Records *(Courtesy Simon Waronker)*

Liberty Records' Los Angeles headquarters, late 1950s *(Courtesy Simon Waronker)*

Cover of *The Surfer Quarterly*, Vol. 2, No. 2, Summer 1961 *(Courtesy* Surfer *Magazine)*

The Capitol Tower, Hollywood, early 1970s

executive Fred Rice contacted *Car Craft* late in 1963, wondering, on the pop culture end, "Who else is into this car thing?" He was referred to Roth, who warned, "I'm into the car thing in a monster way." Rice took Roth at his word and signed him to help formulate a series of "rod and roll" novelty albums, with Capitol A&M man Jim Economides as producer.

Gary Usher was hired to form a studio group for the Roth albums under the stage name Mr. Gasser and the Weirdos (a gasser being a high-performance racer powered by standard gasoline). Usher won the assignment after having proven invaluable several months earlier by assisting Nick Venet in organizing a *Shut Down* car sampler (an assortment of cuts such as the Beach Boys' "Shut Down," "409," a 1958 Robert Mitchum narrative called "The Ballad of Thunder Road," and "Black Denim Trousers" by the Cheers, a short-lived 1955 L.A. vocal trio led by actor Bert Convy, which Usher augmented with material from the Super Stocks studio band he formed for the project.

The Super Stocks consisted of Phil Spector's familiar infantry (known as the Wrecking Crew): Leon Russell, Glen Campbell, Hal Blaine, Billy Strange, Jimmy Bond, Tommy Tedesco, Carole Kaye, Steve Douglas, David Gates, Ray Pohlman, Barney Kessel, Jerry Cole, and others. The group had few qualms about going once more into the breach as hired hitters, this time on behalf of Big Daddy's fictional drag strip gargoyles. Mr. Gasser and the Weirdos' first album was titled *Hot Rod Hootenanny;* its tracks included "The Fastest Shift Alive," "Mad 'Vette," "Eefen' It Don't Go—Chrome It," "Weirdo Wiggle," and "Termites in My Woody."

Roth and *Car Craft* editor Dick Day were united with a piano player and wrote poems keyed to chords from which orchestrations were arranged. At the end of the first day, Economides turned to Roth and said, "When you said you couldn't sing, you were right!" Vocals and spoken characterizations were handled by Usher, Darlene Love of the Crystals, Robin Ward (who notched a number 14 hit on Dot in the autumn of 1963 with "Wonderful Summer"), Bob Klimes, Richard Burns, and Dennis McCarthy. Roth himself provided the chewing sounds on "Termites in My Woody."

Hot Rod Hootenanny was released in November 1963, followed by a *Surfink!* EP with contributions from the Super Stocks and the Weirdos, and a full-length sequel in April 1964, *Rods N' Ratfinks.* All the albums made money.

The main beneficiary of the asphalt-eating rush to capitalize on the car-rock craze was Gary Usher, for whom the phenomenon represented a second-chance career after Murry Wilson spurned him. From late 1963 to the close of 1965, the volume of car recordings he produced, composed, and sang on (often with Brian Wilson's loyal participation) accelerated at a clutch-dropping pace. Besides five post–*Shut Down* Capitol albums for the Super Stocks *(Hot Rod Rally, Big Hot Rod Hits, Thunder Road, Surf Route 101, School Is a Drag),* Usher cowrote four car songs with Roger Christian ("Custom City," "Draggin' U.S.A.," "Rebel Rider," "Shut Down Again") for Annette Funicello's March 1963 *Muscle Beach Party* film soundtrack, with the Honeys performing backing vocals.

He produced the Competitors' November 1963 album, *Hits of the Street,* for Dot, performed vocals and arrangements on portions of Dick Dale's 1963–64 *Checkered Flag* and *Mr. Eliminator* albums for Capitol, and organized the Ghouls (aka the Super Stocks) studio group for the November 1964 Capitol release *Dracula's Deuce* (which included "Be True to Your Ghoul").

Singer Richard Burns and Usher joined some Gassers alumni for *Black Boots and Bikes,* a May 1964 Capitol LP issued under the name the Kickstands. Vocalist Chuck Girard of the Ghouls joined Usher on the Knights' October 1964 *Hot Rod High* album for Capitol, and in May 1965, Usher gathered assorted Ghouls and Gassers for the Revells' Reprise album *The Go Sound of the Slots,* a release boosting the increasingly popular rumpus room diversion of slot-car racing. Usher and the Super/Gasser/Ghouls unofficial glee club sang on the Silly Surfers' 1964 *Music to Make Models By* for the Hawk Model Company and its later Mercury Records incarnation *The Sounds of the Silly Surfers.*

Usher performed and/or produced four Decca albums for the Surfaris that appeared between February 1964 and February 1965: *Hit City '64, Fun City, U.S.A., The Lively Set* (the movie soundtrack that contained material composed by Randy Newman), and *Hit City '65.*

Among the most successful, chartwise, of the many Usher-directed car-rock involvements was the Hondells, a Mercury Records studio act fronted by the Ghouls' Richard Burns and supported by singer-bassist-guitarist Glen Campbell. Notwithstanding the records' credits, Usher produced the Brian Wilson–penned songs "Little Honda" and "My Buddy Seat," which rose to number 9 and number 87, respectively, on the Hot 100.

Others absorbed in the high-velocity car recording rage included a band from the Fontana/San Bernardino area, Jim Messina and His Jesters. Messina coauthored most of the 1964 *The Dragsters* Audio Fidelity album with a transplanted Michigan singer-songwriter named Glenn Frey.

Bruce Johnston recorded with Doris Day's son Terry Melcher in 1964–65 as Bruce & Terry, issuing the Columbia singles "Custom Machine"/"Makaha at Midnight" and "Carmen"/"I Love You Model T." Johnston had recorded with Jan Berry and Dean Torrence in the late 1950s as the Barons; he wrote and sang "I Promise You" for the 1959 sound track of American International Pictures' *The Ghost of Dragstrip Hollow;* and he had been a member of the Gamblers, who cut "Teen Machine"/"Tonky" in 1961 for the independent Last Chance label. He did a solo album on Del-Fi in June 1963, *The Bruce Johnston Surfing Band: Surfers' Pajama Party,* that straddled the asphalt and sea spheres with R&B traveling music such as a cover of Wilbert Harrison's "Kansas City." Johnston sang leads and played piano on the Kustom Kings' April 1964 Smash Records album *Kustom City U.S.A.* and contributed vocals and keyboards to the Vettes' January 1964 MGM album *Rev-up.* Like Melcher, Johnston was part of the lineup that Usher summoned for such Hondells sessions as "You're Gonna Ride with Me."

Melcher produced the Catalinas (another group guise for the Phil Spector studio mafia) on a September 1964 Ric Records album that included Beach Boys covers and two car songs written by singer Bobby Darin, "Boss Barracuda" and "Run Little Rabbit"; Bruce Johnston supplied piano accompaniment. But Johnston and Melcher came within tailgating distance of the music industry's top eliminators (drag winners) when they took charge of the Rip Chords.

Melcher was a staff producer at Columbia Records' Los Angeles office in 1963 when Inglewood songwriters Phil Stewart and Ernie Bringas brought in some songs. Melcher took the two original Rip Chords into the studio, with Jack Nitzsche arranging, Glen Campbell on guitar, and Hal Blaine on drums, and the resultant "Here I Stand" reached number 51 on the Hot 100. Melcher and Johnston cowrote the follow-up "Gone" and backed Stewart and Bringas on vocals, with Campbell and Blaine becoming permanent studio members of the act. The next and biggest Rip Chords hit was a song written by Carol Conners, aka Annette Kleinbard (formerly of the Teddy Bears), called "Hey Little Cobra," named for the Ford Cobra GT; the song sped to number 4 early in 1964.

Next, Jan Berry and Roger Christian gave the Rip Chords a song called "Three Window Coupe," which went to number 28, Bobby Darin writing the B-side, "Hot Rod USA."

Throughout this deluge of car classics, Brian Wilson and the Beach Boys continued to fraternize and offer writing and studio support to their like-minded recording colleagues, most of whom they had seen or socialized with since adolescence. But sometimes all the traffic merging toward the charts got its bumpers locked. After Brian wrote "Little Honda" in 1963, he waited until April 1964 to record it with the Beach Boys and then hesitated releasing it as a single. Gary Usher believed in the song in a way Brian did not, and so Usher had the Hondells duplicate the Beach Boys' arrangement for their own hit version. Meanwhile, Terry Melcher had been asked by Dot Records to find some hits for the commercially stagnant Pat Boone, and he chose "Little Honda" as the trial balloon, Melcher and Johnston laying down all the vocal tracks except for Boone's leads. The day of the Boone session, the Hondells' "Honda" reached the national airwaves, but Melcher finished the Boone single anyway, adding a Melcher-Johnston B-side with his and Bruce's backing vocals called "Beach Girl." Deejays turned Boone's "Honda" single over and played the flip side, making "Beach Girl" one of the last respectable chart achievements of Boone's career.

The Beach Boys' single of "Little Honda," rushed out by Capitol on an EP titled *4-By the Beach Boys*, trailed the Hondells by a solid month and rose no higher than number 65.

During the same interval, Melcher contemplated following the Rip Chords' "Three Window Coupe" with a new Brian Wilson song called "Help Me Rhonda." Brian, though, had big plans for the song and asked Melcher not to issue the cover the Rip Chords had already cut for Columbia. Respecting Brian's wishes, Melcher withdrew his act's record from the release schedule.

New companies and artist reputations were resting on the sustained strength of "rod and roll." Lou Adler, now manager of Jan & Dean, had discovered a new songwriting team in Phil (P.F.) Sloan and Steve Barri, two young Los Angeles talents who worked in the Screen Gems publishing stable. Late in 1963, Adler invited them to furnish Screen Gems clients Jan & Dean with new material. Impressed with their demos, Adler got Sloan and Barri a recording contract of their own with Liberty Record's Imperial subsidiary as the Fantastic Baggys—the Rolling Stones'

Mick Jagger lent the name its adjective in a snide compliment after Adler had played Mick some of the Sloan-Barri songs.

Jan & Dean were deep into their own car song phase: Their new single, "Dead Man's Curve," a Berry-Wilson-Christian song (on which Brian sang), was named for a downhill turn on Sunset Boulevard beside UCLA where noted voice actor Mel "Bugs Bunny" Blanc had just suffered a near-fatal accident. Since Jan (in a Sting-Ray) and Christian (in a Jaguar XKE) often raced each other in casual Saturday night sprints from the stop lights at Sunset and Vine, they wrote those two cars into the lyrics.

Looking for an octane-filled follow-up, Jan & Dean chose a song that Christian and friend Don Altfield had written based on a line from an old Jack Benny TV sketch, "The Little Old Lady from Pasadena," and asked the Fantastic Baggys to join the Honeys on it as backing singers.

Jan & Dean recorded a Berry-Christian-Wilson song, "Ride the Wild Surf," as the title track for the 1964 Columbia film starring Shelley Fabares of ABC-TV's *Donna Reed Show* fame, and Jan & Dean's *Ride the Wild Surf* sound track album featured another Sloan-Barri song, "Tell 'em I'm Surfing." The sound track's liner notes were written by Santa Monica native Fabares, who ended with a warm endorsement of Jan & Dean: "You'll love 'em. My husband and I do"—her husband being Lou Adler, whom she wed in 1964.

The Fantastic Baggys' own LP, *Tell 'em I'm Surfing*, appeared in July 1964, a month prior to the *Wild Surf* album; Adler produced, Chuck Britz engineered, and Hal Blaine arranged.

By September, Jan & Dean had their new album in the stores, *The Little Old Lady from Pasadena*. Its twelve tracks (including two Sloan-Barri songs, "Horace, the Swingin' Schoolbus Driver" and "Summer Means Fun") had extensive backing harmonies by the Fantastic Baggys.

When Adler founded his Dunhill Records label in 1965, his first album was a Steve Barri–Phil Sloan production, the Rincon Surfside Band's *The Surfing Songbook*, which included renditions of the Brian Wilson songs "Drag City" and "Little Deuce Coupe."

To complete this wide and intricate ring of complementary alliances, Brian Wilson decided to produce Shelley Fabares's costar on *The Donna Reed Show*, Paul Peterson, who played Fabares's young brother in the TV series. Peterson, a nineteen-year-old former Mousketeer from Glendale, recorded for Colpix, the Columbia Pictures label for which Fabares had scored several hits, notably the 1962 chart-topper "Johnny Angel." Peterson himself had made the chart with six consecutive 1962–63 singles, among them the Top 20 "She Can't Find Her Keys" and the number 6 hit "My Dad."

Colpix had a big investment in car music in 1964, signing car groups Hit Pack, the Tigers, the Jan Berry–produced Matadors, and Carol & Cheryl (the Conners sisters), for whom Jan Berry and Terry Melcher wrote tunes. Wilson was eager to assist Peterson, whose last chart single was "The Cheer Leader," a song that rose to number 78 in *Billboard* and enjoyed national exposure over the 1963 Christmas holidays.

So Brian and Roger Christian cowrote an emotionally charged anthem for Peterson called "She Rides with Me"; Brian also sang a specially miked and mixed backing vocal on the track. The sound was aurally stirring and technically adventurous, but it didn't even get near the Hot 100. Brian was crushed, feeling he had let Peterson down. Indeed, it proved the close of the actor's recording career.

Others were faring still worse. Dave Marks, now an ex–Beach Boy, literally walked in on the garage practice of Mark Groseclose's Hawthorne band, the Jaguars, and offered to take them over in quest of a label deal. Heads bobbed agreeably. They were renamed Dave Marks and the Marksmen.

Enter Murry Wilson, who had just sold Able and was anxious to expand his management roster. Hearing that the heavily rehearsed Marksmen had real promise, he lured the very musician he had ostracized to Western Recorders for a session he had booked and bankrolled, talking Marks and the band into cutting a new song of Murry's called "Car Party." Hal Blaine and Glen Campbell also contributed. Once the draining and mirthless track was in the can, Dave and his group felt they had had enough of Brian Wilson's dad and refused to go any further. Murry vowed to bar them from L.A. airwaves.

Russ Regan, the man who baptized the Beach Boys, stepped in, liked Marks's own car demos, "Cruisin' " and "Kustom Kar Show," and took the tapes to Herb Alpert, who was roughly two years into the experience of running A&M Records, a company he had formed with close friend Jerry Moss, a twenty-nine-year-old promo man who helped break the Crests' "16 Candles" for Coed Records. A&M had charted singles with the act that Alpert led with his own trumpet, the Tijuana Brass, its biggest being the number 6 instrumental "The Lonely Bull." But A&M had no teen bands, so Dave Marks and the Marksmen became its rock-and-roll firstborn.

"Cruisin' " and "Kustom Kar Show" were recut at Richie Podolor's local studio, with Alpert supplying the clap track and the Honeys singing backup. Due to Murry, local jocks wouldn't touch it. A second single, "Do You Know What Lovers Say"/"Food Fair," was also shunned despite a promo tour second-billed to Jan & Dean, and the Marksmen were dropped.

Warner Bros.' A&R chief Joe Smith signed them for one more single, "I Wanna Cry"/"I Could Make You Mine." Radio avoided it like a leper's kiss. Murry's revenge was that of a rat fink, lowercase. For Marks, the ride was over.

16

• • • •

When I Grow Up
(To Be a Man)

s 1964 unfolded, the effects of stress on everyone were evident. Brian wasn't getting along with Murry. Murry wasn't getting along with Audree. Capitol wasn't getting along with Murry as the representative of the Beach Boys, who were having trouble getting along with Brian. And Brian knew Capitol could no longer succeed financially without rock and roll—which is why the company's attention was suddenly divided between the Beach Boys' next album and an LP by a hot British band that the label had hastily compiled for American release, *Meet the Beatles*.

Capitol was new to rock and roll but learning quickly; contrary to standard practices with its older pop roster, the company found it could release new Beach Boys albums within months or weeks of each other. *Surfin' U.S.A.* appeared in March 1963, the *Surfer Girl* album entered stores in mid-September 1963, and *Little Deuce Coupe* shipped the first week in October 1963. All three LPs were swiftly certified gold by the Recording Industry Association of America. (RIAA began issuing Gold

Record awards in February 1958 on sales of a million records; the gold record total was reduced by 1960 to 500,000 units sold and then revised in 1961 to denote factory billings of $1 million.) Thus, Capitol was looking for more Beach Boys product after the Christmas rush and devised a sequel to its previous car rock compendium, *Shut Down, Vol. 2*; this time, though, it was an all Beach Boys release of new songs.

Capitol's annual gross income for 1961–63 was just shy of $50 million, and its success with the Beach Boys took some pressure off the label's other top sellers: the Kingston Trio, Nat King Cole, and Al Martino. However, Sir Edward Lewis, head of Capitol's British EMI parent company, was disgruntled with the sparse licensing and distribution his U.K. product could expect in the indispensable U.S. market. A case in point was the Beatles, a new group out of Liverpool with two albums, an EP, and four singles presently ruling the British charts—yet Capitol had shown no interest in picking up its option on Beatles records for the States. Capitol surmised that surf and car music as exemplified by the Beach Boys was *the* most lucrative route imaginable, with nothing likely to exceed it.

When Capitol passed on the Liverpool quartet, a firm called Trans-Global stepped in and negotiated rights to lease some of the numerous available Beatles masters to Vivian "Vee" Carter's and Jimmy "Jay" Bracken's Chicago Vee Jay label, best known for its R&B hits with Dee Clark, Jerry Butler and the Impressions, and Gene "Duke of Earl" Chandler. While the deal immediately disintegrated into a nonpayment dispute, Vee Jay went ahead and released the *Introducing the Beatles* album, which failed to reach the charts due to lack of publicity and promotion.

Capitol finally bowed to British corporate pressure on December 26, 1963, and issued a Beatles single of "I Want to Hold Your Hand"/"I Saw Her Standing There," earmarking $50,000 for domestic promotion. Three days later the U.S. label learned what it had been missing: A quarter of a million copies had been sold. By January 10, "Hand" was number 1 and the single's sales were over a million, with purchases in New York stores progressing at a rate of ten thousand units an hour.

Meet the Beatles, originally due in February, was promptly rescheduled for January 20 release. The Beatles were booked for a two-week U.S. publicity tour in February, including a prearranged live appearance Sunday, February 9, on *The Ed Sullivan Show*, plus half-hour matinee and evening concerts on February 12 at Carnegie Hall.

Four thousand screaming fans and hundreds of press were waiting at

New York's Kennedy Airport for Pan American Flight 101 on February 7 when the clipper Defiance landed with the Beatles aboard in first class. Sitting in the aisle seat in front of Paul McCartney—ever in the optimum place at the optimum time—was Phil Spector.

Rattled by the overwhelming reception for the Fab Four, Brian met with Mike Love to share their qualms and construct a strategy to cope with the phenomenon. *Little Deuce Coupe* was their best-selling album to date, although it leveled off at number 4 over the holidays—two positions lower than their previous peak for *Surfin' U.S.A.*

Currently in the can for *Shut Down, Vol. 2* was "The Warmth of the Sun," a forlorn ballad that eulogized Judy Bowles's rejection of Brian and the death of John F. Kennedy. Brian and Mike Love began writing the song at 2:00 A.M. on the day following the assassination, the Boys winding down at the El Dorado Hotel after a concert in Marysville, California, fifty miles from Sacramento. Also completed were the harmony-clad cover of Frankie Lymon and the Teenagers' 1956 gem "Why Do Fools Fall in Love," with perfect falsetto soloing by Brian, and "Fun, Fun, Fun," a projected single that the Boys had cut at Western Studios on January 1. Mike had posed the idea for "Fun, Fun, Fun" following a recent concert trek. En route from a Holiday Inn to the Salt Lake City airport, he told Brian about a girl he knew who had her Thunderbird keys taken away by her father after lying about school-night trips to the library; it seems she had actually been meeting a new boyfriend at a hamburger stand.

Informed by countless Hawthorne evenings spent at Foster's Freeze, Brian and Mike wrote a Chuck Berry–tinged power ballad with a strong undercurrent of feminism: The lyrics celebrated one woman's summer sovereignty behind the wheel of a street racer she could drive "like an ace." With a punchy guitar intro that sprang like the sweetest rogue storm surf or the smoothest high-torque elimination run, "Fun, Fun, Fun" was the musical essence of acceleration, a safari apotheosized.

The Beach Boys hustled the single out, managing a chart debut at number 116 one week after the Beatles had touched the tarmac at Kennedy International, and it later went to number 5. Brian wanted the Liverpool competition to hear Hawthorne's best Top 40 artillery while both bands were still on American turf because the Boys were due to depart for an Australian tour with the Surfaris and Roy Orbison.

The long-term prospect of liberty from the grief of his family fortified Brian each time he found himself having to write, record, or tour to forestall local competition, satisfy the Capitol coffers, or prop up the failings of other members of his filial enterprise. But 1964 was the year he realized his yen for relief and self-realization would be frustrated by forces he was unable to abate.

The Australian journey was envisioned by the Beach Boys as total unfettered immersion in the fruits of their achievements, an opportunity to encounter a foreign fan base and fun-loving culture on unceremonious terms, but the last-minute imposition of Murry Wilson as road manager shriveled the band's expectations. Each previous concert journey on which Murry rode shotgun had dissolved into degrading episodes in which the senior Wilson accosted or fined group members—mainly his sons—for breaches such as lack of "congeniality," inattentiveness to boisterous autograph hounds, or unservile temperaments when packing their gear for the next gig.

Being so far from things familiar, Brian knew his father would overcompensate. Sure enough, Murry was unceasingly tyrannical, mounting an around-the-clock bed check from the moment they alighted in Sydney, ridiculing and smacking Brian and his brothers in front of press and tour promoters, causing misery and calling it loving authority. It was as if Murry had swallowed the perverse ego of his own now-exiled father; Buddy's pneumatic bluster was steadily expanding inside him until it displaced what little endured of Murry's individual will. Murry was becoming the parent he and his own siblings had cast out, doing sinister sentry duty to prevent (and thus ensure) its happening to him.

Returning to Los Angeles by way of Hawaii, where they did a concert, the Boys resumed work on *Shut Down, Vol. 2*, cutting the pleasant but lightweight "Keep an Eye on Summer" and Brian and Gary Usher's livelier and more vocally elaborate "Pom-Pom Play Girl." On February 20, Dennis did a tom-tom-rooted drum solo preserved as "Denny's Drums" and then recorded the lead vocal on Mike and Brian's affectionate "This Car of Mine," about a salvaged racer selected from a row of "old and broken" junkers; Dennis had earlier bought a Jaguar XKE and totaled it the same day, convincing Murry to cosign for a coveted Sting-Ray.

Mike cut a lyrically accessible version of Richard Berry's "Louie Louie" tale of a homesick Jamaican sailor and sang the main vocal on Brian and Roger Christian's gorgeous "In the Parkin' Lot." An overly rehearsed bit of studio repartee and stilted putdowns, also taped on February 20, became filler under the title " 'Cassius' Love vs. 'Sonny' Wilson." And Carl added a serviceable stomp instrumental with "Shut Down, Part II," Mike's noisy sax apparent at the onset. But the best work of a busy day was "Don't Worry Baby," Brian's vision of a Spectorian ballad more ravishing and real than what Phil would have cast for his second wife, Ronnie.

Eager for publicity to coincide with the March 2, 1964, release of *Shut Down, Vol. 2*, the Beach Boys agreed to perform on Steve Allen's daily ninety-minute TV talk show syndicated by Westinghouse. The Boys wanted to whip up a measure of the home viewer frenzy ignited by the Beatles' live *Ed Sullivan Show* performances from Manhattan's Studio 50 and Miami's Deauville Hotel, but Steve Allen's drawing power, once able to dent Ed Sullivan's ratings when Allen had a Sunday variety format opposite Ed's in the mid-1950s, was now greatly reduced in his more-frequent but late-night weekday slot.

A surfing clip courtesy of the Long Beach Surf Club was reeled behind Allen's opening credits announcing guests Samuel G. Kling (author of *The Complete Guide to Divorce*), actor Anthony Perkins, and the Beach Boys. Seated at a squat rostrum recalling *The Tonight Show* desk he formerly manned as its original host, Allen held up the album jacket and introduced the Boys for the first of two songs, "Fun, Fun, Fun" and "Surfin' U.S.A." Although game in their black slacks and open-necked candy-stripe tops revealing their white undershirts, they could not escape the low-budget gist of their surroundings.

The day following the official release of *Shut Down, Vol. 2*, the Boys were back in Western Studios to do a German rendition of "In My Room" in emulation of the covers for EMI-Deutschland's Odeon label the Beatles had done of "I Want to Hold Your Hand" ("Komm, Gib Mir Deine Hand") and "She Loves You" ("Sie Liebt Dich") in Paris on January 29 at EMI's Pathe Marconi Studios. The Beatles, who had played and recorded in Hamburg back in 1961, had acted to serve a popular demand, but the Beach Boys and Capitol had entertained a misguided whim. The Germans preferred the Boys in English, and the Teutonic "In My Room" was not released.

More bothersome was the ad supplement designed by Capitol for publication in national newspapers' Sunday magazine sections starting in April. The headline read: DIG THIS! CAPITOL RECORD CLUB BRINGS TEENERS THE BIGGEST HOOTENANY . . . DANCE PARTY . . . SURFIN' FUN . . . HOT ROD . . . FOLK AND COUNTRY . . . HIT ALBUMS! AND THE BEATLES TOO! Pictured below were all four Beatles hoisting a sign that said HEAR THE

BEATLES, THE BEACH BOYS, AND THE KINGSTON TRIO—NOW! Of the nine albums shown under the Beatles' photo there was *Meet the Beatles,* The Kingston Trio's *New Frontier* . . . but no Beach Boys product. Stapled to the back page of the four-page Capitol insert was a free cardboard disc—"A surprise gift from the Beatles, the Beach Boys, and the Kingston Trio!" that contained the Beatles' "Roll Over Beethoven," the Boys' "Little Deuce Coupe," and the Kingston Trio's "When the Saints Go Marching In." The Beach Boys were worth giving away but not worth billing above the Beatles. Capitol's energies were shifting from the West Coast Yanks to the new blokes in town.

In March, Brian took the Honeys into Gold Star to cut a single for Warner Bros.—his own "He's A Doll" with Ginger Blake and Diane Rovell's "The Love Of A Boy And A Girl" on the flip side. On April 2, 1964, the Boys were again in Western Studios, taping "I Get Around," whose choral complexity, hand-clap accents, and full-band resonance revealed the seasoning gained from their touring. Mike had picked up on the morbid frustration of Brian's basic lyrics, on which Brian bluntly divulged "getting bugged" driving up and down the same old streets while pining for exotic places in which to spend the "real good bread" he was earning. Love salted the verses with aspects of his inbred bombast and fleshed out the chorus with a diversity of whoops and wha-wha-ooh passages.

"I Get Around," with "Don't Worry Baby" on the B-side, entered *Billboard*'s Hot 100 on May 23, leaping over "P.S. I Love You" and declining chart-topper "Love Me Do" to take the number 1 slot for the first two weeks of July—the most resounding triumph in the Beach Boys' tangled transit from the Richie Valens Memorial dance.

Much of Brian's genius involved his ability to enjoy, compound, and redirect the contributions of his companions while allowing himself and his music to be elevated from private bathos to beaming relief. But the atmosphere in such a hothouse environment was delicate. Any chill doomed flowering concepts to a quick wilt or even death on the vine. Emotions had stayed raw within the Wilson group since Australia, and Murry hadn't backed off in his hectoring, prodding Brian in Western Studios during each take for "I Get Around" with criticisms that his bass patterns were undermining the song's structure; Dennis was also the target of scorn.

Mortified, Dennis put his fist through a wall and walked out. Brian paced as Murry persisted in his spiteful criticisms, his son trying to contain himself as he towered over his chunky, belittling father. But then Brian snapped, physically shoving his parent-manager out of his path and, when further challenged, telling the old man he had at last gone too damn far. He was *fired*.

Audree would later tell friends that Murry sank into a grave depression after the incident, taking to his bed for the better part of five weeks. Brian was unmoved, personally or professionally; his father would have no further word in the daily workings of the band. Temporary financial and tour management was transferred to Dave Cummings and Dick Current, former IRS agents whose Cummings & Current accounting firm handled Murry's Able and Sea of Tunes accounts.

At Capitol, Murry had likewise overstayed his diplomatic mission; his constant (though warranted) questionings of Capitol's accounting practices were delivered with a polarizing and theatrically vociferous tone. He didn't like the way Capitol disbursed funds owed to the band, yet he snarled his own affairs by borrowing money for Able against the group's future Capitol checks. He told Voyle Gilmore that a rock-and-roll band bounding from timetable to timetable as it hurried to meet each of Brian's overnight trains of thought could not be docked for studio time the same way Lou Rawls's union sidemen or Nancy Wilson's jazz orchestras were. But Murry made his case the way a mean cop tells a hobo on his beat to move along.

At home, any semblance of family cohesion that the common base of the house on West 119th Street had once conferred was now finished. A spacious new residence purchased by Audree and Murry in the former Quaker colony of Whittier (named for poet John Greenleaf Whittier) only dramatized the absence of an affinity between them after their children had moved away. They could not fill the large new residence with what remained of their feelings for each other, and the gaiety Audree once expected from their marriage was in meager supply. More in evidence were the gruffness, explosive resentment, and sporadic greed of a husband confounded by his haphazard search for sufficiency.

After twenty-six years of living under the same roof, Audree and Murry separated, and Murry bought another house in Whittier with income he was amassing from the Sea of Tunes publishing interests secured from Brian. Audree and Murry would often spend joint afternoons with the Boys but then return alone to their separate addresses.

The Wilsons' exit from the Hawthorne house (which the family vacated but did not sell) hit Carl hardest, as did his parents' estrangement.

Blessed with a disposition that drew none of Murry's choler and all of Audree's kindliness, Carl tended to recall the poignant origins of circumstances now spiraling out of control, such as the fact that Brian had been the one to ask Murry to set his Able company aside in order to defend the Boys' interests, Brian pleading "Dad, please help us. I really wanna be in the music business."

When Murry became the show biz dad any son would dread, Carl could identify for friends the moment the inflated self-image had begun to devour his father: "It was the constant fixing up of the old house. He had a good time doing it, but it started looking so out of place, with people driving by all the time, looking. I really wish he woulda just fucking left it alone."

Carl was still attending Hawthorne High as late as the spring of 1963 (Dennis had been expelled for fighting a year earlier), but harassment from young teachers jealous of his campus status reached a critical level. Cleaning up one day after printing class, Carl was jarred to hear his instructor jeer, "Oh, yes! Look good before you go out there and see your public." Late in his junior year he went to the bathroom without permission and was maliciously marked a truant and suspended. With a ten-day band tour imminent, the length of the suspension made it impossible for him to complete the year and get credit for it since he wouldn't be in class the legal number of days.

Murry went to the principal's office to sign papers authorizing Carl's release from Hawthorne High, and for his senior year Carl was enrolled in Hollywood Professional School. Dave Marks and Diane and Marilyn Rovell also attended this performing arts academy, founded in 1922. Carl found the change to be "a scream—the total opposite of going to public school. It was truly for professionals, for people who worked. It started at 9:40 and got out at twenty minutes to one—a *short* day. I'd tell the lady who runs the school, 'Well, I'm gonna go out shopping,' and she says, 'Ooo-kay. Have a nice time!' " The sumptuous 1964 graduation ceremonies at the Brentwood Country Club were a "weird" augury of the deflection from his lower-middle-class upbringing that success had enforced. Having seen what became of the Loves' hazardous first blush with wealth, he assured himself that the ostentation was "ridiculous."

Absurd in its own right was the education the Beach Boys were getting about the insatiable pressures of feeding Capitol Records' marketing and distribution mill. Unsure how much longer the "surf thing" and "car thing" could continue, the label saturated the market with a surfeit of nonmusical automotive and sound effects records: *The Big Sounds of the Drags; The Big Sounds of the Sport Cars; The Big Sounds of the Drag Boats; The Big Sounds of the Drags, Volume 2; The Big Sounds of the Go-Karts; Breedlove 500+.* Capitol was also looking for the sixth Beach Boys album in its six-part contract option, less than two years after the group had signed on.

Somehow Brian obliged, recording on a staggered schedule during April and May. The Beach Boys' version of "Little Honda" was completed, as was a cover version of Doc Pomus and Mort Schuman's 1959 hit for Brooklyn doo-wop group the Mystics, "Hushabye." Mike assisted Brian in the imagery of what would be the title track of the album, "All Summer Long," coming up with the beautifully evocative passage " 'member when you spilled Coke all over your blouse." Brian conceived the cleverly suspenseful, organ-activated arrangement for the ominous "Wendy." "We'll Run Away," the last of the Wilson-Usher compositions, was an effective we're-not-too-young-for-a-wedding scenario.

"Carl's Big Chance" was the final surf instrumental he placed on a Beach Boys LP; now one of the band's performance strengths was Carl's prowess on guitar, techniques he had acquired from such friends as John Maus of the Walker Bros. making the staccato style of his leads more concise and convincing. Brian's "Do You Remember?" charmed listeners as a sentimental roll call of early rockers—Little Richard, Danny & the Juniors, Chuck Berry, Elvis Presley, Jerry Lee Lewis—and their musical monograms.

"The Girls on the Beach," recorded May 19, was a ravishing Brian Wilson ballad in the "Surfer Girl" mode but more complex in its harmonies and key changes, with Dennis's descant on the "sun in her hair" vocal bridge sounding like a happy-sad recollection of bygone good times with a certain policeman's daughter in the shadow of Manhattan Pier. (The group agreed to let Gary Usher and Nick Venet use the song as the title track to a Paramount beach film scheduled for spring 1965.)

"Drive-In" was yet another nod, "Chug-A-Lug"-fashion, to the flagrant excesses of high school jaunts to Studio Drive-In on Sepulveda Boulevard. "Our Favorite Recording Sessions" sounded like more studio gab saved as padding, but unlike the " 'Cassius' vs. 'Sonny' " segment, it was truly spontaneous. As such, it came closer than anything previously available to disclosing the Boys' taut tête-à-tête (Mike jesting edgily about throwing Brian across the room) as tensions in their relentless studio regime escalated.

"Don't Back Down," Brian's saga of "teeth-gritting" guts in the face

The Spectors Three, 1959: Annette
Merar, Russ Titelman, and Warren
Entner *(Courtesy Russ Titelman)*

Herb Alpert and Jerry Moss,
the founders of A&M Records,
early 1990s

Lenny Waronker (son of Simon),
president of Warner Bros.
Records, 1994

The Beach Boys go collegiate, mid-1960s: Mike Love, Al Jardine, Brian Wilson, Carl Wilson, and Dennis Wilson

Murry's Capitol album, *The Many Moods of Murry Wilson*, October 1967

The withdrawn *Smile* album art, Capitol catalog No. DT2580, December 1966

The Byrds, 1965
(Courtesy Columbia Records)

Randy Newman, L.A.'s sardonic troubadour *(Photo by Andy Denemark)*

Brian and Marilyn Wilson's Bellagio Road mansion, Bel Air, California *(Photo by Suzan Murphy)*

Songwriter/arranger Van Dyke Parks: Groucho Marx in Charles Ives pajamas *(Photo by Carl Studna, courtesy Warner Bros. Records)*

The Beach Boys in concert at the
Hollywood Bowl, November 1, 1963
(Courtesy Capitol Records)

The Beach Boys, 1965
(Courtesy Capitol Records)

The Beach Boys, 1975: Carl Wilson,
Al Jardine, Ricky Fataar, Dennis Wilson,
Blondie Chaplin, and Mike Love
(Courtesy Reprise Records)

Brian in Brother Studios, 1976, during the making of *15 Big Ones*
(Courtesy Reprise Records)

Launch of the "Brian's Back" campaign by Warner-Reprise:
Mike Love, Brian Wilson, Mo Ostin, and Stephen Love

Brian Wilson on the concert stage, late 1970s *(Courtesy Reprise Records)*

The Beach Boys, 1985, following the death of Dennis Wilson *(left to right):* Al Jardine, Bruce Johnston, Brian Wilson, Carl Wilson, and Mike Love *(Courtesy Epic Records)*

Dennis Wilson on his sailboat, *Harmony,* in Marina del Rey with future wife Karen Lamm, May 1976 *(Photo by Suzan Murphy)*

Dennis in 1977 on the eve of the release of his solo album, *Pacific Ocean Blue* *(Courtesy CBS Records)*

Wendy *(top)* and Carnie Wilson, 1993
*(Photo by Deborah Feingold, courtesy
Feingold Studios)*

Brian Wilson, 1988, just prior to the
release of his *Brian Wilson* solo album
*(Photo by Kamron Hinatsu, courtesy Sire
Records)*

of high-tide adversity, was the appropriate capper for the collection. On the maiden pressing of *All Summer Long*, the song was erroneously listed as "Don't Break Down."

A search for locations at which to take photos for the new album's cover brought the Beach Boys back to the setting of their debut *Surfin' Safari* jacket art: Paradise Cove in the North Bay area, seventeen miles north of Santa Monica. Capitol photographers and art directors Ken Veeder and George Jerman were in charge as before; missing were Dave Marks and the yellow pickup truck rented on-site for fifty dollars and then draped with palm fronds to resemble a wood-paneled safari wagon. In their place were attractive blond and brunette models, the two women changing clothes a half-dozen times as they cavorted for snapshots with each band member, making it seem as if each of the Boys had a dynamite honey for the full-swing luau occurring before the camera. But the most genuine moment of the entire shooting was never published or circulated: Dennis surfing.

Denny knew Paradise Cove, a private swimming and fishing area usually closed to surfers, from his teenage coastal stealaways with the nomadic surf rats. Borrowing a board, he paddled out to where there were south swells of about five feet breaking toward the rocks north of the parking lot. Concentrating for once, he judged the speed of an incoming set, turned quickly, and made for the shoulder of a fringing wave, sliding smartly downward across it. Pumping the board in a slight sway to sustain momentum in the small surf, he slowly straightened out in the white froth of the scattering soup as he neared shore. Carl stared, thrilled and proud.

All Summer Long was released on July 1, the day before President Lyndon Johnson signed the Civil Rights Act of 1964, the most sweeping antidiscrimination legislation since the Reconstruction. It would be a long, hot summer, with inner-city rioting breaking out around the country. That same year, filmmaker Bruce Brown expended $50,000 making *The Endless Summer*, a global surf docu-travelogue tailing former gremmie Mike Hynson and cohort Robert August as the Sandals strummed theme music.

The Beach Boys spent most of June and July cutting *The Beach Boys' Christmas Album*, which was Brian's version of the rock-and-roll Yuletide as formerly envisioned on Phil Spector's 1963 *A Christmas Gift for You* collection. The "Little Saint Nick" tune (first released as a single in December 1963) that launched the LP was one more behind-the-wheel epiphany Brian experienced while piloting his new Pontiac Grand Prix to the Wich Stand.

Jan & Dean went into Western Studios on July 29 to record "Sidewalk Surfin'," a tune exalting the semi-accepted, much-censured new sport of skateboarding. Jan Berry had commissioned Brian Wilson and Roger Christian to write a song based on Brian's "Catch a Wave" melody and utilizing the "bust your buns" terminology Jan & Dean supplied. The single's pavement-hopping sound effects were taped outside Western Studios by Jan & Dean, and helped take the track to number 25 nationally, giving the purportedly life-threatening pastime its first anthem.

August began for the Beach Boys with a show at Sacramento's Memorial Auditorium that Capitol Records had allowed Brian and Chuck Britz to tape—at the suggestion of Sacramento promoter Frederick Vail—for a live album slated for October release. A prior Vail-produced concert, minus an ailing Brian, had been performed at the same venue on December 21, 1963, and the best tracks from both were later combined. However, the best introduction by the twenty-year-old Vail occurred at the pre-Christmas concert, so the word "Christmas" was edited from the opening announcement on the album: "And now, from Hawthorne, California, to entertain you tonight with a gala . . . concert and a recording session, the fabulous Beach Boys!"

And they did sound fabulous, the harmonies sweetly pointed, the playing exuberant, the temper of their well-sequenced half-hour both eager and witty. There were enough hits and album highlights ("Fun, Fun, Fun," "Little Deuce Coupe," "In My Room," "Hawaii," "I Get Around") plus histrionic covers (Murry Kellum's "Long Tall Texan," Jan & Dean's "Little Old Lady from Pasadena," Bobby "Boris" Pickett and the Crypt-Kickers' "Monster Mash," Dick Dale's "Let's Go Trippin'," the Rivingtons' "Papa-Oom-Mow-Mow," Dion's "The Wanderer," the Four Freshmen's "Graduation Day," Chuck Berry's "Johnny B. Goode") to convey the vibe of a local surf stomp rather than a showcase set. *Beach Boys Concert* became the group's inaugural number 1 album and for many fans the first live LP they had ever purchased. The high quotient of between-song screams aided the Boys in their battle of repute with the Beatles but also made it necessary to re-record several songs in the studio, later splicing in crowd reactions.

On August 4 the bodies of three civil rights workers (Andrew Goodman, James Chaney, and Michael Schwerner), missing in Mississippi since June 21, were found buried in an earthen dam. On August 7 the

Gulf of Tonkin Resolution was passed by Congress, approving U.S. military action in Southeast Asia. On August 26 the Democratic National Convention nominated Lyndon Baines Johnson for president, but the *Los Angeles Times*'s metropolitan coverage that morning was dominated by the last twenty-four hours of a "frenzied" three-day visit to the city by the Beatles, who had played to a screaming throng of 18,700 at the Hollywood Bowl on August 23.

Natalie Cole, fourteen, daughter of Capitol recording artist Nat King Cole, was driven to the Bowl by her father's chauffeur Ellis Dean. She told the *Times*, "I like my dad's singing better than the Beatles, but the Beatles are cuter than my dad." Supervising the taping of the Beatles' concert for Capitol Records was Voyle Gilmore, with Ken Veeder taking the concert photo.

During their stay the Beatles rented a mansion in Bel Air and ate, swam, and played cowboys and Indians while wearing toy pistol holsters and Mexican blanket waistcoats sent as gifts from Elvis Presley. Cowed by the musical claustrophobia the Beatles' L.A. sojourn and its radio-sustained aftermath created, the Boys were happy to leave town at the start of September for a trip that took them into the Southwest, Northeast, New England, and New York for their own appearance September 17 on *The Ed Sullivan Show*, which went well. The Boys again earned their share of shrieks from young females.

Returning to Los Angeles for a month before the group's first European tour, Brian took up residence in a new one-bedroom flat at 7235 Hollywood Boulevard near Wattles Garden Park. Brian was now keeping steady company with Marilyn Rovell, who was working in a doughnut shop by day and at night doing backup sessions with the Honeys on recordings and demos for Gary Usher, Steve Barri and P. F. Sloan, and the Screen Gems publishing office.

On October 5, NBC-TV premiered *Karen*, a thirty-minute teen situation comedy starring Debbie Watson; it was one of three interlocking Monday night sitcoms centering on life in an apartment complex in Southern California called 90 Bristol Court. The Beach Boys provided the forty-five-second *Karen* theme song, written by Bob Mosner and Jack Marshall, with Mike Love singing lead. Later in the month, the Surfaris released a full-length version of the song as the B-side to their Decca "Hot Rod High" single.

The Beach Boys spent most of October on a promotional junket through England, France, Sweden, Germany, Italy, and Denmark. Brian wrote a lovely new song at his hotel in Copenhagen called "Kiss Me, Baby," its conciliatory lyric showing the extent to which his undefined relationship with sixteen-year-old Marilyn Rovell was becoming more serious.

In November, immediately after boarding a flight to Australia for a second tour, Brian experienced a mild panic attack. Only thoughts of Marilyn soothed his nerves, and he asked the pilot to cable Marilyn. When Brian reached Australia, he phoned Marilyn and asked her to marry him. She was stunned, but Brian was desperate: Nothing was stable in his life.

Brian finally had achieved financial and personal freedom but had no sense of how to partake in them. And he couldn't bear to be by himself. Marilyn, who obviously loved Brian, seemed the anchor for his emotions, the remedy for his fears. On December 7, 1964, Brian and Marilyn were married in a civil ceremony at the city courthouse in Los Angeles, and she moved into his Hollywood apartment.

But Brian's behavior was erratic, his comings and goings unpredictable, his manner uncharacteristically aloof for a newlywed. He admitted smoking marijuana with musician friends and people connected with the talent agencies that handled rock-and-roll bookings. Young and sheltered, Marilyn was distressed by these disclosures. They fought over his strange behavior, his selfish disregard for her feelings, and his lengthy disappearances and marked mood of detachment.

The Beach Boys had been in and out of Western Recorders with engineer Chuck Britz since June 8, 1964, generating more tracks for an album slated for release on March 1, 1965, to be titled *The Beach Boys Today!* "She Knows Me Too Well" was a melancholy, self-lacerating tune about Brian's "weird way" of showing love and inflicting hurt. On June 22, Brian and the Boys recorded "Don't Hurt My Little Sister." The title echoed advice that Diane Rovell had repeatedly been giving Brian regarding Marilyn.

Brian had originally composed it for the Ronettes in another pass at finding a professional link with Phil Spector, but Spector insulted Brian during a meeting about the song in Spector's Hollywood hotel room. Phil made it known he had completely revised "Little Sister" under the title "Things Are Changing (for the Better)," and Spector subsequently dismissed Brian from a Gold Star session at which they were to block out "Little Sister," coolly calling his piano playing inadequate. Brian's version with the Beach Boys restored the tempo, lyrics, and structure first conceived by him.

"When I Grow Up (To Be a Man)" was less than two minutes of reflection on adolescent wiles and adult choices. The Beach Boys cut it in August 1964, with Brian and Mike wondering aloud in the lyrics if they would love their future wives and families for the rest of their lives or be saddled with an abundance of spousal and fatherly regrets. In the background the Boys were heard counting up the ages of indecision from fourteen to thirty.

"Dance, Dance, Dance" was an up-tempo, sleigh bells–laced party track by Brian and Carl that was taped on October 9. Fortifying the raw physics of the piece was Carl Fortina's accordion; Brian would use the soothing respirations of the instrument, usually played by Fortina or Frank Marocco, as a secret emotive weapon on his finest songs over the next four years. Picked as the stalking-horse single for the half-done *The Beach Boys Today!* album, "Dance, Dance, Dance" was due to hit stores the first week of November.

On December 16, the Boys recorded "Kiss Me, Baby" at Western Studios. Brian and Mike traded rapt soliloquies about forgotten grudges and pointless romantic squabbles. Seven days later, on December 23, as Brian was bidding Marilyn good-bye at Los Angeles International Airport and preparing to board a morning plane to Houston for a concert that night, he suddenly sensed she was gazing at Mike Love. Whether her scrutiny of Mike was mindless or meaningful, Brian believed something was oddly askew, if not terribly wrong, and that Marilyn's affection for him might be straying. Agitated, Brian turned away and caught the flight.

Five minutes outside Los Angeles, the screaming started. The tall, dough-faced young man sitting in the forward section, whose manic stares before takeoff had given way to white-knuckled catatonia, had suddenly begun crying and then making jagged, high-pitched yowls as he grabbed at his airline pillow. His traveling companions leaped to his side, trying to pry the pillow from his swollen face.

"Cool it, Brian!" barked Al Jardine.

"My God, what's wrong, Brian?" asked Carl Wilson. "Brian, please tell me what's wrong!"

By now Brian had spun out of his seat and was on the cabin floor, sobbing convulsively.

"I can't take it!" hollered Brian as he rolled and lurched about the plane. "I just can't take it! Don't you understand? I'm not getting off this plane!"

Wilson went on to perform that night, but he awoke at the hotel the next morning with a crippling knot in his stomach and burst into tears at half-hour intervals throughout the day. The group's latest road manager put Brian on the late plane back to Los Angeles, where he was to be met by his mother, Audree. Brian had sent word that he did not want to see his father.

The Beach Boys needed an immediate replacement for Brian so they could continue their tour through the Southwest, South, and Northeast, so a call was placed to Glen Campbell, the versatile studio musician who had just played on the group's session for "Dance, Dance, Dance." Besides being an excellent lead and rhythm guitarist, he was also an accomplished bassist and vocalist who could easily substitute on Brian's instrument as well as his high harmony parts. Campbell agreed to join the group in time for their concert in Dallas.

The band was lucky to secure the road services of Campbell, who earned $100,000 a year as a first-string session musician, often scheduling recording dates around his morning golf games. Born April 22, 1936, near the village of Billstown, Arkansas, Campbell had toured from October 1960 to May 1961 as lead guitarist for the Champs. In the autumn of 1961 he scored a West Coast solo hit (albeit reaching only number 62 nationally) with a single on Crest Records called "Turn Around, Look at Me," a song he cowrote with Jerry Capeheart. A first choice for Phil Spector's recording dates, he was considered by top arranger Jack Nitzsche to be the best young guitarist in Los Angeles.

By late 1964, Campbell's guitar, banjo, and vocals had appeared on over six hundred recorded tracks, ranging from sessions for Rick Nelson, the Kingston Trio, Bobby Darin, Merle Haggard, Dean Martin, *Buddy Greco Sings the Beatles*, and Wayne Newton's "Danke Shoen" to Roger Miller's recent summer hit, "Dang Me"—on which Glen played the distinctive twangy acoustic lead—and Elvis Presley's songs for the film soundtrack of *Viva Las Vegas*.

Campbell had become a semi-regular on ABC-TV's prime-time pop music program *Shindig*, for which he did alternate-week feature stints. He also played in the show's two house ensembles, the Shindig staff band

and the on-camera Shindogs combo, whose combined personnel included Leon Russell, Russ Titelman, Delaney Bramlett, and Elvis Presley's and Rick Nelson's sideman James Burton.

Because of Campbell's demanding schedule as a freelance instrumentalist and sometime actor (pressing obligations included a Wayne Newton session at Capitol to cut "Red Roses for a Blue Lady" and a small part in the Steve McQueen movie *Baby, The Rain Must Fall*), Glen hurriedly passed Brian's bass and harmony baton to surf-pop veteran Bruce Johnston. Mike Love had contacted Bruce and asked him to rendezvous with the Boys for a concert in New Orleans.

Back in Los Angeles, Audree Wilson had gone alone to meet Brian at the airport, intending to take her son to the Hollywood apartment he now shared with Marilyn or bring him back to her new house in Whittier. No, said Brian; he wanted to go home, to Hawthorne, to West 119th Street, to the last safe place he knew.

So they drove the short distance from the airport to the City of Good Neighbors, turning off Prairie Avenue to the bush-shrouded bungalow at the corner of Kornblum Street. Unlocking the screen and panel doors and stepping inside, Brian and his mother were slightly unnerved to find that virtually everything in the house had changed: decor, furnishings, color schemes—Murry had redone the premises completely for the new tenant-buyers who were away at the moment. Underfoot, however, the house's hardwood floors still creaked as they had even after Murry made the boys drive nails between the slats and spread them apart. Brian slowly wandered from room to room while his mother followed, and he gradually wept himself into exhaustion.

At length he sat back down in the living room. Audree told him it was all going to be okay, but he knew the things that would not easily be mended: the quiet he couldn't find outside music; the buzzing at night in his bad ear when he was extremely tired, the noise like static from an ill-tuned radio; the phantom blows from his father that he fended off in the darkness of his dreams; the falsetto singing that brought him spiritual absorption and secret shame; the humiliations of adolescent bedwetting; the qualms and conflicts of adult sexuality; the horror he felt when Judy Bowles ended their engagement by saying she didn't feel as he did; his ambivalent hunger for the girlish affection Marilyn offered him; the utter absence of real friends and confidants in his life other than his mom.

Carl had been closer to Audree, Dennis had always depended on her more to plead his case and intercede on his behalf, but it was Brian who had most clearly seen Audree's hopeful strength and the skill at reassurance that had attracted Murry's admiration. Audree had accompanied him in his childhood singing, in his seminal recordings, and in moments when his emotional temerity ebbed, such as the time he needed someone to assist in purchasing the ill-fated engagement ring for Judy Bowles. Audree helped Brian select the $150 circlet with a small diamond, letting him know the uncertain step was in any event a worthy one, but Brian never got up the courage to offer Judy the token of his love.

In the stuffy stillness of the vacant Hawthorne house, Brian quietly flooded the musty spaces with grief for all the tranquil moments gone. A decade before, on rare occasions when Murry was in good spirits, there had been afternoon trips to Skippy's soda shop up the street from school, where kids in the seventh and eighth grades hung out, and where Brian's mom and dad would take him for a hamburger and a vanilla malt. Brian used to play two-man games of twenty-one-point handball on the Hawthorne High courts until it was too dark to see the black rubber orb. After dinner he had gone to his room to read and imitate the gothic writing style of Edgar Allan Poe as part of his homework for English class, finding its first-person voice and studied pauses a fit template for aspects of his early songwriting. One weekend morning he left the house early with Murry, who bought him his first Fender bass from a music store in South Hawthorne. He had never forgotten the sharp glint in Carl's smiling eyes when he asked his little brother to help teach him to play the instrument.

Looking back, the instances where Brian stuck up for himself or insisted on having fun on his own terms now seemed the most real: his preference for playing center field in varsity baseball so he could sing to himself out of the other players' earshot, the decision to quit varsity football against Murry's wishes when the competitive atmosphere became too oppressive, buying every Kingston Trio album released on Capitol from 1958 until leader Dave Guard left the group in 1961, revering them but resisting Murry's ploys to model the Beach Boys after the trio.

Murry's inability to see the Boys' success through their excited eyes sabotaged many of the professional glories he had once assured the Boys they would find so gratifying when they gained popular recognition. "You guys are winners," Murry would shout. "Go out there and be winners!" But when Brian tied with songwriters Ellie Greenwich and

Jeff Barry in 1964 for six Top Ten hits, a feat for which he was due to get a BMI Award, Murry had no praise for him, instead accusing Brian of getting a fat head.

To come so far and feel so lost—what was next? How could the future regain its appeal? What would make the past seem worth it? Audree had no answer for these queries, but she listened hard and held firm her eldest son's hand. She had memories like Brian's, and shattered expectations, too.

So they sat together in the hush of the bare rooms, and when they were too wrung out to talk or think anymore, they got up to go.

Brian never entered the house again.

17

●●●●

Wake the World

Surfing had finally managed to ease itself out of its adolescence, thanks to the Beach Boys, Bruce Brown, Mike Doyle, Malibu . . . and Australia.

The Beach Boys' rock and roll lent popular mystique and cultural romance to the sport. By virtue of the group's actions, surf songs about one's inner sensibilities and kinship to nature had become synonymous with the pursuit of happiness—and excellence.

Beach Boys Concert was one of the group's most significant albums of the 1960s, though not strictly for musical reasons. As important as the appealingly proficient performances of their familiar songs was the evidence on the record that an American group could inspire the fanatical adulation associated with the Beatles. The high-decibel delirium of the crowd on *Concert* was matched by the good humor with which the band greeted it. Their joshing, larkish modesty paralleled the sly playfulness Americans encountered in the Beatles' summer 1964 movie *A Hard Day's*

Night, which also contrasted the absurdity of audience frenzy with the genuine satisfactions of comradely musicianship.

The pictures in the glossy foldout album jacket layouts for *Beach Boys Concert* revealed a group of friends who took show business conventions lightly but had a hip rein on their own irreverence. Handsome Dennis had sharper drums and a better moptop than Ringo Starr, and his brothers arrived onstage riding the "Little Honda" 90 motorbikes that were the de rigueur means of transport in the realm of teen leisure. "You Meet the Nicest People on a Honda," stated the ad campaigns in *Playboy* and *Car & Driver,* while competitor Yamaha countered with a splashy "Swinging World of Yamaha" promo blitz with waters' edge photos of the Trailmaster 100 Sportcycle.

And the Beach Boys' three-man arsenal of "Olympic white" Fender guitar weaponry (Al's Stratocaster, Carl's Jaguar, Brian's Precision Bass) that flashed on the cover of *Concert,* as well as the cream-cabinet Showman amps and separate Reverb units stacked behind them, testified to the top-flight intentions of the musicians. Listening to Carl's spiky solo on "Let's Go Trippin' " while looking at the album photos, every afterschool rocker knew instinctively that this was a suburban garage band that had grown up right: true to the gnarly roots of the surf milieu but with a sound much evolved from the bungalow blare of its barefoot, just-for-fun forebears.

Filmmaker Bruce Brown scored similar points on a cinematic level, giving the world an athletic and cosmopolitan image of surfing via his feature-length *The Endless Summer.* Enthusiasts who had seen Brown's prior underground surf documentaries *(Slippery When Wet, Surfing Hollow Days)* knew the twenty-two-year-old Dana Point surfer and film buff was a true zealot whose first movie equipment was a spontaneous 1958 gift from Dale Velzy, the board maker who had earned a bundle over the two previous years selling his Velzy/Jacobs Malibu "sausage board." Velzy went with Brown to a local camera shop and shelled out the dough, believing Bruce would do the sport proud.

Unlike the basement Super-8 clips and short-subject VFW hall one-reelers that formed the substrata of the surf cinema, *The Endless Summer* spoke to accidental tourists as well as avid apostles, explaining the wide penetration and expanding possibilities of surfing as its cameras chronicled an equator-crossing search by two adept board riders for the perfect wave—discovered in South Africa's peerless point surf.

While the film's John Van Hammersveld–designed poster became a
dorm and office fixture, admired for the fluorescent sun tones of its
ambiguous high-contrast portrait of surfers, circa dawn or dusk, it was
the prose beneath the silk-screened graphics that convinced the ignorant
of the sweep and sophistication of the sport:

> On any day of the year it's summer somewhere in the world.
> Bruce Brown's latest color film highlights the adventures of
> two young American surfers, Robert August and Mike Hyn-
> son, who follow this everlasting summer around the world.
> Their unique expedition takes them to Senegal, Ghana, Nige-
> ria, South Africa, Australia, New Zealand, Tahiti, Hawaii, and
> California. Share their experiences as they search the world
> for that perfect wave which may be forming just over the next
> horizon.

No matter that Brown only changed his original South Africa–California round-trip itinerary at the last minute when he learned it was fifty
dollars less to book a round-the-globe exploration. No matter that East
Coast film distributors laughed at the box office bonanza *The Endless
Summer* enjoyed at Santa Monica Civic Auditorium when it opened there
in the summer of 1964, dismissing it as a tempest in a regional tidepool.

Two weeks of *Endless Summer* test screenings in the winter of 1964 in
Wichita, Kansas, did better business than *My Fair Lady.* So while Brown
continued to personally narrate West Coast showings at high schools and
colleges in San Diego, San Bernardino, Anaheim, Fresno, Sacramento,
and elsewhere from January to March 1965, he had another print of his
film enlarged to 35 millimeters and showcased it at the Kips Bay Theatre
in mid-Manhattan later that year. The acclaim from the New York–based
media finally secured the first-run national and international theater
bookings he had believed were attainable, and *The Endless Summer* went
on to gross $30 million. A planet chilled by the Cold War, racial turmoil,
and political assassinations had glimpsed the warming glow of a new
grail. And so, as even the Beatles related in their 1964 song of the same
name, the restless spirits of the decade had a new motto: "I'll Follow the
Sun."

Oceanside, California, surfer Mike Doyle provided the leadership for
such pilgrimages when he took first place for 1964 and 1965 in the
newly instituted *Surfer* magazine polls (veteran Phil Edwards had won

the very first poll in 1963). Doyle's recognition was due to his power-oriented, post-hotdogging approach to wave riding, a highly competitive style based on balance, stance, and ambitious control. Doyle inspired serious young surfers to ride for pleasure and technical perfection, *and* to win.

Doyle had come up through the ranks of the West Coast competitions, excelling at the Huntington Beach championships held annually since 1960. His go-for-broke rides at the first official world surfing championships in Australia in 1964 inspired adept Aussie observers such as Robert "Nat" Young, who had a copy of Doyle's ten-foot-six-inch long, twenty-two-inch wide, soft-railed board made for himself.

Doyle's approach to surfing had evolved beyond the hotdogging Malibu appetite for nose rides, head dips, drop-knee cutbacks, hanging fives and tens, trimming (planing across the face of a wave), and stalling—a ride-prolonging move in which one banks up the wave's face to slow the board so that the curl can catch up. The strong, well-developed swell lines of Malibu waves made the skilled execution of these stunts possible. So pervasive was the legend of this blessed surf beach—located midway between Malibu Lagoon and the Malibu Pier—that in the summer of 1963 Brian Wilson and Roger Christian wrote a song (unrecorded) called "Malibu Sunset" in honor of its glories. (The demo of the tune was offered to singer Andy Williams through a relative, who mislaid the only copy of the tape.)

Mike Doyle had learned much from the constant wave-hungry rivalry for the title of "Mr. Malibu" between Mikey "Da Cat" Dora and Johnny "Lizard" Fain, as well as the lengthy foot-over-foot rides of Dewey Weber, Linda Benson, Mickey Munoz, Mike Diffenderfer, Hobie Alter, Bob Cooper, Tom Morey, Terry "Tubesteak" Tracey, and the others who assembled on the first Monday of each September for the annual Malibu luau. Every year they burned the season's grass shacks and toasted "Motherbu"'s marvelously formed right walls at the first point break—located well offshore in a spot directly in front of the beach's landmark Rindge Mansion and flagpoles—which offered nose rides of over three hundred yards. By 1965, Doyle's colleague David Nuuhiwa had turned such Malibu nose trips into a science atop an unmodified nine-foot-six-inch board.

Because a rider of the big Malibu board had to step around its surface to achieve control and acceleration, the hefty (as much as forty pounds) Malibu guns were divided psychologically into three sections, with the front three feet intended for walkups to nose riding, the middle for overall strategic positioning, and the back third for turning, including S- and 8-shaped radical cutbacks, and board-bouncing horizontal "ricochet" reverses of direction.

Large Malibu boards and their flamboyant American passengers had not been seen in Australia since 1956 when a contingent of Yank surfers (Greg Noll, Tom Zahn, Mike Bright, and Bob Burnside) visited for an "Oz" exhibition tour timed to take place during the Melbourne Olympics. Local surfers bought several of the departing exhibition team's Malibu boards, which ranged in length from nine feet six inches to ten feet and had been shaped by Velzy/Jacobs, Noll, and Joe Quigg. Oz manufacturers scrambled to import balsa wood to make knockoffs of the American guns until the 1959–62 renaissance when Greg McDonagh, Scott Dillon, Noel Ward, Barry Bennett, and other Sydney-based shapers began supplying foam boards to hotdogger Jack "Bluey" Mayes and Hawaii-tested Aussie riders such as Bernard "Midget" Farrelly. By 1966 the lighter, foam Malibu guns (with mahogany stringers for lateral strength, laminated wooden noses, and wooden fins) had been fully adopted Down Under, as had the smooth, flowing body actions of the Malibu riding style.

The name Malibu is said to have come from the Chumash Indian phrase *"mala i boo,"* which means "place on the cliff," that is, the ancient village founded on the rise at the rear of the beach, on the east side of the mouth of Malibu Creek. Explorer Juan Rodríguez Cabrillo landed at the mouth of Malibu Creek in October 1542 during the course of another Spain-sponsored quest for El Dorado, the fabled seven cities of gold, and "California," the mythic isle cited by Cabrillo in his July 5, 1542, diary entry. California itself was first named and described by novelist Garci Rodríguez de Montalvo in 1510 in his epic multivolume romance *Las Sergas de Esplandian* (The Deeds of Esplandian). A poetic combination of the Latin words *calida* (heat) and *fornax* (furnace), the word was coined in the following passage by Montalvo, which might have given the modern inhabitants of Malibu some pause:

> Know ye that at the right hand of the Indies there is an island called California, very close to that part of the Terrestrial Paradise, which was inhabited by black women without a single man among them, and they lived in the manner of Amazons. They were robust of body with strong passionate

hearts and great virtue. The island itself is one of the wildest in
the world on account of the bold and craggy rocks. In their
land there are many griffins [a creature with an eagle's head
and wings and a lion's body]. . . . In no other place of the
world are they found.

Montalvo took liberties with the facts, yet by 1966 a creature no less
foreign than the griffin could be glimpsed off Southern California's
shores: An Australian surfer with an eagle's head and a lion's heart had
surfaced to spark the last maturation stage of the sport.

Nat "The Animal" Young arrived in San Diego for the World Championship, riding a 9-foot 4-inch, 22-inch-wide Malibu "short board" that
was also a relatively thin 2¹/₂ inches deep (4 inches being the norm).
With Doyle as an idol and Santa Barbara's George Greenough as stateside
tutor, Young took the short gun he had designed with Aussie Bob Mc-
Tavish and elevated Doyle's competitive attack to drastic "slash and
turn" heights, power-surfing in a manner that laid new tracks in the curl
and confounded Yankee observers with its utter impatience for protracted nose-riding niceties.

The important standards of style, size, and performance that Malibu
had once set were shattered by this wizardly surfer from "Oz." Boards
began to shrink as riders whipped, spun, and sliced the foam with them.
The board and its water-borne trajectory became extensions of the un-
bound imagination, obedient to every mental outburst. What the surfer
could visualize, he could actualize, and the ride became a projection of
his mental and spatial scope. Nothing for surfdom on sea was ever the
same again. The land assault was coming next.

Jan & Dean's "Sidewalk Surfin' " had reveled in its number 25 *Billboard*
peak as 1964 skittered to a close. Having featured two skateboard instrumentals ("Skateboarding—Part 1" and "Skateboarding—Part 2") on
their *Ride the Wild Surf* and *The Little Old Lady from Pasadena* albums, the
singing duo was helping nurture the fad that had first been noted in
1958 editions of *The Hawthorne Citizen* as a plank-cum–roller skates device seen rolling out of shop classes in South Bay high schools.

Now, with the Tokyo Summer Olympics of October 10–24 still fresh
in the public's mind due to the United States winning the unofficial team
championships with thirty-six gold medals, the prospects of eligible new

sports for future olympiads were being bandied in the consumer press. John Severson and the editors of *Surfer* introduced *The Quarterly Skateboarder* in the winter of 1964, announcing in an editorial that

> whenever a new sport comes into existence or an existing sport suddenly gains popularity, its thrills are often compared to other sports. People compare the thrills of surfing to skydiving, bullfighting, skiing, and other exciting individual participation sports. These same comparisons will be made and are being made in the sport of skateboarding. . . . We predict a real future for the sport—a future that could go as far as the Olympics. . . . There is no history in skateboarding—it's being made by you. . . . Already there are storm clouds on the horizon with opponents of the sport talking ban and restriction. . . . It's up to you to see that skateboarding does not become a sport of rebels and radicals. It's a sport for young sportsmen.

On the cover was a shot of Dave Hilton of the Hobie-Super Surfer Team executing a rolling "big jump" over a high bar in West Covina. Inside were ads for skateboards by Hobie Super Surfer Skateboards, Jack's Surf Shop, Surf 'N Ski Slalom Skate, Waimea Bay Skateboards, Roller Derby, Landsurfer, Vita-Pakt (an expansionist citrus products company), Huntington Surf Center (which featured "Phil Edwards" and "Malibu" model skateboards), Skee-Skate of California ("The skateboard that started it all. The original Skee-Skate. Over 1/2 million sold . . . and still the leader!"), and Cooley Associates "Bun Buster" boards ("Made of imported Australian 'Yuba' hardwood . . . has high-quality double-action malleable castings with rink-type composition rubber and plastic wheels").

While Skee-Skate's original three-dollar model and Roller Derby's smallest board had metal roller skate–style wheels, the newer ten- and twelve-dollar boards had clay or hard-rubber wheels and grained hardwood platforms shaped to the basic contours of a Malibu board, with two-way truck wheel mounts for a turning radius based on left-right balancing emphasis.

The Santa Monica Bay Area was cited as "the current capital" of skateboarding. Although oddities such as the metal, three-wheeled Skooter Skate had been available in the Midwest since 1939, it was in

Santa Monica that lifeguard-surfer Larry Stevenson manufactured one of the first modern commercial boards, selling eight the first month and two thousand a day within the next two years. Stories in *The Quarterly Skateboarder* on matters radiating from the Bay region included an interview with twenty-two-year-old surfer Mike Hynson of *Endless Summer* fame. Hynson described informal skateboard slalom courses he and fellow surfer Joey Cabell had created (using their sandals for markers) at idle moments during a recent West Coast to East Coast promotional bus trip arranged by Hobie to promote surfing: "Joey probably came up with the idea first from his skiing experiences. Since then, the only change in downhill slalom skateboarding has been the replacement of the sandals with cans."

Elsewhere in the issue, Hynson was pictured winning a "night rally" skateboard competition at the grand-sounding Laguna Beach Hidden Valley Slalom Run, which was actually a deserted stretch of Hidden Valley Road lit by long rows of car headlights. Mike aced out Cabell and Mike Diffenderfer by two-tenths of a second in the contest, setting a new course record of 27.1 seconds just as the police arrived and cancelled the meet for lack of a town permit.

As photo essays in the issue disclosed, skateboarding was primarily a shoeless affair; even in formal tournaments where one wore protective headgear, feet remained unshod to allow a fully sensitized ride. *The Quarterly Skateboarder* pictorials also showed that skateboarding in storm drains and drained swimming pools was already common in locales such as Whittier, San Diego, and Menlo Park.

Music for the movement was on the increase. An ad drawn by cartoonist Rick Griffin in the back pages of *The Quarterly Skateboarder* publicized a new Triumph Records LP, *The Challengers Go Sidewalk Surfing!*, on which former members of the Belairs, Journeymen, and Showmen joined to record such asphalt-cutaway instrumentals as "Hop Scotch" and "Skinned Shins."

Early stars and seminal influences on the sport were Tommy Ryan, Danny Bearer, Mikey Maga, and Pacific Palisades surfer John Milius, the "father of the kick turn," who taught the move to top competitor Torger Johnson and Hobie trick riders Dave and Steve Hilton.

Johnson took first place in tricks competition at the May 22–23, 1965, Anaheim Nationals, which were televised by ABC's *Wide World of Sports* and covered on all three network news broadcasts. Bruce Logan placed second in tricks on Anaheim's concrete course laid over the turf at the ten-thousand-seat LaPalma Stadium, while freestyle innovator John Freis took first place overall. Women were prominent in the sport from the start, notably Laurie Turner, Coleen Boyd, and Pat McGee.

Bun Buster was among the Southland skateboard firms that sold a cumulative 50,000 boards in 1964, and in March 1965 a toy buyer for Gimbel Brothers of Philadelphia told *The Wall Street Journal* it foresaw springtime sales of 250,000 units. Vita-Pakt expected its gross 1965 sales to grow threefold from the previous year, to $100 million, and an Italian manufacturer bragged to *The Journal* that its European production had hit 50,000 a month.

Sure enough, all projections for 1965 were dead-on, with the domestic volume of purchases bettering fifty million skateboards. The nation's toymakers were ecstatic, yet the sport's initial life span was about to expire simply because few sidewalk surfers saw the skateboard as a toy. The young sportsmen and women mentioned in *Quarterly Skateboarder* wanted a high-performance board whose suspension, design, and traction could withstand, not just *respond* to, the probative freestyle demands of their playground, swimming pool, back street, and drainage tunnel proving grounds. Yet most skateboards were built with flimsy suspension and remounted steel skate rollers that could neither absorb the impact of nor offer the stability for trick riding. Hard-composition clay wheels had a tendency to overheat from the friction of heavy use and disintegrate when they hit a pebble; wheels with a higher hard-plastic makeup literally braked on contact with stones or stray gravel, sending riders hurtling headfirst over their boards.

Alternative wheel substances were tried, including dense cardboard, but all wore out too quickly under slalom conditions. The thick board surfaces were too stiff and unresponsive to curb-hopping leaps and subtleties of terrain, and wheels were positioned too far forward and aft to assist in the cantilevered kick turns and counterpoised seesaw spins that were the "guava" and "rad" award winners at meets.

Public safety was trumpeted as a deterrent to sustained popularity in assorted municipalities, with the shore town of Shrewsbury, New Jersey, attracting attention when police seized skateboards. By the spring of 1965, Montclair, New Jersey (which had a famed long and winding course on newly paved Fairview Place), and Jacksonville, Florida, had made national headlines by issuing public safety ordinances banning street and sidewalk surfing. But devotees knew the real reason for the sport's decline by summer's end was the inadequacy of the boardware.

In Los Angeles, the issues of public health and safety and overheated conditions were not confined to clay skateboard casters. On Wednesday, August 11, 1965, most of those who could be were at the beach when Watts, a largely African-American community less than five miles from Hawthorne, exploded in the bloodiest race disturbance thus far in American history. The spontaneous six-day eruption of rage and frustration among that ghetto's poor left 34 people dead (29 of them black residents of Watts), over a thousand injured, 3,438 adults and 514 juveniles under arrest, and $200 million in property damage.

The white press called the Watts upheaval—which was detonated by a drunk-driving arrest—a "riot," and Mayor Sam Yorty blamed the matter on "communist influences." But a UCLA study immediately afterward showed one-third of the residents of the precinct located mere blocks from where Murry and Audree Wilson had lived together as newlyweds would call their neighborhood turmoil a "revolt." Isolated from the rest of the city, with jobs scarce, general goods and services inferior or nonexistent, medical and transportation facilities sorely lacking, and institutionalized police racism and brutality blatant (cops called billy clubs "nigger knockers," and in the Seventy-seventh Street police station a picture of Eleanor Roosevelt bore the inscription NIGGER LOVER), Watts was an open pit of despair.

Further post-disturbance surveys of Watts citizenry showed children commonly reaching adulthood without ever once having set foot on the beaches of Los Angeles County. A commission to determine the causes of the disorder was appointed by Governor Edmund G. "Pat" Brown and headed by ex–CIA director John A. McCone. One hundred days after the tribulation, the commission issued its findings: The tumult in Watts, it stated, "had not been a race riot in the usual sense but an explosion—a formless, quite senseless, all but hopeless protest.

"So serious and so explosive is the situation," the McCone Commission warned, "that unless it is checked, the August riots may seem by comparison to be only a curtain-raiser for what could blow up one day."

The land of sunshine promised much, and often delivered it, but it was increasingly displaying not only its limitations but also the subtle snags in the sameness of its physical and emotional atmosphere.

"It started to bother us, doing this same stuff, because we thought we were trapped," said Carl Wilson of the Beach Boys' musical output in 1964. In February 1965, Carl and the rest of the group were again in Western Recording Studios laboriously rehearsing the vocal balance for the single version of "Help Me Rhonda," a song of Brian's centering on a sulky opening lament devised by Mike Love: "Well since you put me down I've been out doing in my head . . ."

Between Carl's guitar noodling on the Kingsmen's arrangement of "Money," nervous jibes about the Vietnam draft, and engineer Chuck Britz's scoldings ("Fellas, Brian, have the guys loosen up. You got a beautiful tune here. Loosen up! You're so tight, I can't believe it!"), Brian and the Boys were having a good time homing in on the track. Al Jardine was ready for the lead vocal overdub—his debut as lead singer on a Beach Boys record (excepting "Christmas Day" on the group's Christmas album)—when Murry Wilson arrived in the control room.

Murry said he knew the band didn't want him to come down, "and that's why I got drunk."

"You're not drunk," Brian soothed.

"Murry, you shouldn't drink," said Mike sadly.

"And all we're asking you for," Murry continued, joining Al at the microphone in the studio proper, "is a little syncopation. Listen, 'Da-doo-doo-dee-dee-dee-DA bo-ba-DA-dee-BA-doo-da.' "

"Those aren't the words, Murry," said Al.

"No, no, listen," Murry groused. "Syncopate it a little. What are the words?"

"I don't know," said Al, discomfited. "Ahh, 'Since you put me down I been out doing in my head . . .' "

"Show him how to do it just once, Dad," said Brian from the control room. "Then he'll do it."

"All right, sing it, sing it!" said Murry.

" 'Since you put me down . . .' " Al began.

"No," Murry corrected. " 'Since you put down, boo-dee-dee-BA-ba-dee-dee-BA-dee-da.' Go on, go on that kick. 'Ba-doo-doo-doo-doo-doo-doo-BA-dee-dee-ba-da. . . .' Got it? You know what I mean?"

"I got it," said Al.

"Let's go," said Brian to Murry. "He's got it now. Don't sing with it. Let *him* sing it once."

"Do you want me to leave, Brian?" said Murry testily. "Your mother and I can leave now if you want."

"No," said Brian to his father. "I just wanted you to let *him* sing it."

"Did you really get drunk?" Mike asked.

"For the first time in my life," said Murry.

"Oh, bull," said Brian in a kindly but impatient tone. " 'First time' . . . "

"Brian said, 'Come down and relax,' " Murry joked with pained sarcasm, "so I did."

The session went downhill from there.

"Brian, fellas," said Murry, now seated with Audree in the control room. "I have three thousand words to say. Quit screaming and start singing from your hearts, huh? So you're big stars, but let's fight. Let's fight for success. Okay. Loosen up. Be happy. You got any guts, let's hear it. . . ."

BRIAN: "Dad, that was only eighty-two words."

MURRY: "I said three thousand. Come on, Brian, knock it off."

DENNIS: "That's only ninety-five."

MURRY: "You guys think you're good? Fellas, as a team we're unbeatable. Come on, let's go."

BRIAN (groaning): "Goddamn it. That really gets me. I've got one ear left, and your big loud voice is killing it. My ears are killing—"

MURRY: "So Audree and I leave, okay?"

BRIAN: "No. All I ask is that you just put that hand mike about five hundred feet away from you. Chuck, start, please."

The session resumed. Then stopped again.

MURRY: "Brian, your voice is too shrill on this harmony kick. Sing from your heart. Can we hear a chord? Just a chord like we used to when we used to sing clear records. Okay?"

The group struck a unison harmony chord. It was flawless. They resumed cutting the chorus.

MURRY: "Carl, can I hear your part? I can't even hear you, dear. Come on in and sing it. You've been low for two hours."

BRIAN: "Come on in the door, Carl."

MURRY: "What's the matter? You made too much money, buddy?"

BRIAN: "No."

MURRY: "Let's sing from our hearts. I know you're not taught this way much, but I'm your father. Come on, fellas. We need the honest projection that we used to have."

BRIAN: "You wanna have the '409' sound, right, on 'Help Me Rhonda'?"

MURRY: "When you guys get too much money, you start thinking you're going to make everything a hit. Now listen, let me tell you something. When you guys get so big that you can't sing from your heart, you're going downhill."

BRIAN: "Downhill."

MURRY (angry): "Downhill! Son, son. I'm sorry. I've protected you for twenty-two years, but I can't go on if you're not going to listen to an intelligent man, against many people trying to hurt you."

BRIAN: "Are you going now?"

MURRY: "I . . . no. . . . This is awfully unfair for you to—"

BRIAN: "Are you going or staying? I just wanna know."

MURRY: "What do you want? If you want to fight for success, I'll go all out."

BRIAN: "No. We don't want to do that."

MURRY: "You think you got it made?"

BRIAN: "No, we don't. We would like to record in an atmosphere of calmness, and you're not presenting that."

MURRY: "Look, Brian. I love you. Your mother loves you. . . . Son, success never comes easy. Success never comes from phony singing for money."

BRIAN: "Why don't you go tell Johnny Rivers that?" [Rivers, aka John Ramistella, a New York City–born, Los Angeles–based singer-songwriter-producer, had recently had his third pop hit on Imperial Records with Harold Dorman's "Mountain of Love."]

MURRY: "I don't care who you tell. Dick Dale, Capitol Records, anybody. You sing from your hearts. Forget it." (To Audree): "I'm sorry, dear. We're never coming to another recording session." (To Carl): "Carl, I'm so sorry."

CARL (long pause): "I'm sorry."

AUDREE (softly, getting up to go): "I'll talk to you all later."

MURRY: "I know, I'm not drunk. The kid [indicating Brian] got a bit of success, and he thinks he owns the business. I'm so sorry, dear. I'm so sorry. I want Capitol to praise these tunes because you can't compete with the brains that are trying to hurt you. Please remember that you can only— I'm sorry, I can't talk anymore. . . . You can only fight from the bottom of your hearts. You forget to sing from your hearts." (To Brian): "You do it, but the other guys are coasting."

BRIAN: "Why don't you tell Dennis that. Who's not singing from—?"

MURRY: "Chuck and I used to make one hit after another [snapping his fingers] in thirty minutes. You guys take five hours to do it. You know why?"

BRIAN: "Times are changing . . . times are changing . . . times are changing . . . times are changing."

MURRY: "Because you guys think you have an image. Don't ever forget . . . honesty is the best policy. Right, Mike?"

MIKE: "Yes, sir."

MURRY: "You know what I'm talking about. We've had our differences, but you know what I'm talking about. . . . Okay, forget it."

BRIAN: "Times are changing . . . times are changing."

MURRY (to Brian): "Forget your image as a producer, dear. You can live for two hundred years if you grow."

BRIAN (sighing): "I don't know what you're talking about."

MURRY: "Okay. Forget it." (To Audree): "Let's go."

After Murry departed, Brian was able to supervise the completion of the "Rhonda" single session, with Hal Blaine and Glen Campbell assisting on the instrumental tracks. Unlike the inferior January 1965 try placed on the *Beach Boys Today!* this time the group's vocal backing was brighter, simpler, and more subtly overlaid, and Brian added livelier bass, plus pounding piano and a bracing guitar break. A so-so LP track was transformed into a hit, soaring to number 1 in the May 29 edition of *Billboard* and staying there for two weeks.

Beach Boys Today! climbed to number 4 nationally, but noting the strong public preference for the single arrangement of "Help Me Rhonda," Bruce Johnston talked Brian into putting it (labeled as such) on the group's next album.

The Beach Boys were prospering, but Carl Wilson still worried that they were "trapped . . . into having to sing about a certain thing." By March 30 the Boys were in the studio once more, cutting an LP due for release in June titled *Summer Days (and Summer Nights!!).*

18

Break Away

Murry had divested himself of his heavy machinery business and was no longer involved in the day-to-day life of his family. Now he forged a career as a gentleman publisher and outfitted his Whittier home to suit that self-image. He built a music room addition that was almost four hundred feet in length and had a cathedral ceiling, and he filled it with Beach Boys mementos, a built-in stereo system, and a fine piano. At the far end of the room was a stained-glass window illustrating the Sea of Tunes logo, a string of musical notes stretched across the ocean. Outside were a patio and pool at which he entertained clients.

A profound sentimentalist with an unappeasable need to be respected, he was most comfortable with equally unrefined, demonstrative, and ceremonious people willing to allow his open attempts to court them. These qualities interlocked perfectly with the rituals of a publishing ambassador who traveled steadily to meet middle-management people in the radio, retail, and publishing industries, garnering their favor with flattery, perks, and awareness of the issues and urgencies of their regional power bases.

Because he was honest, because he liked hardworking, uncomplicated people who liked him, and because he meant all of what he said to those he approved of, never forgetting a promise or reneging on an agreement, Murry made many friends for the Beach Boys in the midsixties. Each personally solicited ally appreciated the boisterous brio of "the Beach father" and returned it with a goodwill that sometimes endured for decades.

Murry took his chief mission to be the constant revitalization of the Beach Boys catalog, ensuring that chain stores and mom-and-pop outlets were well stocked with back-title albums and singles, that radio stations had the full range of old Beach Boys releases for any gaps in their playlists, and that managers regularly heard new ideas to market and program them in a timely or topical fashion. Frequently traveling overseas on business and pleasure trips, he regularly bought unusual trinkets and multipurpose gifts in bulk, shipping trunks of them back home for later use as tokens of gratitude.

On excursions through France to meet with local publishing executives, Murry would purchase cases of a pleasant but inexpensive perfume, and a swing to the Far East would find him returning with dozens of kimonos bought wholesale, either of which he would later give out to program directors, regional distributors, and record store owners in Minneapolis, Nashville, Phoenix, Seattle, Sacramento, Denver, Salt Lake City, and other cities he had energetically primed to support the Boys' music year-round. (It was in this spirit that Brian wrote and recorded "Salt Lake City" on March 30, 1965, for the forthcoming *Summer Days [and Summer Nights!!]* album as a tribute to the town's fan base. The Salt Lake City Downtown Merchants' Association would be permitted to press up to 1,000 limited-edition promotional singles of the track, which ended with the line "We'll be coming soon.")

Understanding that the bulk of the record industry's loyal human attachments were predicated on fanlike boosterism and reciprocal rituals of partisanship, Murry would conclude a meeting with a local disc jockey or advertising manager by confiding, "This business can really take its toll on relationships and home life. For instance, when was the last time you came in your front door at the end of a long day and still had the wisdom to tell your wife or girl you love her?

"Here," he'd advise, producing an already gift-wrapped bottle of his bulk-purchased French fragrance, "give this to the woman in your life tonight, with best wishes from my sons and me."

Since the world of records and retail was still barely out of its Big Band/Hit Parade salad days, both the older and younger personnel he encountered were charmed by these schmaltzy gestures, which made an increasingly cutthroat world seem cozy. Moreover, any present or compliment from the parent of the Beach Boys could be interpreted as a personal message or keepsake from the Boys themselves.

Murry had always been extraordinarily generous toward his children as far as satisfying their material desires, buying them go-carts, surfboards, musical instruments, clothes, automobiles, and all the other outward signs of love that father Buddy Wilson's uncertain income and selfish instincts had denied him and his siblings. In this sense Murry was consistent in his intention to countermand the cold and ungiving aspects of his own rearing. Such largess would often go awry, however, as Murry sought to attach various arbitrary rules and strictures to such gifts, the issue of control never far from the surface.

When Murry realized his dismissal as the Beach Boys' manager did not impinge on his ability to enhance the fortunes and repute of the family act, he welcomed the freedom to operate outside the inhospitable work environment of the studio.

The propagation of the Beach Boys' back titles—on whose visibility and brisk sales Murry's livelihood now depended—would not have been possible, however, had Murry not railed when Capitol repeatedly threatened to overlook the group amid the onslaught of the Beatles. Maintaining hours-long vigils outside the offices of important Capitol executives such as singles promotion manager Al Coury and A&R executive Karl Engemann (producer and brother of singer Bob Engemann of Capitol's Lettermen), Murry stemmed the skepticism and laxity toward the Beach Boys that enveloped the Capitol Tower once the Beatles sales behemoth made other artists on the label's pop-rock roster seem like also-rans.

Fred Vail, the concert promoter who pushed Murry and the Beach Boys to quadruple their early tour income by promoting their own shows, was one of the people who worked closest with Murry between 1963 and 1965 in building awareness of the group. While he made no attempt to excuse fatherly flaws and the coarse extremities of Murry's foolish pride, Vail had a high opinion of Murry's contributions up to 1965—"He makes Capitol maintain the Beach Boys as a priority"—that was shared by such Beach Boys intimates as Roger Christian and, surprisingly, given all their flare-ups and fallings out, Gary Usher.

"I'd love to write one of those essays on 'The Most Unforgettable Person I've Ever Met' for *Reader's Digest* about Murry Wilson," Vail would tell friends and associates of the Boys. "The guy's like an old-fashioned drill sergeant. He's loving and protective and at the same time gruff and very, very assertive. He can be humble and he can be arrogant. He can be a proud father and he can be a screaming manager. He's very physical, grasping your hand and giving you a solid shake or slapping you on the back. He's always fair, paying me my worth and also giving me bonuses depending on the outcome of the concert. But walking the tightrope between father and uncle, manager and taskmaster is too difficult for him."

Murry's fragile sense of personal dignity was forever in jeopardy because of the early humiliations inflicted by Buddy Wilson, and his inability to stand apart from that past when presented with any possible reproof of his authority frequently warped his judgment.

An incident that occurred after Murry's firing at the "I Get Around" session and just before his disastrously tipsy attempt at rapprochement during the recording of "Help Me Rhonda" signaled for many the improbability of Murry's future as his sons' chief advisor. Brian was working with Chuck Britz at Western Studios on early takes of "When I Grow Up (To Be a Man)" when a sheepish Murry poked his head in. Jan Berry, who was recording next door at United Studios with Dean Torrence and Lou Adler, heard that Murry was hovering nearby. Aware that Brian was fed up with his clumsily despotic dad, the impish Berry quickly hatched a practical joke. Murry had never forgiven Brian for giving the "Surf City" hit to Jan & Dean—the publisher-parent still widely denounced Jan Berry as a "song pirate"—so Berry strode into the Beach Boys taping dressed in the costume of a buccaneer, a makeshift patch covering one eye and a kerchief tied over his head. At the sight of Berry, Brian and company exploded in glee, everyone instantly getting the gag's reference. Seeing his own son helpless with laughter at the expense of "a father's protectiveness," Murry was apoplectic with fury.

The highly charged political environment around Murry and the Boys eventually leveled off, and as he came to accept their schism as a saving grace, Murry discerned the value of his more remote but less debilitating position as publisher. He turned forty-eight in the summer of 1965, and a slower pace was prudent. All probably would have been well had Murry not broken his own cardinal rule, the one he invoked to punish Dave Marks. It was Murry's precept that the family business must be protected against all rivals and insurgents who might be armed with privileged information or an insider's advantage.

And Murry betrayed it. He summoned all he knew about the Beach Boys, and he used that knowledge to try to compete with them. The band Murry selected for this commercial assault had initially been known as the Renegades, a Westwood/Pacific Palisades–based rock and blues group. Drummer Rick Henn, lead guitarist-saxophonist Eddie Medora, bassist Vince Hozier, keyboardist Marty DiGiovanni, and rhythm guitarist Steve O'Reilly played sock hops and twist clubs throughout Los Angeles County. Medora and DiGiovanni had joined guitarist Byron Case and his Snow Men group for a Challenge Records recording date with producer Kim Fowley in December 1963 to cut an instrumental single, "Ski Storm"/"Ski Storm Pt. II," which earned airplay on KFWB.

Challenge Records subsequently signed Medora, Hozier, DiGiovanni, O'Reilly, and Henn as the Rangers, and they issued two singles in 1964, "Justine"/"Reputation" and "Mogul Monster"/"Snow Skiing." The latter record was a response à la "Ski Storm" to the seasonal surf bum/ski bum sea-to-mountains migrations prevalent in western youth culture. Medora and DiGiovanni were fellow students of Carl Wilson's at Hollywood Professional High, and Carl set up an audition with Murry; the dutiful son confided to his school friends that if Murry found new protégés, maybe he would spend less time pining for the band he had originally represented.

After a fourteen-hour audition during which Murry also tested the group's aptitude for vocal harmonies, he offered, "Well, I guess you boys are hungry for success."

Signed to Capitol Records' Tower subsidiary by A&R executive Eddie Ray, the group was renamed the Sunrays, an acronym for Mur*ry* Wil*son*, who wrote both sides of their treble-steeped debut single "Car Party"/"Outta Gas." The single tanked.

Rick Henn wrote the featured track on their next single, "I Live for the Sun," which was released in June 1965 and did well on KRLA's "Disc Derby" morning program (the band goosing the response by phoning frequently to request the song), ultimately progressing as far as number 51 on *Billboard*'s Hot 100. The cocky O'Reilly left the group afterward due to personality clashes with Murry, and Byron Case took his place on guitar. The other members found Murry eccentric but were grateful for the attention he paid to their tour logistics and daily working conditions, ensuring that they ate in the best restaurants, stayed in nice lodgings, and were not pushed any harder than a well-booked itinerary required.

"Andrea," the Sunrays' next single, showed significant chart improvement, getting as high as number 41 nationally and bolstering Tower's belief in an album, for which Murry brought in pop and mood music producer Don Ralke and Hial King of the Newports as arranger and vocal coach. Also recruited were studio musicians, including Hal Blaine, Earl Palmer, and Carole Kaye.

On the road and for numerous television appearances (*American Bandstand, Shindig, Hullabaloo, Where the Action Is*) the Sunrays were dressed in regulation Kingston Trio uniforms: white chinos and striped sport shirts. But the band was not enamored of traditional surf music, preferring R&B in the Chess Records mold, the departure from the regional surf-instrumental norm making them a well-received act on bills with the Four Seasons, Sonny and Cher, and the Beach Boys.

While the Boys felt fresh animosity toward Murry for blatantly casting the Sunrays on record and in publicity campaigns as a Beach Boys clone, the band members had a cordial backstage rapport with one another. Because of the Sunrays' competent four-part harmonies, live instrumental prowess, and the R&B-angled content of their sets, they invariably made for an excellent warm-up act, as noted in a *Los Angeles Times* review of a Hollywood Bowl concert with the Beach Boys where they were well received by a crowd of thirteen thousand.

Murry was losing patience with the slow but steady progress the Sunrays were making and reasserted control over their repertoire, insisting their next single be a country song, "Still." Radio programmers and their audience were perplexed by the sudden left turn, and the single's upward crawl halted at number 93 after two weeks on the Hot 100.

Tower issued three more Sunrays singles, "I Look Baby, I Can't See"/"Don't Take Yourself So Seriously," "Just 'Round the River Bend"/"Hi, How Are You," and "Loaded with Love"/"Time," this last being misperceived by Murry and others as a drug song. By late 1966 the Sunrays' prospects were fading, and Vince Hozier had received his draft notice. Murry told the group he didn't know how to proceed any further, and they accepted his decision, feeling he had been, in Hozier's words, "a hell of a good man to us."

Yet the experience left Murry depressed, disaffected, cognizant of the fact that he had betrayed his own code. As a Christmas gift the Sunrays recorded a special song that thanked their mentor-manager for the measure of success he had made possible. When Murry heard the acetate, he began to cry, telling the Sunrays between sobs, "It sounds like shit. You should have let me mix it."

Tears were also shed in the other wing of the Wilsons' professional sphere. Brian disclosed in a band meeting near the end of recording and mastering *The Beach Boys Today!* that he would no longer travel and perform with the group; he would stay home and function as head composer and studio conceptualist.

He foresaw a beautiful future for the group, but the only way they could achieve it was if "they did their job and I did mine." Mike's eyes welled up; Al Jardine wept and got stomach cramps; Dennis picked up an ashtray and told people to leave the room or he'd hit them with it. Only Carl remained calm, accepting Brian's logic and knowing it would be up to him, as the group's best musician, to lead the stage band from that day forward. Once the tears had ceased, Carl went from member to member and described how the new plan would unfold. Numb but reassured, each nodded at his instructions. No longer the baby brother, Carl had taken charge.

The Wilsons' first cousin Steve Korthof (son of Audree's brother Carl) was appointed equipment manager, Dick Duryea was hired as road manager, and Roy Hatfield was enlisted to coordinate tour publicity.

Glen Campbell concluded his temporary Beach Boy status with a few additional tour stops as Carl taught Bruce Johnston the rest of Brian's bass and vocal parts. Conversely, Brian himself had taken an interest in Campbell, who had a contract with Capitol Records; Brian offered to compose and produce a single for Glen. Brian collaborated on the project with Russ Titelman (now an Aldon/Screen Gems staff writer), who enjoyed swapping Phil Spector anecdotes with the Beach Boy.

Titelman and Wilson cooked up two songs: "Sheri, She Needs Me" and "Guess I'm Dumb." Brian chose the latter as most appropriate for Campbell. Originally cut for the Beach Boys on October 14, 1964, with Campbell on guitar, the unissued song was recast on Glen's behalf in April 1965 and released on June 7, 1965, with the credit "Arranged and conducted by Brian Wilson," but it proved too impressionistic for Campbell's pop-country audience. "Dumb" did at least appear on *Billboard*'s weekly Bubbling Under the Hot 100 survey, and three months later, Campbell had his first chart success with Buffy Sainte-Marie's "Universal Soldier," followed by a trio of solid country hits: "Burning Bridges," "Gentle on My Mind," and "By the Time I Get to Phoenix."

On April 6, 1965, Bruce Johnston was given backing vocal responsibilities on a new tune of Brian's tentatively called "Yeah, I Dig the Girls" but soon retitled "California Girls." Brian wrote the melody in his and Marilyn's Hollywood apartment, the song's underlying organ surges conjuring a carnival midway. Mike Love provided lyrics based on Brian's assertion that "everybody loves girls" the whole world over. Johnston's falsetto backing was so close to Brian's in its contours that the group regarded its naturalness on the track as uncanny. Carole Kaye's bass line on the track aped Brian's playing with equal weight. In both cases he taught them their parts and then marveled at their effectiveness.

On April 9, 1965, Johnston was appointed Brian's official replacement, sealing the pact with an evening concert in Wilmington, Delaware. That same night the Astrodome, the world's largest air-conditioned all-weather arena, opened in Houston, Texas. The pop touring business was evolving into an aggressive year-round enterprise, and revenues from concerts were rising to a level equal with or greater than record sales, which made public appearances a financial and career necessity.

By April 30 the Beach Boys were engrossed in principal recording for the *Summer Days (and Summer Nights!!)* album, Carl doing his very first lead vocal as a Beach Boy on Brian's "Girl Don't Tell Me," about a romance renewed from the previous summer. Music was supplied by the band without additional support: Denny drummed, Carl picked and strummed, and Brian played the celesta.

In May, the Beach Boys adapted the Crystals' "Then He Kissed Me" as "Then I Kissed Her." Brian neatly melded the Wilson and Spector production styles of wall-high resonances and warm personal detail. Mike sang the lead vocal on Brian's "Amusement Parks, U.S.A.," a song that paid passing homage to Freddie Cannon's 1962 smash "Palisades Park." Also that month the Boys cut the classic slow dance instrumental "Summer Means New Love."

On May 24 the group recorded "The Girl from New York City," Brian's female-focused reply to the hit of the previous January, "The Boy from New York City," by the Newark, New Jersey, quintet the Ad

Libs. But "You're So Good to Me," a track done the same day, was one of Brian's best arrangements of the decade; its "la-la-la" chorus and Motown-like tambourine-and-foot-stomp percussion reinforced the affectionate narrative about the rewards of belief in a partner's best qualities. The "kinda small" and "such a doll" lines and other fond phrases of recognition that Brian sang so convincingly were bouquets to Marilyn for putting up with his erratic moods.

The polar opposite of Brian's grateful side exhibited on "You're So Good to Me" was reflected as the May 24 sessions continued on "I'm Bugged at My Old Man," a rancorous Fats Domino–influenced parable about Murry's many teenager persecutions. It was as unsparing an indictment as any son could assemble, and as such it became the definitive parents-as-laughingstock rip.

Rather than have the record end on such a derisive note, an a capella good-night song called "And Your Dreams Come True" was added to the May 24 workload; the construct was that of a parting kiss for a young woman whose wedding was one more summer away.

In spite of Carl's long-range sense of dread about *Summer Days (and Summer Nights!!)*, the album rocketed to number 2 and stayed there for one week, and the single from it, "California Girls," reached number 3. It was kept from the top slot by the Beatles' unyielding "Help!" and Bob Dylan's "Like a Rolling Stone."

No longer under the yoke of Murry's sense of studio etiquette and reluctant to fulfill Capitol's request for a Greatest Hits album for the Yuletide shopping season, the Beach Boys allowed themselves an extended burst of September frivolity in Western Studio number 2. Over the course of four sessions and some lighthearted rehearsals, Brian and crew brought in wives, girlfriends, and colleagues such as Dean Torrence, along with beer, acoustic guitars, a harmonica, one Precision Bass, and some bongos for recordings that were less an actual party than a happily contrived folk hoot.

As the tape rolled, songs were discussed, toyed with, and then embarked upon or abandoned (the discards including "Smokey Joe" and the Rolling Stones' "[I Can't Get No] Satisfaction"). The incidental clatter of traversing conversations was substantial, but attempts at silencing the bullshitting in the background were few and fruitless. In order to prevail over the discord, the Beach Boys grafted the hootenanny bravado of the Kingston Trio's 1959 *From The Hungry i* album onto a protracted live pass at "Bull Session with 'Big Daddy,' " and they sang with innate grace and heart.

"(Baby) Hully Gully," last heard at a Hawthorne High assembly, was resurrected, as were oldies such as the Everly Brothers' "Devoted to You" and the Dyna Sores'/Dante and the Evergreens'/Hollywood Argyles' common 1960 hit "Alley-Oop." Johnny Rivers's rendition of "Mountain of Love" received a fresh airing, as did the Crystals' "There's No Other (Like My Baby)." Al Jardine tackled Bob Dylan's "The Times They Are A-Changin' " and watched it crumble into "Heart and Soul."

Dean Torrence entered the studio on September 23 just as a rendition of the Regents' 1961 hit "Barbara Ann" was taking hold, so Dean doubled Brian's vocals as Brian kept the beat with a tin ashtray. All hands joined in on vocals and claps, with Hal Blaine on tambourine, and the jangly spell approached the spirit of a revival. The group also ventured into hilarious burlesques of their "I Get Around" and "Little Deuce Coupe." But the boldest move was to cover three Beatles songs: "I Should Have Known Better," "Tell Me Why," and a surprise highlight of the album, "You've Got to Hide Your Love Away," with tender lead vocals by Dennis.

While the band considered the resulting album a trifle, the public thought it was terrific. Home taping had come into vogue, and evidence that an informal Beach Boys gathering would have the same craggy charm as any reel-to-reel copy of a college frat house sing-along was somehow fascinating.

From the moment the album was released on November 1, 1965, purchasers pored over the copper-toned cover pictures of the "party" (actually a Manhattan Beach house photo shoot staged after the fact) as well as a bonus perforated cardboard insert of fifteen wallet-size snapshots. And they listened with delight to each vehement *sssh!* and disruptive giggle as the musicians tried to direct the mood by delving into "sensitive" songs such as "Devoted to You," the Dylan track, and Denny's Beatle hymn.

Most tellingly, people sang along with the album at their own parties, feeling that the American art of making one's own domestic fun had been adroitly captured and disseminated for global consumption. Notwithstanding the genuine amity caught on tape, *Beach Boys' Party!* was the Beach Boys' most powerful California illusion to date, which is why it went to number 6 nationwide, with its "Barbara Ann" single at number 2 for two weeks running. The LP became a must-have record for every hip holiday get-together from Turkey Day until the Feast of Saint Valentine.

One of the most imposing photographs on the album's jacket was a portrait of a tanned, bare-chested Dennis with his bronze-skinned fiancée, Carole E. Freedman, a willowy, raven-haired eighteen-year-old of stunning beauty. Carole was born in Michigan, raised in Los Angeles, and married previously, with an infant son named Scott, whom Dennis adored and vowed to adopt. The couple was married on July 29, 1965, and the new family took up residence at 2600 Benedict Canyon Drive, a four-bedroom house with a stable and several acres of property.

Brian gave Marilyn what amounted to an advance first anniversary gift on October 13, 1965, when the Beach Boys recorded "The Little Girl I Once Knew" as a self-contained single for late autumn release. Opening with a reflective guitar figure, the song is the first-person account of a fateful reencounter with a young woman from the narrator's childhood, whereupon the passive observer becomes a transfixed suitor, critical of how her current boyfriend holds her and determined to steal her away. The particulars are indistinguishable from Brian's abrupt turnabout in his affections for Marilyn, on whose family couch he once indifferently crashed, only to later beg the little girl of the house for her hand in matrimony.

Two days after the "Little Girl" session, Mike Love tied the knot for the second time, taking the hand of the former Suzanne Celeste Belcher. The match took place under a cloud. Six months earlier, Mike had been named in a paternity suit by twenty-two-year-old secretary Shannon Ann Harris, who claimed the Beach Boys singer was the father of her baby daughter Shawn Marie. Court-ordered blood tests at the Wilshire Medical Laboratories, Inc., that were filed on March 2, 1965, established "Paternity is possible." But on April 26, 1966, Judge Frank C. Charvat ruled that "plaintiff has not established by a preponderance of the evidence that defendant is the father of the minor plaintiff." A motion for a new trial was denied and appeal rights were renounced in exchange for a $9,500 payment by Love to the child, who—despite the judge's ruling—grew up using the surname Love.

Suzanne Love became pregnant with her first child by Mike, a daughter named Hayleigh who was born on December 27, 1966. As individuals the Beach Boys were experiencing both the brackish shallows and the shore-pounding peaks of high-risk lives, their rides and spills taking place under the scrutiny of envious and irked gremmies and hodads. They had sold their lifestyle and its surfing metaphors to America the same way Southern California and its golden pioneer allegories had been bartered to their forebears, and bystanders wanted to feast on the bounty of the gamble won.

There is a phrase—the "sparkle factor"—in surfing that describes the glistening effect the sun has on the water as it furls and trundles. The intense, rolling twinkle of refracted light is strongest in the early morning and late afternoon when the sun is at its sharpest angle in relation to the waves. At such moments, to be padding down the beach or poised in the surfing lineup out where the water begins its swell formations is to be privy to the sublime. The only sight more intoxicating—and privileged— is that of the "sparkle room," that is, the inside of the curl as the board traverses the long line of a Malibu-style wave. And the sole thing better than the sparkle room by day is the sparkle room lit by a full moon, the beauty of its fierce brevity tempting some to madness.

The elemental lure of the sun was pleasure enough for the average seeker, but others would settle for nothing less than the sparkle room or its simulated equivalent. And that became a problem because no sparkle room could be expected to last.

Brian first dropped acid in the spring of 1965 after he and Marilyn had relocated to a two-bedroom apartment on Gardner Street near her parents' house. Marilyn was not present when her husband took a dose of the undiluted LSD. Brian told his fearful wife later that it had been a spiritual confrontation with God. He seemed exhilarated. He seemed distraught. He never seemed the same again.

Public notice of the proliferation of "LSD parties" in Los Angeles initially came in the form of a July 1962 article in *The Journal of the American Medical Association* written by psychiatrist Sidney Cohen and colleague Keith Ditman. *The Los Angeles Times* took note and discovered that the California Narcotics Bureau was unaware of the practice, which had been taking place in Beat Generation literary circles since the 1950s. LSD-25, as it was formally called in pharmacological circles, had been discovered on April 16, 1943, in Basel, Switzerland, when Sandoz Laboratories research chemist Albert Hofman fell ill with hallucinations while synthesizing his twenty-fifth compound of a solution of lysergic acid diethylamide derived from a toxic rye fungus known as ergot. The experiment was part of an ongoing search for drugs to treat migraine head-aches, and he had absorbed the crystalline solution through his fingertips.

In a lab report Hofman characterized his chemically induced delusions as "an uninterrupted stream of fantastic images of extraordinary plastic-ity and vividness, and accompanied by an intense kaleidoscopic play of colors." On April 19, approximately forty-five minutes after ingesting a dose of one millionth of an ounce in a glass of water, he feared for his sanity, believing his ego was suspended in space and his body lay dead on the sofa below him. A kindly neighbor who brought a cup of milk he had hoped would counteract the baneful effects now appeared to be a "malevolent insidious witch." Hofmann endured the mental suffering for hours yet awoke the next day feeling fine.

But his "problem child," as he called LSD, would attract the attention of the CIA, which conducted clandestine testing with unwitting human guinea pigs in the 1950s and 1960s. At the same time the drug became a preoccupation of visionary novelist-screenwriter Aldous Huxley, a British aristocrat transplanted to Los Angeles, who ordered forty-three cases of LSD from Sandoz in 1955. In 1963, on his deathbed at a friend's house on Mulholland Drive, Huxley requested an intramuscular injec-tion of LSD.

LSD spread in Los Angeles entertainment and psychiatric circles by way of Perry Bivens, a diver who worked for producer Ivan Tors's 1957–61 syndicated TV series *Sea Hunt.* Bivens turned his Beverly Hills psychia-trist friend Oscar Janiger on to the drug, who in turn gave it to novelist Anaïs Nin.

A Veterans Administration counterpart of Janiger's, with whom he had mutual friends, was psychiatrist Sidney Cohen, who worked at the Los Angeles Neuropsychiatric Hospital. In his experiments Cohen intro-duced the drug to analysts at the Rand Corporation in Santa Monica as well as provided it through an intermediary to cancer specialist Mortimer Hartman; he gave it to actor Cary Grant, who told reporters during a press conference on the set of the 1959 film *Operation Petticoat* that the drug made him feel "born again."

When Sidney Cohen published his paper on LSD parties in the AMA journal, acid was already well known in surf music circles, the song "LSD-25" having appeared on the B-side of "Moon Dawg," the 1961 World Pacific single by the Gamblers, the Hollywood band helmed by drummer Sandy Nelson and keyboardist Bruce Johnston.

In February 1965 clinically potent acid of bootleg origins was circulating widely in the Haight-Ashbury district of San Francisco, the product of an alliance between University of California at Berkeley chemistry major Melissa Cargill and Berkeley dropout Augustus Owsley Stanley III, who as a serviceman had worked in radar and electronics while stationed at Edwards Air Force Base. Owsley's refined compound was first sold to distributors as powder or a light blue liquid that could be titrated onto sugar cubes, but Owsley preferred making his own 250-microgram tablets and selling them at two dollars a "tab."

Owsley found a less casual collaborator in Berkeley mathematical physics major Tim Scully, and they became friends with the Grateful Dead (for whom Scully built sound equipment) as well as Acid Test and Trips Festivals author-promoter Ken Kesey and cohorts the Merry Pranksters. In 1965 poet Allen Ginsberg declared that acid dispelled the conditioned behavior that commences in childhood, and in September of that year, *San Francisco Examiner* journalist Michael Fallon updated the beatnik term coined by *San Francisco Chronicle* columnist Herb Caen to describe Ginsberg's behaviorally reconditioned generation; by means of Fallon's reinvention of Norman Mailer's "hipster" badge, the post-Beat bohemians who congregated in the Haight's Blue Unicorn cafe became "hippies."

In Los Angeles, Marilyn and Brian were fighting about drugs, and she grew upset enough to move out of their latest apartment to a temporary flat on Detroit Street that was near her parents' place. One of Brian's new drug-taking associates was Santa Barbara College graduate David Van Cortlandt Crosby. David, son of Academy Award–winning cinematographer Floyd Crosby and his socialite wife, Alphi, was born in Los Angeles on August 14, 1941, and did early-sixties recording *(Jack Linkletter Presents a Folk Festival)* with the Les Baxter Balladeers.

World Pacific engineer-producer Jim Dickson, an A&R scout for Elektra Records, extended free demo time to Crosby and the group called the Jet Set, which also included native Chicago guitarist James Joseph McGuinn III, novice New York drummer Michael Dick aka Clarke, and Missouri guitarist Harold Eugene Clark, formerly with a Kansas City act called the Surf Riders.

Of the four, the most seasoned players were Clark and McGuinn. Clark, born November 17, 1941, in Tipton, Missouri, had cut a local single in 1955 with a group called the Sharks and had been a member of the New Christy Minstrels, playing on their *Merry Christmas* and *Land of*

Giants albums. McGuinn, born July 13, 1942, to James and Dorothy McGuinn (authors of the best-seller *Parents Can't Win*), was a frustrated folk singer. He had been tutored on banjo by Frank Hamilton of the Weavers, toured and recorded with the Limeliters and the Chad Mitchell Trio, did session work for both Judy Collins and Tom and Jerry (the latter soon renamed Simon and Garfunkel), served as a Brill Building song-writer for Bobby Darin's publishing company, and cowrote "Beach Ball," a July 1963 Beach Boys soundalike single for Capitol Records that was released under the name the City Surfers (the other players being pianist Terry Melcher and drummer Bobby Darin).

The members of the Jet Set had become acquainted in their favorite watering hole, the Troubadour, where McGuinn appeared playing Beatles songs and rock treatments of folk standards on a twelve-string acoustic guitar—an innovative idea that caught the other players' fancy, especially Gene Clark, who sometimes duoed with McGuinn. The group played there and made a point of going to a local movie theater to see the Beatles' *A Hard Day's Night* for schooling in the correct comportment of a rock act.

Dickson produced one exploratory Elektra single ("Please Let Me Love You"/"Don't Be Long") with the Jet Set, which insisted on using the pseudonym the Beefeaters. They were bolstered on the tracks by Ray Pohlman, the Phil Spector session bassist who'd become music director of *Shindig,* and drummer Earl Palmer.

The Beefeater single died, and the need for a better bass player than Crosby led Dickson to recommend Chris Hillman, a San Diego guitarist who had appeared on the Scottsville Squirrel Barkers' *Bluegrass Favorites* album and performed with the Golden State Boys (whom Dickson re-named the Hillmen over the course of months of demoing them at World Pacific).

Looking for material equal to the Jet Set's new lineup, Dickson asked promo man Jack Mass for an acetate of an unreleased Bob Dylan song called "Mr. Tambourine Man" that Dickson had heard in concert. The group was reluctant to cut it until Dylan stopped by World Pacific in the fall of 1964, intrigued when he heard they were rehearsing it. The Jet Set's World Pacific demo version deleted many of Dylan's lyrics and re-structured his slack version into a rock song that featured Michael Clarke's drumming in march tempo and McGuinn's new Rickenbacker twelve-string electric as the axis.

An audition by the Jet Set for local promoter Benny Shapiro had

McGuinn, Crosby, and Clark singing along with their demos, the layered live and tape harmonies thrilling Shapiro's daughter Michelle with their Beatlesque ambience. Shapiro later mentioned the charm of the moment to Columbia Records' jazz star Miles Davis, who passed the tip on to his label. Allen Stanton, CBS's West Coast A&R rep, subsequently signed the group, on November 10, 1964, with Jim Dickson and partner Ed Tickner acting as its managers.

Terry Melcher, now a Columbia staff producer working with Paul Revere and the Raiders, was assigned to guide the sessions. The first Columbia recording date was January 20, 1965, for a new arrangement of "Mr. Tambourine Man"; Melcher adjusted the tempo to resemble the measured glide of the Beach Boys' "Don't Worry Baby." McGuinn, Crosby, Clark, and Hillman were on vocals, but McGuinn's twelve-string was the only instrument hoisted by a band member. The rest of the music was played by session men picked by Dickson: Larry Knechtel (bass), Jerry Cole (rhythm guitar), Leon Russell (keyboards), and Hal Blaine (drums)—each of whom happened to be a hero of Melcher's because of his contribution to Beach Boys records.

"Mr. Tambourine Man" was released as a single on April 12, 1965, with Gene Clark's ballad "I Knew I'd Want You" on the flip side. The group, which had been appearing at the chic Ciro's nightclub, was riding through Los Angeles in a black station wagon they had purchased from folksinger Odetta when KRLA spun their single three times in a row. Crosby and his compatriots drooled. Within weeks it was the number 1 song in the nation, marking the advent of a new-fashioned California sound: folk rock.

But one of the group's greatest secret satisfactions was its resolve to discard the name Jet Set in the interregnum of signing with Columbia and re-recording "Mr. Tambourine Man." The decision came after all the members had been invited to Ed Tickner's house for a Thanksgiving dinner revel, and the festive discussion was thrown open to different monikers. Mention of a Dino Valenti song called "Birdses" led to Tickner's well-received nomination of "The Birds," although sympathies arose for a Beatles-like variant spelling, with the orthography of explorer-aviator Admiral Byrd's surname winning out. Best of all, Tickner agreed, was the presence in the name of "the magic 'B,' as in Beatles and Beach Boys."

19

●●●●

Here Comes the Night

Brian Wilson was taking cues from the Beatles. The Beatles were taking cues from the Byrds, who were taking cues from the Beach Boys, the Beatles, and Bob Dylan.

In October 1965, Dylan had done his first recording with a band called the Hawks; the sessions produced a song called "I Wanna Be Your Lover," its antecedent in John Lennon's and Paul McCartney's "I Wanna Be Your Man" as obvious as it was obeisant. During that same month the Beatles were in Studio Two of EMI Studios on Abbey Road in London cutting "Norwegian Wood (This Bird Has Flown)" for *Rubber Soul,* the somber song contemplating the meaning of life's missed chances.

On November 17, Brian Wilson recorded a ghostly instrumental with horn and reverb guitar in Western Studios, which he tagged "Run James Run" but later retitled "Pet Sounds." Far removed from his delicate augury of youthful infatuation on "Summer Means New Love," "Run James Run" was a vision of solitary flight, a long night drive with the windshield dashed by a downpour. Tambourine, triangle, and guiro denoted the wipers battling the showers, and two empty Coca-Cola cans clunked by Brian in a sound booth described a disoriented mind peering into the gloom. Silly-seeming in its ingredients, it was crisp and shuddersome to the ear.

The Beatles' album *Rubber Soul* was released in the United States by Capitol Records on December 6, 1965, and broke all previous sales records for an album: 1.2 million copies were purchased in nine days.

George Harrison's much-remarked use of the Indian sitar on the album track "Norwegian Wood" had occurred at the encouragement of the Byrds. In August 1965, Jim McGuinn and David Crosby had spent a Los Angeles evening with John Lennon and George Harrison during which they sat in a large bathtub tripping on acid and strumming guitars while Crosby told them about Ravi Shankar. Crosby's knowledge grew out of a recent Shankar session at World Pacific to which Jim Dickson had taken David, and the Byrds had been listening to tapes of Shankar's music ever since.

The Byrds' freer sense of rock and its cultural and philosophical boundaries was manifest on their December 1965 *Turn! Turn! Turn!* album. Their heavenly electric limning of the title track (originally adapted by Pete Seeger from the Book of Ecclesiastes), Dylan's "Lay Down Your Weary Tune" and "The Times They Are A-Changin'," and McGuinn's "He Was a Friend of Mine" dashed all preconceptions of rock and roll as a three-chord cakewalk. The tolling monastic triad of McGuinn, Crosby, and Clark's vocal harmonies brought popular music a quasi-religious nobility built upon the rock of Hillman's heart-throbbing bass.

Terry Melcher received considerable credit for the cloistered otherworldly gloss of the production on the Byrds' first two LPs, McGuinn conceding that Melcher's "association with the Beach Boys and Jan and Dean and also being in the Rip Chords gave him that creamy California sound that he superimposed on the rough-edged folk-rock sound that we were doing, and I think . . . it gave a luster to it that it wouldn't have had." But the band bounced Melcher in December by means of a letter to Columbia executives signed by all five members. Although they were the top live band in Hollywood, Melcher wouldn't allow them to play anything and everything on their albums.

Also in December 1965, Brian and Marilyn Wilson reconciled and bought a large house on Laurel Way in Beverly Hills, where Brian now smoked pot openly as he listened to *Rubber Soul*, telling friends, "This album blows my mind because it's a whole album with all good stuff! I'm gonna try that, where a whole album becomes a *gas*. . . . *Rubber Soul* is a complete statement, damn it, and I want to make a complete statement, too!"

While Dylan, the Beatles, the Byrds, and the Beach Boys were locked in a dreamy, determined dance with rock destiny, the world seemed unprepared for 1966, a year during which the pleasures of hot rod and sports car recreation would face social curtailment as 52,500 fatalities and 9 million injuries were reported in traffic accidents, and Ralph Nader, author of *Unsafe at Any Speed*, crusaded for (and got) anchored seat belts and other sweeping auto safety laws. In the meantime, army draft calls increased as U.S. troop strength in Vietnam grew to almost 400,000, and a peace march on the Washington Monument saw 63,000 protesters vowing to vote for antiwar candidates.

Feminist Betty Friedan founded the National Organization of Women; the phrase "black power" was popularized by new Student Nonviolent Coordinating Committee chairman Stokely Carmichael; James Meredith, marcher for black voter registration, was wounded by gunfire; and Dr. Robert Weaver's appointment as Secretary of the Department of Housing and Urban Development made him the first black cabinet member in U.S. history.

Medicare, the federal medical insurance program, was instituted. And multiple homicides by Charles Whitman (fourteen), Richard Speck (eight), and Robert Benjamin Smith (five) spawned the expression "mass murderer."

Star Trek, freeze-dried coffee, and London's mod fashion look were introduced. TV's wildly popular *Batman* program flooded the nation with related toy merchandising and pop recordings (the Marketts' number 17 "Batman Theme" and Jan & Dean's number 66 "Batman"), and the manufacture, sale, and possession of LSD would become illegal in every state in the Union.

Brian returned to Western Studios on January 24, 1966, to cut "You Still Believe in Me," one of a series of songs he wrote with acquaintance Tony Asher, a jingles writer for the Carson/Roberts advertising agency. Brian blended the "Believe" track with vestiges of a 1965 ballad called "In My Childhood" that included bicycle bell sound effects, and on the twenty-third studio take he achieved the sound he wanted. That same day the Byrds recorded the raga-flavored "Why?" as well as the modal beginnings of the John Coltrane–inclined jazz-rock track "Eight Miles High," the lyrics to the latter song inspired by the altitude commonly reserved for military aircraft plus the "touchdown" of a Byrds tour in London in August 1965.

In February and March 1966, Dylan did two tour-interrupted sessions at CBS Studios in Nashville, Tennessee, recording such tracks as "Sad-Eyed Lady of the Lowlands," "Stuck Inside of Mobile with the Memphis Blues Again," "Visions of Johanna," "Leopard-Skin Pillbox Hat," "I Want You," and "Just Like a Woman." He also cut a parody of the Beatles' "Norwegian Wood" called "4th Time Around," and a track mixing Salvation Army street Americana with drug metaphors that seemed a promising single, "Rainy Day Women #12 & 35."

Due to the widening use of marijuana and LSD, drug colloquialisms were gaining candid popular usage, and articles in *Time, Newsweek*, and the daily press chronicled accounts of acid overdoses, acid suicides (notably Jack Linkletter's twenty-one-year-old sister, Diane), and even purported acid murders. Disturbed by the prospect of a permanently tarnished corporate image as a drug purveyor, Sandoz notified the U.S. Food and Drug Administration on April 7, 1966, that they would halt production of LSD-25, cancel all research contracts, and turn all stores of the chemical compound over to the federal government.

"Eight Miles High" was released as a single backed with "Why?" and opened on the *Billboard* charts in the April 9, 1966, issue, eventually reaching number 14 despite criticism that the A-side was about drugs—Crosby insisted that although the Byrds wrote the song on amphetamines, it was only about plane travel.

On April 13 Brian was in Gold Star Studios coordinating the vocal tracks on "I Just Wasn't Made for These Times," another song written with Tony Asher that features early use on a pop record of the theremin, the electronic fluctuant-pitch instrument devised by Russian inventor Leon Theremin and utilized as eerie punctuation in the Bernard Herrmann score of the 1951 science fiction classic *The Day the Earth Stood Still*. Not unlike the peace-seeking alien in the movie, Brian sang that he was looking for a place where he could fit in and speak his mind.

On April 14, five days after the U.S. chart debut of "Eight Miles High," the Beatles entered Studio Three at EMI's Abbey Road studio to record "Rain," a John Lennon track written in homage to the Byrds' electrosonic interpretation of Dylan's "Mr. Tambourine Man."

In the April 16 issue of *Billboard*, Dylan's "Rainy Day Women #12 &

35" entered the charts, its back-alley metaphysics mobilizing a new pop audience that rapidly pushed it to number 2.

On May 24–25, 1966, the Byrds recorded a treatise on Einstein's theory of relativity by Jim McGuinn, "5D (Fifth Dimension)." The searchingly psychedelic title track of their forthcoming third album, it featured iridescent keyboards by Van Dyke Parks, a friend of Terry Melcher's who had done session work with Paul Revere and the Raiders and had a new solo single on the MGM label, "Come to the Sunshine." A waltz-time trip through the light-speed fantastic, it ratified the Byrds' private fight for creative independence.

With *Rubber Soul* a blockbuster and *Blonde on Blonde* and *5D (Fifth Dimension)* due in June and July, respectively, most of the killer B's had prepared their major pronouncements. Now the industry looked to Brian Wilson, who had quit the road, as he explained in a fan magazine piece headlined BRIAN WILSON: WHY I STAY HOME, in order to stay in his new house in Beverly Hills and

> plan the new direction of the group. . . . I wanted to move ahead in sounds and melodies and moods. . . . For a month or two I sat either at a huge Spanish table looking out over the hills, just thinking, or at the piano playing "feels." . . . Feels are musical ideas, riffs, bridges, fragments of themes. A phrase here and there. . . . I wanted to write a song containing more than one level. . . . A song can, for instance, have movements, in the same way as a classical concerto, only capsulized.

As Bob Dylan sang on *Blonde on Blonde*'s "Visions of Johanna": "Little boy lost, he takes himself so seriously."

Pet Sounds was to be an analysis of romance, centering on the theme of a young man growing into manhood, falling in love and out again; chasing the wrong partners and disappointing the right ones; longing for an ideal relationship and forsaking the worth of the flawed ones, all the while on a forlorn, almost picaresque quest for the reasons behind his emotional restlessness. Based for the most part on Brian's personal life, it was a poignant, sometimes uplifting but ultimately dispiriting work that catalogued a succession of failed relationships. Much of the pessimism and dejection that pervaded the album's thirteen selections were tied to the marital problems that Brian and Marilyn were experiencing at the time.

"Wouldn't It Be Nice" was the story of a young couple contemplating marriage through the prism of their preliminary, crushlike captivation. In one of the numerous textural vocal formations Brian conceived for the album, Brian sang the bravely declarative verses, and Mike Love did lead vocals on the more speculative and wishful lyrics at the bridge. Backing vocals had the air of conflicted bouts of conscience and impulse, Brian asking Dennis to sing his parts through cupped hands as if proffering intimate advice. Each time Mike's part spoke of mere prospects, Brian had the backing harmonies charge in with spooky statements of chiding impatience like "Run, run . . ." Hal Blaine played the drums with an orchestral sense of drama, and an accordion was the dominant mid-range instrument.

"You Still Believe in Me" was an interior monologue of self-doubt, exploring and debating Marilyn's patient capacity to forgive Brian's self-ishness and creative absorption. Contrasting the rude force of their frequent breakups with the softer tone of their reconciliations, Brian admits the only time he feels in control of the relationship is when she's providing the stability, although he's unable to be what she wants him to be. There is no resolution of the problem, Brian concluding that he wants to "cry." The track commences with piano strings being hand-plucked and muted as the keys are struck, Brian and Tony Asher reaching into the console to manipulate the wires and dampers to create the tremulant "soft-loud" pianoforte effect. Finger cymbals, harpsichord, and bicycle bells convey the song's fragile state of mind.

Having decided to absent himself from the Beach Boys' concert life and the anxieties it caused him, Brian wrote "That's Not Me" about the thoughts that went into his choice. Even though Mike Love later sang the verses and doubled Brian on the chorus, the lyrics were by Tony Asher, and they excelled, like the rest of the album, at allowing Brian's audience to partake of the most sensitive aspects of his compositional motivations.

As an ad copywriter accustomed to turning fact-gathering discussions with clients such as Mattel Toys into prose that bespoke their perspective on their own products, the friendly and unaffected Tony Asher was a superb sounding board for Brian's psyche. And since Asher had largely given up on commercial music and settled comfortably into the advertising world by the time Wilson contacted him, he had little inclination to distort Brian's themes for his own careerist aims or divert them from their essential concerns.

The son of Warner Bros. Films staff producer Irving Asher and silent film star Laura La Plante (Universal Pictures' top female lead of the 1920s), Tony was born in London on May 2, 1939, shortly before England's Lord Mountbatten enlisted his father to make British army training films to aid the war effort against the Nazis. More than two decades later Tony joined Carson/Roberts just as it was making its historic pitch to Ruth and Elliot Handler of Mattel to begin the campaign to sell toys on television; the Handlers risked the future of their firm on the viability of the million-dollar strategy.

When Carson/Roberts's Mattel slogan ("You Can Tell It's Mattel—It's Swell!") clicked, Asher found himself writing vastly popular ads and jingles for the Barbie and Chatty Cathy dolls. Asher's sudden role as Brian's on-call wordsmith had been a snap decision owed to the Capitol-pressured Brian, who continued to dodge the label's aim of releasing a Beach Boys greatest hits album. Brian had recalled Asher from a past meeting in which the sometime songwriter presented some of his material, so he phoned Tony at his office, and the copywriter-composer cleared his schedule to permit the collaboration.

Asher was a handsome, earnest, fairly straitlaced personality who wanted nothing from his association with Brian beyond the efficient use of the leave of absence he had taken to assist him. Brian was perceived as a temporary employer, and Asher went to Laurel Way on time each morning with his small black notebooks in order to serve him—but Tony quickly recognized the differences in their work ethics. He would wait calmly for hours while Marilyn struggled to roust Brian from bed, and it might be late afternoon and several meals and misadventures later before the boss would join the lyricist at the piano for discussion of Brian's ideas.

Happily, Asher respected those ideas and labored long to put them into words that were true to Brian's conversational tone while cogent enough to advance the scenarios of the songs. Few facets of Brian's unstructured home life were shielded from Tony, whether they were tiffs with Marilyn or interludes of marijuana and hash intake, but when songwriting at home or in the studio was done, Asher went back to his own life until 9:00 A.M. the next business day.

Since the Beach Boys were off on an Asian tour and had other concert commitments during the composing of the music, the toil was divided between teaching the wordless arrangements to studio players and revising the rough drafts of lyrics. This would be the first Beach Boys album on which the band itself never played a single note, which removed all previous restrictions. The music tended to determine the final editorial shape of the words, so Brian would bring dubs of the three- and four-track tapes of the music beds back to the Laurel Way house as catalysts for the writing.

"Don't Talk (Put Your Head on My Shoulder)" was a peaceful meditation on romantic tranquility, yet it might just as easily have been a song of reunion for any loved ones. A distant cymbal is struck with clocklike rhythm, and Brian's most unrestrained falsetto is borne forward by bowed cellos and tympani rumbling in the background; such adornments also invoked the milieu of a requiem.

"I'm Waiting for the Day," written in 1964 by Brian and Mike Love, was an early attempt to evade surf or car topics and concentrate on relationships—in this case adult relationships since the song's spokesman is willing to woo a love prospect by first helping mend her heart as a forbearing friend. The flutes, strings, kettle drums, acoustic guitar, and beseeching organ strains in the fifty-eight seconds before Brian's vocals begin are a matter-of-fact testament to his ability to compose using Beach Boys harmonies as coloration only.

Brian played some new material over the phone to Mike Love in Japan, but the group was largely unconsulted on all aspects of the record. They returned from their travels to find that Brian needed them just for vocals—and that he had inflexible plans for how and where they would be added.

Brian had intended to put harmonies to "Let's Go Away for Awhile," whose title he contemplated changing to (or appending with) the watchwords "And Then We'll Have World Peace." In any event he ultimately disregarded the lyrics Asher penned for the plaintive piece and left it vocal-less, the soft horns, vibraphone, piano, and dashes of strings constituting a piquant jazz nocturne.

In the sixteen months after his 1964 breakdown on the plane, Brian experienced two more episodes of nervous collapse during which concepts of God and prayer took on greater, albeit undogmatic, meaning. Marilyn's reasonable nature was sometimes an astonishment to him, given the chaotic and overwrought background he had come to accept as commonplace. As he withdrew further from the Beach Boys and depended on her to ground him again after periodic descents into chronic dope smoking and LSD trips, the open "God Only Knows" question of where he would find himself without her support became a fearful mantra in the back of his mind—and then a full-fledged song, with Carl executing the magnificent lead vocal. Prior to recording the track, Brian and Carl prayed.

"I Know There's an Answer" was originally cut at Western Studios on February 9, 1966, six days after Carl Wilson married Annie Hinsche, daughter of a prominent Beverly Hills real estate broker. Previously titled "Hang on to Your Ego," the lyrics were drafted by current Beach Boys road manager Terry Sachen. But Mike Love spurned the track when he heard it, denouncing it as an arrogant "doper song" stemming from one too many acid trips, and refused to have anything to do with its vocal completion. Hoping to avoid a rift with the Mike Love–Al Jardine faction of the band, which feared public reaction to Brian's downbeat direction, and the Carl Wilson–Dennis Wilson–Bruce Johnston bloc, which saw the music as a lovely progression to which Brian was entitled, Brian rewrote the song.

On the original solo vocal Brian exhorted listeners to hang on to their egos even though they would likely lose the fight; in the new version Mike alternated the first lines of the verses with Brian—who sings that he had to find the "answer" by himself—and then Mike supplied the backup vocal tracery. Still, the music retained its idiosyncratic charm, with banjo and kazoo underpinning the rhythm section.

Mike did the lead vocal on "Here Today," a rumination on the ephemeral nature of love among the smitten and flirtatious. The pounding rush of harmonies on the choruses gave the other Beach Boys a sense of familiar terrain, but they were less pleased when the melody dropped out in the middle to allow a pendulate bass line to go it alone until it converges with some remote carney keyboards. Brian intended to use Love prominently on other cuts, but Mike told him he found some of the lyrics so "offensive" and "nauseating" in their psychedelic suggestiveness that he would not participate further.

The final track on the album was "Caroline No," a song suggested by Brian's high school crush on slender blond cheerleader Carol Mountain, now married but still living in Hawthorne. In a burst of slightly stoned heartache, he cursed himself for never finding the gumption to approach the comely pom-pom girl and confess his enamored state, and the lyric scenario flowed out.

Brian foresaw "Caroline No" as "a story about how, once you've fucked up or once you've run your gamut with a chick, there's no way to get it back. It takes a lot of courage to do that sometimes in your life. It's a pretty love song about how this guy and this girl lost it and there's no way to get it back."

The track's sense of desolation was seamless, from the hollow knell of the percussion that began it (actually Hal Blaine rapping on the base of an empty Sparkletts' watercooler keg) to the concluding sound of dogs barking at a passing train.

"I just felt sad," Brian summarized, "so I wrote a sad song."

In keeping with Brian's concept of calling the new Beach Boys album *Pet Sounds*—"because we specialized in certain sounds. . . . The songs were our pet *sounds*"—he had taped his two pooches Banana and Louie as they howled; he also spliced in the roar of freight cars barreling past a railway crossing signal.

After adding the dogs to the song, Brian turned to Chuck Britz and said excitedly, "Hey, Chuck, is it possible we could bring a horse in here if we don't screw anything up?" Britz replied: "I beg your *pardon?*"

Capitol followed its usual modus of issuing Beach Boys singles well in advance of completed albums, releasing "Caroline No"—at Brian's personal urging—on March 7, 1966. Capitol and Beach Boys product manager Nick Venet knew Brian was the sole singer on the record and that the Beach Boys had not otherwise participated, so they listened for once to Brian's thinking: "I've always used the word 'spiritual' in my life and my career, and the high, pretty voices and mellow instruments all add up to something spiritual for me. I get a little bit paranoid about being made fun of for my voice, but if I release a song under my name, if I could get a single going, it will be a spiritual release for me, and I'd have a hit."

Thus, it was decided the credit on the single and its picture sleeve would be "Brian Wilson" rather than the Beach Boys. Unfortunately, in acceding to Brian's personal and artistic aims, Capitol confused a constituency waiting for new Beach Boys product. Moreover, Brian's name was far from a household word, and since there was no substantive press campaign to accompany the 45, it met with mixed trade and commercial response, running out of steam at number 32.

Brian's joy with the solo single's immediate appearance on the charts turned to disgust and depression when the record hovered below the top 20 nationwide and then went into freefall. Business is business, however, and Capitol's concession to Brian's independent will had come with a catch: A single that Brian had cut back in July (music) and December (vocals) 1965 would be retrieved from the vaults as the next Beach Boys single.

The song, broached by diehard folkie Al Jardine, was "The Wreck of the John B.," last heard on the Kingston Trio's album *From The Hungry i* in an adaptation by poet–folk archivist Carl Sandburg and Lee Hays of the Weavers. Also known as "John B. Sails," the song was a traditional chantey of the Bahamas, telling the saga of the ship's tragic grounding off Nassau as viewed through the bloodshot eyes of its unhappy crew. The remains of the ill-fated *John B.* lay undisturbed in the shoal at Governor's Harbor until they were excavated in 1926, and the publicity raised the popular profile of the commemorative ditty.

Composer-conductor Alfred George Wathall, who taught at North-western University's School of Music, conceived a modern arrangement of the song in 1926–27 while serving as master arranger and composer for WGN, the *Chicago Tribune* radio station, and it swiftly became a favorite in the folklorist circles in which Sandburg, the Weavers, and Woody Guthrie moved.

While Wathall prescribed the meter of "The John B. Sails" as *moderato melancolico,* Brian hatched a triumphant, uptempo reading whose glockenspiel grace notes emphasized all of the song's humor and none of its sodden woe. The Beach Boys' cascading a capella interlude on "Sloop John B," which was cut in one take, gave the single a visceral elegance without precedent on Top 40 radio, and it hit the *Billboard* charts on April 2, 1966.

Jan & Dean were seeing poor results in 1966 from their foray into the folk idiom: a *Folk n' Roll* album that sold badly despite the inclusion of their treatment of P. F. Sloan's "Eve of Destruction," which used the same music tracks as former New Christy Minstrel Barry McGuire's number 1 hit. Preoccupied with his impending medical school exams, Jan Berry was driving to an appointment at his local draft board on April 19, 1966, when he lost control of his Sting Ray and swerved into a parked truck, the mishap killing three people and leaving Jan in a coma from which he later emerged with partial brain damage. On May 3, 1966, while Jan was recuperating in the UCLA Medical Center, Liberty released the single "Popsicle"/"Norwegian Wood."

"Sloop John B" reached number 3 in the Hot 100 on May 7, 1966, after a five-week ascent. Despite the fact that the song had absolutely nothing to do with the rest of *Pet Sounds,* it became the album's identity element and selling point when the finished album was shipped to stores on May 16, 1966.

Derek Taylor, former *Daily Express* reporter and the Beatles' public relations coordinator, had been working as the Byrds' publicist when he was hired by the Beach Boys to unveil *Pet Sounds* in London. Taylor arranged a reception at the London Hilton, at which Marianne Faithfull, John Lennon, and Paul McCartney joined a flock of chic guests who listened intently. Afterward, Lennon and McCartney went back to Paul's house and began writing "Here, There and Everywhere," whose preamble ("To lead a better life . . .") was directly inspired by the musical preludes Brian had composed for *Pet Sounds*' "Wouldn't It Be Nice" and "God Only Knows."

While the British critics were effusive in their praise and the American musical community almost dumbfounded in its admiration, the words- and image-minded U.S. press was largely silent about *Pet Sounds*, overlooking altogether Brian's fertile use of eight-track recording (one composite track for instruments, the rest for vocals) and hesitant to acknowledge artistic dimensionality from an act it had already dismissed. And the cover art by George Jerman, which showed the Boys feeding bread bits and Fritos to goats at the San Diego Zoo, was deemed too quaint.

Capitol's *Pet Sounds* promotion was modest, and despite a climb to number 10 in *Billboard*, sales were sluggish, the release escaping the notice of many regular Beach Boys fans but attracting numerous first-time buyers, among them Linda Eastman, erstwhile namesake of Jan & Dean's 1963 hit single and now a widely published rock photographer. During the same period she photographed Brian at home for a book project and was startled at how many delicatessen refrigerators he had in his house.

Capitol didn't issue a single to herald the in-store status of *Pet Sounds* until August 1, 1966—three months after the album's release. But Capitol's strategy included the *Best of the Beach Boys*, which was rushed to a well-primed retail reception in time to enter the *Billboard* charts several weeks before the issue (August 13, 1966) in which "Wouldn't It Be Nice" debuted. The *Best of* anthology briskly went gold, soaring past *Pet Sounds* to number 8 on the strength of a slick and pervasive ad campaign. Commerce hit a home run, art was forced to bunt. Brian returned to a darkened dugout. (Wilson was faring better in *Billboard* than Phil

Spector, whose "River Deep, Mountain High" production opus with Ike and Tina Turner failed to reach the chart in May, sending an abject Phil into seclusion.)

Tony Asher left the field for his former profession, returning to Carson/Roberts to create jingles and advertising music for Mattel's Liddle Kiddles minidolls and Hot Wheels gravity-powered race cars. He later formed his own jingle and TV-commercial production companies—Producers Music Service and Paisley Productions—while occasionally penning songs with prominent writer Roger Nichols (Paul Williams's collaborator on many of the Carpenters' hits); the Asher-Nichols material, such as "Love So Fine," was recorded in 1967 by Herb Alpert.

Brian Wilson settled back into his Laurel Way lair, crushed by the commercial anticlimax of *Pet Sounds* but determined to distract himself with the insular creative realm he had conjured. Brian smoked a bit more dope, dawdled at his refrigerators, dropped a bit more acid, and pondered life's simple twists of psychedelic fate as diagrammed in such current paths of hippie wisdom as the I-Ching, tarot cards, astrology, Tantric Buddhism, numerology, acid mysticism, and Subud (an Indonesian organization whose ritual theories of names had prompted the Byrds' Jim McGuinn to change his to Roger in late 1967).

Despite his deep disappointment, Brian felt he was not yet out of the running in the "complete statement" pop tourney, believing he possessed an ace in the hole, a turn of the tarot he had begun preparing in the Gold Star studio A control room as far back as February 18, 1966. There were twenty-eight takes on the first day's taping for the ambitious song's basic track, Brian shouting after the second try to "Hold it please, let me hear the organ—*perfect*—we'll go with that! . . . Organ, Fender bass, and piccolo!" Rough lyrics by Tony Asher were used only for guide vocals as Brian pressed onward with the project, shuttling between United, Western, Sunset Sound, RCA, and Columbia studios as he wore out the engineering acumen of Chuck Britz, Larry Levine, Bruce Botnick, and anonymous others.

On April 9, 1966, Brian was exclaiming "Great take!" for the twentieth attempt in *that* session. The twentieth bid on May 4 found him asking "Who can stay and overdub bells and tambourine?" The fifteenth pass on May 27 found Brian seemingly satisfied, saying, "That was it, man, beautiful." But "Let's do it with *perfect* feeling" was the plea of the producer on the fifth take of the September 1 taping, as recording continued.

Although it began as an R&B tune, the marathon piece had something to do with the wavelengths people emitted and received from one
another. One rejected lyric fragment of the song in progress described
how a look in a woman's eyes made Brian intercept something he
couldn't explain, something "weird" from her that "comes in so strong"
and made him "wonder" what people were "picking up" from *him*.

20
• • • •
Time to Get Alone

Lenny Waronker was in his car, headed down Franklin Avenue in Los Angeles in October 1966, when he first heard "Good Vibrations." There had been tremendous hype beforehand about the Beach Boys single, much talk about the months and money (some $16,000) that Brian Wilson had spent in the studio to create a self-contained jukebox masterwork. So it was amazing, thought Waronker, that all the skeptical Los Angeles AM stations immediately made it the Pick Hit of the Week. And every producer in town was talking about the 45 because it was a four- or five-part song that broke new ground. The twenty-three-year-old Waronker was stunned by it all—especially the bold, crazy edit in the middle of the track, at the juncture after the harmonica went into a wordless vocal upsurge and then stopped dead. As he drove and listened, he decided it was the biggest musical feat in single form that he had ever heard, and he suspected he would feel that way for a long time to come.

"Good Vibrations" was a delightful synthesis of the thematic and stylistic strong points of the current psychedelic surge, complete with harmonies. Mike Love had authored new lyrics to replace Asher's stilted, Brian-filtered mysticism, dictating them to his wife Suzanne as they rode on the Hollywood Freeway from Burbank to Columbia Studios for the umpteenth taping of the track. While Brian tossed in enough exotic instruments (sleigh bells, jew's harp, wind chimes, harpsichord, flutes, organ, and theremin) to make Phil Spector envious, he sacrificed none of the Beach Boys' prepossessing airiness. Carl and Mike sang like bell-bottomed seraphim on "Good Vibrations," and it became the variegated but coherent statement that Brian had endeavored to make with the self-conscious *Pet Sounds.* The best part was that he managed it all in three minutes and thirty-five seconds, and so it became the band's biggest-selling number 1 single.

Lenny Waronker had an indirect relationship with Brian through Van Dyke Parks, who had met Wilson on the front lawn of Terry Melcher's Cielo Drive home in Los Angeles in late 1965. On April 22, 1966, Lenny Waronker left his post as a promo man and song plugger for the Metric Music division of Liberty Records and joined Warner Bros. Records' A&R staff. Waronker had admired Parks's MGM singles ("Come to the Sunshine"/"Further Along," "Number Nine"/"Do What You Wanta?"), and was equally enthused when Parks played him a new song he had written called "High Coin."

Warner's was then juggling a host of pop and psychedelic Bay Area acts that label vice president Joe Smith acquired through the April 1, 1966, purchase of San Francisco–based Autumn Records from former KYA deejay-entrepreneurs Tom Donahue and Bob Mitchell (who was ill with Hodgkin's disease), and KSOL disc jockey turned Autumn producer Sylvester "Sly" Stewart.

The Autumn roster boasted the Beau Brummels ("Laugh, Laugh"), Bobby Freeman ("C'mon and Swim"), the Mojo Men, the Vegetables, and a Santa Cruz group called the Bermuda-Clad Tikis (Ted Templeman, Richard Yost, Edward James, and Richard Scoppettone). Smith needed an A&R man to fly with him to San Francisco, listen to Autumn Records' tape archives, and assess the producibility of the defunct company's artist lineup, so he recruited the just-hired Waronker.

Lenny's first two production assignments were the Mojo Men and the Tikis, and the latter had opened assorted shows for the Beach Boys. Waronker asked Parks to help him groom the two bands, Van arranging material and doing production coordination while Lenny found some material. Waronker went to Screen Gems Publishing and picked an as-yet-unreleased Buffalo Springfield song, written by Richie Furay and Steve Stills, for the Mojos: "Sit Down, I Think I Love You."

Parks applauded the choice, Stills having once played guitar in the Van Dyke Parks Band. For the Tikis, Waronker selected Paul Simon's "The 59th Street Bridge Song (Feeling Groovy)" but worried that the Tikis' name was not right for such a classy tune. The droll Parks recommended that the band be redubbed Harper's Bizarre so that he "could weed out my love of Cole Porter/Depression-era songwriting."

When both of the singles Waronker oversaw became smashes, he had the clout to empower Parks, and Van Dyke produced Harper's Bizarre's *Anything Goes* album for Warner's, which included several Randy Newman songs, including "Happy Land" and "Debutante Ball." The group scored another hit with the title track and also recorded Parks's "High Coin" (as did Bobby Vee, the West Coast Pop Art Experimental Band, and the Charlatans).

Late in 1966, Parks was signed by Joe Smith at Lenny Waronker's urging as a solo artist. Parks's first release was an atmospheric cover of Donovan's "Colours" under the pseudonym George Washington Brown. Warner's was impressed when a *Village Voice* writer who discovered it on a Greenwich Village jukebox gave it a good review. Parks got $12,500 in seed money to develop an album of his own compositions to be called *Looney Tunes,* and he drove out to Palm Desert in a Volvo purchased by Brian Wilson to write the material. Parks had also been hired by Brian to write lyrics and arrange music for a project of Brian's titled *Dumb Angel,* which was conceived as a sort of aural free-for-all.

The forces converging herein represented dramatic reversals of fortune for all parties concerned, namely, Warner Bros., Waronker, Parks, and of course Brian. In each case, because of their new affiliations, their lives and business interests would become forever altered—and forever intertwined.

Warner Bros. Records was founded at 10:00 A.M. on March 19, 1958, by Jack L. Warner, Sr., president of Warner Bros. Film Studios, who flew from Hollywood to New York on one of the last pre-jetliner transcontinental propeller-plane flights in order to formally incorporate the label.

Jack's grandfather Benjamin Warner came to America from Poland with his family in the 1880s, settling in Baltimore in 1888, the year after the incorporation of the City of Burbank, California. The family moved around the Midwest as Ben and sons Harry, Albert, Sam, and Jack tried cobbler, butcher, and bicycle repair businesses before brushes with vaudeville (Jack singing in blackface in front of illustrated slide shows in Youngstown, Ohio's Dome Theatre) had led to a nickelodeon, film distribution, and finally a film production company: the Warner Feature Film Company.

Its first movie, in September 1912, was a silent three-reeler titled *Peril of the Plains.* In 1916 the Warner brothers moved their production equipment (one camera) to a barn in Hollywood. By 1925 the company was also running KFWB radio (the "WB" was for the Warner brothers) in Los Angeles when KFWB engineer Nathan Levinson returned from a New York trip gushing about a "talking picture" demonstration he had seen at Bell Laboratories. On June 25 of that year, Warner's signed a deal with Western Electric to develop "sound" motion pictures (initially only syncronized music and audio effects); the Goldman, Sachs investment house backed their joint purchase of Brooklyn's Vitagraph Studios for the creation of Vitaphone soundies, which trickled out.

It was not until Harry Warner bought a Broadway play with music called *The Jazz Singer* and filmed a version—only allowing star Al Jolson's ad-lib dialogue "You ain't heard nothin' yet, folks!" into the sound track at the last minute—that the new era of "talkies" began. Opening in New York on October 6, 1927, *The Jazz Singer* helped double national movie attendance to ninety-five million people a week, also multiplying by tenfold the one hundred sound theaters then extant.

Warner Bros. had just finished filming Spencer Tracy in the film adaptation of Ernest Hemingway's *The Old Man and the Sea* when Jack Warner announced the appointment of James B. "Jim" Conkling, former president of Columbia Records, as president of the Warner Records subsidiary. Located across from Warner Pictures' Burbank lot, the record company's headquarters was the vacant top floor (above the machine shop) of a two-story auxiliary building at 3701 Warner Boulevard. Warner Bros. Records' first recording artist was Connie Stevens, star of the Warner's TV series *Hawaiian Eye,* whose sales on her debut LP *Conchetta* (the name on her birth certificate) were slight.

The label's first hit was actor Tab Hunter's last: a honking-sax remake of the Andrews Sisters' 1941 standard "(I'll Be with You in) Apple Blossom Time," produced by A&R trainee Karl Engemann and arranger Don Ralke. It inched up to number 31, but Hunter, aka Arthur Klem, had been pistol-hot two years earlier with his number 1 Dot Records single "Young Love." Passions had plainly cooled.

Warner's second hit, with Ralke and Engemann still in charge, was by TV's *77 Sunset Strip* star Edd "Kookie" Byrnes and guest Connie Stevens: "Kookie, Kookie (Lend Me Your Comb)." Ralke's own stream of indefinable, unsellable albums for the label was typified by his *Never Heard Gershwin with Bongos*. It was in April 1960 that Warner's finally took off with the Everly Brothers' first Warner's single, the number 1 "Cathy's Clown," and the classic comedy album *The Button-Down Mind of Bob Newhart*.

Over the hills in Hollywood, Frank Sinatra announced plans to leave Capitol Records as a result of simmering royalty disputes and start his own label, and the Chairman of the Board did as he vowed. On December 15, 1960, Reprise Records was born, its name taken from the Old French musical term meaning "to play and play again." On a whim Sinatra selected a steamboat as the label's logo. Sinatra hired Verve Records' controller Morris "Mo" Ostin to be Reprise's administrative vice president and gave him a stern mandate. "He didn't want to have any rock-and-roll artists," Ostin later explained to Warner executives. "He wanted what he thought were quality types of artists and the kind of operation that consisted of music he himself represented. He was adamant in this position."

In 1963, Warner Bros. acquired the somewhat indebted Reprise and its Rat Pack roster of Sinatra, Dean Martin, Sammy Davis, Jr., plus a few loose cannons: Trini Lopez, Dodgers pitcher Don Drysdale, Les Baxter, Art Linkletter (TV host and parent of Jack and Diane), and Jack Nitzsche, who was enjoying the sea air with "The Lonely Surfer."

Three years later, as Lenny Waronker surveyed the rock landscape on Warner-Reprise's behalf, the parent label's top sellers were comics Bill Cosby and Allan Sherman and folk trio Peter, Paul and Mary. At Reprise, Sinatra had just unleashed an unstoppable number 1 single that he had cut on April 11, 1966, called "Strangers in the Night"; the lead guitarist on the session (playing in E-flat with a capo) was Glen Campbell.

Waronker grew up in Beverly Hills and Pacific Palisades. His earliest friend (prekindergarten) was Randy Newman, who lived around the block from Waronker for most of their boyhood. (Both families' California ranch houses were built by the same architect.) When Randy and Lenny weren't playing sports in the Newmans' backyard, sitting at the midsize Steinway piano in Randy's room, or hiding out in the little house they had built in the great Brazilian pepper tree on the Newmans' front lawn, they were frequently sitting in hushed awe on some Twentieth Century–Fox soundstage while Randy's uncle Alfred led a sixty-five-piece orchestra through film synchronization for a project such as *The King and I.*

To return the favor, Lenny would bring Randy to his father Sy's office to hear tapes of forthcoming singles by Bobby Vee, Gene McDaniels, or Eddie Cochran. The easygoing Oklahoma-born Cochran and Lenny liked each other; the day Eddie solemnly played "Summertime Blues" for the senior Waronker's approval, Lenny was sitting there and spouted, "That's great!" The single jumped to number 8 and became Cochran's biggest career hit. Afterward, with every subsequent Cochran single, the need for Lenny's endorsement became a running joke. The shared jest ended on a Sunday morning in April 1960 when the phone rang at the Waronkers' home in Pacific Palisades with the news that Cochran had been killed in an auto crash in Chippenham, Wiltshire, England. Sy Waronker and his son were devastated, and the next person a tearful Lenny called was Randy Newman.

While attending University High, Lenny and Randy sometimes skipped school together to drink beer and talk about girls. But music was always the linchpin in their mutually supportive fellowship, the two teenagers figuring out jazz arrangements for pop songs and vice versa as an idle exercise. As Carole King and Gerry Goffin began to generate hits with their Brill Building output, Waronker would bring the sheet music and demos to Newman's house, saying, "Listen, these guys are doing this, and they're not as good as you are."

The first song Waronker and Newman recorded together was Randy's arrangement of the Elvis Presley song from *King Creole,* "Lover Doll." Lenny produced the track at Liberty Studios in 1960 while his father was away, sneaking in Randy, guitarist-singer Pat Carter, and fledgling Metric Music singer-songwriter Jackie DeShannon. Nothing came of the session, and Waronker went on to USC to study business and music. Randy enrolled at and dropped out of UCLA but attained a Metric contract in 1962 as a writer, a milestone he and Lenny celebrated.

Much later, in the week before Waronker assumed his post at Warner Bros., he and Randy departed for Palm Springs on a four-day motel vacation, during which they smoked grass, took amphetamines, jumped in the pool, played gin rummy, ordered room service, and fantasized about the future. Those dreams began to come true for Randy in 1966 when Judy Collins recorded "I Think It's Going to Rain Today" for her *In My Life* album, and they flourished on September 15, 1967, when Mo Ostin signed Newman to Warner Bros. Records. Randy's first album, *Randy Newman Creates Something New Under the Sun,* would be produced by Lenny Waronker and Van Dyke Parks.

Parks was born on January 3, 1943, the youngest son of Richard Hill Parks III and the former Mary Joy Alter. Parks senior had been a member of John Philip Sousa's Sixty Silver Trumpets and piloted a dance band to pay his way through medical school, and he became a distinguished neurosurgeon, neurologist, and psychologist, the first to admit black patients to a white southern hospital, South Florida State. Mary Joy Alter Parks was a Hebraic scholar.

Van Dyke, a clarinetist and coloratura singer ("I had a wider range than Yma Sumac") in junior high school in Lake Charles, Louisiana, went on to attend the Columbus Boychoir School in Princeton, New Jersey, for six years, had a contract with the Metropolitan Opera, and sang under the baton of Arturo Toscanini. In 1955, after some television and stage acting, he appeared in Grace Kelly's last film, *The Swan,* with Alec Guinness and Louis Jourdan. Parks also appeared in the "completely lackluster" German TV series *Heidi* in 1957.

By the time Van Dyke Parks was fourteen, his father was practicing medicine in a suburb of Pittsburgh. Van Dyke studied classical piano at Carnegie Tech in quest of a fine arts degree but dropped out after two and a half years to take a job playing clarinet in the CBS-TV studio band of *Art Linkletter's House Party.* When the gig fell through, Parks remained in the West and traveled up and down the California coast with his eldest brother, Carson; he boned up on Mexican music, and the two played for their supper. He became proficient enough on *raquinto* guitar to do a guest shot with Los Tres Ases in the Mexico pavilion at the 1964–65 New York World's Fair.

In pursuit of a supplementary income, Parks became acquainted with songwriter Terry Gilkyson ("Memories Are Made of This") and through him got to play and arrange on the sound tracks of several Disney movies *(Savage Sam, The Moonspinners, The Jungle Book).* Parks was briefly in Gilkyson's Easy Riders group, toured New England with the Brandywine Singers, and returned to Los Angeles with the song "Come to the Sunshine," which landed him his MGM deal, the single reaching number 16 in Phoenix, Arizona, which is where Steve Stills sat in with his combo.

There was a demand in mid-sixties Hollywood for session pianists, so

Van Dyke set aside his Mexican guitar and took any keyboard dates he could get—precisely the line of employment he sought from Columbia producer Terry Melcher the day he made Brian Wilson's acquaintance and got the *Dumb Angel* gig.

"Brian sought me out," Parks explained to the curious, "because he had heard about me from some mutual friends, a neighborly couple who later fell into disrepute with the Wilson clan because they were experimenting with psychedelics. People who experimented with psychedelics —no matter who they were—were viewed as 'enlightened people,' and Brian sought out the enlightened people."

He and Brian would hang out, exchange ideas, and ultimately work on an album—to be titled *Smile*, or what Brian called "a teenage symphony to God"—that would weave Wilson's luminous melodies with Parks's ruminous monologues. The rest of the Beach Boys scorned Parks when he couldn't give them a stringent explanation of his elliptical Edith Sitwell–on-sensimilla lyrics. ("Columnated ruins domino" was one descriptive snatch from the song "Surf's Up.") But Van Dyke's contributions were prized by Brian, whose career priorities were undergoing convolution.

Brian ordered new Beach Boys manager Nick Grillo to have carpenters and teamsters come to his house with eight truckloads of refined beach sand and dump it inside a little wooden wall erected around the periphery of the house's hefty dining room. It was, in effect, an indoor sandbox into which Brian's Chickering grand piano was set. Now he could wiggle his toes in the beachlike grit while he composed *Smile*, and he would never have to glimpse Manhattan Beach again. A tent of expensive multicolored cloth was suspended from the ceiling in an adjoining room that was used for infrequent "business conferences." Those meetings were often chaired by David Anderle, whom Brian had brought in to develop the notion of the Beach Boys' own record label, to be called Brother Records.

Anderle was the manager of Van Dyke Parks and also of another new friend of Brian's, Ireland-born singer-songwriter Danny Hutton, who issued a luckless 1965 single, "Why Don't You Love Me Anymore?"/ "Home in Pasadena," on A&M Records' Almo subsidiary, and then managed a middling chart ascent (to number 73) with his "Roses and Rainbows" on Hanna Barbera Records. But the followup—"Big Bright Eyes"/ "Monster Shindig"—nosedived, and two hapless 1966 singles for MGM neatly described Hutton's dilemma at the point he encountered Brian:

"Funny How Love Can Be"/"Dreamin' Isn't Good for You" and "Hang On to a Dream"/"Hit the Wall." Hutton would go on to lucrative success with his then-coalescing group Three Dog Night (which Brian would soon produce on a new song, "Time to Be Alone," under his suggested name of Redwood), but the festivities surrounding *Smile* found Danny in a quiet period.

Brian's Beverly Hills home and the numerous studios he used for the *Smile* sessions became havens and/or rallying points for a loose group of musicians, friends, and hangers-on, some who liked company when they tripped or partners to whom they could pass the hash hookah. The climate around their host was described to others as "carefree" and "very spacey."

"It's always an amusing decision," Parks told associates, "whether to leave your shoes on or take them off when you step into his piano sandbox."

Less amused were the other Beach Boys who returned from a tour of England to discover Brian's world in disarray and their next album overdue. They were by turns ecstatic, confused, disappointed, and appalled by the music Brian unveiled in a series of listening sessions. The band decided the tracks they heard could not be released in their present form. Brian went into shock over the verdict, but his attitude slowly took on the tenor of an artistic about-face.

"That *Dumb Angel*, we *never* finished it," he stated years afterward, "because a lot of that shit just bothered me—but half of the shit we didn't finish anyway. Van Dyke Parks did a lot of it; we used a lot of fuzz tone. It was inspiring 'cause Van Dyke is a very creative person, and it was a boost to me because he had a lot of energy and a lot of fresh ideas, so that energy has helped me. But a lot of the stuff was what I call little 'segments' of songs, and it was a period when I was getting stoned and so we never really got an album; we never *finished* anything!

"Why? Because we got off on bags that just fucking didn't have any value for vocals! A lot of tracks just weren't *made* for vocals, so the group couldn't do it! We really got *stoned!* We were too fucking high, you know, to complete the stuff! We were *stoned!* You know, *stoned* on hash 'n' shit!"

The psychic turning point seemed to be a piece of music known formally as "Mrs. O'Leary's Cow" but commonly referred to by Brian as "Fire." The music aimed to approximate fire itself—its basking, sizzling, and suffocating properties—and was played by L.A. session musicians under the direction of Brian and Van Dyke Parks. During a mercifully breezy interval, Marilyn Wilson went out and bought red plastic children's fireman helmets for everyone to wear the day of the final session. Brian, bare-chested, found the environment stimulating and then frightening. A blaze erupted across the street from the recording studio one night. Not long after the track was done, there was a rash of sizable fires in the Los Angeles basin. Brian told people he destroyed the "Fire" tapes because he felt his music had caused the conflagrations and that the incidents made him cease all work on the record. ("Yeah! And it made me think that was a stupid thing to do—so I stopped! It scared me away!")

Up until the Beach Boys' decision to can the original *Smile* album, Capitol had every intention—even though they never received a final master—of releasing it as the next Beach Boys record under catalog number DT2580. At least two different versions of an album jacket had been designed, differing only slightly. It was a primitive full-color illustration of a "smile" storefront, its display windows filled with sundry mounted and pedestaled smiles, and presided over by a curly-haired proprietor and his prim wife (both attired in turn-of-the-century garb), who were also smiling. Apart from its visual incongruities, it could have been a tyke's drawing of any of the dozens of emporiums that lined the main streets of Hutchinson, Kansas, in the 1920s, including the shops at which Brian's uncle Charlie and other relatives had worked. On the back cover of the LP jacket prototypes was a black-and-white photo of the group, including Bruce Johnston, surrounded by astrological signs. Brian was not in the picture.

The original titles of *Smile*'s aborted cuts were "Old Master Painter," "Surf's Up," "The Grand Coulee Dam," "Who Ran the Iron Horse," "You Are My Sunshine," "Our Prayer," "Bicycle Rider," "Cabin Essence," "Heroes and Villains," "Indian Wisdom," "You're Welcome," "Holidays," "Barnyard," "Child Is Father of the Man," "I'm in Great Shape," "Wind Chimes," "Wonderful," and "The Elements Suite," which consisted of "Mrs. O'Leary's Cow (from the Fire)," "Vega-Tables (from the Earth)," "Good Vibrations (from the Air)" and "I Love to Say Dada (from the Water)."

Capitol printed a booklet of abstract illustrations interpreting Parks's equally abstract lyrics, and the label ran several advance ads for the record. One two-page spread touting the success of "Good Vibrations"—

"No. 1 in the USA, No. 1 in England"—also pictured one of *Smile*'s LP cover mockups with the caption COMING—WITH THE GOOD VIBRATIONS SOUND! The text for another ad read: *"Look!* Listen! *Vibrate! Smile!* It's Brian, Dennis, Carl, Al, and Mike's greatest ever! Contains 'Good Vibrations,' their all-time biggest-selling single, other new and fantastic Beach Boys songs . . . *and* . . . an exciting full-color sketchbook look inside the world of Brian Wilson!"

What Brian's world actually looked like then, the public would never get the chance to see. Behind the scenes, as all plans for *Smile* were scrapped, professional and private turmoil reigned. On January 3, 1967, Carl Wilson refused to step forward to be sworn in for the U.S. Army after receiving his draft notice. He stated that he was a conscientious objector, and a court battle would rage for four years before he was permitted to perform community civic duties in lieu of uniformed military service because of his moral convictions. And in March 1967 the Beach Boys sued Capitol in the first of what would be many writs and legal disputes over the accounting of royalties.

Eager to impose a physical distance between Brian and his clinging non–Beach Boys entourage, Marilyn encouraged Brian in his desire to relocate to larger lodgings. She sold the Laurel Way house and moved Brian and little else besides his grand piano to a mansion at 10452 Bellagio Road in Bel Air that had once belonged to Edgar Rice Burroughs, author of *Tarzan of the Apes.* Marilyn had a high brick wall with an electronically controlled gate erected around the outermost boundaries of the estate. Brian hired workmen to paint the haciendalike building a bright purple, but when neighbors got a partial look at the impending color scheme, a Bel Air Citizens Committee called a community-wide meeting that culminated in a terse demand. Brian relented and had the house redone in a more sedate pale yellow.

Work inched forward on a reconstituted incarnation of *Smile,* now to be called *Smiley Smile.* The Beach Boys dropped their suit against Capitol in exchange for permission to release the album under the new Brother Records imprint, and engineer Jim Lockert was contracted to help the Beach Boys edit, remix, and otherwise reorganize the overwhelming amount of raw tape into something comprehensible. A portable studio was installed in Brian's Bel Air living room so that he could be drawn back into the herculean task of fulfilling his earthbound obligations. New songs ("With Me Tonight" and "Gettin' Hungry") were created by Brian and Mike to fill the yawning gaps left by the gutted material. Though

Brian balked at adding the commercial "Good Vibrations" single to this revamped edition of his fallen masterpiece, he was overruled.

The lengthy "Heroes and Villains" track from *Smile*, which contained some of Parks's wittiest and most accessible lyrics, was carved down to three minutes and thirty-eight seconds and floated as a trial balloon to gauge the market for the delayed album. It got no farther than number 12.

During the extended time span in which Brian and the Beach Boys had engaged in mental/musical hide-and-seek, the Beatles had released their brilliant *Revolver* (August 8, 1966) and their epochal *Sgt. Pepper's Lonely Hearts Club Band* (June 2, 1967) in the States. All the ground rules for rock and roll had been changed, this time for good. And Brian could not go home again; the Hawthorne house had been sold.

Capitol created new artwork for *Smiley Smile*, an illustration of a diminutive smile cottage in the midst of a soft green jungle of flowers and simpering beasts. Above this cartoon-Gauguin tableau, the album title and the Beach Boys' name were hand-drawn in a flowing dark green script with orange piping.

No Beach Boys album ever had more advance publicity, and the appetite it whetted among eager fans for a full-length epic the equal of "Good Vibrations" was tremendous. Some devotees even tried calling the pressing plants to obtain an early copy. Released on September 5, 1967, *Smiley Smile* would be the poorest chart showing to date of any Beach Boys album, rising no higher than number 41. The trite, stillborn tracks heard on vinyl were taken by many true believers to be a veritable slap in the face.

Coming upon the innocent-looking emerald cover art, other less anticipatory pop consumers mistakenly assumed the Beach Boys had made an album for tots. It seemed as if a child were father to the band.

21
• • • •

It's Getting Late

For some it was the Summer of Love, for others it was the Long Hot Summer. In June 1967, Carole Wilson filed for divorce from Dennis Wilson after repeated separations and disagreements, charging that Dennis had struck and brutally beaten her with his fist before, during, and after the period during which "the plaintiff was pregnant with the minor child of the marriage"—Jennifer B. Wilson, born February 25, 1967.

Dennis had originally filed for divorce from Carole on December 21, 1966, after one year, four months, and twenty days of marriage, charging that Carole had "treated plaintiff in an extremely cruel and inhuman manner and has caused plaintiff great and grievous mental and physical suffering." That action was "dismissed upon my wife's promise that she would be a dutiful wife," as asserted in court papers, and the couple had temporarily reconciled.

Now Carole was announcing the demise of a pairing that had never been viable for either partner, their incompatibility compounded by the surplus of material goods they shared: the large Benedict Canyon Road house, two Ferrari sports cars, one Rolls-Royce sedan, three horses, one ski boat, and the tedious list of other possessions, bank accounts, and laundry and telephone bills addressed in the legal papers. Desperately in love, desperate in their lives, wed at the peak of the Beach Boys' renown, both from broken homes and bringing all the unfinished business of their former lives into vows taken too young and in haste, they would fight in the Superior Court of the State of California for the next seventeen years over issues pertaining to property settlements and child support for Jennifer. Dennis had also adopted Carole's son Scott from her previous marriage, and while Carole retained custody of the children, Dennis's bonds to them were loving and lasting. He would always find it easier to connect with kids than adults.

In January 1965, as Dennis and Carole were beginning to get serious with each other, he sang the lead vocal for one of Brian's most upsetting and prophetic songs, "In the Back of My Mind." The lyric concerned the rationalization of fears and the hardship of surmounting that habit. The inability to sustain happiness, the incentives to bolt and run, the logic of self-doubt in a dubious world, the alarm of losing a paramour whose best attributes are irreplaceable—all the song's fatalistic angles were given a sincere reading by Dennis as a crying saxophone crept along behind him. The track seemed to fall apart at the end, the melody adrift and disjointed and the narrative collapsing around a tinkling discord redolent of shattering glass.

As if anticipating America's impossible image of the perfect surfer boy and girl as depicted on the back of *Beach Boys' Party!* "In the Back of My Mind" assumed the proportions of an anti-anthem, one more clue to the receding future that was continually overlooked by the players and the listeners.

More evidence accumulated with the approach of June 16, 1967, the day of the opening round of performances at the three-day Monterey Pop Festival. Set between San Francisco and Los Angeles at the seaside site of the former capital of California, the community and its concert were located on a bay named for the Count of Monterey, the ninth Viceroy of Mexico. Rich in California lore and upstate-downstate rivalries, the city also represented the perfect remove from the dying agendas of the old rock order and the coming-out fete for the new.

The Monterey Pop Festival was first envisioned by promoter Benny Shapiro and wealthy entrepreneur Alan Pariser, who approached singer-songwriter John Phillips about it in Phillips's home on April 4, 1967, sharing the idea with Phillips's wife Michelle and their dinner guest, singer Paul Simon. The Phillipses' singing group, the Mamas and the Papas, were to be the headliners. The concert was later produced in its final, charitable form by Lou Adler (owner of Dunhill Records, the Mamas and Papas' label), John Phillips, and their attorney Abe Somer. Terry Melcher and Johnny Rivers matched the $10,000 that Adler, Phillips, and San Francisco promoter Bill Graham put up to fund the idea, and Paul Simon also anted up, each joining a board of directors that would include Paul McCartney, Mick Jagger, the Byrds' McGuinn, Smokey Robinson, and Brian Wilson.

The Jimi Hendrix Experience, signed by Reprise Records' general manager Mo Ostin for $40,000 on April 22, 1967, was scheduled to appear, as were the Grateful Dead, which had been signed by Warner Bros. Records' general manager Joe Smith on December 28, 1966. The Association, an act on Warner's Valiant Records subsidiary, also agreed to play. The final bill included Johnny Rivers, Simon and Garfunkel, Big Brother & the Holding Company featuring Janis Joplin, the Steve Miller Blues Band, Buffalo Springfield, Eric Burdon and the Animals, Beverly, the Paupers, Lou Rawls, the Electric Flag, Quicksilver Messenger Service, the Paul Butterfield Blues Band, the Who, Al Kooper, Canned Heat, Country Joe and the Fish, Otis Redding backed by Booker T. and the MGs, Moby Grape, Hugh Masekela with Big Black, Jefferson Airplane, Laura Nyro, Ravi Shankar, the Group with No Name, the Blues Project, the Mamas and the Papas, the Byrds, and the Beach Boys.

Fifty thousand fans bought the $3.00–$6.50 tickets and came to watch, as did Augustus Stanley Owsley III, with a batch of "Monterey Purple" acid custom-cooked for the occasion. The Beach Boys were due to follow the Byrds on Saturday, June 17, the second evening of the festival, but they didn't show: Brian and the band were too demoralized to make it. But the Who did, Pete Townshend smashing his guitar and Keith Moon demolishing his drums for the first time on an American stage at the crescendo of "My Generation."

Jimi Hendrix, who won a backstage coin toss for the right to follow the incendiary Who for his U.S. stage debut, concluded his performance with a feedback-fueled rethinking of the Troggs' 1966 hit "Wild Thing," tossing in a few bars of Sinatra's "Strangers in the Night" as the song barked and scampered to a peak. Then Hendrix rubbed his Stratocaster suggestively against the tall bank of amplifiers, feedback in full shriek, loosed his guitar strap, laid his axe on the stage, and doused it with lighter fluid. He planted a kiss on its smooth finish and then set it aflame, staggering offstage into history. "And you'll never hear surf music again," Hendrix warned on "Third Stone from the Sun," a track from his debut *Are You Experienced?* album whose final recording was done in England on April 4, 1967, just as the U.K. release of the *Surfer Girl* album was climbing the British charts as a last-minute substitute for *Smile. (Are You Experienced?* reached U.S. stores in August 1967.)

After the Monterey festival there was a symposium at Mills College in Oakland in which disc jockey Tom Donahue described a community approach to rock radio that would incorporate the conviviality of a record collector spinning beloved album cuts in the basement for his compadres. Donahue got his chance to see his concept fly when, after almost two years of relative idleness following the sale of Autumn Records, he took a job in mid-1967 doing a free-form, eight-to-midnight show on KMPX-FM, a foreign language radio station on its last legs. Listeners loved the evening menu of unedited rock. Assembling a new staff, removing all sloganeering station ID pitches, paring conventional commercials to a bare minimum, and attracting hip sponsors from the Haight community, Donahue moved forward with programming that featured historical, thematic, and flow-oriented "sets" of album tracks and launched the free-form format that made possible the further propagation of the music played at Monterey.

The summer weekend Donahue's KMPX-FM adventure went on the air, Joe Smith hosted a record party for the first Grateful Dead album at a Polish hall in North Beach. By the fall of 1967, Donahue's style of radio was the new standard. Back east, New York City's WNEW-FM began a "progressive" format in November 1967 with a 250-title album track playlist.

When friction arose between Donahue and station owner Leon Crosby, Donahue staged a strike at 3:00 A.M. on March 16, 1968, the intransigence of the warring parties leading to the defection of Donahue and his staff and concept to Metromedia's former classical outlet, KSFR, which was rechristened KSAN. In emulation of KSAN, rock music on FM radio and the album-oriented (or AOR) format became the formidable broadcasting forces of the next decade.

Russ Solomon, a Sacramento retailer who as a sixteen-year-old in 1941 ran a used-record concession in his parents' drugstore in the Tower Theatre building, pushed ahead with his own collateral brainstorm of a deep-catalog store to suit the free-form listeners' consumer tastes, opening a huge records-only Tower Records outlet at Columbus and Bay streets in San Francisco. New records were stacked in beguiling piles on the floor, unique bazaarlike exhibits were conceived, underground magazines and community-action flyers were displayed, specially commissioned replica paintings of album jackets were later posted outdoors, and the physical abundance, enticing informality, and casual sense of richness that characterized the California retail revolution were emphasized.

But the Beach Boys, a staple of the Top 40 AM power structure, were not especially welcome on these freewheeling new air lanes, nor were they accentuated in the bright and overflowing aisles of Tower Records. They seemed to have no apparent musical comments to make on the burning issues of the day, whether the steadily escalating Vietnam conflict or the corresponding strife in America's inner cities: Twenty-six died in race riots in Newark, New Jersey, and forty-three people were killed in street disturbances in Detroit, Michigan.

Released on December 4, 1967, the Beach Boys' *Wild Honey* album was an R&B outing whose title was a jocund takeoff on Brian's health food diet and a flip reference to the distaff surf "honeys" of yore. Recorded in the living room of Brian and Marilyn's Bellagio Road home, its cover art was a blurred photo of the large stained-glass window the band looked at every day as they laid down tracks.

The title song kicked off promisingly with a theremin before crumpling into a strained vocal by Carl that was further hampered by an extremely thin instrumental and harmony mix. Mike and Brian had intentionally written the song in a style approximating that of Stevie Wonder, but the lighthearted stab at funkiness was ineffective; as a single it crawled to number 31 on the Hot 100 and expired.

Also unconvincing was Carl's starchy cover of Wonder's "I Was Made to Love Her." Slightly better was "Here Comes the Night" (not the 1965 hit for Them but a Wilson-Love song), which was a more straightforward attempt at white soul arranged with help from Curt Boettcher, the talented twenty-three-year-old who produced "Along Comes Mary" and "Cherish" for the Association.

Brian's best production work on *Wild Honey* was "Darlin'," a high-energy rewrite of Sharon Marie's 1964 "Thinkin' 'Bout You, Baby" that lifted off with an astringent horn accompaniment and stayed airborne, giving the Boys a number 19 hit. The rest of the album's songs were branded by a word dropped prominently at the start of "Aren't You

Glad": "precious." Typical was "I'd Love Just Once to See You," which segued from a detailed monologue about dishwashing to an unctuous sexual come-on, Brian noting that he'd love but once to see his inamorata "in the nude." Lyrically, the low point was "Let the Wind Blow," in which the group opined that a higher power should let the bees "make honey" and let the "poor find money," but most important, please let the girl of their dreams stay where she was.

"Love Won't Wait," advised Murry Wilson on an appalling instrumental album that Murry induced Capitol to release in October 1967 called *The Many Moods of Murry Wilson*. Its cover art was a grid of twenty photos of young female models, and its hope was to ape the highly successful series of more than a dozen mid-fifties Capitol mood music albums (*Music for Lovers Only; Music, Martinis and Memories; Lonesome Echo*, and so forth) by famed comedian-composer Jackie Gleason.

But whereas Gleason had acumen in this area, as well as top studio orchestras led by trumpeters Bobby Hackett and Pee Wee Erwin, Murry had only journeyman arranger Don Ralke (*Never Heard Gershwin with Bongos*) to fall back on. Despite the uncredited inclusion of Al Jardine's composition "Italia," neither Murry's LP nor its single, "The Plumber's Tune"/"Islands in the Sky," located an audience, and the cost of the project was said to have been buried in the Beach Boys' own year-end accounting ledgers. Thankfully, *Wild Honey* offered a sales rebound after the sorrows of *Smiley Smile*, moving up as high as number 24 in *Billboard* after it debuted in the December 30, 1967, issue, and *Best of the Beach Boys, Vol. 2* would eventually sell better.

The Beach Boys pursued new directions as Mike Love's burgeoning interest in transcendental meditation and the teachings of Indian guru the Maharishi Mahesh Yogi blossomed. In January 1968, Linda Eastman photographed the Beach Boys and the Maharishi at the Plaza Hotel, each band member holding a flower as the guru beamed at them from his perch on the couch in his suite. And in February 1968, Mike Love and the Beatles, all of them attired in flowing white *kurta* tunics, traveled to the foothills of Rishikesh above India's Ganges River to meditate at the Maharishi's ashram. After eleven weeks (Paul and friend Jane Asher departed at the nine-week mark, Ringo even earlier) the remains of the Beatles' troupe tired of the yogi and the roving eye he was thought to cast on their female companions and exited his ashram. John Lennon wrote a snide song ("Sexie Sadie") in memory of his stewardship at the feet of the Maharishi, aka Sadie.

Mike Love found more lasting comfort in the Maharishi's doctrines, and in April 1968 he gave the Boys a song testifying as much ("Transcendental Meditation") for their *Friends* album. The otherwise undogmatic and ultra-gentle record, cut in Brian's Bel-Air house and Los Angeles's I.D. Sound Studios, got the group as high as number 47 in the late spring with its handsome-sounding three-quarter-time title track.

In May 1968, during the span when Suzanne Love gave birth (on May 23) to her and Mike's second child, Christian, the Beach Boys made the mistake of mounting an anachronistic just-the-hits concert trek that depended on its costar, the Maharishi, for a stab at social relevance. With Dr. Martin Luther King, Jr., just murdered and the Maharishi keeping his own flower-strewn counsel, few could fathom the dizzy cavalcade, and only two hundred fans wandered into a tour stop at New York's Singer Bowl. (A summer tour of the South was canceled in the wake of the King slaying, and the assassination of Robert Kennedy in June further pinched the nation's capacity for the Beach Boys' puzzled detachment.)

Despite its dulcet charms, the friendless *Friends* album got no farther than number 126 on *Billboard*'s album chart after its July 1968 release. Yet Brian proclaimed the peaceful album to be his favorite after *Pet Sounds* and held fast to that opinion for the next twenty-five years.

Country rock was the new trend in California music. The Byrds' album *Sweetheart of the Rodeo*, produced by Gary Usher for Columbia, appeared in July 1968 and amazed listeners with its reverent rockish handling of songs by Merle Haggard and the Louvin Brothers as well as its entrancing new material by Gram Parsons. Parsons soon joined with Chris Hillman to form the Flying Burrito Brothers, attracting ex-Byrds Michael Clarke and a Minneapolis picker named Bernie Leadon.

In the face of such changes, Mike Love rescued the Beach Boys from creeping public contempt by bringing a slice of bittersweet nostalgia to the June 1968 sessions for the Boys' *20/20* album. "Do It Again" was a lyric occasioned by a day Mike had spent surfing with high school buddy Bill Jackson at Trestles Beach, a treasured, albeit illegal, surf rat rallying point located in front of the U.S. Marine Corps' Camp Pendleton Reservation off Highway 101. The day was azure, the swells on the upper and lower segments of the break line were great, and Mike wrote the words as a diary of the day's events.

Brian took Mike's verses, borrowed the rhythm from the Frogmen's 1961 hit "Underwater," and devised a distinctive production signature by running a series of press rolls on a snare drum through a tape-delay system, achieving a sexy metallic buzz that was sandwiched with a clap track to make the single seem to detonate. Magnificent in every respect, "Do It Again" was fed through the AM Top 40 pipeline and carried the Boys to a decent Top 20 hit.

Another excellent song on the *20/20* collection was "I Can Hear Music," a canny production venture by Carl utilizing a Phil Spector–Jeff Barry–Ellie Greenwich song recorded previously by the Ronettes. Carl's revision was vastly superior to the original and would give the Boys a number 24 hit.

Van Dyke Parks's solo album, entitled *Song Cycle* rather than *Looney Tunes,* was released by Warner Bros. in November 1968. A lovely pastiche —antic, affecting, lullingly surreal—it was the aural equivalent of Groucho Marx in Charles Ives's pajamas, and it became one of the most acclaimed albums in pop history.

The New Yorker called it "a milestone of American pop music," *Esquire* named it "high record of the year," *Hi-Fi/Stereo Review* said it was "Record of the Year," and *Time* termed it "all shimmering beauty." After Warner's sold about ten thousand copies of *Song Cycle*, Stan Cornyn, Warner Bros. Records' director of creative services, initiated a full-page ad campaign in *Crawdaddy* and *Rolling Stone* magazines with the headline: HOW WE LOST $35,509.50 ON "THE ALBUM OF THE YEAR" (DAMMIT), which was followed in due course by another full-page ad with the headline TWO WEEKS LATER, AND IT STILL LOOKS BLACK FOR "THE ALBUM OF THE YEAR." (Twelve years later, *Song Cycle*'s sales would total 14,411 units.)

When Randy Newman's first album sold only forty-seven hundred copies that same year, Cornyn had the cover redesigned and embarked on a similar two-part campaign (Headlines: ONCE YOU GET USED TO IT, HIS VOICE IS REALLY SOMETHING, followed by WANT A FREE ALBUM? OKAY). But Newman's Lenny Waronker–produced sequel, *12 Songs,* eventually sold over fifty-two thousand copies, and other groups like Three Dog Night started recording his songs.

Warner's support of Parks and Newman never ceased, but each artist succeeded in getting Cornyn to discontinue his outré ad campaigns.

"Bluebirds over the Mountain," completed in November 1968 for the Beach Boys' *20/20* LP, was a new version of New York rockabilly singer Ersel Hickey's minor 1958 hit. An oddly exuberant tale of a failed love affair, it charted modestly during the last shopping days before Christmas. Also in December, Murry Wilson produced three of his songs for the Honeys ("I Think It's Gonna Be Alright," "Come to Me," and "[Let's

Take a] Holiday") at Sunset Sound Recorders in Hollywood. Capitol refused to release the tracks.

On Christmas Eve, 1968, Suzanne Love legally separated from Mike Love, the resultant divorce proceedings a disagreeable study in the extremities of post-marital acrimony. Suzanne charged Mike with "cruelty" and "adultery." Mike countercharged with "involvement with 'hippies' and people associated with drugs" and "committing adultery with Dennis C. Wilson." Suzanne denied the charges, alleging that "husband has himself been described as a 'hippy.' " Mike next complained in a court-filed declaration that Suzanne told him "she has experienced hallucinations in which the devil had sexual intercourse with her in the presence of others," adding that she allegedly told Mike "that I am 'the devil' and that she is 'Jesus Christ.' " Suzanne discounted the incident as a case of indigestion. Mike was awarded custody of the children, and Suzanne was allowed court-circumscribed visitation rights.

A more credible intersection of the devil and the Beach Boys had taken place during the April 1968 recording of *Friends*. Dennis Wilson had been introduced by a Patricia Krenwinkle to a grifter from Ohio named Charles Milles Manson. Manson would stealthily try to glom onto Dennis and Terry Melcher (who both deflected the would-be troubadour when he sought a recording contract) in much the same fashion that he skimmed whatever he could from every other Hollywood notable with whom he arranged an introduction.

On August 9, 1969, the insidious menace Manson brought to the entertainment community was horrifically manifested in Terry Melcher's former home on Cielo Drive, where Manson and his "family" murdered pregnant actress Sharon Tate and four others. The killings continued the following night with attacks in Los Feliz on Leno and Rosemary La Bianca. Manson and his accomplices were convicted of the crimes in 1970 and sent to prison, with any requests for parole repeatedly denied.

The B-side of "Bluebirds over the Mountain," entitled "Never Learn Not to Love," earned notoriety as having been derived from "Cease to Exist," a song written by Manson. Dennis maintained "Never" was recorded in reaction to nefarious long-haired "acid" vagabonds of the period such as Manson, and that it was revised several times before its final version was cut on September 11, 1968.

The Beach Boys' contract with Capitol was due to end on June 30, 1969, the same month former member Dave Marks released his second, rather good but roundly ignored album on Imperial Records with a four-piece band called Moon. The Beach Boys sued Capitol, on April 12, 1969, maintaining that an ongoing audit of the company's books found substantial underpayments. Capitol released "Break Away," a single written by Brian and his father (who used the pseudonym Reggie Dunbar) that stopped at number 63, but the company soon allowed their Beach Boys catalog to fade from their inventories.

In a settlement reached with Capitol, the Boys retained ownership of *Pet Sounds* and all subsequent albums. But Murry Wilson had already decided to divest himself of his own publishing interests, suspecting the commercial clout of Brian's songs had run its course. In November 1969, Sea of Tunes was sold to Irving-Almo Music, the publishing division of Herb Alpert and Jerry Moss's A&M Record corporation, for $700,000 cash. All monies went to Murry.

In March 1970, Brian's uncle Johnny Wilson died, with only Johnny's brothers mourning the loss of their sibling, who was divorced with no children at the time of his passing. At last at peace, Johnny was buried in Fairlawn Cemetery in Hutchinson, Kansas.

In June 1970, Don Henley and his band Shiloh arrived in Los Angeles. Henley and bassist Michael Bowden rode in Henley's 1967 SS 396 Chevelle, while guitarist Richard Bowden and his wife, Shane, followed in their Buick Elektra, and keyboardist Jim Ed Norman drove a Ford van pulling a U-Haul trailer full of equipment. The band lived with Kenny Rogers of the First Edition for a few weeks, then moved to Howard's Weekly Apartments on Laurel Canyon Boulevard. Rogers's wife, Margo, managed Shiloh for a while, but the Texas country-rock act was going nowhere.

Meanwhile, Henley met Glenn Frey and J. D. Souther at the offices of Amos Records, Shiloh's Bell Records–distributed label. Henley and Frey began hanging out at the Troubadour, and Frey asked Henley if he wanted to go on the road with him in a band backing singer Linda Ronstadt. Henley jumped at the chance to make $200 a week touring, as did the Bowden brothers, Bernie Leadon, and Randy Meisner. After four months backing Ronstadt, the band had its own sound. With Henley, Frey, Meisner, and Leadon as the nucleus, the band became the Eagles, signed with David Geffen's Asylum label, and went to London to cut their first album with Rolling Stones producer Glyn Johns.

Dennis Wilson was remarried on August 4, 1970, to former restaurant employee Barbara Charren (a son, Michael, was born six months later), and on December 4, 1970, Denny released a single on Stateside Records,

"Sound of Free"/"Lady," with keyboardist Daryl Dragon; they performed as Dennis Wilson and Rumbo.

On August 29, 1970, Van Dyke Parks was appointed director of audiovisual services of the Warner Bros. Records Television Films Company. His objective was to create ten-minute promotional films for Warner-Reprise acts, shorts that could be shown in first-run movie theaters and/ or on late-night television. As abbreviated art films and mini-documentaries, they could conceivably be bought with federal funds by music and film schools; the then-distant plans to develop a cable TV channel for Warner Bros.' use was also mentioned as a potential profit center.

Song-length, musical film shorts called Panoram Soundies had been tried in a jukebox-style format by the Mills Novelty Co. during the 1940s, and the Beatles filmed promotional TV/movie theater clips in 1967–68 for "Hello Goodbye," "Hey Jude," and "Revolution," but no record company had ever established an in-house department for the production of what would prove the forerunner of music videos. Parks, who composed music for the Datsun car company's TV commercials, convinced some of the top advertising directors and camera crews in the business to shoot 16-millimeter concert, documentary, and theme promos for Ry Cooder, Joni Mitchell, Captain Beefheart, Little Feat, Randy Newman, the Esso Trinidad Steel Band, and Earth, Wind & Fire. The results were good to excellent (although Joni Mitchell objected to animated nudity in her clip), but Warner's Mo Ostin could not justify expenditures of a half-million dollars for music films with no viable means of distribution or dissemination. A year after Parks assumed his post, the audiovisual services department was dissolved, and Van Dyke, as Stan Cornyn put it, was "orphaned" (although he continued to release his own acclaimed albums for Warner Bros., such as *Discover America* [1972] and *Clang of the Yankee Reaper* [1975]).

The Beach Boys were uncertain of their next collective move, but manager Nick Grillo attracted the interest of Mo Ostin at Warner's. Soon thereafter the Boys received great press after Michael Klenfner, a longtime associate of Bill Graham's organization, joined with booking agent Chip Rachlin to secure the group a February 1971 date at Carnegie Hall. Hosted by WNEW-FM deejay Pete Fornatale, the captivating two-hour concert was a watershed event and led Klenfner to persuade Jerry Garcia and Bill Graham to let the Boys jam with the Grateful Dead after the Dead's encore at the Fillmore East on April 27. According to *Billboard,*

"From their opening 'Heroes and Villains' to the closing of 'Good Vibrations,' the Beach Boys combined the best of their many standards with different material and treatment, producing a contemporary feel."

The Boys had a new social currency and a new label, but Warner's was a different company in the early 1970s from what it had been in the early 1960s. Joni Mitchell, Frank Zappa, James Taylor, Neil Young, Van Morrison, Little Feat, the Doobie Brothers, Fleetwood Mac, and Alice Cooper had helped tutor the label in the ways of extracting profit-cum-art from pensive singer-songwriters, biker/hippie bands, and obtuse pop savants.

The first Beach Boys album proffered to Ostin, *Add Some Music to Your Day*, was rejected but came back in much-amended form as *Sunflower*. Gone were Brian and Al's "Good Time," "I Just Got My Pay," and "Take a Load off Your Feet, Pete," Al's "Susie Cincinnati," Dennis's "Fallin' in Love," and Brian's "When Girls Get Together." Among the new songs was one Lenny Waronker had heard Brian perform alone at Brian's Bel Air house. "Cool, Cool Water" affected Waronker so deeply that he made a note to himself: "If I ever get the opportunity to produce Brian, I'd encourage him to do something that combined the vividness of 'Good Vibrations' with the noncommercial gentleness of 'Cool, Cool Water.' "

As indicated by Ricci Martin's relaxed, toddler-filled group photograph on the cover, *Sunflower* was the Beach Boys' most outgoing and unconstrained recording at its current six-member strength. Having finished with Capitol and fielded pre-Reprise interest from MGM and CBS Records, the Boys were in the grip of a fresh optimism that extended to their creative interrelationships. Brian was a recommitted participant, working happily during 1969 to help the band amass approximately four dozen tracks. One factor spurring the Boys' revived studio zeal and adventurism was Stephen W. Desper, a talented engineer hired in 1968 whose skill at mixing the *Friends* album for stereo had impressed Brian. Desper thereafter played a central role in setting lofty recording standards for *Sunflower* and its follow-up, *Surf's Up*, which were chiefly created in Santa Monica at the newly built Brother Studios.

The liner copy for *Sunflower* boasted that the LP "utilizes the most advanced recording techniques in the industry today," listing various production tools that encompassed seven different microphones, and a computer-controlled mastering lathe with a Neumann SX-68 helium-cooled dynamic feedback cutterhead. It also noted that a 3M sixteen-track tape deck and a custom-built thirty-position Quad-Eight mixing console had "provided extreme flexibility and special effects for this album."

This high-tech inventory was not merely saber-rattling, as the surging throb of Dennis Wilson's breath-stealing "Slip On Through" exhibited. A serpentine bass line, inside-out drum patterns, and the queerly clangorous knell of a cow bell launched the introductory song's kaleidoscope of four-tiered vocals: one layer of intersecting harmonies, another of organ and hornlike washes of phase-shifted sound, a third stratum of wordless punctuations or percussive phrases like "believe, believe," topped off by Dennis's beautifully insistent lead singing. A clutter-free triumph of arranging flair, "Slip On Through" was also a sophisticated step beyond the dream-walking *Pet Sounds* esthetic, and it rocked hard thanks to convulsive drum breaks and nimble conga tattoos.

Next was Brian's "This Whole World," whose rhythmic floor was an impeccable vocal parquetry of various tonal parts. Carl's graceful intonation on the heartfelt lyric about global amity made unsurpassed use of his swooping falsetto range and his catch-in-the-throat vocal sob to convey the emotional breadth of the music's message. The song's ability to traverse a half-dozen separate moods and settings in an evolution of less than two minutes was similarly arresting, making the quasi-elongated "This Whole World" the most ingenious of Brian's many mini-opuses.

The "World" track's extended fade was also a deft transition into the gradual build of the song that followed, "Add Some Music to Your Day." Written by Brian with Mike Love and friend Joe Knott, "Add" was the eldest Wilson's consummate appraisal of music as the great equalizer and companion of the common man. The song started with hushed praise for the "Sunday morning gospel" that began the week for many citizens and then traced music's gentle but pervasive daily influence as it poured from neighbors' homes, dentists' offices, the carts of ice-cream vendors, and the altars of wedding ceremonies, gladdening passersby as much as direct participants.

Dennis's "Got to Know the Woman" was one of the few Beach Boys songs that could honestly be called funky, its tinkly Dixieland piano a perfect foil for the coarse frivolity of the verses, which contained a boorish come-on to the object of one's lowest bump-and-grind fantasies. Increasingly caught up in the track's pulsative groove, the singer's absurdly overstated ardor has pushed him by mid-song into open embarrassment, his familiar macho pose toppling into a knowing laugh that listeners could share.

Brian and Bruce Johnston penned the dazzling "Deirdre," a stroll-tempo devotional to an idealized, red-haired goddess; its stippled use of flutes plus the spacey filtering and compression techniques in the vocal mixes gave the final track a celestial grandeur. Side one of *Sunflower* concluded with "It's About Time," a flat-out rocker by Dennis, Al Jardine, and writer Bob Burchman that was the first-person account of a fallen artist nearly destroyed by his fruitless search for "a lost elation." The Santana-like Latin pivot of its percussion gave the song a nice tension, and the personal renewal described by the song's central character triggered a driving guitar break that made his second chance seem both plausible and thrilling. An undidactic commentary on rock indulgence and self-redemption, it was also a wishful scenario regarding Brian Wilson's sporadic troubles.

"Tears in the Morning" on side two was Bruce Johnston's melodramatic but ably sung story of a love asunder; its string section, tactical Broadway-style pit drumming, Parisian accordion, and horn/piano coda were vaguely redolent of Sinatra's Nelson Riddle–arranged songs for films such as *Can-Can* and *Pal Joey*. The unusual approach for modern rock-pop was redeemed by the track's production clarity, which made for a neat contrast with the eerie, buzzing reverberance of Brian and Mike Love's ghostly love vow, "All I Wanna Do."

"Forever," by Dennis and buddy Gregg Jakobson, and "Our Sweet Love," a Brian-Carl-Al collaboration, were pristine ballads that would not have been out of place on *Pet Sounds* but for their absence of pessimism. "At My Window," Al and Brian's ode to a bird on a sill, was a childlike consideration of a good omen and served as a fit prelude to the meditative innocence of "Cool, Cool Water," which incorporated a portion of the spooky, droned canticle of "I Love to Say Dada" from the shelved *Smile* album.

Use of such *Smile* remnants foreshadowed the resurrection of "Surf's Up" from that failed project as the saturnine title track for the Beach Boys' second Brother-Reprise album (which was originally to be called *Landlocked)* and also paved the way for the equally moody brilliance of Brian's " 'Til I Die," a highlight of the latter record.

At the conclusion of recording for *Sunflower,* the group had a great deal of finished material in the can ("Games Two Can Play," "Walkin',"

"Lady," an instrumental called "Carnival"), with only the frisky "Take a Load off Your Feet" surfacing in 1971 on *Surf's Up*. The direction the Beach Boys would take in the 1970s would be determined by audience reaction to the keen self-assurance of *Sunflower*. When the commercial response was one of utter disinterest, that direction swerved downward, away from the hopefulness that had characterized the group's new beginning.

Although one of the Beach Boys' finest albums, *Sunflower* sold a piddling number after its release on August 31, 1970, sparking four head-scratching years at Warner's during which Brian was seldom seen. (He had little direct involvement in *Surf's Up*, opposed the title song's inclusion, and fought to overcome group objections to " 'Til I Die.") Brian did peek from the shadows when he coproduced a euphonic album on United Artists Records in July 1972 for Marilyn Wilson and Diane Rovell under the name *Spring* (rechristened *American Spring* for Europe). Not to be outdone, Stephen Love coordinated a self-titled record of sister Maureen Love's harp music for the Love Records label in 1973. And brother Mike had remarried, meeting new wife Tamara Love at a TM course.

Skateboarding rebounded as a sport in 1973 when former enthusiast Frank Nasworthy discovered that cast-molded polyurethane wheels, used in making roller skates, would solve all skateboarding's traction and control problems. Nasworthy, a surfer living in Norfolk, Virginia, came upon barrels of the wheels in the Purcellville, Virginia, factory of Creative Urethane while visiting a friend. Urethane roller skate wheels had been made in the 1950s, but the long-wearing properties of the early versions were offset by low speed potential because of the plastic's softness. Soft wheels roll slower than hard wheels, but Creative Urethane owner Vernon Hitefield had solved the spongy, speed-inhibiting snag with his denser-cast wheels, loose ball-bearing casing to aid in acceleration.

Nasworthy took a box of forty with him to California in 1971, and by December 1973 he was selling eight thousand wheels a year to surf shops in San Diego County. He and Creative Urethane were having difficulties with shipping demands and billing schedules, however, and Nasworthy sought to push the company beyond the manufacture of replacement wheels for roller-rink skates.

Forced to go out on his own, Nasworthy formed Cadillac Wheels in 1973 and began designing his own wheels to meet high-impact street and contest specifications. In early 1975 he licensed his five models of wheels to the Encinitas-based Bahne and Company (makers of surfboards and windsurfing boards), becoming their design consultant, and sales moved toward the million mark. Skateboarding was fully resurrected, mightier than ever, and *Skateboarder* magazine also revived.

Everything creaky was suddenly cool again, with California's outdoor youth and speed culture reborn. Ed Roth was even once more the darling of the custom car shows. All that was missing was Brian. He didn't appear on the Beach Boys' most substantial chart appearance of 1974, a guest shot as backing singers on Chicago's "Wishing You Were Here" from the *Chicago VII* album. Produced by James William Guercio for Columbia, the single featured Al, Carl, and Dennis in a vesperslike chorale on the vocal refrain, and it reached Number 11 in the Hot 100 that autumn.

Not until 1976 would the most notorious hermit in rock finally reemerge, and when he did, it proved more disturbing than his disappearance.

22
• • • •

Getcha Back

It was a stark, surreal tableau. Brian Wilson, now thirty-three, was seated before a handsome Hammond B-3 organ in the center of the Beach Boys' splendid, twenty-four-track Brother Studio on Fifth Street in Santa Monica, his massive form suspended in the cold blue expanse of a giant circular stained glass window depicting our solar system that loomed behind him. The air was electric with tension, and Brian's thick-fingered hands were trembling so badly they could scarcely find their proper places on the keys. Mercifully, the organ was not turned on.

"Come on, Bri," cousin Stan Love cajoled softly. "Play your new song. Play 'California Feeling.' "

The bearded potbellied man at the Hammond smiled weakly, brushed a veil of stringy brown hair from his downcast eyes, and sighed with exasperation. "Damn," he exhaled in his high raspy voice. "I'm *so* nervous, but I *will* relax."

One hardly recognized the man at the organ. He bore no resemblance to the lanky, dough-faced teenager who sat atop the bright yellow, palm-festooned pickup truck on the cover of *Surfin' Safari*, one thin hand clutching a surfboard and the other shielding his eyes from the beach glare as he peered out at the rolling Pacific. Fifteen years and 75 million records later, Brian Wilson, the singer-composer-producer *extraordinaire* who had elevated one of the most phenomenally successful vocal and musical groups to a permanent place in American folklore, was slumped over a silent keyboard in a soundproof room a half-hour drive from where that first album photo was shot; he was overweight, overwrought, and scared shitless.

"Come on, Brian," Stan continued. "Play it. It's a *great* song."

Stan Love, sandy-haired former forward with the Baltimore Bullets of the National Basketball Association and the younger brother of Mike Love, was Brian's current confidant and salaried chauffeur. He was also his bodyguard. Skinny Stan, elbows on the organ top and eyes trained on his stout responsibility, was trying to put his charge at ease.

"What's the song like?" Brian was asked by a visitor.

"I don't know," he murmured. "It's got a *feeling* to it. . . . There's something about it that's very *warm*. It's sort of a Bill Medley–Brian Wilson combination."

How does the tune go? What are the lyrics?

Brian straightened up, rolled his hefty shoulders back, and showed a brave, childlike smile. "Heck," he allowed, "I should . . . I should just sing it!"

He flicked the power switch on the organ and adjusted the volume with the foot pedal. Brian's rubbery fingers hovered above the Hammond's bared teeth. Uncertain, they stiffened, and he formed two chords, faltered, and then began to sing:

> I was walking down the beach in San Onofre
> It was such a beautiful day
> The wind was blowing through my hair
> And the sun dances in the morning sky
> When you're driving through L.A.

In that way, on that day in the spring of 1976, Brian Wilson told the world that the beach was back.

The bizarre myths surrounding Brian in the years since signing with Warner Bros. had come to rival the fables the Beach Boys had fostered about Southern California. His neighbors in Bel Air whispered that he was a hashish head, that he lived on candy bars and milk shakes, that he was unduly dependent on his family for spending money and mobility, that he locked himself in his bedroom and stayed there for six straight months. They were amazing stories, and most were true.

Brian's freedom of movement was hampered in part by the loss of his driver's license after he was involved in several automobile accidents. "I knocked my head—got a lump on my head—on the last one," he explained. "That was about three years ago. I haven't had my driver's license since. They took that away from me. Now I just get driven."

Stan Love apparently didn't take Brian every place he wished to go; on the precious few occasions he traveled unescorted, Brian was ill-equipped to do so. Friends told of infrequent visits by Brian in taxis for which he had to borrow money to pay the fare.

"Brian seems to have a problem getting spending money," said a prominent producer and friend, who told of several private lunches with Wilson in 1975 that ended on a humiliating note. "Brian would ask me if he could borrow fifty dollars," he maintained. "I'd always give it to him, but after a few times I started to wonder why the hell Brian Wilson, who has made millions of dollars in the record business, didn't have any money of his own. I couldn't understand it. He told me he wasn't sure who had control over his money or even the deed to his house."

Carl Wilson would have to explain in 1976 that drugs were a reason for Brian's repeated pennilessness when in public.

"There was a thing where Brian kept on giving people money to 'score.' Not for himself but for themselves. It's like he was giving a guy every week a few hundred bucks, and a very well known guy at that. And so what the business office did was they put Brian's wife . . . ah, took Brian's signature off the checks for a while until he could become more responsible about it."

Equally puzzling were the circumstances surrounding a 1975 production deal that Brian "requested" with Equinox Records, Inc., an RCA-based production company headed by Terry Melcher and surrogate Beach Boy Bruce Johnston. At the time Brian had little in the works but ennui, so he signed a contract with Equinox to produce thirty-six sides over an indefinite period of time. The generous terms included a bonus advance of $23,000 and what Johnston then described as "probably the highest production royalty any producer's ever received."

When Brian was paid the $23,000 bonus, he begged that the money be placed in a separate bank account from his wife's, which was done. Shortly afterward, according to a prominent figure close to the deal, the account was closed and the money transferred to an account at a different bank in Marilyn's name.

Once the Equinox deal went through, Brian worked with Melcher on only four basic tracks, among them versions of Frankie Lymon and the Teenagers' 1956 hit "Why Do Fools Fall in Love" and Elvis Presley's single of the same vintage, "Money Honey." The tracks did not turn out as planned. Mysteriously, Brian refused to finish them.

"He wouldn't go all the way," said Melcher. "He wouldn't even touch anything in the control booth; he acted as if he was afraid to. He'd offer suggestions, but he wouldn't go near the board. He knows his reputation, so he makes a lot of unfinished records. Sometimes I feel that he feels he's peaked and does not want to put his stamp on records so that peers will have a Brian Wilson track to criticize."

W ell, that's it. That's the song."

Brian shut off the organ and sat back, relieved but expectant. As he dabbed his forehead with his damp shirt sleeve, he kept sneaking looks at his visitor.

"Do you like . . . I dunno—do you *like* the song?" he finally wondered aloud, his voice loud and squeaky.

The total exhaustion in his features was chilling. If a man could wash his face in fear, as if it were some milky, implacable liquid, surely this was the way it would emerge. He overwhelmed those who came close to him with the sensation they were meeting a man with a broken heart.

But what of the song? Even in its crude form the churchlike "California Feeling" was one of the best gospel ballads Brian had written since "God Only Knows." Yet, strangely, it was not necessarily part of the project on which he was presently at work.

" 'Palisades Park' and 'Blueberry Hill'!" he gushed, referring to the 1962 Freddie Cannon hit and the 1956 Fats Domino smash, "that's what we Beach Boys are working on right now! Everybody's coming in this afternoon, and we're gonna work on those! Yep, we're trying to get back together so that we can keep our economy going. See, we don't want to go broke, and what little stuff we have to work with, well, we're trying to utilize that because . . . well . . ."

The Beach Boys were back in the studio to sharpen their rough tapes of "Blueberry Hill" and "Palisades Park," two songs that would eventually appear on what Dennis Wilson described as "one of three albums we're working on simultaneously to fulfill our commitment to Warner Bros. It's very possible that one will be an all-oldies album. We've wanted to do that for a long time, and Brian's into that. The other two could take the form of a double album of all-new material that stretches from hard rock and roll to these wordless vocals we've been doing that sound like the Vienna Boys Choir."

The oldies album was slated to include the Five Satins' 1956 single "In the Still of the Night," the Drifters' 1963 "On Broadway," and "Tallahassie Lassie," the 1959 Freddie Cannon song. Among the original songs (all titles were tentative) were "Ding Dang," "10,000 Years," and "Rainbow" by Dennis; "Gold Rush" by Al Jardine; "Glow, Crescent, Glow," "Lisa," and "Everybody's in Love with You" by Mike Love, and Brian's "California Feeling" and a tune called "Transcendental Meditation Song."

As Dennis talked about what "everybody" was involved in, he was alluding to what he characterized as "the original, Hawthorne-era Beach Boys."

"Carl sings the lead on 'Palisades Park,' " Brian explained. "He did it in one take. I might ask him to add more 'Let's Go Trippin' ' guitar to the song, but I'm still thinking about that."

What made Brian decide to resume an active role in the band?

"Well, I looked at the guys, and they looked kinda sad," he explained. "They didn't look happy; they looked like something was wrong. I said to myself, 'Hey, maybe they're upset because we're not having any hit singles! Maybe they're mad at me! I checked into it, and sure enough, as soon as we did 'Palisades,' everybody was happy again. Know what I mean?"

Brian smiled wanly. It was an embarrassed, painful upturn of his lips; more the gallant gesture of an excruciatingly shy man than any demonstration of happiness. He was dressed in baggy dungarees, scuffed track shoes, and a print shirt with a vaguely orange floral design that had long since been washed out. The limp, faded shirt was unbuttoned in deference to a swollen paunch that, like the rest of Brian, was pale and translucent, like the underside of an albacore.

He was not the quietly handsome man he had been; his body was rather disproportionate because of the added bulk, his head seemed too small atop his barrel frame, and his long arms and legs flowed awkwardly from their now-drooped torso. Yet Brian retained a singular charisma, and when left to himself there was a dignity in his open heart and insouciant demeanor that was striking. His round, lightly whiskered face was placid, practically expressionless most of the time. The action resided in his small eyes: One moment they revealed nothing, floating dull and glassy in their pinkish sockets; an instant later they were ablaze with a dark fire, scanning the room from side to side, up and down, in a slow, unsentimental scrutiny, as if gauging the relative worth and importance of everything present, discarding with detachment what wasn't useful as a tool or a toy.

Whose idea was it to record "Blueberry Hill" and "Palisades Park"?

"Oh, I thought of those!" Brian boasted with a vacant grin. "I sat around and thought, 'What would be good?' And it took a little time because then I thought, 'Oh, the guys are gonna think I'm sloughing off by getting oldies instead of originals.' But now I think they agree.

"If you find the right song and do that good rendition . . . well, when people think of my music, Beach Boys music, they think of a . . . *spirit.*"

And that spirit was presently three albums in arrears?

"Whew! Whoa!" he hooted. "Who said that? *Dennis* said that? Well, let's— hell, the fact is we're behind commitment. And, okay, I'll tell you what happened: We got lax, very lax, slack, whatever, and we let too much time go by, and now we're three albums behind." A worried look flashed across his face. "Three albums, that's a lot of albums. We could get sued, I suppose."

Brian's train of thought was interrupted by the entrance of Earle Mankey, a member of the Brother Studio engineering crew. He informed Brian that it was now 3:30 P.M. Brian had scheduled a session for 1:00 P.M. but didn't arrive until 2:30. Mankey said it was too late to call in session musicians who were standing by, but there was plenty of time to dub down the "Blueberry" tape.

"I think we should keep Mike Love's voice as the lead," Brian told

Mankey, "and then, if my brother and Mike want to play, we'll do a track."

Stan, still leaning against the organ, mumbled something about Dennis singing lead on the song.

"What's this about Dennis doing the lead?" Brian demanded.

"Oh, that's just what Carl said," Stan allowed with a shrug. "He thought that Dennis might want to do the lead on 'Blueberry' because he has a raspier voice."

"Beware of hurting Mike," Brian cautioned. *"Really,* Stanley." Brian burst into nervous laughter. "Boy, what is this I'm facing? The Wilsons *and* the Loves? I'm outvoted?"

The urgency of Brian's question seemed mutually crushing. A dozen years earlier the idea of overruling him in the studio would have been unthinkable.

"Nah," Stan said sheepishly. "You're right; Mike should stay."

Mankey moved to go, somewhat confused. Brian told him to start playing the "Blueberry" tape in the control room, and he'd be in shortly. Minutes later the engineer's booth was bursting with a lonesome slapback bass being goaded forward by the ghostly plip-plop of what sounded like a timbal stuck under a dripping faucet as Mike's breathless intro crept into the foreground: "I found my thrill. . . . The moon stood still—"

On "still," Love was joined by the rest of the group in a thunderous harmony refrain as a host of horns, guitars, drums, and organ cut loose. The feel was muddy and unpolished, but the track possessed the same felicity that turned their live version of "Barbara Ann" into an infectious 1966 single.

Brian jumped up when he heard the music and began walking around the studio, snapping his fingers idly and acting as if he were looking for something. He peered behind the grand piano in the corner and then squinted up at the ceiling.

"Hey!" Stan called out. "Come on back here!"

"Oh," said Brian, caught in an errant cocoon of concentration. "Excuse me."

He dutifully returned to the organ bench.

"Hey, they sound really tight," he bubbled in reference to the two oldies currently being completed. "I like them both, and I think they're both hits. 'Palisades Park' has an edge, though, because it's upbeat. . . . It wasn't a spectacular production; we did everything in one take. We wanted it to be kind of mediocre with a good beat and a simple vocal to reach people that way because we have a little problem."

A little problem?

"Yeah. See, we used to be real *arty*, you know? And at times it only sold to a select few, but if we could just get *commercial*, I believe we could sell records . . . and be back in the action!"

Back in the action? The Beach Boys tipped the scales for million-dollar sales of 1974's number 1 *Endless Summer* (a title recommended by Mike) and 1975's *Spirit of America*, two gold-status Capitol anthologies of early gems, and they continued—minus Brian—to be one of the few surefire box office concert attractions in the world. Brian, however, seemed mortified by those developments. In his eyes the Beach Boys were an aimless studio band that stayed on the road cranking out his aging triumphs to avoid confronting their creative debilitation; what was once Brian's forte had now become the group's greatest pitfall: hit singles.

Brian paused and looked away, as if reevaluating that path of thought. When he turned back, he was frowning.

"We've been off the [top ten] singles chart for *eight years*," he said, "and that's a long time not to be having any hits and stuff. So we would be really pleased if we could get something that the masses would like.

"I personally have been *long* forgotten from the writing," he stated morosely. "Everybody's saying, 'You're a great writer, a real genius.' But it's been a long time, and it will be a shock to reenter. I mean, I'm going through shock myself right now."

He riffled through the pockets of his jeans and extracted a dented pack of cigarettes, lighting one hastily. He was about to resume his melancholy disquisition when a tanned, athletic surfer type in overalls, sweatshirt, and sneakers strolled into the studio. Dennis Wilson, his moppish hair blithely disheveled and sporting a two-day beard, flashed his good-natured grin around freely—until he spied Brian's cigarette.

DENNIS (irritated): "What are you doing *smoking*, Brian? Huh? Listen to your voice! You're starting to get hoarse! Don't be stupid! Put out that cigarette *now!* Take two puffs and put it out!"

BRIAN (indignant): "No! I'll finish it, and then I'll stop. I have no more cigarettes."

DENNIS (to Stan): "Man, what is *this?* I thought you were gonna help him stop that damn smoking."

STAN: "Hey! What can I do?"

DENNIS: "Take the cigarette out of his *hand* and put it in the ashtray. There's too much damn smoke around here as it is." (To Brian): "Put it out!"

BRIAN (holding up the cigarette): "When this thing reaches the butt to the filter—"

DENNIS: "Brian! Two puffs and then put it out!"

BRIAN (voice cracking): "What are you *talking* about? *I'm smoking my cigarette!*"

DENNIS: "How many have you smoked today?"

BRIAN: "Four."

DENNIS: "Honest to God?"

BRIAN (smirking): "Four packs."

Dennis, furious, stalks off.

Brian returned to the piano bench. "What year is this?" he asked Stan.

"Nineteen seventy-six," Stan answered blankly.

"Okay," Brian ruled, "so finally it's 1976, and we're still riding on our past success. I mean, I've gone on *that* for I don't know *how* long!"

"*Too* long," Stan offered. "How's that?"

"Really," said Brian with a crooked smile. "Like, okay, we'll get a song and we'll go halfway and we won't follow through. Fine. I kick myself in the ass for it, and then I come back and try again. It's almost like a guy who gets knocked down; he has to keep getting back up until he gets himself together. That's how it works. All I care about is that I want everyone to be happy. If these sessions aren't fun, then fuck it! It hasn't been for a while, and that's why we said, 'Fuck it!' for a few years.

"In the last two years all I ever cut, all I *ever* recorded, was skimpy little bits and pieces, little fragments," he confessed. "Something happened to my concentration—I don't exactly know what, but it weakened for some reason—and I lost the ability to concentrate enough to follow through. But that's my own problem because of hangups I have.

"There's something called instinct, okay? And if your instincts start to lead you, then fuck, that's *where it's at.* And if they lead you astray—" He didn't complete the sentence.

"But you have to get a feel for *instinct* versus *opinion*," he asserted. "If you say, 'Palisades Park' and get that *feeling*—then it's straight ahead! If you don't, and start thinking too hard, well, that's what makes me retreat.

"I get too mental," he admitted sadly, "and I don't think I follow my instincts as much as I should. I used to—shit, for years in a row! I mean *instinct*. I used to think the hits up one after another." He snapped his fingers rapidly. "Then I got too *thoughtful* about it, and I fucked up. So I suppose I have to get back on my fucking feet and trust my instincts and go with them a little.

"There's a lot of different ways to go," he said. "One way is very mental, trusting in your mind. The second is kinda going with your instincts. And the third would be *force*. If the first two fail, the last sets in, but that can work, too.

"A lot of people use plain, sheer force to get where they want to go. Others say, 'Hey, man, this is the direction!' And they ride it. Hell, I've seen a lot of force, where you force something on somebody for his own good. You just say, 'Oh, goddamn, I *know* this is right for you!' And you can be right . . . sometimes.

"What we have to do," he decided, "is find the best ten songs we can and do an oldies but goodies thing. We could do 'Sea Cruise,'' and I'd like to do 'Ruby Baby,' because I think Dennis could do the lead on that real good. We could do 'Working in a Coal Mine,' too."

He sang, "Working in a coal mine, going down, down! . . .'

"See," Brian counseled, "the trap is, there's an awful lot of commerciality that we're exposed to, and that's intimidating. Even if the stuff isn't really art, there's something about a commercial record . . . that *special* something. We released a few good records, and they bombed in the face of more commercial stuff. 'Sail On Sailor' was very arty, but it was a damn good record and it bombed. When that happens, it's a little defeating."

"Sail On Sailor," which charted in 1973 at a peak of 79 but then reentered the Hot 100 in 1975 and rose to number 49, was the Beach Boys' best-selling single since signing with Reprise.

"We were ahead of people in some ways during our early Warner's period," Brian conceded, "but we were not commercial. I don't know if there's a real problem or not about this commercial idea, but what bugs me is to go into a studio, and if I still have a defeatist mind, I say, 'Aw, it's good, but it's not gonna sell.'

"Eight years with *no* hits," he said, sulking. "Eight years without something the kids'll buy on instinct. Ahhh, but look at Sinatra. Thirty-five years in this business, and he can't get a hit single! Phew! Who knows what the fuck people are thinking?

"Even during the Beach Boys' bad times, other people imitated us. It's very *easy* to imitate us, so in that respect the Beach Boys are still happening. But there's a funny thing called doing your own thing. If you're not actually projecting something of your own, it's too easy to fall down that elevator shaft and get *panicky*.

"That's why I say it's better now to have a winning attitude. I didn't always, but by God it works! You've got to at least think you're a winner, even if it hurts to say it!

"But since we got back from Holland, we haven't recorded diddly-womp, and I don't know what the fuck for. I don't know why."

As far as Warner-Reprise Records was concerned, the Beach Boys had been a grave commercial disappointment over the last five years, and the label thought it knew why: insufficient evidence of the Brian Wilson touch. Only time would tell if Brian's new Norman Vincent Peale pathology would be parlayed into profitable records, but in the interim all the bosses in Burbank wanted to know was, "Where's the product?"

Alas, the Beach Boys had had that question mark hanging over their heads for so long that what was once a sword of Damocles was beginning to resemble a halo. As Dennis Wilson put it in 1976, "I was talking to Brian the other day about the fact that the band hasn't released a new record in a long while, and he said, 'Well, good things take time.' "

"The best-selling Beach Boys album on Warner Brothers?" mused David Berson in 1976, as executive assistant to Warner Bros. chairman of the board and CEO Mo Ostin, and a man responsible for dealing with the Beach Boys on a daily basis. "That's a tough one. If you considered *The Beach Boys in Concert* album"—a two-record set released in November 1973—"as more than a single record, well, obviously *In Concert* is the only Beach Boys album that went gold. It did not go gold because it sold enough copies to push a single-record package into the realm of a gold record, however. But because it was a double-record set and because it had a greater retail price, it went gold if you pro-rate the sales via the price and you call one of those albums one and three-quarters albums or one and a half albums, or whatever . . . and that was the biggest-selling album."

What Berson was trying to explain was that the Beach Boys had managed only one gold record on his label, and it was a struggle. While Capitol racked up platinum awards for Beach Boys records a half-decade after the group had departed the company, Warner-Reprise's catalog with the group seemed lost at sea. To add insult to undertow, Reprise had not done as well as it hoped with the four post–*Pet Sounds* LPs the Beach

Boys obtained from Capitol in 1972 and repackaged on Brother-Reprise as two-record sets: *Smiley Smile/Friends* and *Wild Honey/20/20.*

"The initial album, *Sunflower,* which may be the best album the Beach Boys ever recorded, did not sell many copies," said Berson, "and we were very, very disappointed. *Surf's Up''*—issued in July 25, 1971—"was a very, very big album for us—to a large extent, I think, because Brian Wilson was still involved, but it did not go gold. The next album, the double-record set of Carl and The Passions' *So Tough/Pet Sounds''*—issued in May 1972—"was our worst-selling Beach Boys album."

Chronologically, that left *Holland* and *The Beach Boys in Concert.* The latter was originally submitted to Reprise as a single record, was rejected, resubmitted as a double album, and was nearly rejected a second time. *Holland,* released in January 1973, also was rejected once, but that was a story in itself.

> Concentrating on their widely recognized obsession—techno-logical advance—they took off for Holland where the surf's *never* up and went through some half a million dollars settling in and arranging for nearly four tons of flying studio, a proto-type for the future, to be brought from America. The evidence of the whole incredible adventure is on their new album, sim-ply called *Holland.*
> —from a Warner Bros. press kit, November 1972

"It was Jack Rieley's idea to go to Holland," said Brian Wilson in 1976. "We met him one night when he walked into our health food store." For a year Brian was part-owner of a health food store in West Hollywood called the Radiant Radish, until the store closed on July 29, 1970. "He walked in and said, 'Hi, I'm Jack Rieley from NBC News.' And I said, 'Hi.'

"He said, 'I've got a show over on KPFK. Come on over and do an interview.' So we took a liking to the guy, and he joined us as a manager and a singer and a songwriter; a really stimulating person. He had a deep voice.

"So after a while we were tired of California, and Jack Rieley said, 'Let's go to Holland and do some concerts!' So the band went over and stayed and did an album."

The "concert" the Beach Boys scheduled was an appearance on a Dutch TV spectacular called *Grand Gala du Disc.* After the show, the band

and their families remained in Holland, deciding to make Amsterdam the base of operations for their European tour, and then spent several months in the Netherlands countryside recording their fourth Reprise LP. When the tour ended, they set up shop in a converted barn in rural Baambrugge with the recording equipment from Brian's Bellagio Road living room and additional matériel. Then they sent for Brian and his brood.

Wilson's wife and two daughters (Carnie, born April 29, 1968, and Wendy, born November 16, 1969) arrived, but Brian was another matter. Twice he set out for Los Angeles International Airport to catch flights, and twice he decided for some unknown reason to turn back. On the third attempt Brian boarded the plane, but when it landed in Amsterdam, there was no sign of him, except for his passport and a ticket made out in his name that were found on his empty seat. After an hours-long search, he was located in the airport's duty-free lounge, fast asleep on a couch.

Brian's last three Beach Boys offerings—excepting his December 23, 1974, "Child of Winter" Christmas single—were all on *Holland:* "Funky Pretty"; "Mount Vernon and Fairway," a twelve-minute fairy tale set to music that Brian wrote while in the Netherlands; and "Sail On Sailor," which was written and recorded in Los Angeles.

Mike Love, golden-haired but unignorably balding, and dressed in sandals, white chinos, and a long woolen jacket woven in a colorful Indian design, was perched on a stool in a corner of Brother Studios in the spring of 1976, watching through a large glass window as Brian mixed "Blueberry Hill" in the spaceshiplike control room. Earle Mankey, trying to be encouraging, kept asking Brian what he thought about "more saxophones, more echo, more bass drum, more . . ."

Brian, stone-faced and bent over the board, was completely oblivious, sliding his fingers up and down the rows of dials, twisting this, turning that, engrossed in a once-familiar gambol.

"Ah, yes," Love whispered to himself, immensely pleased by the total picture. "It's just like old times," he said, remembering the period during the 1950s when he was still living with his family at the corner of Mount Vernon and Fairway in the View Park/Baldwin Hills section of Los Angeles. "You know that line in Brian's fairy tale about 'distant lights'? Well, that was from my bedroom upstairs, which had a fantastic view. We used to sleep in the bunks, and I'd have a transistor radio under the covers. . . . You remember that part in the fairy tale about the prince's 'magic transistor radio'? Well, that came from *that*.

"Brian thought up the idea of the fairy tale in Holland, and we all thought it was great how the whole thing came together. We all loved working on it, and from the start we thought it made a great little 'present' to go with *Holland*. So that's what we did. Don't you love it? Isn't it wonderful?"

Forty-five minutes later, Brian gave his version of the fairy tale record's inception.

"The fairy tale? Okay, let me tell you. Well, we were in another country, we were in Holland, and I just sat around and drank apple sap—that's like apple cider—and just sat around and dreamed. And one night I was listening to that Randy Newman album called *Sail Away*. So I started playing the album, and I was sitting there with a pencil and I started writing. And I found that if I kept playing the Randy Newman album, I could stay in that mood. It was the weirdest thing; I wrote the whole fairy tale while listening to that album. It was the weirdest little mood I created.

"I was thinking about Mike Love's house, and I just wrote, 'There was a mansion on a hill,' and then later on, in my head, I created a fairy tale.

"But anyhow, so I had the fairy tale, but nobody was ready for that. *Nobody.* I remember, Carl said, '*What?!*'

"Then . . . Oh, I know what happened! I got fucked up; I got depressed. So Carl did all the editing on it and even did part of it himself when I wasn't there. It was really a thrill; the first time we'd ever done anything that creative. I wanted it to be on the album, but they said, 'No! It's too long.' We argued and all, and I was depressed. So they finally compromised by saying, 'Okay, we'll slip it in that package as an extra record or something."

Reprise was not pleased with the original version of *Holland* and spurned it, soon after it was submitted, as a "weak" album. The Beach Boys—who had dropped a personal fortune on the escapade—"freaked," according to one Warner Bros. Records employee, who added, "It was bloodshed; everybody went wild." It seemed that the company had been waiting for something easily marketable to offset the *So Tough* fiasco and so it was unmoved by the fairy tale and impressionistic cuts such as Jardine and Love's ten-minute "California Saga," as well as unhappy with the absence of a strong single.

From there, the sequence of events took a somewhat gothic turn.

With *Holland* in limbo and tempers flaring, a business associate close to the problem decided to contact several people near Brian in the hope that Brian either had, or could be induced to compose, a surefire single suitable for inclusion on the album. Among those approached was Van Dyke Parks. Parks was said to have shown up in the executive offices of Warner-Reprise "minutes" after he was telephoned, carrying a cassette of a song called "Sail On Sailor," which Brian had first drafted in the early 1970s.

The following description of what was on Parks's cassette was supplied by a source close to the Beach Boys who was present when the cassette was first played.

"Brian was playing that song ['Sail On Sailor'] on the piano. It was completely different words. He's singing different words; much better words. It was one of the most curious things I've ever heard.

"It begins with Van Dyke saying, 'Brian, there's something you gotta do for me, man. I want you to sit down at the piano, and I want you to write a song for me. Lyrics, melody, everything. I want you to do it right on the spot.' Brian says, 'I'd do anything for you, man, but would you do something for me?'

"Van Dyke says, 'I'd do anything for *you*, Brian.' So Brian says, 'Hey, you gotta convince me, Van Dyke, that I'm not insane.' He keeps repeating over and over again, 'Hypnotize me into thinking that I'm not insane. Convince me that I'm not insane.'

"Van Dyke says, 'Cut the shit, Brian. I want you to write this tune right here.' And the cassette goes on for about fifteen minutes. As you can imagine, there's a lot of halts in it. He's trying to do the words at the same time, too. So when he runs out of words, he stops playing and starts again."

At Reprise's insistence, the Beach Boys recorded what proved to be a rewritten version of "Sail On Sailor," with Blondie Chaplin, new Beach Boys supporting guitarist, singing the lead. Brian is said to have had no hand in the production of the final song.

To understand Brian Wilson it always helped to get an update on his younger brother Dennis, who persisted in living the lifestyle of the sea and sun while Brian remained indoors, daring or being dared to distill it into songs. "I don't know why everybody doesn't live at the beach, on the ocean," said Dennis in May 1976 with a bemused shake of his head. "It makes no sense to me, hanging around the dirty, ugly-as-shit city. That's why I always loved and was proud to be a Beach Boy; I always loved the image. On the beach you can live in bliss. You wake up and fall out into that water, go fishing, go sailing, go—"

The rest was drowned out by a noisy flock of gulls that dipped and soared in the cloudless blue sky of a gusty spring day in Santa Monica Harbor, polishing the Scottish brass fittings on *Harmony,* a magnificent fifty-foot, twin-masted ketch that he rebuilt from scratch in 1975 with "a couple of Yugoslavian guys."

Dennis would remarry the following week, on May 21, 1976, to model Barbara Karen Perk Lamm, former wife of keyboardist Robert Lamm of the rock group Chicago. (Dennis had divorced second wife Barbara Wilson in August 1974; they had two sons, Michael and Carl, the latter born in December 1972.)

"Look at this," said Dennis, taking time out from polishing the shine on one of the guardrails of the sailboat, whose hand-carved winged pelican under the bowsprit indicated the sailboat had originally been named the *Watadori* (Bird of Passage) when it was built in Japan in 1950 by the Azuma Boat Company. Dennis licked his callused thumb and pushed it across the weathered deck. "See how the grain comes out in this wood when it's wet? This is *teak;* it's made to look beautiful when it's all wet out at sea. This boat looks okay now, but it's best when it's in action."

The boat appeared to have something in common with Brian Wilson. "He could still stand to lose a few pounds of gut," said Dennis, "but I think I understand why he took off for a few years. He wanted to rest and felt there was no sense living in the past. He's been through a lot of tremendous emotional changes and setbacks from taking drugs and not understanding them, among other things. Brian's a reclusive, sensitive, vulnerable guy, and he was probably one of the most famous people in the world at one point. That *completely* got to him.

"But the thing I wonder about is where does Brian's creative spark come from? Not his subjects or anything, but his spark. What makes it so great for me is that I really don't know. There's a mystery behind Brian, even to *me.* Creatively, where in the fuck does the guy go? Where is he coming from?"

Dennis tossed his polishing rag into the hold and went down into the large galley opposite the aft cabin, a living/sleeping area with four large windows and outfitted with Oriental rugs, a set of drums, and an electric piano. He sprang back up moments later with a frozen cream pie that he proceeded to shovel into his mouth with a small plastic fork.

"People always thought Brian was a good-time guy until he started releasing those heavy, searching songs on *Pet Sounds* and all, but that stuff was closer to his own personality and perceptions. . . . My father used to go to pieces when he heard stuff like 'Caroline No.' . . . By the time people get an accurate picture of Brian Wilson—if ever—he's gonna be far beyond them again, and I can dig his frustration.

"For instance," said Dennis, "I wrote a song intended for *Holland* about Vietnam. I got the image of a soldier—me—dying in a ditch, and I ended up doing a song about it. The soldier began feeling, 'Why the hell am I here?' Then the coldness started to move up his body, from his feet to his legs, to his chest . . . until he was dead. See? It was too negative! How could I put that on a Beach Boys album?"

The great thing is, at least I feel that you can put *anything* on a Beach Boys record if you can get that *feeling*," said Brian Wilson at Brother Studios, sealing the pact by downing his third consecutive glass of orange juice. "Boy, this stuff is good for you!" he said as he placed his glass on the counter in the kitchenette. "I'm writing a song about how people should forget about hot dogs and hamburgers and eat good food."

As the rest of the Beach Boys hustled around the complex, intent on various errands, Brian fretted in a tiny-tot voice about the strict diet and athletic regimen he'd been on; he was also pondering the transcendental meditation techniques he had been introduced to by Mike Love.

"It gives me a chance to see a side of life I don't see often," he stated as Love looked on approvingly. "But I sit down in a chair—I don't fold my legs like a yogi because my legs are too big because I'm out of shape. So, jeez, it's a big *pain*."

Love's face fell, and the ever-waggish Dennis Wilson came into the room, spinning a new snare drum head on his index finger. "Hey, Dennis," said Brian, "are you going to the meeting at Carl's house?"

"Yeah," said Dennis. "You coming?"

"Nah," said Brian. "I don't like business meetings. . . . I feel like a piece of material there."

Moments later, standing alone in an adjoining room, a somber Dennis spoke of his older brother in a blunt, advisory tone.

"Listen, Brian Wilson is not a good-looking human being, yet his music is beautiful. Look at Nat King Cole; he looked like a real piece of shit, but he had a beautiful voice. Look at Aretha Franklin; she would scare me in a dark room, yet her voice is fantastic. Roy Orbison, too. The thing I listen to is the *music.*"

With a half-day's work under their belts, Dennis, Mike (and Stan) decided to take a short break and ambled into the cozy, plant-filled lounge in the front section of the "Brother Building." They were lying about on the stylish 1940s beach furniture, shooting the breeze, when Brian entered and sat down on the couch.

STAN: "Brian! Hey, how ya feeling, buddy?"

BRIAN: "Okay."

DENNIS: "Hey, Brian. I was telling Mike and Stan that I saw a musical in New York the other day called *The Wiz*. It's a black *Wizard of Oz*. The whole cast is black, and the score is all soul music, man! Brian, you should go to New York for a few days soon and see *The Wiz*. Hands down, it's the best musical I've seen."

STAN (excited): "Brian, let's go to New York in a week or two and see the play!"

BRIAN (uneasy): "Are you kidding! New York—that's a *lonely* place, with all those tall, dark, unfriendly buildings."

STAN: "Well, why don't you take your lonely friends with you?"

BRIAN: "No deal."

DENNIS (diplomatic): "Well, New York *can* get a little weird. When I was there last week, I did a few interviews."

BRIAN (softly): "Someone should interview my psychiatrist."

DENNIS: "What was that, Brian?"

BRIAN: "I saw a doctor today. Somebody should talk to *him*. You know what he told me? He said, 'Okay, we're gonna start on *self-nourishment.*' I didn't know what that was. He said, 'Read this little piece of paper.' He handed me the piece of paper, and I said, 'Read it to me.'

"It said, 'I love you.' Turns out you're supposed to read this to yourself.

"The doctor said that you're supposed to tell yourself you love yourself and you trust yourself. It's a whole weird thing. You're supposed to read the paper three times a day for five minutes each time, no matter *where* you are, saying 'I love you, I love you' to yourself, and all these other different thoughts; they're all written on little pieces of paper. It's supposed to be called nourishment; it's supposed to help you. It's a really weird idea.

"Heck, I lost the paper. I thought the guy was crazy."

The doctor in question was Eugene E. Landy, a pricey, Pittsburgh-born clinical psychologist, licensed in California and Hawaii, who practiced a controversial "twenty-four-hour therapy" in which, according to a paper Landy wrote on the subject, the therapist "maintains total contact with the patients . . . in their own environment."

Marilyn Wilson had been instrumental in bringing Landy into the picture in order to get Brian functioning again as a recording artist, but the Beach Boys organization also sanctioned Landy's treatment.

The dyslexic, hyperkinetic son of a physician and a therapist, Landy's test at the University of Pittsburgh at the age of five revealed an IQ of 150; he dropped out of school at twelve but eventually completed his education, earning a B.A. in psychology at California State in 1964, an M.S. in psychology from the University of Oklahoma in 1967, and a Ph.D. (in philosophy) from the same university in 1968. He made his initial reputation treating problem adolescents and drug addicts, and training Operation Headstart, Job Corps, Peace Corps, and VISTA volunteers in rehabilitation procedures. He also worked with returning Vietnam vets with dope habits and published the *Underground Dictionary*, a glossary of drug and street jargon for practical use in dealing with denizens of "the other side of life."

And there appeared to be another side to Landy's life, too, the psychologist often asserting that he spent his prepsychology days working in record promotion for RCA, Decca, Coral, and Mercury records. Landy maintained that he "discovered" fellow Pittsburgh native George Benson, whom he had encountered playing the ukelele on a street corner. Landy took the adolescent Benson—later to become a noted jazz guitarist and singer—to New York and got him a deal for one (unsuccessful) single with RCA; but, according to Benson, the two parted ways when Landy sought excessive control of Benson's career.

"My people developed a distrust for [Landy]," stated Benson, "when he made them sign a power of attorney that they didn't understand, and he got all my mail and all my checks."

In Landy's paper on twenty-four-hour therapy, he would similarly insist on "complete patient dependency on the therapist and total control of the patient's life," noting that the central theme of his patient treatment was that "people behave in ways that mask their inadequacies, whether real or imagined, as they function in the world. They do so by creating facades and external support systems, while engaging in interpersonal power games to get what they want."

According to Landy, his celebrity client list included rock star Alice Cooper and actors Rod Steiger and Richard Harris. Yet it would be Landy's affiliation with Brian Wilson that attracted the majority of the publicity he seemed to cultivate, lending new shades of meaning to the notion of people with inadequacies "engaging in interpersonal power games to get what they want."

The following morning, Brian, dressed in the same shirt he had worn the day before and the same scuffed track shoes, and a pair of navy blue pants with wiggly white lines running down the outside of either leg, was jogging along a portion of UCLA's cross-country course.

Stan Love, trim and confident in a lemon-colored warmup suit, was urging him on. "That's it, Bri. . . . There's no hurry. . . . Enjoy yourself."

It was the first day of Brian's Stan-inspired physical fitness program, and as he took the hill, shirttails flapping, he looked to be having a good time.

After the run, Brian and Stan located a shady spot under some pines where they held each other's ankles while they did some sit-ups. Brian did ten. Stan did eleven.

"You know, I dig running," Brian told Stan as they walked back to the car. "Were you surprised I could go that far?"

"I was very surprised when we were going back up that hill," Stan replied as they sped off, "because going up the hill is a lot tougher."

"Yeah!" said Brian, breaking into a hacking cough. "Now let's go home and get some orange juice."

"Brian," Stan pleaded, pounding for emphasis on the steering wheel of the silver gray Mercedes he was driving, "you're not gonna get rid of that damn cough until you quit all that damn smoking!"

It was a glorious day in Southern California. The air was crisp and bracing, and the sun leaped through the windshield like a wild animal as

Stan and Brian descended a steep grade on the UCLA campus and then rode out onto Sunset Boulevard.

"You know, coughing is good for you!" Brian chirped hoarsely. "It's good because it makes your face flush and it gets the blood rushing to your head! It gets everything moving!

"Whoa," Brian moaned as the Mercedes caught the full slope of the incline. "Boy, this is a big hill. And look at those guys!" he said, pointing at several joggers headed in the opposite direction. "I don't know how those guys could do that if they smoked like me. Probably couldn't, huh?"

" 'Course not," snapped Stan, eyes on the road. "And if you think this hill is something, check out this sharp turn coming up here. I mean, it's like 'Dead Man's Curve' or something."

"Dead Man's Curve!" Brian whooped. "Did you know I helped write a song called that for Jan and Dean? Did you, Stanley?"

Love slowed the Mercedes as it reached the main entrance to Bel Air, slipping past the guard gate and police station and onto Bellagio Road. A Spanish-style villa and manor was visible on the left. Pulling up to the iron gates, Stan leaned out of the car window and pressed a button on the intercom. There was a pause and then a small speaker barked a harsh "Hello?"

"Marilyn? . . . Yeah, it's Stan."

There was another pause as the gates noiselessly swung wide. The car followed the winding driveway around to the back of the house, past a sign stuck in the grass: DRIVE CAREFULLY. CHILDREN AT PLAY.

Stan parked the car between the garage and a hurricane fence that enclosed a large mosaic-tiled swimming pool.

"What do you want to do now?" Stan asked Brian as he climbed out of the car. "Do you want to go right into the house?"

"Well," Brian whined, "I'm not sure."

"Hey, I've got an idea!" Stan announced with a knowing grin. "Let's shoot some hoops!" Without waiting for a reaction he sauntered into the garage and emerged with two basketballs. Brian and Stan took shots for fifteen minutes, Stan commenting on Brian's form. Brian had a good shot but could not dribble. When he missed or fumbled, he blamed it on his loose shirttails: "Damn! My fucking shirt keeps getting in my way!" Stan ignored him until the remark became a redundancy. "Come on," Stan finally chided. "No excuses."

Poised in another attempt at overcoming his apparel, Brian became embarrassed and let the ball drop from his hands, then headed into the house.

"Wait a minute, buddy!" Stan hollered consolingly. "You didn't make that last shot! You should always make the last shot before you call it quits."

The idea seemed reasonable to Brian, and he returned, grim-faced, to complete the unfinished chore. Seven tries later he hooked a beauty into the net: *swish!*

"Nice work, buddy," Stan congratulated him, and he walked on the veranda to the front door. "See, you should always end on the right note. Always. You oughta know that by now."

Once inside, Brian headed straight for the kitchen and a row of refrigerators, where he removed a carton of orange juice and poured himself a tall draft. "Gimme those vitamins!" he gasped between gulps.

To the right, off the kitchen, was a well-appointed dining room overpowered by busy wallpaper with a botanical motif that gave one the vague sense of stepping into the cover of *Smiley Smile*. Beyond lay the main parlor, which opened onto an array of large rooms and a stairway winding upward. Underfoot was a thick pile carpet with a sculptured design resembling a whirling pool of water. Several steps down on the right was a comfortable den dominated by a Norman Rockwell print that hung over the mantelpiece. Nearby was a 1930s telephone booth, complete with crank-style magneto phone. The den's left wall was glass from floor to ceiling and revealed a small courtyard with gurgling fountain. The rest of the room was taken up with dark wood furniture, a billiard table, and Brian's Chickering piano. On the piano bench the opening bars of "California Girls" were illustrated in black-and-white needlepoint.

Adjacent to the den was a huge rectangular living area furnished with chunky, overstuffed couches and chairs covered in dark shades of velvet. At the far wall, sun streamed through the *Wild Honey* stained-glass window depicting an array of flowers and bees. The sixteen-track studio console on which the *Smiley Smile, Wild Honey, Friends,* and *20/20* albums were recorded was gone. Brian had to be content with a six-foot console unit built into the wall that powered four JBL Studio Monitors hanging from the ceiling. Beneath the one nearest the *Wild Honey* window was a six-foot-by-four-foot Advent VideoBeam TV screen.

Stan stretched out on the longest couch, located beneath a row of picture windows overlooking another veranda and the property's rolling, manicured grounds. Parallel to the couch was a husky stone fireplace over which hung a small needlepoint sign, a gift from the singer Cher; it read KEEP IT LIGHT.

Brian walked in, toting a half-glass of juice, and plopped down on one of the shorter couches, making small talk.

"Hey, I love Bacharach and David!" he said. "They did two of my favorite songs. They did a thing called 'My Little Red Book.' I love that, and I might record it." He burst into song: " 'I just took out my little red book/The minute you said goodbye!' "

What was the second of his favorite songs?

"The second song? I don't remember . . . but I liked the Beatles! I thought melodically they were very creative."

Didn't he feel in fierce competition with them?

"Yeah, well, it's a business," he instructed.

Was he flattered by "Back in the U.S.S.R.," the Beatles' 1968 homage/sendup of "California Girls"?

"I didn't even recognize that until someone said something," he confided without expression. "I thought it was really adorable. And . . . I think the Stones are one of the best groups. I like 'Goin' Home.' "

Had he been back to Hawthorne lately?

"Ho!" he exclaimed, shivering slightly. "I wouldn't want to. I'd be scared to death just to go back there." Then, almost to himself: "I don't know why. It's scary enough in Bel Air."

The talk shifted to his upbringing and his parents, particularly Murry, who had died on June 4, 1973, the official cause of death ascribed to "acute myocardial infarction" due to "coronary atherosclerosis." Murry had been suffering from heart disease for a year, and when his fatal coronary came, he was dead within fifteen minutes. Murry was buried in Inglewood Park Cemetery; his wife Audree was appointed executor of his estate, which was appraised at $266,674.51.

Just before Murry's death, Brian explained, the Beach Boys had planned to record a love song written by Murry called "Lazzaloo." "The song was five and a half minutes long," said Brian. "It was about an exotic love affair in Turkey. Dad was a little ballsy," Brian muttered somberly. "He had a lot of balls. With him, everything was 'punch'! He really tackled things. Really got behind them. He believed in a little punch.

"Yeah, my old dad helped. I won't forget him. My dad made an album. I have the album, but I don't want to play it because he died."

That said, Brian rose hurriedly, went to an upright piano in the corner of the living room, and started hammering out an aggressive melody that was unrecognizable. Brian's face remained blank.

When he retook his seat, there was the barest trace of a smile on his pale lips, and he began chatting about his childhood, how he was "a baseball *fanatic,*" a B-plus student, and an athletic and musical companion to his cousin Mike.

"Mike had a lot of hassles with his folks," Brian said, as Stan Love looked up, suddenly interested. "I'd be on the phone saying, 'Hey, Mike! I'm gonna come to your school tomorrow at locker-room time' because we used to run track. And I'd hear his dad say, 'Get off that goddamn phone! I'll bust your fuckin' nose all over your fuckin' face!' He used to say that to Mike."

After a few more minutes of talk, Brian stood up again as if responding to some unexpressed whim and moved to leave the room. He got as far as the parlor when he wavered. "I'm gonna take a rest," he said tentatively. "I don't know what to do here. I don't know what to do."

Receiving no suggestions, he returned to his chair, drawn by the VideoBeam, which Stan had switched on to watch a tennis match between Chris Evert and Evonne Goolagong.

"Is she good?" Brian asked Stan, pointing to Evert.

"Sure she is!" Stan replied. "She's the best in the world."

"Really?" said Brian with awe. "She's young."

Chris Evert tossed her racket in the air in victory, and as it floated across the VideoBeam screen in a slow-motion replay, the graceful blur seemed momentarily buoyed by a burst of laughter emanating from the veranda. The front doorbell rang, and a short pleasant-looking brunette in her late twenties appeared from the rear of the house. Dressed in a well-tailored gray corduroy jumpsuit and sneakers, she opened the door with a gracious greeting ("Hiya, kids!") and admitted three little girls, each eight to nine years old and lugging an overnight bag.

The brunette aimed them toward the kitchen. "Go right on in the back. Wendy's waiting for you. I'll fix you all hot dogs."

Marilyn Wilson turned, walked over to Brian, and sat on his lap. "Honey," she told him, "Wendy's friends are arriving for the slumber party. They're gonna be here all day and night. I hope they don't drive you crazy."

"They won't," he replied firmly.

"Marilyn has a new single," Brian explained, brightening, and went over to a shelf in search of it.

"I don't think it's over there, honey," said Marilyn, who strode out and then reappeared moments later with a cassette. "Here it is, Brian. Here it is!"

Brian took it from her and put it in the tape deck.

"This is Marilyn's new single," he said dryly. "It was recorded at Western Studios. I did the instruments. I played all that's here, and Marilyn did the background voices."

The music began to spill out of the monitors. Unpolished but engaging, it had the unmistakable hallmarks of a record with a B. Wilson byline: simple, dampened drums; snappy, accordionlike organ; a melodic yet commanding bass line; and loads of un-Dolbyized emptiness to heighten the strategic use of echo. If Brian was indeed playing everything, he had coordinated his efforts well. The track was a remake of the 1957 Jimmie Rodgers hit "Honeycomb." Marilyn's vocals were a bit flat and her phrasing ungainly, but there was genuine appeal when she and her husband teamed up for multitracked harmonies in the choruses.

Marilyn swayed with the beat as the music played, but Brian stood stiffly at the tape deck. As "Honeycomb" faded, Marilyn grinned. Brian, in an oddly cautious move, leaned over as if to kiss her on the cheek, then hesitated. There was an awkward second before his wife noticed, comprehended his intentions, and then offered her cheek to him with a consenting tilt of her head. He planted the tiniest peck and then straightened and spoke in a dramatic tone as if needing to overcome the din of the now-ended tape.

"She's got a great voice! She's one of the best singers I've ever heard in my life!" Then, in a more conversational tone: "If I could produce any artist, I'd produce my wife, Marilyn Wilson—or I'd produce Bobby Goldsboro."

"Anyone who heard what I have been able to hear over the past month, in the most casual situations, *on this piano*—Brian Wilson's recent works—would be astounded by his development and evolution," Van Dyke Parks vowed in May 1976, patting the spinet at which he was seated in his Hollywood apartment.

A slight, bespectacled thirty-three, Parks spoke with a voluble expressiveness worthy of William Jennings Bryan or a carnival barker. He politely declined to discuss the making of "Sail On Sailor," relegating his role in its path to finished recording to "a simple act of moral support.

"There has been a great deal of attention paid—and it's been a divisive issue—on whether or not Brian Wilson would do any more recording 'by himself,'" Parks asserted. "He should have been permitted by now to record a solo album. Brian has appealed to Warner Brothers since [the Beach Boys signed] there, to do record production on his own.

"Now it may be for some legal reason, as a secretary of an executive would put it, that Brian has not been permitted to work within the reasonable boundaries of his own initiative. But I see no reason why he should not be producing records by himself, and I think he could do that easily.

"One time Brian said to me that he had asked an executive of Warner Brothers for some money to produce an album, and an underexecutive, to which he had to address himself finally, offered him a figure that it is safe to assume could not on any real basis provide for an album. It was inadequate for an album or even a single; it was an insulting figure, and even Brian Wilson is capable of being insulted. . . .

"You must understand that Brian developed a new volume of sales for the record industry. He developed a new sense of economics. So you can understand how subject he could be to . . . resentment or hate. And he hasn't displayed any. Still . . . justice denied is justice denied."

According to David Berson, Brian approached Warner Bros. in the mid-1970s about doing a solo album.

"Yes," said Berson, "and the decision on that was always up to Brian. Needless to say, whatever he wanted to do, we would love for him to do."

Was a budget of $5,000 quoted to him for a single, perhaps?

"He was supposed to record something for five thousand dollars? If it were a single or if it were a side, it's quite possible," said Berson. "He approached me directly on any number of occasions, and I've always encouraged him. I don't think that we ever really talked about money, except on one particular occasion where he seemed to be serious and I actually got that fire lit in me and said, 'Hey, maybe this guy's really gonna do it.' And I think we talked about money, and he characterized the offer as being more than sufficient and in fact one of the most generous he had ever received.

"There were advisors that he consulted who disagreed and didn't think the offer was so generous. Marilyn said, 'How can you insult my husband that way?' and Brian asked her to leave the meeting. He said, 'Get out of here! This is a very generous offer, and I want to continue this meeting in spite of what you think.'

"But there's always been an outstanding offer to him and an understanding between him and myself, and between him and Mo [Ostin], that whenever he wants to do something, we'll certainly support him and back him up and pay for it.

"The plans are always the same: There are no plans because you don't know what Brian's gonna do. You're never certain whether his proposals are going to evaporate in thin air in the next minute. Anybody who gives a shit about the record business and is aware of Brian Wilson—and that's got to be anybody who is aware of almost anything—knows that a Brian Wilson project has got to be worth a lot of money. But they always seem to be transitory enthusiasms for him."

One enthusiasm of Brian's in 1976 that Carl Wilson hoped would not be transitory was his then-current interest in returning, on a limited basis, to live concert performances. It was the Beach Boys' custom to pay Brian a portion of the net profit from their tours, but they preferred he made the money in a more animated fashion.

"When we started to become active again, around 1970," Carl recalled, "we did a thing at the Whiskey A Go Go"—at Sunset and San Vincente in Hollywood—"and Brian lasted two sets one night. Then, after the first set the next night, he had to go home because his good ear was really hurting him, and it made him dizzy. His right ear is deaf, except once in a while when he's exposed to a really *loud* noise; then he kinda hears a rattle, but it hurts his good ear. Then, because of problems in his inner ear, his equilibrium gets screwed up.

"I've always kinda had a gut feeling that it was going to clear up, but that doesn't mean shit. He had an operation [in the late 1960s] that was supposed to be a success according to the surgeon attending at the time, but he still doesn't hear much out of his right ear.

"I'm dying for Brian to hear stereo. I want so much for him to hear with both ears because of all people he would love it.

"Before we started working on the new albums, Brian was bored as shit. If conditions were right and he was up to it, I would love for him to play with us. You know, Brian and I wrote one song for this new album called 'Good Timin'.' It's got a lot of counterpoint on it, lyrics overlapping." Carl recited: " 'You need good timin'/Lay down your worries/It takes good timin'/Lay down your troubles . . .' "

Neither "Good Timin' " nor "California Feeling" would appear on *15 Big Ones,* the fifteen-track, fifteenth anniversary Beach Boys album released July 5, 1976, by Brother-Reprise Records. Of the songs recorded in Santa Monica between January 30 and May 15, 1976, the originals were "It's OK," "Had to Phone Ya," and "That Same Song," all written by Brian and Mike; "T M Song" and "Back Home" written by Brian; and "Everybody's in Love with You" by Mike Love. Al Jardine's "Susie Cincinnati," first recorded by the Beach Boys late in 1969 as a B-side and later deleted from *Sunflower,* was included in a new rendition.

The oldies on *15 Big Ones* were "Palisades Park," "Blueberry Hill," 1956 hits "A Casual Look" by the Six Teens and "In the Still of the Night" by the Five Satins; the Dixie Cups' 1964 hit "Chapel of Love"; the Righteous Brothers' 1965 single "Just Once in My Life"; a medley of Little Willie John's 1958 R&B weeper "Talk to Me" and "Tallahassie Lassie"—and the album's big single, Chuck Berry's "Rock and Roll Music," in a version that vaulted to number 5. A second single, the slice of summertime advocacy called "It's OK," made it to number 29.

A jerry-built and almost brazenly unrefined album, *15 Big Ones* profited by a sizable press blitz that attended a "Brian Is Back" campaign (Mike's brother, band manager Steve Love, came up with the slogan). *15 Big Ones* went gold, and Brian even made a few furtive appearances in selected concerts. But something was wrong—with Brian, with the Boys. Something that hit records could never fix.

23
• • • •

That Same Song

L ooking like an orphan of a hurricane, Brian Wilson made a guest
appearance on NBC-TV's *Saturday Night Live* in November 1976.
Seated at a piano positioned in a prop sandbox, a beach ball at his feet,
the obviously petrified Brian played, as best he could, a solo keyboards
and vocal version of "Good Vibrations." Just out of camera shot, Dr.
Landy held up cue cards that read RELAX and, ironically, SMILE.

Less a performance than a pointedly exploitative skit about a singer
suffering from clinical stage fright, the segment was live television at
its most distressing and the latest in a litany of ill-conceived, Landy-
coordinated media events involving Brian. Shortly after the program, the
two-hundred-dollar-an-hour doctor was no longer in charge of the composer's personal recovery.

The Beach Boys themselves were no less able to relax or smile when
beset by the icy tailwinds from the lucrative but critically lambasted *15
Big Ones*.

"I was unhappy with the oldies—absolutely," Dennis admitted in

320

September 1976 as he sat at an electric clavinet in Brother Studios, his sun-bronzed fingers forming chords as he blustered. "The album should have been one hundred percent originals. We had enough Brian Wilson material to do it; I was disappointed [that the group] wouldn't follow through with that. Steve Love, Mike Love, and Alan Jardine were pushing to get it out—it was just a big push. They'd rather just get it out there than take time with it and develop it. Carl and I were really upset.

"It was a total vote; everyone stood in the studio and raised hands over the tunes. I was blown out of the water, but I don't want to sound negative—just critical. I'm very excited for Brian, but I don't want him to lay back, the way he's been doing with oldies."

During the latter half of that same afternoon, Carl Wilson reclined on a chaise lounge on the deck of his home on Broadbeach Road in Malibu and seconded his brother's disaffection with their latest record.

"The truth is, Dennis and I were hoping that Brian would go back to the main plan," began Carl, who had been discreetly serving as the Beach Boys' de facto producer since *Smiley Smile*. "Dennis and I had a picture of doing an album of oldies as a warm-up and then doing another album. But as it happens, we started to do the new stuff and then Brian said, 'Well, I've recorded enough. I don't want to record any longer, and the album's finished.'

"I believe that Brian was consciously underproducing the album, and that was his choice—we deferred to him. But when we voted to do it that way with those particular songs, I left the studio right there on the spot because I was very disenchanted. Thing is, then I came back and worked my ass off because I support my brother professionally and personally. . . . We choose to be in this group. . . . If we didn't want this group, we'd all split right now because we don't need it. . . . But I think people get off on relationships."

Further insights into these relationships could soon be gleaned from Bruce Johnston and the Wilson brothers' resultant solo LPs: three records—two modest, one marvelous. Johnston's *Goin' Public*, produced by Gary Usher and released by Columbia in May 1977, had remakes of "I Write the Songs," his Grammy-winning number 1 hit for Barry Manilow, and two Beach Boys standards he had written, "Deirdre" and "Disney Girls." A harmless calling card for his songwriting skills, it had no other subtext, and it failed to chart.

The pair of LPs made by the Wilsons, however, had ensued as Dennis and Carl backed away from day-to-day disagreements within the group, signing individual deals with James William Guercio's CBS-distributed Caribou Records label for their respective projects: *Pacific Ocean Blue* (original working title *Freckles;* released September 16, 1977) and *Carl Wilson* (issued, after several postponements for Beach Boys–related duties, on March 27, 1981).

Carl had dabbled before in extracurricular endeavors. In 1970 he produced an eponymous Brother Records LP (distributed by Capitol's Starday-King subsidiary) for the Flame, a South African rock band from whose ranks the Beach Boys would draw drummer Ricky Fataar and guitarist Blondie Chaplin. The two musicians were hired in 1971 for the Boys touring band and became full-fledged members of the group in 1972, recording and contributing to the songwriting until the period preceding work on *15 Big Ones.*

Carl and brother-in-law Billy Hinsche co-produced Dean Martin's son Ricci for the 1975 Capitol single "Stop, Look Around"/"I Had a Dream" and an Epic album, *Beached.* These projects were upbeat, forward-looking affairs that took Carl out of his quiet, contemplative milieu. In contrast, the *Carl Wilson* album, which peaked at number 185 in *Billboard,* had a prettily sung but morose and enervated disposition, culminating in the disturbing stasis of "Seems So Long Ago."

While no less pessimistic, *Pacific Ocean Blue* was infinitely more promising. Dennis discovered a gruffer and tougher curve on the Beach Boys' rash optimism, his Little Feat–esque rhythm shifts and Captain Beefheart–as–surf rat vocal tendencies carrying the enthralling record to number 96.

As in the lauded but little-seen film *Two-Lane Blacktop* (1971) in which he costarred with singer-songwriter James Taylor, Dennis instinctively knew how to invoke the dingy hoodoo of his darksome youth, each dream-walking annunciation of this outsider-agnostic ranking with Brian's best tracks for its aching self-disclosure. Dennis poured his soul *and* his instincts into the incantatory arrangements, which foreshadowed the fervid wiseguy woe of such artists as Tom Waits. Dennis had made a brilliant album, but he still could not get the attention of the people who were most important to him—his family, his musical peers, his more thoughtful compatriots—and he would quickly come to see that recurring predicament as a permanent impasse.

In November 1976, Capitol Records put out a second live Beach Boys album, *Beach Boys '69—the Beach Boys Live in London,* which actually had been recorded at Finsbury Park and London's Palladium in August and

December 1968. It was one of two concert records Capitol had in its vaults, the other being a 1967 Hawaii performance collection whose coy official title had been *Lei'd in Hawaii*. (Also dating from this era was *Stack-o-Tracks*, an August 1968 Capitol release of fifteen Beach Boys tracks *sans* vocals that were intended as a sing- and play-along novelty; it failed to chart and was deleted from the Beach Boys catalog for the next twenty years.)

The twelve-track *London* album hopped to number 75 over the winter, remaining on the *Billboard* album chart for ten weeks and evidently putting a sales crimp in Warner's next Beach Boys LP, already announced for spring.

On April 11, 1977, Brother-Reprise Records released *The Beach Boys Love You*, which went as high as number 53. It was the closest Brian had yet come to a solo album. With the exception of his and Mike Love's "Let Us Go On This Way," a song called "Good Time" that he and Jardine had placed on the 1972 spring LP, and the doggerel "Ding Dang" he had written with former Byrd Roger McGuinn, the material was entirely Brian's: "Roller Skating Child," "Mona," "Johnny Carson," "Honkin' Down the Highway," "Solar System," "The Night Was So Young," "I'll Bet He's Nice," "Let's Put Our Hearts Together," "I Wanna Pick You Up," "Airplane," and "Love Is a Woman."

Although Brian had turned his guileless regard to such topics as planet-gazing and airplane rides (both interests and/or highlights of his boyhood), the music miraculously transcended its Crayola conventions and formed an affecting portrait of a man trying to redefine his shattered personality.

"I'm a very neurotic person; neurotic and nervous and uptight all the time," Wilson explained in March 1977. "I can't help it. There's nothing I can do about it, and I don't know why. Meditation doesn't help me like the Maharishi said it would—it just doesn't do shit for me. I've given up on it."

As for other avenues of rehabilitation, Brian confirmed that Dr. Landy "withdrew from the case about two months ago. He had some difficulty with my business manager, and they decided to go their separate ways. Now I'm seeing someone else twice a week, Dr. Steve Schwartz; he's a very mild man, doesn't have much to say, just listens.

"In my program with [Dr. Landy] I was being monitored every twenty minutes by him. [He had] control of my life legally through the commitment of my wife—my wife committed me to him—because I had gotten very low with drugs and got myself in a bad position mentally, physically, and emotionally. I was taken over by the doctor, and I straightened up. He definitely helped me. It cost over a hundred thousand dollars—he charged me a hell of a lot per month."

Wilson added that in retrospect he was not entirely pleased with his doctor's decision to book him on *SNL:* "I was a little put out by that. I'm not generally used to being alone; I haven't gotten used to that, and it's difficult for me. I have a lot of difficulty pulling things off for myself, but I did it alone and it worked out."

Landy defended his actions, saying he felt "it was an excellent idea" to have Brian on *Saturday Night Live* and thought his detractors had misunderstood his motives for doing so. "Four of these shows, and he would have been doing them with no problem. When a person works out of fear, they have to adjust to the environment, and each environment is new because it's fearful in the beginning. That was a fearful situation.

"As a one-shot [live performance] it was a terrible thing, but *not* if we'd done the four or five we were planning on. By the fourth one you would see the flow that really is there when we sit down in his living room together and fuck around—or in the studio.

"We were ready to do more. It was taken out of my control by emotional responses rather than knowledgeable decisions. That's the way most Beach Boys things are, though." Perhaps. But Landy neglected to mention that Brian had done several live performance stints just prior to the unsettling *SNL* telecast—including an appearance playing and singing solo on *The Mike Douglas Show,* summer tour dates that year with the Beach Boys, and an NBC-TV special taped in June 1976 called *The Beach Boys: It's O.K.*—with Brian showing no improvement whatsoever in his professional ease.

In any event Brian had already been productive in a more customary studio setting. Prior to *The Beach Boys Love You,* Brian had produced *Adult Child,* an unreleased album that contained twelve songs: "Life Is for the Living," "Hey Little Tomboy," "Deep Purple," "H.E.L.P. Is on the Way" (which was originally intended for *Sunflower*), "It's Over Now," "Everyone Wants to Live," "Shortenin' Bread," "Lines," "On Broadway," "Two Can Play," "It's Trying to Say," and "Still I Dream of It."

After *The Beach Boys Love You,* the group tried to fulfill its Warner-Reprise contract with a second Christmas album. The company was said to be highly skeptical that Brian appeared anywhere on *Merry Christmas from the Beach Boys.* The record contained such tracks as "Santa's Got an Airplane" (which was the "H.E.L.P." song with new lyrics), "I Saw Mommy Kissing Santa Claus," "Holy Evening," "Winter Symphony," "Go and Get That Girl," "God Rest Ye Merry Gentlemen," "Oh Come All Ye Faithful," "Hark, the Herald Angels Sing," "We Wish You a Merry Christmas," and "Michael Row the Boat." But the seasonal gambit was shelved.

Family disputes impacting on the group included an ongoing quarrel spearheaded by Dennis and Carl over Steve Love's role as the group's manager and business advisor, a vehement tussle that saw the Beach Boys break up before the eyes of *Rolling Stone* writer John Swenson on the tarmac of Newark Airport on September 3, 1977, Al Jardine's thirty-fifth birthday. A week later the band members would bury the hatchet, but management of the Beach Boys would became the responsibility of Carl's personal advisor, former Elvis Presley road manager Jerry Schilling.

Tamara Love, Mike's third wife, by whom he had a young daughter named Summer, was about to be divorced. And Dennis's seven-month marriage to Karen Lamm also ended, in divorce, on September 19, 1977. Dennis had earlier responded to court-filed declarations by Lamm about their relationship by maintaining in a sworn statement of April 13, 1977, that he "had never lived together with respondent as husband and wife" and that Karen's "purported love for me is based entirely on mercenary motives and nothing else." However, property and spousal issues between them had not been decided.

Shortly thereafter, Dennis and Karen reconciled and remarried in July 1978. Karen's attorney, Marvin Mitchelson, moved to have the property action between them dismissed "with prejudice," meaning that the case was closed and could never be reopened. Two weeks later Dennis *again* filed for divorce, now free of any property claims by Lamm. The second divorce became final in June 1980. Lamm was said to have received monthly payments of $2,000 until February 1983, and then $1,000 a month until a personal loan was repaid. Soon afterward, Dennis began a two-year relationship with Fleetwood Mac singer-songwriter Christine McVie.

On Independence Day, 1978, Carl and Annie Wilson separated after twelve years together that had produced two children, sons Jonah (born March 22, 1969) and Justyn (born October 19, 1971). Carl filed for dissolution of their marriage thirteen months later, with legal arguments over modification of spousal and child support issues persisting for another decade.

Eleven days after Carl's home life disintegrated, Marilyn and Brian separated, Brian moving out of the Bellagio Road house. Brian petitioned for divorce six months later. Awaiting settlement were extensive joint assets ($400,000 in escrow from the sale of the Laurel Way house, the Bellagio house's $450,000 trust deed, acreage on the Hawaiian island of Kauai, personal effects, and life insurance), limited partnerships with the Beach Boys in everything from undeveloped land in California and Hawaii to a Motel 6 in Texas, office and industrial real estate, two aviation plants, and shares of monies from Brother Records and Brother Publishing.

Marilyn and Brian agreed to a stipulation for the appointment of a judge *pro tempore* to make the final determination of the division of assets, choosing Joseph A. Wapner, former presiding judge of the Los Angeles Superior Court, who was soon to be a national television star as magistrate for real-life small-claims issues in the syndicated half-hour TV series *The People's Court.*

A native of the Dayton Hills section of Los Angeles, Wapner filed a forty-two-page Marital Agreement Settlement that halved with Solomonic precision all of Marilyn's and Brian's worldly goods, awarding Marilyn such holdings as "one 1978 AMC Cherokee, bearing California license plate WENDY 22, and one 1970 Mercedes 280 SE, bearing California license number CARNIE," in addition to 50 percent of the furniture, $260,618.30 from the proceeds of the sale of the Laurel Way home, and one-half interest in all rights, royalties, and receipts for musical compositions created by Brian during the marriage, the songs ranging from "Don't Hurt My Little Sister," "Wouldn't It Be Nice," and "California Feeling" to "Let Us Go On This Way."

Marilyn would have custody of Carnie, then twelve, and Wendy, eleven. Brian was given reasonable visitation rights, and neither parent could remove the children from the state of California for periods in excess of thirty days. All in all, it was a carefully administered parting.

The Beach Boys' final Brother-Reprise album, to be accepted in fulfillment of the group's contract with Warner's, was supposed to be called *California Feeling,* but both the track and the title were nixed in favor of the provisional tag *Winds of Change.* When the record finally reached stores in September 1977, it was called *M.I.U. Album* since at Mike Love's behest much of it was recorded—as was the second Christmas record—on the campus of Maharishi International University in Fairfield, Iowa. Produced by Al Jardine and keyboardist Ron Altbach, *M.I.U. Album* was an innocuous product, spawning a Buddy Holly cover single, "Peggy Sue," that squeaked to number 59. The album levitated as far number 151 and then vacated the charts—the identical *Billboard* run *Sunflower* had achieved eight years earlier when the Beach Boys were rescued by Reprise.

If the Boys seemed a little stale, skateboarding was getting *crispy,* continuing to build from its underground years. Innovations like the sealed bearing had rendered board wheels dirt- and jam-proof and capable of high velocity, official speed trials for the sport clocking in riders such as Sam Puccio at 54 miles per hour. Pool riding became an accepted subgenre of skateboarding, and guerrilla pipeline assaults on government defense projects utilizing mammoth (twenty-two feet high or better) concrete pipe assemblies were immortalized in magazine spreads and the rad rumor mills. Handstands, "berts" (one-hand pivot turns), and other freestyle moves once familiar on street corners were now practiced at formal skate parks, and top skaters such as Stacy Peralta and Russ Howell did well-attended exhibition tours.

The Ramones, Devo, and the B-52's were the rock sounds of choice among hardcore skateboarders, and Tony Alva took the overall World Professional Title in February 1977 at the Hang Ten Championships in Carlsbad. The 1978 Signal Hill Speed Trials saw Roger Williams of Huntington Beach top out at 59.92 m.p.h. in a skate car.

Wider skateboards with upturned noses, concave decks, and kicktails veered into vogue to assist in flat-surface "tic-tac" nose-swing acceleration, gutter climbs, curb grinds, acid drops, slides, fancier kick-turns, and ollies (standing jumps with the board, feet remaining on the deck). Prices for boards now ranged from $100 to $3,000 for a custom aluminum Ermico windfoil speedboard. Building a backyard ramp became the modern equivalent of joining the Boy Scouts or taking Outward Bound training, as skateboarders went increasingly vertical with "shredding" moves like the elevator drop, backside air, hand-plant invert (a sort of fluid handstand turn off the "coping" or high edge of the ramp), and no-hands ramp ollies. Helmets, elbow pads, and knee pads were hip garb for grinding, slamming, and bailing.

By 1979 street boarding and "skate punks" had gone wild, with wall skating and more radical ollies, inverts, slides, acid drops, lugelike "coffins," rock-and-roll curb spins, street pole turns, and boosting moves (running leaps off standing objects) that required "rail slider" grips lining the right and left underedges of the wide boards. The rail sliders aided in stability while grinding along curb-, ramp-, and park bench edges, besides preventing the graphics on the underdecks of boards from being marred.

Late in 1980, Kevin Thatcher became the founding editor of the San Francisco–rooted *Thrasher* magazine, whose informal motto of "Skate and Destroy" showed a determination to proclaim the alienated urges and renegade skating styles of the sport. *Thrasher* shipped its premier issue in the first month of the new year, and as it became the shredder's bible, its rebellious stance rapidly embraced the skate rock ethos exemplified by bands such as Jody Foster's Army, the Drunk Injuns, the Big Boys, Minus One, and Faction, a San Jose combo whose music trumpeted street boarding's capacity for risk and trespass.

Street boarding proved a massive influence on surfing. Turning moves copped from concrete—like "berts"—slowly converged with capers learned during the mid-sixties' rise of rounded plywood skim boards, which rode the inches-thin surface of flat surges at the water's edge. Foam skim boards led to tapered chest-high fiberglass skim boards for riding the shore break, with Laguna Beach recognized as a nerve center for the adrenalized scene.

Also stimulating a radical, romping attitude in the surf was the Boogie board, a pliable polyethylene cross between a sled and a wave board. Invented in 1974 by Tom Morey and manufactured by Morey's and his partner Germain Saivre's Carlsbad plant, the Boogie had turned-up "vaccuum track rails" along its sides, eliminating the need for a fin to facilitate steering. Boogies sold in assorted sizes from $29.95 (small) to $50 (large), with a full-size Boogie surf gun available for $100. Boogies had caught on in a big way by 1978, selling upward of seventy-five thousand annually because of their safety and portability.

In 1978 the Boys began to implement a 1977 $8 million deal with CBS Records in conjunction with Caribou Records. This contract, quietly signed as the group's agreement with Warner Bros. was nearing fulfillment, had been a source of disgruntlement on the part of Warner's since it still had several albums pending in what became a lame-duck relationship. In due course CBS Records would become unhappy with its end of the bargain.

The first record release in the CBS pact was *L.A. (Light Album)*, issued in March 1979, whose disco remake of the Boys' "Here Comes the Night" went to number 44. The album was largely produced by Brian Wilson surrogate Bruce Johnston, back in the fold after a late-1970s hiatus.

At Huntington Beach, aka Surf City, fights and cursing were heard in the lineup of the crowded breaks while as many as 150 surfers vied for the morning's menu of decent waves. "Dropping," or slipping into and riding the inside of a wave already occupied by a rider, was the mortal sin of surfing—but now it was a commonplace. And if somebody from Rincon or Port Loma paddled out at Surf City, he or she might get pounded. "Two Much Pressure" was the epigram on T-shirts worn from Point Conception to the Coronado–Imperial Beach bowls, and every boardhead knew what it meant: localism. IF YOU DON'T LIVE HERE, DON'T SURF HERE or HAZARDOUS TO TOURISTS were the standard graffiti warnings spray-painted on most beach signs. The territorial imperative was parodied yet codified in 1979 by the independent band Surf Punks, led by Dennis Dragon, a sometime participant during the late 1960s and early 1970s in the Beach Boys' tour band. The brother of occasional Beach Boys keyboardist Daryl "Rumbo" Dragon of the Captain and Tennille fame, Dennis was also the son of Carmen Dragon, conductor of the Glendale Symphony and a well-known studio engineer. But his Surf Punks became the lighthearted lightning rod for an aggressive sensibility from 1979 onward when they released three indie albums: *Surf Punks, My Beach,* and *Locals Only.* The music inspired a fanatical following among serious surf locals thanks to songs from *My Beach* (which sold more than fifty thousand copies in a year) such as "Punch Out at Malibu" and "Somebody Stole My Stick."

When the new shorter "sticks" became popular, shrinking below nine feet, to seven feet and then six feet or less, their sheer numbers in the water legitimized the quick turns and *aggro* tactics necessary to pilot them. Veterans knew that the sport of kings and sorcerers was getting violent. *Surfer* published "Some Rules of the Road" by Jim Kempton in 1979, ten basic tips for "cooperation, respect, and alert caution." It was heartbreaking for old-timers to see that somebody needed to be told to say "Leave me some room, please"—even after "inadvertently" dropping in.

And then came the "surf nazis," a new breed of bullyboys—complete with swastikas stenciled on their beach haunts. Spreading out of the South Bay, surf nazis were described by surfers at El Porto, an unincorporated stretch of Los Angeles County shoreline between El Segundo and Manhattan Beach, as "cutthroats who will cut you off and do anything for a wave. Anything."

In 1980 the Surf Punks played a concert in Ventura County where they themselves became the brunt of localists who denounced them as "Southers," the audience antagonists also braying that they should "go back to Malibu!" After the unruly show, the band's car was rammed by a bus.

In March 1980 the Beach Boys released *Keepin' the Summer Alive,* an album produced entirely by Bruce Johnston that generated a number 75 single with "Goin' On."

But Buddy Wilson could not go on. Living alone at 1040 West Sixty-eighth Street, a brisk stroll from the first proper dwelling his wife and kids had inhabited within the Los Angeles city limits, he had become increasingly incapacitated by heart disease. With no one disposed to care for him on a constant basis, Buddy had entered the Southwest Convalescent Center on Cerise Avenue in Hawthorne, and on May 29, 1981, he died there of coronary arrest at the age of ninety-one. His son Douglas "Skeeter" Wilson, then living in Encinitas, made preparations for Buddy's unembalmed remains to be burned at the Harbor Lawn Crematory in Costa Mesa. William Coral Wilson's ashes were scattered at sea by the Neptune Society. A life of restless scuffling and bitter frustration begun in a Kansas cradle in February 1890, back when Benjamin Harrison was in the White House and Los Angeles was a town of only 50,000 citizens, was finally at a close.

W ith his wife and children out of his life, and his brothers, cousins, and friends in the Beach Boys' extended family more and more estranged from one another, Brian Douglas Wilson, now forty-three, had nobody to look after him, either.

Having been brought back into the public's consciousness, Brian was indispensable to the Beach Boys' future viability as a force in popular music and the entertainment industry, a point always underscored by the weak showings of records that lacked his full vision. *Ten Years of Harmony (1970–1980),* a holding-pattern anthology, languished at number 156; Mike Love's *Looking Back with Love* solo outing, produced by Curt Boettcher for Boardwalk Records, did not chart; and *Youngblood,* Carl's second solo album, also never charted in *Billboard.*

But the balance of power in the Beach Boys had irrevocably shifted, and it was now a voting bloc of members that decided all artistic and business issues. No one wanted a return to the autocratic studio fiats of Brian's heyday, where what he said and felt and sang was law. They just wanted him healthy. And they also wanted him happy, although they were too unhappy themselves to know how that might be accomplished. Most of all, they wanted him under control . . . either their own or that of somebody paid to assume the task.

Since 1976, when Dr. Landy left the Beach Boys' employ, Brian had been under the care of a host of doctors, psychiatrists, and psychiatric nurses, each of whom kept him in reasonable health but none of whom could compensate for the essential emptiness of his personal life, and none of whom were willing or qualified to play the role of disciplinarian. Indeed, Brian hadn't had such a figure in his life since his father, Murry, and when Murry died in 1973 the trauma of that unresolved filial power struggle had plunged Brian into a bedridden, drug-addled depression from which he had yet to recover.

Audree, who was herself in delicate health, was getting too old to look after her son, and his brothers did not want to share a roof with him. Someone had to be found to keep him well and also useful to the Beach Boys' enterprise, someone who would enforce a strict system of rules.

Lacking a willingness to look for fresh candidates, the thoroughly exasperated Beach Boys and their advisors, who now included new manager Tom Hulett of the Concerts West organization, decided to re-trace their steps and approach the therapist whose professional modus was an avowed "twenty-four-hour" regimen. As this psychologist had asserted in his published paper on his technique, he aimed to develop total control of the patient's life, adding that "most people outside of the patient's circle are fearful of such a person upon whom so much dependency is placed and who exercises extreme control."

These were also the reasons that Brian and the people within his family circle had been fearful of Murry Wilson.

24
• • • •
What's Wrong

Whoa, Brian!" yelled a grinning, sunglass-adorned black man from the passenger seat of a speeding yellow Ferrari as he called out in 1985 to a preoccupied jogger headed in the opposite direction. The big-boned runner responded with a small wave as he loped along the shoulder of Old Malibu Road, then his tanned, bearded face brightened with a slight grin as he picked up the pace on his daily six-mile jaunt. Only in Southern California could one encounter the cloistered likes of Stevie Wonder bidding good morning to rock-and-roll recluse Brian Wilson as each commenced another day of pop prominence.

Wilson, dressed in white shorts, windbreaker, and Nike sneakers, wore the glowering expression of one either lost in grievous reflection or rudely awakened from a protracted slumber as he pressed on. The sun intensified. Sweat appeared in droplets at the edges of his copper and gray whiskers. His freckled skin lost all its light wrinkles as it relaxed on his small, squarish countenance, and it was not difficult to see the features of an open, pained boy that still lurked behind time's abrasions on the man.

Several hundred yards to his left lay the Pacific, rolling and breaking with a mid-spring vigor. Brian's slack features stiffened again as a blustery ocean breeze raced up through the thick pockets of yellow gazanias and reddish purple rosea ice plants that coat the stepped Santa Monica Mountains rising on his right. Perched on a broad shell in the middle distance was the handsome campus of Pepperdine University, whose huge swimming pool and Nautilus-equipped gym Wilson used on a thrice-weekly basis. Thanks to athletic advisors kept on retainer, Brian was in sensational shape, perhaps the best since he had played third-string quarterback for the Hawthorne Cougars. As he leaned into the gradual incline and rounded a wide turn in the road, he began to sprint.

"At this rate you could break forty-seven minutes and set a new record," shouted Evan Landy, the twenty-three-year-old son of Brian's self-described "round-the-clock shrink" of the last two and a half years. "Go for it, Brian, go for it!" Sure enough, Brian hit his stride on the return trip and clocked in at forty-six minutes and forty-five seconds. Heading toward the guard gate in the Malibu colony, he walked back to his comfortable two-story beach house in a buoyant frame of mind.

Variously described as "manic depressive," a "paranoid schizophrenic," "mentally disturbed," or a "victim of drug-induced neurosis and/or psychosis," Brian had perhaps suffered most of all from what friend Van Dyke Parks called "an absence of unconditional love—love that had no contingencies, no hooks, no fine print, no exploitation in the subclauses."

"I always knew in my heart that exercise was where it was at," Brian enthused as he caught his breath, his eyes showing a curiously sad cast, "but I never had the guts to get out and do it until Dr. Landy came along and forced me to get the message. He initiates the times when I do it, but I'm all for it, you know. I *endorse* it.

"I've written seventy songs in the last two years, and I'm still roaring. And I'm really excited about the new Beach Boys album; we're just gonna call it *The Beach Boys,* 'cause we've had enough dumb titles in the last few years.

"You can't feel good about doing nothing. It's a fact of life," Brian said with finality as he pressed a buzzer on an intercom affixed to a high, blind redwood plank fence and then walked into a narrow courtyard leading to his rented house. He took the back porch steps two at a time and entered the kitchen with a sheepish flourish of his outstretched arms. Seated around the expansive cooking and eating areas were Chad, a rangy, wiry-haired psych student and part-time helpmate around the premises; Stephanie, a petite blond French woman in her early twenties who acted as cook and au pair; and Carlos Booker, a robust young man from New Jersey who worked, as did the rest of the staff, for Eugene Landy. Booker had been the "house manager" since Brian relocated here from a previous Malibu residence. Brian, who was never permitted to be alone, paid for all of them.

Each was introduced by Brian with the awkward overearnestness of a first-time cabin boss in a summer camp. Chad was helping Stephanie prepare a noon breakfast. Carlos was seated at the kitchen table, carefully cataloging the half-dozen shallow boxes containing neat rows of cassette tapes filled with takes of Brian's recent song demos.

Brian surveyed the activity with a faint air of wounded detachment. "Usually I do all the cooking," he said pensively, "but I got a late start this morning. I'll . . . I'll . . . make toast!" he announced. Then he turned and sauntered through the high-ceilinged, many-windowed white living room, magnificent views of sea and sky prominent on all sides, and ascended the stairs to his exercise room to peer into the mirror, surveying the gun-shy figure suspended there. *"Boy,"* he sighed sadly, his shoulders slumping; he decided against more exertion, excusing himself to wash up.

He crossed the hall to the master bedroom with its small patio over the beach and moved past the battered brass bed covered by a rainbow-patterned comforter, past a Los Angeles County Museum print from a Monet exhibit and a Celestial Arts poster-poem entitled "The Spectrum of Love," and into the bath, shutting the door behind him. The most prominent item on the second floor, firmly taped to Brian's valet, was a large sheet of paper on which a one-word note was written in bold capital letters: BEEPER!

A few minutes later the sound of a running shower could be heard, Brian's plaintive tenor raised above the rushing water: "Cover me, cover me, I'm looking for a lover who will come on in and cover me!"

Reappearing after a half-hour, humming the opening bars of "California Girls" to himself, Brian was wearing white canvas loafers, white chinos, and a blue and white Santa Monica souvenir T-shirt. He began popping slices of white bread into the toaster.

A fruit salad, a steaming bowl of eggs, and Brian's proud pillars of toast were set out on the dining room table beneath a large vintage portrait of the Beach Boys, circa 1963, an unpublished shot from the pictures taken for the *Surfer Girl* album jacket. As the food was being passed around, Brian called a halt and asked Carlos to "put on 'Blue.' "

"Huh?" said Carlos.

"Please put on 'Blue,' " Brian repeated. "Play it a little bit loud."

Carlos hesitated, knowing that there was no copy of *Blue*, Joni Mitchell's 1971 Reprise album, in the beach house.

"Nah," Brian corrected, "I mean 'Rhapsody in Blue.' It's my favorite. It sends me back to being a little boy, being a baby."

Asked about the BEEPER sign posted upstairs, he lifted his shirt to reveal the electronic beeper paging unit attached to his belt.

"I wear it every day, all day," he said, "in case we go somewhere and Dr. Landy wants to get in touch with us. He beeps us, and we go to a phone and call him."

Everyone else at the table adjusted his or her clothing to reveal similar beepers secreted on their persons, as if signifying membership in some fraternity. There was a sudden sensation of airlessness in the room.

"We have a house project going on," Brian volunteered. "We have a communal living situation my doctor set up, and it includes these staff members and me. I've been feeling pretty good. We're having a lot of fun. I get to bed around eleven-thirty every night, and I get up around ten. I usually make a little tea in the morning and relax for about a half-hour, and then I exercise. Then I try to write songs. I've become more stable; I'm not as radical. I don't take drugs like I used to. I'm much more refined."

After brunch, as the diners took their plates back into the kitchen and washed them (house rules), Brian began to ponder his adolescence aloud, drawing a conscious line of demarcation between his "tough" years (meaning his childhood) and his "great" years, which coincided with his senior year at Hawthorne High, and the independence his musical performances at school assemblies presaged.

"In my last year of school . . . I was *very* happy," he recalled haltingly. He crossed the sunroom of the beach house and seated himself in an overstuffed chair before a picture window that opened on a brick patio. In the distance a bevy of giggling children dodged the riplets on a sandbar. "I wouldn't say I was popular in school, but I was associated with popular people." He spoke with a tinge of awe mingled with befuddlement, as if uncertain he was delving into his own past or that of an old acquaintance.

"Anyhow, later on, when the Beach Boys got rolling, I started to become a little better on the chick circuit. It kinda got slowly developed. It wasn't something that overnight was *wow!*

"All these chicks—they were after Dennis! When we first got going, the chicks would stomp on our asses to get to Dennis behind the drums. *Den-nis! Den-nis!* And we'd watch the chicks run by. And then later on I began to get a reputation with the chicks, kind of as a lover boy kind of guy, but in a very subdued way. I was subtle, you know? I'm not like Dennis was. I'm not a real cocksman. I'm a subtler kind of guy. I do it all on the conversational level. I get across my thing by just talking."

How were things between him and his ex-wife? Was he in touch with their children?

"I never am," he declared flatly. "I hardly ever talk with them. They're living in Encino, in the San Fernando Valley. I'm going through a bachelor period in my life."

Brian decided to play "Male Ego," a bonus track on *The Beach Boys* CD that became the B-side to "Getcha Back," the first single from the album.

"Male Ego" was a ditty about mustering the courage to relate to women on an equal basis, creaky in its lyric content but without the juvenile traits of Brian's songs on *The Beach Boys Love You*. The jittery, huff-and-puff quality that ran through his singing on the last four studio LPs had abated, replaced by a quirky forthrightness that was disarming.

"These days," Brian said, "my themes are still love, mostly love—but adult love; a level of maturity, a higher level, a more refined kind of love."

Things weren't always so stable and reflective in Brian's corner of the world. When he initially moved to this house in January 1983, it was amid charges by his former nurse-companion, Carolyn Williams, that he had been "kidnapped" on January 16 from a hospital bed and "shanghaied" to Oahu. Williams asserted in a prepared statement that she was being evicted from Brian's old Malibu address, where she had been staying since April 1982, without Brian's knowledge or approval. At the Kahala Hilton in Honolulu, Wilson held a press conference in which he countered, "We are trying to get rid of her, yes, so that we can sell the house. It sure is weird."

Dr. Landy offered his own overview of the peculiar turmoil. "No one thought there was hope for Brian," said Landy, "but four people decided to take the shot anyhow: his brother Carl; Carl's manager, Jerry Schilling; Brian's lawyer, John Branca; and the Beach Boys' manager, Tom Hulett. They got together in January 1983, took Brian away from these other people, and called me. I said, 'There are certain conditions. I want him in a hospital first; I want to check the man out physically.' "

Brian weighed 320 pounds when he was admitted to Cedars-Sinai Hospital, and he was in a chemical daze from the recreational drugs he had been taking, as well as from the psychotropic drugs and antidepressants prescribed for him. According to Landy, Brian had been living on four steaks a day, along with a steady diet of cigarettes and alcohol. The obese Beach Boy was put on a biomedical diet of intravenous vitamins and entered a program of what Landy termed "heavy detox."

"We put Brian through every test imaginable to see what food allergies he had, the levels of medication in his bloodstream. This man was on so much shit! He had forty percent lung capacity and no liver!"

After two weeks Brian was flown to Hawaii with his doctors for another fourteen days of reorientation. In Los Angeles, Dr. Arnold Dahlke, the man who shared Landy's Westwood practice and helped him formulate his twenty-four-hour therapy, prepared a new living situation for Brian with a three-person staff that would be rotated every two months or so. Brian arrived in Hawaii on a Sunday. Monday morning, Landy suggested he and Brian take a walk.

"No, no, no," said the Beach Boy.

"How about a drive?"

"Okay."

The two men and the other doctors got into a rented Chrysler convertible and rode a quarter-mile to a beach.

"Let's go look at this pretty beach," said Landy, "then go to breakfast."

"Okay."

After a few minutes Landy motioned for Brian to follow him.

"How we gonna get to breakfast?" said Brian, unnerved.

"I'm gonna walk," said Landy. "It's only another quarter of a mile to the restaurant."

"How am I gonna get there?" said Brian, trembling. "I can't walk that."

"Well, we'll come back for you."

"You're . . . you're gonna *leave* me here!" said Brian.

"Unless you walk with us," Landy answered, nodding. "Or you can wait in the car."

Brian walked gingerly down the beach toward the coffee shop.

The year 1983 had been relatively quiet for the Beach Boys, the biggest excitement occurring just prior to the annual July Fourth Mall celebration in Washington, D.C., when Secretary of the Interior James Watt uninvited the band as headliners, opting for singer Wayne Newton. The Reagans were embarrassed by the uproar that attended the snub, presenting a mortified Watt with a mock trophy of a foot with a hole in it for shooting himself thusly. The Beach Boys were asked to pay a White House visit on July 17 and posed for photographers.

Privately, however, Brian remained wary of what he called "our Beach Boys–White House associations" and did not want to be seen as allied with the Reagan administration.

" 'Bipartisan' means you don't take sides," said Brian. "We have that image with the public. We're not known to America as either Democrats or Republicans. I just know we have a following and can draw a half-million people on a July Fourth."

Restlessness was another factor adding to the Beach Boys' malaise. Al Jardine had been a real, albeit under-recognized, asset, but lately he seemed more interested in ecology and movements to protect the California coastline, especially the areas around his Big Sur ranch, where he now lived with second wife Mary Ann. And when the frequent Wilson-Love squabbles escalated, Al usually sided with Mike.

Bruce Johnston had often accepted the role of mediator in such arguments but begged off as the internal turmoil worsened, the members fighting in public, sometimes on stage. Dennis, who was on unusually tense terms with all members of the group, had recently formed a romantic bond with Shawn Marie Love, Mike's alleged child by Shannon Ann Harris, whom Dennis had met through his own daughter, Jennifer. A casual friendship had evolved into ardor, and Shawn became pregnant, giving birth on September 3, 1982, to a son, whom Dennis named Gage Dennis Wilson. On July 28, 1983, Dennis and Shawn were married, a development that strained Dennis's brittle standoff with Mike Love to the breaking point. A mutual restraining order prohibited Mike and Dennis from provoking each other in or out of the spotlights.

With Dennis also undergoing financial difficulties that forced him to sell *Harmony*, his cherished sailboat, the youngest Wilson brother was at his lowest ebb, drinking excessively while being intermittently treated at St. John's Hospital for alcohol dependency under the name Charles Wilson. In his more lucid moments, Dennis had attempted to resume recording for his second solo album, *Bamboo*, which included the tracks "He's a Bum," "(I Found Myself in a) Wild Situation," and "Alone."

Five months after his latest marriage, on December 28, 1983, while diving off the boat slip in Marina del Rey where *Harmony* had formerly moored, the thirty-nine-year-old Dennis drowned in thirteen feet of fifty-eight-degree water. Dressed only in cut-off jeans and a face mask, he had been retrieving personal memorabilia that had fallen or been tossed off the *Harmony* during his tempestuous years of ownership. An autopsy showed he was legally drunk.

Shawn insisted on a burial at sea, the nineteen-year-old widow stating it had been Dennis's wish; a special dispensation was granted by the White House for funeral arrangements normally reserved for deceased naval personnel, and Dennis Carl Wilson was so interred.

The problem with Dennis," said Brian in 1985, shifting nervously on the couch in his Malibu house after his post-jog shower, "was that he was totally out of control. He had a little bit of a hassle with his wives, a divorce situation. He was married five times [including the two weddings to Karen Lamm], so he got clobbered in the divorce laws. So did I.

"Carlos told me there was a message on my answering machine at this other house down the street that we used to live at," he continued, his voice growing quieter. "I went in there, and this guy Jerry Schilling, who's Carl's manager, told me, 'I'm sorry to have to tell you that Dennis drowned.'

"I felt real *strange*. It's a weird feeling when you hear about a death in the family, a weird trip. It's not something you can really talk about or describe. I got tears after about half an hour. Then I saw it on the news and thought, 'Oh, God, there he is, lying there dead.' I was blown out by the whole idea that he *drowned*, although I just let it lie; I didn't fuck with it, I didn't think too much about it. I let it lie.

"He and I were pretty good buddies," he said, rising slowly from the couch. "It pissed me off when he drowned because I felt I wasn't just losing a brother, I was losing a friend, and that compounded it even more."

Brian excused himself in a near-whisper and left the room.

Released in June 1985, *The Beach Boys*, the last album for CBS/Caribou, rose to number 52, the Boys' highest chart level in eight years, and it spawned one of the group's biggest singles in almost a decade, "Getcha Back."

Artistically, *The Beach Boys* was nearly as strong as *Sunflower*, the banners of its felicity being the harmonies, which had rarely been more smartly and adroitly lush, making one appreciate anew that there were no other voices that could duplicate that singular sound; the digital recording technology, which in the hands of Culture Club producer Steve Levine and engineer/programmer Julian Lindsay made the above refinements possible without cluttering the tracks for what had optimally been a consummate studio act; and Carl Wilson's singing. The exquisitely ominous "It's Gettin' Late," with its churchy, rippling vocal mesh, was a fitting vehicle for whole-souled lead singing redolent of his hearty candor on *Holland*. Indeed, there was such an embarrassment of vocal riches from Carl's quarter that it was difficult to overapplaud any one high point: "Maybe I Don't Know," "She Believes in Love Again," the tender "Where I Belong," and Stevie Wonder's "I Do Love You," Wonder himself furnishing much of the track's instrumentation.

Also enjoyable was "California Calling," a cooperative writing effort between Brian and Al Jardine on which former Beatle Ringo Starr played drums, and "Passing Friend," a song provided by Culture Club's Boy George and Roy Hay.

"I think there is a feeling with this album that we've crossed over into a new realm of well-being after a terribly trying and rocky time," said Carl in 1985. "And people are up to hear us. I got a charge out of the David Lee Roth hit with 'California Girls' [number 3 in March 1985, Carl doing backing vocals]. Ted Templeman [the former Harper's Bizarre band member who produced Roth's remake for Warner's] wondered if I'd be put off if he asked me to sing on the track, and I said, 'Hell no!'

"As for the Beach Boys, we're taking advantage of the most advanced recording technology once more—that was always a facet of the best stuff we've done in the past," Carl continued, noting that *The Beach Boys* album was the first recorded with the audiophile-friendly CD format in mind. "The digital approach is so new, and it can be quite tedious until you learn it. I was pleased for Brian and also for Alan that they dug in in England and later in Los Angeles and figured it all out with the help of Steve Levine and his partner, Julian Lindsay. Almost everything on the record was programmed note-for-note, sound-for-sound, beat-for-beat, and then we wouldn't hear it until we sent it through a computer."

Research into the digital technology that underlies the CD began at Bell Labs in the 1930s. Digital music recordings later aired on Japan's NHL broadcasting system, and Decca created digital recording for the BBC in 1969. Sony's head research scientist Heitaro Nakajima developed digital albums issued by Nippon/Columbia in the early 1970s, and in 1977 the Phillips company introduced the analog laser disc that could "read" audio and video information by means of a laser beam. In 1978, Sony agreed to merge its digital signal processing with Phillips's optical disc expertise to conceive the compact disc. A twelve-inch format capable of holding thirteen hours of music was rejected in favor of a twelve-centimeter size with a sixteen-bit sound resolution system. The final format was chosen, according to Heitaro Nakajima, because it could accommodate Beethoven's Ninth Symphony. On October 1, 1982, the first commercial CD was introduced in Japan: Billy Joel's *52nd Street* album. In September 1984, the first CD manufactured in the United States was Bruce Springsteen's *Born in the U.S.A.*

"In the Capitol days," said Bruce Johnston, "they had Duophonic sound, which was *bad* stereo. Brian took us to a new high aurally with *Pet Sounds,* and then we had a breakthrough with *Sunflower. The Beach Boys* is a new chapter, a marriage of the Beach Boys' vocabulary with the playing and arranging of the 1980s."

"It was both a pleasure and a nightmare," added producer Steve Levine, regarding the instruction in digital programming the Beach Boys needed to employ the technology for their first CD release. "Like any group that's been around for so long, the Beach Boys are set in their ways. And, of course, they usually had Brian as their producer. The Fairlight synthesizer and all the rest was so alien to Brian and the group, but then it slowly began to dawn on them how enormous the potential was. The harmonies, particularly, are finally the idealized actualization of what we've had in our minds all these years when we think of the Beach Boys."

All that was missing was Dennis, yet his presence on *The Beach Boys* was haunting. "Getcha Back," for instance, opened with the lockstep snare pattern that the undexterous drummer made a badge on the band's earliest sound. "The snare drum on the record," said Carl, "was taped in the racquet ball court at the Century West Club in Los Angeles." Brian and Steve Levine had conspired to re-create Dennis's garage pounding as a subtle tribute. On the back sleeve of the LP and CD packaging was the inscription THIS ALBUM IS DEDICATED TO THE MEMORY OF OUR BELOVED BROTHER, COUSIN AND FRIEND.

"God, my mom had to beat them to let me in the group," Dennis admitted in 1977 during a lunch break at the Mexican restaurant across from Brother Studios. "She said, 'Come on, Brian, let him in, or it'll break his heart!' Mike and Brian went, 'Nah, we don't want him.' But then Brian softened up, gave me a hug, and said, 'Aww, what the hell.'

"Around the time when we put out the first live Beach Boys album we were doing a show with the striped shirts on and the whole bit, and I found myself totally gazing at Brian, thinking, 'This guy's my brother?' I was famous because some guy was beautiful, and I got the chance to play drums and sing with him and take part in this great ride.

"God," Dennis said, his eyes welling up, his voice choked with wistfulness and then with laughter as he wiped his tears away with his hand. "What a lucky fuckin' honor!"

The full participation of Brian on *The Beach Boys* was distinctive but ably integrated—and therefore more dignified than on recent former albums. He was responsible for five collaborative songs on *The Beach Boys,* and on three of those tracks his vocals were voluble yet oddly detached; the lyrics on "Crack at Your Love," "I'm So Lonely," and "It's Just a Matter of Time" simply didn't sound like Brian talking. The credits on the album sleeve held a strange and instructive revelation: Dr. Eugene Landy was listed as their cowriter.

Interviewed for *California* Magazine during the production of *The Beach Boys,* Landy was quoted as saying, "I'm practically a member of the band. . . . Brian's got the talent to make the music. . . . He's the creator. The other band members are just performers. So I'm the one who's making the album."

Shortly after lunch at Brian's house in Malibu, Landy arrived to check on his patient. Brian was in the den where he wrote, hunched at the

Schafer & Sons upright, drifting in and out of "I Dream of Jeannie with the Light Brown Hair" and then on to new melodies.

"Brian always plays that old chestnut when he's thinking out loud," said Landy, a short, thickset, balding man with a constant, eruptive laugh.

Landy and Wilson were an unlikely pair, the doctor still hyperkinetic and effusive to the point of obnoxiousness, while Brian remained a diffident man who lived for the most part in his head. Comparing the Brian Wilson of 1982 with the Brian of 1985, the decision made by Carl Wilson, Tom Hulett, and Jerry Schilling to rehire Landy might have helped save Brian's life—which is precisely what Carl and company hoped for. But now, two and a half years later, Landy was still on the job, and for all appearances to the Beach Boys, his presence could continue indefinitely. Landy's motives and ethics in serving as Brian's highly paid therapist and a gainful participant in Brian's songwriting and recording reputation were being called into question by the other members of the group.

In his Malibu den, Brian had his own question: Would someone like to hear a couple of his newest songs, compositions he had written entirely on his own?

Brian put on a pair of horn-rimmed glasses and began to sift through the sheet of lyrics on the piano easel, a flurry of titles flicking by: "I've Been Through This One Before," "The Lost Song," "What's Wrong with Starting Now," "Walking on Water," "A Bad Time Soon Forgotten," "Baby Let Your Hair Grow Long," "Black Widow," "Melt Away," "Wondering What You're Up To Now."

He settled on three songs—"Angel," "You," and "Water Builds Up." After another flourish of scattered chords, he began to play "Angel," a slow, piquant lament similar in texture to "Caroline No." "You" was another pungent ballad. "Water Builds Up" had the exuberant might of "You're So Good to Me" or, interestingly enough, "Break Away," the 1969 single Brian wrote with Murry. Perhaps not coincidentally, "Water" was a treatise on anger and how to manage it.

"I'm finally going to do a solo album," Brian boasted when he was finished playing. "I should have done one a long time ago, but I didn't have the confidence or the discipline. I was on too big of a bum trip.

"I'm gonna do it all myself, I think," he added. "I'm gonna do it all in the booth, by machine. I'm gonna use the new digital equipment they have now. I'm thinking of calling it *Nighttime*, which has always been the time of day I like best."

It would be a night to remember, and Seymour Stein, president of the Rock and Roll Hall of Fame and director of the Warner Bros. Records–distributed Sire label, wanted to share it with Lenny Waronker, now president of the Warner-Reprise organization. Shortly after the Hall of Fame's 1987 ceremonies for the second annual induction dinner, Stein visited Waronker to tell him how he had decided to sign Brian Wilson to a solo deal.

"I knew Brian was a shoo-in as an inductee when he became eligible in '88," Stein recounted a month after the ceremony in his typically breathless tone. "So I invited Brian to the dinner to let him see what it was like and to act as a presenter for the great songwriting team of Jerry Leiber and Mike Stoller ["Hound Dog," "On Broadway," "Jailhouse Rock"]. I spoke to Brian on the dais, and I said, 'My God, seeing how nervous you are is calming me down!'

"But Brian was so good, giving a speech and singing 'On Broadway,' that I ran to the phone in the Waldorf and called this friend of mine, Andy Paley, who was producing a record for me in England. 'You're not gonna believe who I just had the greatest conversation with!' I told Andy. 'I spoke with Brian Wilson!' "

Paley was a former Sire artist—he and brother Jonathan Paley had cut their 1978 *The Paley Brothers* album at the Beach Boys' Brother Studio—and a Beach Boys fanatic, so he gave Stein a flurry of obscure Brian Wilson data with which the Sire chief could impress the singer during the latter part of the Hall of Fame evening.

"And it did!" Stein said with a laugh. "We shook hands in the banquet hall, and several weeks later I went out to Malibu to sit in the little music room in Brian's house and listen to about sixty of his best songs, from which I chose eighteen. And as part of the written deal, I stipulated that someone be brought in to supervise Brian's time, and I appointed Andy Paley as that person."

Paley, who had produced two albums for Jonathan Richman and the Modern Lovers and played with acts as diverse as the Shangri-Las and the Patti Smith Group, immediately went to work with Brian—although a short break came in January 1988 when the Beach Boys were inducted, as expected, into the Rock and Roll Hall of Fame.

With or without Brian, the band had sustained a steady comeback since its twenty-fifth anniversary in 1986, doing well with a single produced by Terry Melcher that revamped the Mamas and the Papas' "California Dreamin' " and featured a twelve-string electric lead by Roger McGuinn. Also mustered were a TV special *(The Beach Boys: 25 Years Together)* and a Capitol anthology *(Made in the U.S.A.)* that was a choice cross-section of evergreens, recent hits such as "Getcha Back," and new material such as "Rock and Roll to the Rescue."

Carl was also in better humor, having remarried late in 1987, to Dean Martin's daughter Gina. (At their wedding Brian sang a song he wrote for the occasion, "Carl & Gina.") But the press had been savage toward the Boys as they rebounded, news of Brian's solo plans heightening insecurities among some members. Mike Love's prickly Hall of Fame acceptance speech was marbled with resentful remarks ("chickenshit!") toward perceived adversaries. Mike himself was the object of reproof for contributions to George Bush's campaign and the politically conservative Parents' Music Resource Center; and he had found no lasting marital partner, his matches in the 1980s with Sue Damon, Cathy Martinez, and Sharon Lee coming undone. Of all the Beach Boys, Mike remained the most outspoken—drawing return fire as a result—yet it was his relentless drive that had ensured the Boys beat the odds as rock relics, prodding them to tour and record.

Months after the Hall of Fame induction, the Beach Boys notched a number 1 hit with "Kokomo," a platinum single off the Elektra Records sound track to the Tom Cruise film *Cocktail.* Written by Mike, Terry Melcher, and John Phillips of the Mamas and the Papas, "Kokomo" was critically dismissed as escapist pop, but its public status as a party anthem helped the Boys' 1989 *Still Cruisin'* album go gold. *Cruisin'* was comprised of mostly Love-coauthored songs that the group had previously placed, partially at Mike's urging, in assorted films *(The Big Chill, Lethal Weapon 2, Troop Beverly Hills, Soul Man, Good Morning Vietnam)* that were aimed at young or nostalgic audiences.

By 1988 the Beach Boys bestrode a new summit as an SRO tour attraction, and Mike would canvass crowd members at each concert about their age range. Requesting a show of hands for those twenty-five years or older, half the throng regularly thrust their arms up. Inquiring how many were twenty-five or *younger,* the other half of the audience would leap to its feet with a giddy roar.

With Brian's solo record under way and some observers taking sides, there was a sense, though largely unspoken, that Brian Wilson was now in competition with the band he had formed.

"Besides evaluating material for Lenny and Seymour," Andy Paley explained early in 1988, "I could tell Brian if he was repeating himself in any of his stuff by incorporating some tiny thing from an obscure old tune. I kept him honest with himself as well as looking forward.

"We started recording about ten months ago, and after a while, when Brian realized I could play a number of instruments, we started jamming and then writing music together to flesh out the songs. Brian hasn't been around other musicians much for the last few years. He cloistered himself. In some ways that's okay, but it's also essential to have somebody to interact with to allow special human accidents to happen: an idea, an absentminded riff that clicks, a little piece of counter-melody."

"The idea of turning out just hits had been both hammered and programmed into Brian at an early age," said Waronker in the spring of 1988, "until he finally rebelled around the time of 'Good Vibrations' and adopted what I respectfully call an arts-and-crafts attitude. Unfortunately, the diminishing commercial reception to the latter work in the late sixties and early seventies, coupled with the self-destructive scene he descended into, inflicted hurts and aversions he still carries.

"When I confronted him with the suite concept, he was shocked, logically assuming the company would be hit-conscious—which is true. But while stuff like 'Surfer Girl' first spurred me into record production, it was the rest of his more expansive music that helped keep me there. I told Seymour that to *not* have Brian do one of the more experimental things he used to do before he went into hibernation would be, well, ridiculous. We compromised by confining the idea to just one extended-length song."

So Waronker began meeting informally with Brian and Andy as the ubiquitous Dr. Landy looked on, tossing out themes for an elongated piece. A notion Brian had for the aural purview of an urban Saturday— from children playing and people shopping to the bustle of weekend nightlife—was briefly explored and then discarded. Unusual musical genres were also nominated as raw material, from Hawaiian folk chants to American campfire songs and lullabies.

"Nothing jolted Brian," said Waronker, "and that's the depth of reaction it takes to capture his muse."

Finally, just before another appointed discussion with Paley and Brian at a restaurant in Brentwood, Waronker paused in a nearby bookstore. "I bought some coffee table movie books, which are my passion," he recalled, and he took them along to the meeting. As Brian and Paley leafed through the picture books, pausing at some stills from Howard Hawks's *Red River*, Waronker blurted out, "How about a cowboy song?"

"Give me a title!" Brian insisted.

"Rio Grande," Waronker replied, referring to the John Ford film classic.

"Hmmmm, Big River," said Brian to himself, according to Andy Paley. "That's a good place to start."

Work on the piece was slated to begin on October 1, 1987, the date, as it happened, of an L.A. earthquake and aftershocks that caused eight deaths and $350 million in property damage.

"For three days," said Brian, "we worked downstairs in my piano room."

"Both Brian and the tremors took some adjusting to," said Paley.

The result was a fanciful but quite affecting piece of rock impressionism, by turns grim and Zane Grey–like. "Rio Grande" worked as a dreamy delectus of cantina keyboards, bunkhouse harmonica, and the banjo of a forsaken frontier, regaling listeners during a journey through the Old West of the American imagination—and its wicked actualities, among them the Cherokee Trail of Tears.

The passage was fraught with hostile forces, flash storms, and unexpected pleasures (night-blooming jasmine, for one), but the mighty river loomed throughout as a symbol of redemption. "I wanted to go at my own pace with the solo album and find some spiritual release," said Brian in 1988. "The song reflects that."

With the most elaborate track in enviable shape, thoughts shifted to the refinement of the rest of the material. To ensure technical excellence in the CD age, Seymour and Lenny courted the knowhow of Russ Titelman, now a respected Warner Bros. staff producer. Titelman had made acclaimed LPs with Randy Newman, including *Good Old Boys* (1974), *Little Criminals* (1977, which yielded the number 2 hit "Short People"), and *Trouble in Paradise* (1983), besides producing records for James Taylor, Little Feat, Rickie Lee Jones, Chaka Khan, George Benson, and Steve Winwood—with whom Russ shared a Record of the Year Grammy Award in 1987 for Winwood's *Back in the High Life* album.

Titelman was excited about the quality of the songs Brian had amassed, as well as his willingness to work hard on multilayered tracks such as "Love and Mercy" and "There's So Many," for which Brian had to record vocally demanding interlocking overdubs. But Titelman was dismayed by the edict of isolation Landy had set down for Brian, whereby Landy would change studios every few weeks so Brian would not, in the words of one production staff member, "form any lasting new professional relationships." In all, eleven studios were used for *Brian Wilson.*

"He doesn't want to lose control over Brian," said Titelman in 1988 in reference to Landy. "He's had to give up some control of his patient and now is terrified of losing the rest."

Brian himself was dumbstruck one afternoon to see Andy Paley pick up a studio phone and call his mother. Brian confessed to Andy afterward that he hadn't talked with his own mother "in three years."

"Doctor Landy doesn't like me to be in touch with my family too much; he thinks it's unhealthy," Brian revealed one day in 1988 during a car ride with a studio guest that left him momentarily free from Landy's constant monitoring (although he still wore his beeper).

But while Landy was monitoring Brian, the office of the Attorney General of the State of California was monitoring Landy. On February 16, 1988, the state Attorney General's office, acting as attorneys for the executive officer of the state Psychology Examining Committee for the California Board of Medical Quality Assurance (BMQA), charged Landy with "illegally prescribing drugs" to Brian Wilson, "gross negligence" in unlawfully prescribing those drugs, and "gross negligence" in maintaining a dual relationship as "business manager, business advisor, executive producer, and co-songwriter with his patient while also serving as his therapist; in each of these instances [Landy] has been involved in a 'dual,' 'triple' or 'quadruple' relationship with his patient."

According to the formal accusation filed on behalf of the BMQA by the Attorney General of the State of California, between July 1982 and May 1983—a time during which Landy was being entrusted with helping Wilson through a period of what Landy had called "heavy detox" from Wilson's illicit drug habits—Landy himself had allegedly "prescribed, administered, and furnished drugs and controlled substances" to another patient, a female identified only as "R.G." The accusation further claimed that Landy himself used these substances, which included cocaine and amyl nitrate, as he allegedly engaged in sexual misconduct such as intercourse and forcible sex acts with the female patient under his treatment.

Although Landy steadfastly denied the allegations of cocaine and amyl nitrate use and sexual misconduct with female patient R.G., he did admit that he unlawfully administered drugs to Wilson. Landy and his attorney reached an agreement with the BMQA on February 14, 1989. Landy consented to surrendering his license to practice in the state, and the disputed accusations relating to sex and drug improprieties with patient R.G. were terminated. As part of the agreement Landy also conceded that he would make no application to seek his reinstatement to practice psychology in California for at least two years. In 1992, according to Deputy Attorney General Robert McKim Bell, Landy "requested the reinstatement of his revoked license from our client, the Board of Psychology. The board opposed the reinstatement request, and he ultimately dropped it."

As early as 1978, Audree Wilson was accusing Landy of being "exceedingly greedy" regarding his fees for treating Brian. Between 1983 and 1986, for instance, Landy and his team of assistants looked after Brian while sharing in his lifestyle for a fee of some $420,000 a year for these services.

According to Stan Love, "When Landy was brought back the second time to treat Brian, it was arranged that the Beach Boys would give one full road share of tour proceeds a month to cover the treatment [which then cost $200 an hour]. About two years later Landy came back and said he needed more money to treat Brian, but the Beach Boys didn't have more to give Landy, so Carl gave away 25 percent of Brian's publishing to Landy in order to cover the costs of perpetuating the Landy program. I have copies of all the papers that verify these contracts and agreements."

As the Sire-Reprise album, now titled *Brian Wilson,* developed into a viable project, both the family and the Warner's-appointed production staff grew outraged with Landy's behind-the-scenes behavior. Seymour Stein reached the point where he mistrusted certain communications purportedly from Brian, suspecting they actually represented the thoughts and directives of Landy.

On May 5, 1988, Stein received an unsigned letter sent from Landy's office fax machine that seemed to express Brian's concerns; it was insisted that Russ Titelman's coproduction citation be removed from the album credit for the song "Walkin' the Line." The reason given in the fax was that Brian had allegedly added new musical and vocal elements to the final track that made it sound more "expansive" and more "interacting."

Five days later Stein replied to the fax, and he sent his letter not to Brian but to Landy. Stein's "Dear Gene" letter was a scathing corporate memo that derided Landy's "use of sixty-four-thousand-dollar-words like interacting and expansive." Gathering steam in his denunciation, Stein mockingly wrote, "The end result, minus some Landyisms and catchphrases, read like what might have been a 1940s Freddy Bartholomew script for a B-grade movie, 'Young Thomas Edison.' I view this letter as the venting of frustration . . . to retain control of a project that has, to all intents and purposes, been completed but for the continued and mischievous meddling of a starry-eyed and somewhat greedy psychologist . . . attempting to place his stamp firmly on this Brian Wilson solo effort and in so doing gain some degree of credibility in a new field. . . . We have all just about had it with your behavior."

Throughout 1988, Landy found himself continually at odds with Stein, Lenny Waronker, and producers Titelman and Paley over proper professional credits for the recording. The Titelman-Paley team was particularly incensed when, after Wilson had composed songs in the studio by himself or with others, Landy would arrive with his companion, Alexandra Morgan, and quickly supply new lyrics to those songs.

As *Brian Wilson* neared its delivery deadline in order to make Sire-Reprise's July 1988 release, Landy angered Sire and Reprise executives by demanding certain additional co-writing credits for himself, while fighting to remove the production and authorship credits of others.

In Ground Control Studios in Santa Monica in the late spring of 1988, Brian played the final mix of the entire album for the production staff and visitors, saying he was overjoyed with it. A few hours later, after Brian had left the studio, Landy asked a visitor if he would be interested in hearing "our version, mine and Brian's" of the album, whereupon Landy played an alternate mix, heavily accented by strings and other intensely lush touches à la Murry Wilson. When Landy pressed the listener for a critical opinion, he was told the alternate mix sounded unreleasable, at which point a red-faced Landy immediately phoned Waronker's office in the visitor's presence and left the message that Waronker should go ahead and release "Russ's" version of the album.

Brian Wilson garnered rave reviews, but the album got only as far as number 54 in *Billboard*, though both its "Love and Mercy" and "Nighttime" singles did respectably saleswise. The album had cost Sire-Reprise approximately $1 million to finish, and the parent company spent handsomely on advertising and promotion. But critical acclaim had to share space in the international press with withering accounts of Landy's actions. Lenny Waronker and Seymour Stein both privately expressed the feeling that the negative association with the defrocked therapist had severely hurt Brian commercially.

Faced with the option of issuing a second solo album by Brian Wilson in collaboration with Landy, Sire-Reprise listened to and then rejected that record, titled *Sweet Insanity.*

Still, it was important to Landy to keep up appearances while treating Brian. On Monday, March 27, 1989, the same date on which the state official accepted the surrender of Landy's license for admittedly administering drugs illegally, Brian was scheduled for cosmetic facial surgery at Century City Hospital in Los Angeles, at first for the removal of some wrinkles but eventually for a full face-lift. But surgeon Stephen Zacks postponed the procedure due to his alarm at the amount of medication—including Inderal, a heart medication—that Brian was on, reportedly deciding not to proceed in the patient's present condition due to a drop in his heart rate. Brian told friends that the sudden removal from the strong psychotropic drugs was "horrible," saying he had "never felt so bad in his life." The face-lift was eventually performed on Thursday, March 30, 1989.

At the time Brian recorded his solo album, his personal business card listed not his Malibu home address but rather the office of his psychologist. Landy was no longer licensed to treat Brian, but according to family sources (some of whom had become involved in litigation concerning Brian's assets) Landy had managed since the late 1980s to consolidate ownership of Brian Wilson's contemporary creative output under an official corporate "partnership" dubbed Brains and Genius, in which, according to Landy, he and Brian split all proceeds equally. Landy said the title of the company was a deliberate misspelling: "It's really 'Brian and Gene,' but we decided to call it Brains and Genius because we're both dyslexic." (Asked later on if he was dyslexic, Brian answered, "No.")

When questioned late in 1991 about the future of his business relationship with Brian, Landy said Brains and Genius is "in the midst of being disassembled; Brian and I are in the process of going in separate directions" in order to "prove to the industry and his family that Brian is really well." Yet, the next moment, Landy said he envisioned future songwriting collaborations with Brian and revealed that they had also recently signed a new joint "development deal" for writing and producing records. Landy also alleged he was currently completing negotiations on a four-album contract for Brian with a label he would not disclose, adding, "We're about to go to a better deal than the one Brian had with Sire-Reprise." Brains and Genius's office facilities, then located in West Los Angeles, included a full recording studio.

Asserting his expertise in the area of recording, Landy told *Billboard* magazine in an interview taped on September 20, 1991: "I worked my way through school cutting records. I cut 'Eve of Destruction' with Barry McGuire—remember that? That was for Horizon Records; I was a producer on Horizon Records."

When Landy's comments appeared in print on October 5, 1991, songwriter-producer P. F. Sloan wrote a letter to *Billboard,* published in its November 2, 1991, issue under the headline THE BIG LIE:

> As composer and coproducer of the Barry McGuire record "Eve of Destruction" (No. 1 in *Billboard,* Sept. 25, 1965), I wish to make it clear to the record-buying public that Dr. Eugene Landy's claim to have coproduced the record with Steve Barri and Lou Adler is a big lie and a fabrication of his ego.
>
> I have never worked with Dr. Landy (Brian Wilson's so-called Svengali therapist). Who could possibly be fooled or impressed by his phony claims to any real talent?
>
> I hope this will set the record straight and that it in some way helps Brian Wilson.
>
> P. F. Sloan
> Los Angeles

Brains and Genius was set up to administer a host of prospective joint song publishing, record, film, real estate, and book deals. Among them was the purported 1991 memoir by Brian—in which Landy's role in his life was glorified and his family's denigrated—and for which Landy received one-third of the $250,000 royalty advance and co-owned the copyright through Brains and Genius. In October 1922, Mike Love questioned the legitimacy of the book and sued various parties involved in it for defamation. The suit was settled in February 1994 with a payment to Love, who issued a press release quoting Brian as having stated in sworn depositions that portions of the book were "absolute bullshit," "absolutely fiction," and "all garbage." (Months later, Carl Wilson and Audree Wilson also sued the book's publisher and Brian's former therapist for a reported $15 million.)

These matters also coincided with a lawsuit by Brian against A&M Records' Irving-Almo Publishing division and the law firm of Mitchell, Silverberg & Knupp of Los Angeles, charging fraud and malpractice in Murry Wilson's sale of the Sea of Tunes song catalog, for which Brian received nothing. According to Stan Love, "The desire for *more* money by Landy was why he prodded Brian to press the A&M suit." (Brian would receive a $10 millionsettlement in this dispute.)

In 1990 a number of suits and petitions were filed in Los Angeles Superior Court in support of the selection of a legal conservator for Brian Wilson, due to his alleged mental incapacity. Those filing notices included Stan Love, Carl Wilson, Audree Wilson, and Brian's daughters, Wendy and Carnie Wilson, all calling for the appointment of someone other than Landy to look after Brian. Family sources said the impetus for the conservatorship battle was the alleged redrafting in 1989 of Brian Wilson's will, in which Landy was named the chief beneficiary.

"That was the move that made me file my petition," said Stan Love in September 1991. "Two former employees of Landy's approached me about the will, and the attorneys for the Wilson family [Carl, Wendy, Carnie, Audree] now have signed affidavits from these former Landy employees in which they state that they saw a new will drafted by Landy in which Landy was going to get 70 percent of Brian's estate and publishing, with Landy's girlfriend Alexandra Morgan getting 10 percent and Brian's daughters each getting 10 percent. [One affidavit cites slightly different percentages.] The witnesses say in their affidavits that the will was being readied for Brian's signature."

Confronted with the allegations of a redrafted will in the fall of 1991, Landy at first demurred, saying, "Who needs to be fighting in family fights? I've never seen Brian's will; he's never told me. I've heard these same things, too. I don't think that Brian is going to tell anyone what's in his will." However, Landy expressed knowledge that some redrafting of the will did indeed take place. "That's something that he wrote a year or two ago, I guess, and put it—as I understand it—in his lawyer's safe."

"I think that Dr. Landy has *really* taken advantage, no question about it," Carnie Wilson told *Rolling Stone* in 1991. "When my dad has been off drugs, he's whispered in people's ears, like 'He's really got control of me.

I'm afraid to leave him. I'm afraid.' That will end soon. Because karma is the most powerful thing on earth, and the rat is going to get it. He is going to get it real good."

In a December 13, 1991, settlement in Santa Monica Superior Court over the conservatorship issue, Brian agreed to allow an independent conservator to be appointed to oversee his affairs. The settlement also forced a minimum of three years' separation of Landy from Wilson, restraining and enjoining them from "contacting with each other either directly or through intermediary(ies) in any manner whatsoever, including, but not limited to, by personal contact, telephone, print media, mail, facsimile, wire, computer, or C.B. radio or any other method now known or hereafter to be developed."

The court order by Judge Hiroshi Fujisaki also stipulated that "Brian Wilson and Eugene Landy are each restrained from directing any business of the other, whether financial, personal, or otherwise. Brian Wilson and Eugene Landy are each restrained from acting on behalf of the other in any capacity or for any purpose whatsoever. Brian Wilson and Eugene Landy shall immediately cease, withdraw from, and terminate all business and/or financial relationships with each other."

Back in Landy's office in 1985, during the day on which Brian held his Malibu luncheon/listening session for *The Beach Boys,* Landy had reaffirmed his determination to get Brian back on his feet, while also reasserting a doctrine of quasi-parental managerial control. "I'm the father who won't fuck him," Landy insisted. "And what I want for him nobody can say isn't good: I want him to be honest. I want him to be self-sufficient. I want him to be competent. The goal is to do without me."

Landy even contrasted the "freedom" for which he was preparing Brian with the parasitic songwriting relationship Murry Wilson had previously sought. Landy felt that when Brian's musical skills first emerged, Murry should have simply taken pride in his familial status as Brian's protector and been content with that. "It's amazing that Murry wasn't happy with what he had," Landy concluded in 1985. "You'd think he would have just been happy with what occurred. He had a once-in-a-lifetime situation."

As for Brian Wilson, he had been trapped in a *twice*-in-a-lifetime situation.

25

You Still Believe in Me

The evening program was called "East Meets West: The Musical Legacy of Both Coasts," and the artists invited to talk and perform their songs on March 14, 1994, at Manhattan's Algonquin Hotel included the Mamas and the Papas, Scott McKenzie of "San Francisco (Be Sure to Wear Flowers In Your Hair)" fame, and the former leader of the Rascals, Felix Cavaliere. What brought many in the audience to the latest symposium in the Songwriters Inside-Out series, however, was the chance to see Brian Wilson's face-to-face encounter with Ronnie Spector, ex-wife and vocal firebrand behind the high-walled sound of Brian's most storied musical rival.

"Gosh, there's Ronnie Spector, right in front of me!" Wilson exclaimed nervously as he took his place at the piano in the Oak Room, saying he was uncertain if he had ever before met the lead singer of the Ronettes.

"Once," Ronnie replied. "Twenty-one years ago. You wrote 'Don't Worry Baby' for me. I didn't know then I had so much to *worry* about,

Brian," Spector added, the audience chuckling at the droll reference to her difficult years with the legendary producer.

"It's true," she continued, recounting the "Don't Worry Baby" episode. "It was a follow-up to 'Be My Baby,' and you came running into Gold Star Studios and said, 'I wrote a great song for you!' But of course my ex-husband didn't do the writing on it, so . . ."

Is fate the justice of what could never be, or is it the fulfillment of the tests that had to come? According to William Ellery Channing, hero of fellow humanist Ralph Waldo Emerson and apostle of Unitarianism, "The ties of family and country were never intended to circumscribe the soul. If allowed to become exclusive, engrossing, clannish, so as to shut out the general claims of the human race, the highest end of Providence is frustrated, and home, instead of being the nursery, becomes the grave of the heart."

In the 1880s, the Sthole brothers and other Swedish congregants at the Emanuel Lutheran Church in Hutchinson, Kansas, would have understood the message in Channing's maxim and found solace in its benediction of their restless desires and curiosities. When William Henry Wilson died in 1948 on the wind-whipped tableland of the Great Plains, so distant from the sleepy corner of Meigs County, Ohio, from which he had set forth, there was an organist and two choristers at his memorial service whose hymns, "The Lord Is My Shepherd" and "Saved by Grace," indicated that they and the deceased's survivors knew the meaning of Channing's sentiment-free sermon.

One can depart from all things familiar and spend a lifetime traversing alien territory in search of knowledge, liberty, or the retracting shadow of satisfaction, yet there may be no greater accomplishment than finding and holding fast to the sum of one's better self. In the end, perhaps, we give nothing else, we leave nothing else, we have nothing else but the one innate thing with which we began.

And to say one possessed it still in the last ebb of life would be an astonishing thing. It would be the sound of "Don't Worry Baby," somehow softening an unlikely heart and thereby altering by tiny degrees the compass of a destiny. It would be the hope of "Saved by Grace," a prayer set to music in the belief that goodwill freely given is the greatest and most dependable mercy. It would be the ballad of America, the social experiment for which California became an ultimate destination and the Wilsons uneasy exemplars.

Truly, the Stholes and Korthofs, Loves and Rovells, Jardines and Johnstons, Wallichs and Sinatras, Ostins and Waronkers, Parkses and Paleys, Newmans and Titelmans, Alperts and Mosses, Berrys and Torrences, McGuinns and Roths, Handlers and Spectors, and dozens more had no inkling what a great latticework their lives would become. And when Paul McCartney and his wife of seven years, the former Linda Eastman, took their daughters Heather and Mary to meet Brian Wilson in Los Angeles in 1976, and the former Beatle laid a gentle hand on the back of the trembling Brian's neck to hug him close and say thanks for *Pet Sounds*, there seemed few remaining divergences that time could not correct.

Shawn Love Wilson, Dennis's widow, was a virtual outcast at the point she and their son Gage were left destitute by her new husband's death. She fought the Transamerica Occidental Life Insurance Co. for years afterward for the right to be included, along with Dennis's four children by previous marriages, in the disbursal of his million-dollar life insurance policy—while also battling with what had been diagnosed as inoperative stomach cancer. In an emotional decision in 1986, Shawn won her legal battle, a Los Angeles Superior Court jury deciding that she and her three-year-old son were entitled to a $400,000 death benefit. The insurance company also agreed to settle with Shawn for undisclosed terms in the "bad faith" phase of the trial. At last reports, her cancer was in remission, and she and her son had made a new beginning.

In March 1990, one year after the Berlin Wall was pulled down, more than seventeen thousand defense workers in Southern California lost their jobs as the Cold War joined the Space Race as modern anachronisms. The breakout of peace spelled the twilight of prosperity in Aerospace Alley, but since the Southland had been the derivation of new national industries since Glenn Martin built Southern California's first plane in 1909 in a former church in Santa Ana, residents trusted that the region's knowhow could be retooled in the service of high-tech products other than weaponry.

In surfing, Americans reclaimed dominance of the sport from the Australians, with Kim Mearig and Freida Zamba winning women's world championships in the 1980s, and Tommy Curren and Kelly Slater extending the U.S. run of men's championship titles into the 1990s. (Surfing made a further return to its popular roots in 1993 when Derek Ho became the first Hawaiian world champion.) Old-guard American fans were heartened by Curren's repeated title wins because Tommy learned to ride with the time-honored single-fin boards, rather than the ultra-rad triple-fin thrusters currently cramming Southland surf spots.

The waves had become so congested in areas like Huntington Beach that information highway–attuned surfers now relied on computer-generated forecasting services—which predicted surf conditions up to two weeks in advance—to avoid fin-lock in flaccid waters. Night surfing also became prevalent, Malibu's Surfrider Beach filling up even on moonless evenings with surfers who wore helmet-mounted headlights and wet suits with fluorescent markings.

On May 25, 1990, producer Gary Usher succumbed to cancer in Los Angeles at the age of fifty-one. Shortly before his death, Brian Wilson visited him. Together they sang songs they had written, and they held hands and wept.

Summer 1990 began with the reappearance on the charts of *Pet Sounds* as its compact disc release (with three bonus tracks) crowned the full-catalog appearance of the Beach Boys' Capitol-era albums in the CD format—each with additional unreleased cuts to please hardcore disciples.

June 1990 saw the release of "Problem Child," a rockabilly-pop Beach Boys single from the film of the same name about a youth's struggles to be adopted. Terry Melcher produced it for MCA Records.

On December 2, 1990, Charles L. Wilson, Buddy Wilson's baby brother, died in Hutchinson, Kansas, at the age of ninety-one and was buried in Section 2, Lot 160, Space A in Fairlawn Cemetery with a granite marker to note his passing.

On March 21, 1991, Leo Fender, whose mass-produced electric guitars gave surf rock and the Beach Boys their distinctive power, died in Fullerton, California, at the age of eighty-two. Afflicted with Parkinson's disease, Fender perished en route to the hospital after being discovered unconscious at his home. On July 11, 1991, Roger Christian died of kidney and liver failure in Tarzana, California. The coauthor of "Little Deuce Coupe" and "Shut Down" was sixty-seven.

On December 26, 1993, Garnet Sthole, Edith's brother, died at the age of ninety in Hutchinson and was also buried in Fairlawn Cemetery. Garnet was the last surviving family member to have bidden his sister good-bye and good fortune before she boarded the Santa Fe Scout with her children, bound for Southern California.

Much as Sunkist ads in the *Hutchinson News* once enticed William

Henry Wilson and his family tree to California and its citrus pleasures, Beach Boys songs licensed in the 1980s and '90s to Sunkist soft drinks ("Fun, Fun, Fun," "California Girls") enhanced a comparable proposition. Southwest Airlines, Nissan Vans, and General Motors of Canada also used the group's material to help encourage the public to accede to its wanderlust.

From Högsby parish, Smaland, Sweden, and from Holland, England and Scotland and Ireland's northern province of Ulster, across New York State, Ohio, Kansas, Minnesota, Louisiana, Illinois, and California, the descendants of the families that made up the Wilsons in the nineteenth and early twentieth centuries have become dispersed in great numbers.

For all the Wilsons who hailed from Hutchinson, there would be many more thriving elsewhere in Kansas as well as Phoenix, Arizona; Twin Falls, Idaho; Fayetteville, Arkansas; Jefferson City, Missouri; Roy, Utah; New Castle, Delaware; Wheeling, West Virginia; Wausau, Wisconsin; Detroit, Michigan; Pine View, Kentucky; Philadelphia, Pennsylvania, and numerous other large and small towns across the country. Among this wealth of Wilsons across the United States (and in Britain, too, where some had established new ties) there were many who did not know the range and modern renown of their own ancestry. Nonetheless, they often resembled William Henry, Buddy, Edith, Murry, and their various offspring to a remarkable degree.

In 1987 a group of scientists from Yale, MIT, and the University of Miami School of Medicine confirmed by means of molecular biology that a trait such as chronic depression can be genetically inherited. The findings were one more step in the ongoing investigation of heredity and the role it plays in determining the shared characteristics of a family tree. While many Wilsons have endured a legacy of melancholia, still more have restored their spirits with music. Up to the present there have been innumerable Wilson banjo pickers, harmonica players, mandolin strummers, guitarists, organists, pianists, fiddlers, whistlers, and singers.

Most notably, Carnie and Wendy Wilson formed a vocal trio in 1986 with childhood friend Chynna Phillips, daughter of John and Michelle Phillips of the Mamas and the Papas, and recorded two multi-platinum albums, *Wilson Phillips* (1990) and *Shadows and Light* (1992) that yielded six hit singles, including two number 1's: "Hold On" and "Release Me." In 1993, Carnie and Wendy Wilson issued a well-reviewed Christmas album whose single, "Hey Santa," was a strong seasonal pop release with its own unique flavor, and in 1994, Carnie Wilson and her father Brian released a duet of "Fantasy Is Reality"/"Bells of Madness," written by Brian, singer Sam Phillips, and bassist Rob Wasserman on Wasserman's acclaimed *Trios* album.

As for Brian and the Beach Boys, in 1992 the group released an album, *Summer in Paradise*, on its own Brother Entertainment label, the record coproduced by Terry Melcher and Mike Love (who was remarried on April 24, 1994, to Jacquelyn Piesen). And Matt Jardine, Al's percussionist son, now tours with the group, Matt's strong vocals also fortifying the high harmonies on "Hushabye," "Don't Worry Baby" and "Surfer Girl."

In 1993, Brian Wilson was reunited with Van Dyke Parks for a Warner Bros. album-in-progress called *Orange Crate Art,* consisting of Brian's vocal interpretations of Van Dyke's songs. The title track was a remarkable document, likely to be regarded as one of the most moving vocal arrangements Brian has ever recorded. (Brian and Van Dyke later entered the studio in July 1994 to collaborate in scoring George Gershwin's "Rhapsody in Blue" for choral harmonies.)

But the most important Beach Boys release of the last fifteen years was the assembly by archivist-producers Mark Linnett, David Leaf, and Andy Paley of *Good Vibrations—Thirty Years of the Beach Boys,* a five-CD boxed set of essential, rare, and unreleased sides that was issued by Capitol in 1994 to coincide with the group's thirtieth anniversary. With a thoroughness that incorporated requests gathered from fan clubs and serious collectors, Beach Boys historian David Leaf (author of the highly praised book *The Beach Boys and the California Myth)* and his two more technically oriented production cohorts constructed an ingenious recording schematic that ranged from basal recordings at Candix, Capitol, and Reprise, to the decisive few with CBS/Caribou, Brother, and Elektra.

Of 142 tracks amassed, an initial eighty covered the 1962–69 Capitol years. Most startling among these sides was the thirty admixed minutes from the unavailable *Smile* sessions—the most cohesive sampling of demos, fragments, inchoate productions, and finished tracks yet collated from that miscarried opus. While it was clear on the *Good Vibrations* treatise that Brian's self-critical reassessment of 1976 ("We got off on bags that just didn't fucking have any value for vocals") had validity in terms of the *Smile* material's structural conventions, the otherworldly tilt of these newly reunited experiments made it hard to listen to the thirteen-track portion of the boxed set and then heedlessly press onward; many critics and fans preferred to linger within the curious spell of the chimerical pop digression rather than return too hastily to the realm of accepted hit radio fare.

And while the half-hour cameo from *Smile* whetted the appetites of camp followers for a physically whole future release, Leaf held out dim hopes for that prospect, warning in the boxed set's sixty-page companion booklet that it was implausible to consummate a project that had never actually reached a conclusion: "As so many sessions from that era are incomplete, unpolished, or lost, it is impossible to construct a finished album."

The *Good Vibrations* set also contained thirty-three tracks spanning the early-to-mid-1970s Reprise era; the latter section featured four outtakes from *Sunflower* and two tender ballads ("It's Over Now" and "Still I Dream of It") from the still-unreleased "big band"–flavored *Adult Child* album. But the greatest delicacy of the boxed aural banquet was the twenty-four-track "Special Bonus CD" of previously unavailable alternate versions of Beach Boys classics, among them the original demo for "In My Room," shelved session takes of "God Only Knows," "Good Vibrations," "Wouldn't It Be Nice" and "California Girls," and the homespun, vocals-only harmony tapestries of pop motets like "Wendy" and "Hushabye." In each instance the unadorned evidence was that the Beach Boys were the prime vocal unit of their generation and among the most resourceful in the chronicles of American songcraft.

As a result of its shrewd archival prospecting and discriminating presentation—including clever use of a wealth of rare photos and memorabilia ensconced in an oblong case embossed with a photo reproduction of an antique balsa wood surfboard—*Good Vibrations* singlehandedly restored the Beach Boys' reputation. And it paved the way for Capitol's massive mid-1990s CD reissue of each original Beach Boys album in scrupulously remastered form.

In August 1994, Mo Ostin announced his departure as chief executive officer at Warner Records, and his hand-picked successor, Lenny Waronker, was offered the post. But in October 1994, Waronker (whose contract as president would expire in 1995) declined to become CEO, admitting his decision "will come as a shock to many people." Ostin's departure, and Waronker's reluctance to sign a new deal to lead the company, seemed to mark the twilight of an era for a uniquely nurturing label whose warmth toward its artists often gave it the aura of a family guild.

The Nelsons, a TV family that had once been so emblematic of the

Wilsons' hopes for themselves, was also passing into history. Harriet Nelson died in Laguna Beach, California, in October 1994; she had lost husband Ozzie in 1975 and son Ricky in 1985.

For all the future held as the Wilsons headed into the year 2000, there were some things beyond the family's reach. The house at 3701 West 119th Street in Hawthorne no longer existed. "It's all torn up and gone," Brian confided in 1994. "They put a highway through. I'll never forget that place." The legacy of Dennis Wilson, his life and his trying times, would also endure. The strongest memory that Scott Wilson, Denny's adopted son, would always have of his father was one that began under water. In his mind's eye Scott saw himself sinking into the darkness of the sea, helpless, losing his breath. Meanwhile, his father was diving, diving, finding nothing, and diving again. In a last frantic effort, Dennis dove once more, somehow bumping into his submerged little boy. Seizing Scott by the shoulders, Dennis and his son burst through the surface of water, back into the light.

What Scott recollected was the day as a child when his dad took him on an outing on California's Salton Sea; they had been test-driving a new speedboat when, without warning, its steering mechanism broke and the boat swerved violently, the force of the sudden turn sucking Scott out of his life jacket and plunging him into the sea. Scott Wilson was recalling how his father risked his own life to save him.

In times of loss, in times of thankfulness, in times of remembering, there is a certain prayer, thought to be British in origin, that is known to some of the Wilsons. Passed from kith to kin, it sustains them as well as summarizes the family's philosophy of life:

Give us, Lord, a bit o' sun
A bit o' work and a bit o' fun.
Give us in all the struggle and sputter
Our daily bread and a bit o' butter.
Give us health our keep to make
And a bit to spare for others' sake.
Give us, too, a bit o' song
And a tale and a book to help us along.
Give us, Lord, a chance to be
Our goodly best, brave, wise and free.
Our goodly best for ourselves and others
Till all men learn to live as brothers.

California Calling: Afterword and Acknowledgments

First and foremost, my thanks to Brian Wilson for his help on this book as well as for his generous cooperation in decades past for all my journalism preceding it for *Crawdaddy, Rolling Stone, Musician, The New York Times Magazine,* and numerous other publications. Brian made himself available for many personal and telephone interviews, including a half-dozen between 1984 and 1994 that were expressly for this project. Since 1975 he has repeatedly invited me into his homes, his work environments, and/or his private thoughts to share memories of childhood, adolescence, and adult peaks and valleys. In December 1975 for *Crawdaddy*, Brian granted me the first interview about his professional reemergence with the project that would become the *15 Big Ones* album, and he allowed me to spend considerable time with him early in 1976 for a two-part twenty-thousand-word story for the same magazine.

In the decades that followed I talked with Brian and the other Beach Boys (Carl Wilson, Dennis Wilson, Mike Love, Al Jardine, Bruce Johnston) on numerous occasions for a host of other articles on the band. On

the July 4 weekend of 1988—several weeks prior to its commercial release—Brian debuted his *Brian Wilson* solo record on my internationally
syndicated radio series for Westwood One Networks, and he gave me his
first prerelease print interview on the subject for *The New York Times
Magazine*.

Over the years many of the interviews I conducted with Brian were
arranged with the assistance of Dennis Wilson, with whom I became
acquainted during my years as managing editor of *Crawdaddy*. My professional relationship with Dennis Wilson was especially cordial, and it endured from 1975 until we fell out of touch late in 1982 after I had
resigned as a senior editor of *Rolling Stone* in order to pursue various book
and broadcasting projects. Dennis usually called at my home or office
whenever he was in Manhattan, and I did likewise when in L.A. We
sometimes got together over lunch in New York or L.A. to discuss the
Beach Boys at length, but often we just chatted on the phone about his
latest personal and professional experiences and his evolving perspective
on the group. Sometimes Dennis spoke in confidence; other times he
rambled on discursively and for the record about the substance of his
early life. Aspects of these latter conversations informed portions of the
book, particularly chapters seven to nine.

The sum impression gained from my talks with Dennis was that he
was a warm, poignantly troubled, but painfully honest man. An organic
point he repeatedly made that is threaded through this text is his belief
that he grew up largely alone, leading an existence whose searching
trajectory frequently extended beyond the bounds of his other brothers'
and friends' parochial movements and concerns. Dennis said that as a
boy he would come and go in his own household without the close
monitoring accorded Brian and Carl, and he felt it was because he somehow did not or could not inspire the caring and scrutiny that both his
siblings did. As a consequence Dennis sought a familial brand of interest,
acceptance, and even forgiveness in most of the attachments of his adult
sphere. By the time I first encountered Dennis in 1975, he had come to
acknowledge these sad truisms openly, identifying them as a source of
the hurt that became a permanent aspect of his spirit.

The aim of this book has been to gain a greater understanding of
Brian's, Dennis's, and the other Beach Boys' personal development, of its
deeply felt expression in their music, and of these matters' unique collateral relationship to the social and historical milieu from which the Beach
Boys sprang.

For the generational span of the Wilson family history, I am grateful primarily to Charles Wilson, younger brother of William Coral Wilson, and to Garnet Sthole, brother of Edith Sthole. My interviews with them, including discussions during my trip to Hutchinson, Kansas, in December 1986, were invaluably enlightening in terms of grasping the emotional and territorial sweep of the Wilson family saga. I am also grateful to other members of the Wilson and Love families for interviews and/or helpful responses to detailed research questions, most notably Mary Wilson Bell, Murry's sister; Milton Love and Stephen Love, Mike's father and brother; and Lois Wilson Murphy, a cousin of Charles Wilson, with whom I shared archival family documents after corresponding with her at Charlie's encouragement.

In terms of help in my genealogical research, I wish to thank Ted Rosvall of Rosvall's Royal Books, Falkoping, Sweden; Christopher Olsson, executive director of the Swedish Council of America; Lief Carlsson of the Emigrant Institute, Vaxjo, Sweden; Arlene H. Eakle of the Genealogical Institute, Salt Lake City, Utah; the American Genealogical Lending Library of Bountiful, Utah; the Irish Genealogical Office on Kildare Street in Dublin, Ireland; Minnesota researchers Paula K. Warren and Beatrice M. Ahl, and the Section of Vital Statistics Registration of the Minnesota Department of Health; Karen Werry of the Meigs County Genealogical Society; Denise O' Connor of the Renville County Genealogical Society; the National Archives Microfilm Publications of the Library of Congress; the Registrar-Recorders Office of Los Angeles County, California; Inglewood Park Cemetery of Inglewood, California; and Fairlawn Cemetery of Hutchinson, Kansas.

For in-depth historical information illuminating or paralleling the family histories I was researching, I wish to thank Connie Menninger, Marylou Anderson, Daniel Fitzgerald, Larry Jochims, and Sarah E. Judge of the Kansas State Historical Society; Marilyn Dean Mitchell, Jean Gaeddert, and Cheryl Canfield of the Hutchinson Public Library; Blaine Lamb of the California State Railway Museum Library; Joe Lyle of the Planning Department of Southern California Rapid Transit District; Richard D. Martin of the Peabody & Essex Museum; Meigs County Pioneer and Historical Society; Renville County Historical Society; Escondido Historical Society; Irene Kratzer of the Cardiff-by-the-Sea Chamber of Commerce; Mary E. Manley of Goodyear Tire and Rubber Company; D. W. Ramsey of the Wichita Public Library; Claire H. Peters of Sunkist Growers, Inc.; Dan McGinnis of Wham-O Co. in Pasadena, California; the

Northrop Corporation; Harriet K. Stamos of Revell Incorporated; Mattel Toys; Donna Luhrs of KTLA-TV; John Meyer of AiResearch/The Garrett Corporation; the Greater Hutchinson Chamber of Commerce; the Hawthorne Chamber of Commerce; Laura F. Brown of the Steamship Historical Society of America; Bank Wright of Mountain and Sea Publications; South Gate Chamber of Commerce; the Surfrider Foundation; the Malibu Chamber of Commerce; Tom Quintana of the City of Hawthorne Office of Public Information; the Huntington Beach Public Library; Steve Fjeldstein of the Huntington Beach Community Services Department; UCLA University Research Library; Orange County Genealogical Library; and Kathleen Shilkret of the Los Angeles Area Chamber of Commerce. I also thank Janet DiMartino, publications manager of the Los Angeles Area Chamber of Commerce, for assistance in obtaining permission to reprint the Chamber's 1929 motorists' map.

For permission to reprint historical photos, I wish to thank Janet Evander of the California Historical Society; Martha Ybarra of the Security Pacific National Bank Photograph Collection; Thomas D. Norris of the Kansas State Historical Society; Blaine Lamb of the California State Railway Museum Library; the History/Photo Collection of the Los Angeles Public Library; Kathy Flynn of the Peabody and Essex Museum, Salem, Massachusetts; the Bureau of Vital Statistics of the California State Department of Public Health, Sacramento, California; the Inglewood Chamber of Commerce; Capitol Records; A&M Records; Warner-Reprise Records; Charles Wilson; Dennis Wilson; Lois Wilson Murphy; Ed Roth; Simon and Lenny Waronker; Russ Titelman; the Timothy White Collection; and the Hawthorne Chamber of Commerce. Heartfelt thanks to Mark Summers for the fine illustration of William Coral Wilson.

My thanks to Charles Barker, Stein-Mason Studios, Boston, for extensive photographic services in the reshooting and technical restoration of many of the archival shots published here.

For information on surfing history I want to thank John Severson, Steve Pezman, and Steve Hawk of *Surfer* magazine as well as its many contributors over the years. My thanks to *Surfer* for permission to reprint early covers of their superb publication. I'm grateful also to various veteran surfers, including Larry Gordon and the late Dewey Weber, for insights into the backgrounds and techniques of the great early board makers. Gratitude also to Bob Brown of the Hobie Company; the United States Surfing Association; Ken Johnson of the International Surfing Festival; the United States Surfing Federation; and many others.

My thanks also to Petersen Publications and the editors of *Hot Rod*, especially Lee Kelly and Deborah A. Bailey, for sending me a wealth of information about hot rods in general as well as the magazine group's history. Of all the important figures in the world of hot rods and car customizing, none was more generous with his time, advice, and archival insights than Ed "Big Daddy" Roth, and I deeply appreciate the lengthy interviews he granted me and the rod and Rat Fink memorabilia he provided. Thanks also to Donnelly Simmons of the United States Auto Club, Earl "Mad Man" Muntz and Tee Vee Muntz for their help and cooperation.

In the world of skateboarding I'm especially thankful to Frank Nasworthy, Bob Baine, Stacy Peralta, and Ed Riggins and Kevin Thatcher of *Thrasher* magazine for their time, insights, and historical materials.

The chronicles of the leading Los Angeles–based record companies could not have been researched without the help of extensive interviews and assistance over the years from Simon Waronker (Liberty Records), Joe Smith (Capitol and Warner-Reprise), Mo Ostin (Warner-Reprise), Lenny Waronker (Liberty and Warner-Reprise), Herb Alpert and Jerry Moss (A&M Records), and Seymour Stein (Sire Records).

At Capitol my thanks also to marvelous Maureen O'Connor and Bob Bernstein, and to Sandy Friedman, Carol Ross, and Cheryl Ceretti at the Rogers and Cowan public relations agency for their enormous aid over the years with regard to the Beach Boys. For help during the Beach Boys years at CBS Records, a special thanks to Eliot Hubbard.

I'm also deeply grateful to Dick Dale, Dean Torrence, and Ry Cooder (all three of whom wrote for *Crawdaddy*) for their viewpoints over the years on surf music, skateboarding, Hawaiian culture, and related musical data. Thanks as well to Randy Newman and family, Van Dyke Parks, Russ Titelman, Andy Paley, Joni Mitchell, Bonnie Raitt, Lowell George, Jerry Garcia, Bob Weir, and James Taylor for personal insights over the years into behind-the-scenes operations within the Warner's artists roster. Much gratitude to Don Henley for his boyhood and early Eagles history, and the Texas-California connection. Gratitude also to Roger McGuinn for interviews during my Associated Press and *Crawdaddy* days on the early history of the Byrds. I am also grateful to the late Tom Hulett for information on management of the Beach Boys. Thanks to George and Olivia Harrison for helping verify various Beatles-era details.

I would also like to thank Stan Cornyn and Pete Johnson for their help in grasping the history of production, promotion, advertising, and creative services at Warner Bros. Records, including the label's developmental timeline, mammoth past release schedules, and innovations such as its irreverent *Rolling Stone* ads and *Circular* newsletter. Sincere thanks also to Steven Baker in A&R for his enthusiasm, diplomacy, archival advice, and wisdom concerning the overlap of surf culture and the footloose side of fine arts in Southern California. In Warner's publicity, my thanks also to Liz Beth Rosenberg, Alan Rosenberg, Donna Russo, and Karen Moss.

I extend a very special thanks as well to Bob Merlis, senior vice president and director of media relations for Warner Bros., and to Gene Sculatti, former editor in chief of *Waxpaper* (1976–79), Warner's famed promotional magazine. Bob and Gene are scholarly Beach Boys believers who furnished me from 1984 to 1994 with a steady stream of wonderfully instructive clippings on California culture.

Heartfelt thanks also to Howard Lander at *Billboard,* and Bill Flanagan and Mark Rowland of *Musician* magazine for much support, timely advice, and assistance. My thanks to Michael C. Koehn for the trusting loan of his Hawthorne High class yearbooks and the clippings he sent me.

Wherever the thoughts of certain figures in this book are described or characters are quoted in the text at distant historic points, the reader should be aware that this material was obtained from the reminiscences of the subjects themselves, their associates and contemporaries, or family members who shared their inherited information on what took place and/or what the principals told them had taken place. During interviews, people were continually asked what was recalled or passed down from the principals regarding their stated impressions, opinions, mindsets, and recollective expressions regarding past events.

Recording dates, session personnel and comments from studio logs that appear throughout the text have been corroborated whenever possible by checking the information against the actual notations found in decades worth of American Federation of Musicians (AFM) contract sheets, and in existing session reports from Western Recorders, Gold Star Recording Studios, and Warner Bros. Studios. Where such dates or details conflict with those formerly cited on liner notes or in published interviews, favor was given to the facts found in the contract sheets, since they were filled out and signed by the participants during the sessions. In cases of multiple demo/preliminary session dates, the one yielding the released track was cited. Quoted dialogue from recording sessions is transcribed directly from archival studio tapes of those conversations.

Military records for the Wilsons, including the enlistment and discharge papers of male family members who served in the U.S. armed forces during the span covered in the book, were obtained from the Kansas State Historical Society or other state and federal archives. Memories of family members regarding details of military service, battlefield engagements, etc., were corroborated whenever possible with the respective records of the various battalions and companies in which the soldiers served. The author is especially grateful for the assistance of Dan Fitzgerald of the Kansas State Historical Society, Sgt. Charles A. McHenry of Company C of the 339th Machine Gun Battalion, and the staff of the National Archives.

Court proceedings described in the text are derived primarily from the official transcripts of those proceedings, including depositions and declarations filed during the course of the cases. My sincere thanks to my attorney, Bruce C. Fishelman, and the offices of Stanbury, Fishelman and Levy for a solid decade of assistance in obtaining all available public court records for virtually every contract, case, and dispute filed in Los Angeles County that involved the principal figures in this book.

Many thanks to Calvin W. Torrance and Robert McKim Bell, deputy attorneys general of the State of California, for their kind help and assistance with regard to documents pertaining to the California Board of Psychology's investigation of Eugene Landy's professional practice in the state. Readers of this book should be aware that at the request of the Department of Justice of the State of California, portions of my past writings on Brian Wilson and the Beach Boys were entered, with a signed declaration, into the official record for the proceedings regarding the above investigation of Landy.

Among the most indispensable supporters of this project were respected Beach Boys historian David Leaf and his wife, Eva, herself a longtime friend and confidante of Brian Wilson's. David and Eva read every page of the manuscript and offered many excellent suggestions. David's personal and professional overview on Brian and the Beach Boys is an exceptional one, and his friendship as a fellow journalist and Beach Boys enthusiast has been uncommonly enriching. No true Beach Boys fan should be without Leaf's book, *The Beach Boys and the California Myth*, as well as the superb CD boxed set he coproduced and annotated, *Good Vibrations: Thirty Years of the Beach Boys*, and no devotee should miss the BBC-TV special on Brian, *I Just Wasn't Made for These Times*, directed by Don Was and organized and researched with Leaf's help.

Other fellow Beach Boys reporters who deserve special mention are Jules Siegel, Tom Nolan, Paul Williams, David Felton, Ken Barnes, Pete Fornatale, John Swenson, John Blair, Dominic Priore, Stephen J. McParland, Rob Burt, Neal Umphred, Ken Sharp, Scott Cohen, Edward Wincentsen, Brad Elliot, Billy Altman, Richard Cromelin, Jerry Lazar, Peter Reum, and John Milward.

Much gratitude to the Widener Library of Harvard University, the Boston Public Library, the Los Angeles Public Library, and the Hutchinson Public Library, wherein the author perused hundreds of books and articles pertaining to life from the late 1800s to 1994 in the United States, particularly Kansas, Ohio, Illinois, Minnesota, and of course California. The Widener Library was also helpful for inquiries into emigrant culture as it pertained to Sweden, Holland, Ireland, Scotland, and England as well. And a special thanks to Alex Von Hoffman of Harvard University for his support, research assistance, and advice.

Readers with suggestions or additional information deemed suitable for inclusion in future editions of the book are encouraged to write to the author in care of the publisher.

My thanks to Jim Stein, my agent, and to Owen Laster and Erica Spellman of the William Morris Agency, as well as Jim Silberman and Sonny Mehta for their early belief in this book.

Much thanks also to my patient and endlessly encouraging editor, Bill Strachan, as well as John Macrae III, Amy Hertz, and Raquel Jaramillo for their generous help and faith. I am enormously proud to be in my second decade as a Henry Holt and Company author.

There is a personal side to my interest in Southern California that transcends respect and admiration for the people whose stories are told here. My own family's relationship to the region is a modern but dynamic one, dating back to my older brother Doug's experiences while stationed in the late 1950s at Vandenberg Air Force Base near Lompoc in Santa Barbara County. Doug's vivid affection for Southern California was a delight to our family back in the tough old mill town of Paterson, New Jersey, and it galvanized the spirits of six siblings raised on the Mickey Mouse Club and *Walt Disney's Wonderful World of Color*. Similarly influential were Doug and my brother Denny's enthusiasms for hot rods (worked on in our garage) and pin-striping (a service Doug and Denny performed quite expertly throughout the neighborhood), which dovetailed with aeronautics (my father worked for Curtiss-Wright) and other speed- and style-oriented teenage passions of the Jet Age.

When my dad died of a heart attack in 1964 at the age of forty-eight —shortly after having moved the family to the suburb of Montclair, New Jersey—my mother suddenly found herself raising five school-age children on her bookkeeper's salary (albeit supplemented with assistance from my two eldest brothers). Underscoring this responsibility was the realization that she had never traveled anywhere outside the state— other than Washington, D.C., during her honeymoon—and neither had most of her children.

Stirred by Doug's fond anecdotes of the Pacific Rim and recollections of her late husband's own vows to relocate us there, my mom ultimately spread a map on the dining room table, chose the temperate port city of San Diego as our destination, sold off our big old house on Grove Street, and moved the brood west in 1971.

Although I was away in college at Fordham in the Bronx, my proper home was soon a world away in Point Loma and later in Pacific Beach. The novelty of this shift was offset by the initial culture shock, but watching the renewal, however bumpy in spots, that my family underwent during the 1970s by virtue of its exposure to the welcoming vitality of Southern California was wonderfully heartening. And my youngest brother Davy's adolescence as an avid blond surfer was an engaging reminder of Doug's earlier stints as a surfer on pinstriped hardwood boards in the Southland during his years in the service.

The first record I ever purchased with my own money was "Surfer Girl," bought in the autumn of 1963 with cash from my afterschool job as a soda jerk at a local drive-in. But I never fully appreciated the Beach Boys' milieu until it actually became a part of my own heritage. Thus, *The Nearest Faraway Place* also describes an indelible province in my own mind and heart.

Finally, my humble appreciation to my loving wife, Judy, whose belief, understanding, and tender reinforcement made this endeavor possible. I hope our sons will grow up to be Beach Boys fans, too.

Bibliography

Maps

Atchison, Topeka and Santa Fe Railway System, 1922. Courtesy of the Manuscripts Department, Kansas State Historical Society.

Automobile Club of Southern California. *Street Map of Central and Western Area, Metropolitan Los Angeles.*

Bartholomew, John C., ed. *The New York Times Atlas of the World, in Collaboration with* The Times *of London.* New York: Times Books, 1983.

California Coastal Access Commission. *California Coastal Access Guide.* Los Angeles: University of California Press, 1982.

Cardiff-by-the-Sea Chamber of Commerce. *Cardiff-by-the-Sea.* San Diego: Hart Enterprises, 1989.

Greater Hutchinson Chamber of Commerce. *Hutchinson, the Best of Kansas, Map/Brochure.*

Los Angeles Area Chamber of Commerce. *Los Angeles Motorists' Map,* 1929.

Hawthorne Chamber of Commerce. *Hawthorne City Map and Guide.* Santa Fe Springs, Calif.: Chambers Publishing Co., 1980.

National Geographic Society. *Coastal California.* Washington, D.C.: National Geographic Society, 1993.

———. *Southwest, U.S.A.* Washington D.C.: National Geographic Society, 1992.

Rand McNally & Co. *California.* Deluxe Edition. Rand McNally Map Services Co., 1991.

———. *Greater Los Angeles Freeway System.* Rand McNally Map Services Co., 1991.

Santa Monica Convention and Visitors Bureau. *Santa Monica Visitors Map.* Santa Monica, Calif.: Graham, Silberg, Sugarman, 1990.

Skvaril, Joseph. *A Visual Perspective of Greater Los Angeles and Downtown Civic Center.* Edmonton, Alberta, Canada: World Vision Design, Ltd., 1984.

Books

One of the challenges of this project was confirming the reliability of details preserved in memory, often across a lifetime. Among the books that were particularly helpful in verifying the accumulated knowledge, perceptions, reminiscences, and reflections of the people in this text were the following:

Ainsworth, Ed. *Journey with the Sun: The Story of Citrus in its Western Pilgrimage.* Los Angeles: Sunkist Growers, Inc.

Anderson, Fred. *Northrop, an Aeronautical History: A Commemorative Edition of Airplane Designs and Concepts.* Century City, Calif.: Northrop Corp., 1976.

Armitage, Merle. *Homage to the Santa Fe.* Yucca Valley, Calif.: Manzanita Press, 1960.

———. *Operations Santa Fe.* New York, 1948.

Atchison, Topeka and Santa Fe Railway Company. *Twentieth Annual Report, 1922: Fiscal Year Ending December 31, 1922.*

Atherton, Gertrude. *California, an Intimate History.* Freeport, N.Y.: Books for Libraries Press, 1914.

Bacon, Tony. *The Ultimate Guitar Book.* New York: Alfred A. Knopf, 1991.

Bacon, Tony, and Paul Day. *The Fender Book.* San Francisco: Miller Freeman, Inc., 1992.

Bakker, Elna. *An Island Called California: An Ecological Introduction to Its Natural Communities*. Los Angeles: University of California Press, 1984.

Balfour, Victoria. *Rock Wives: The Hard Lives and Good Times of the Wives, Girlfriends, and Groupies of Rock and Roll*. New York: Beech Tree/Quill, 1986.

Ball, John H. *Surf Riders of California*. Los Angeles: Norman Whale, 1947.

Banham, Reyner. *Los Angeles: The Architecture of Four Ecologies*. Baltimore: Penguin Books, 1973.

Bascom, Willard. *Waves and Beaches*. Garden City, N.Y.: Anchor Books, 1980.

Bayler, Stephen. *Harley Earl and the Dream Machine*. New York: Alfred A. Knopf, 1983.

Bean, Walton, and James J. Rawls. *California, an Interpretive History*. New York: McGraw-Hill, 1983.

Betrock, Alan. *The I Was a Teenage Juvenile Delinquent Rock n' Roll Horror Beach Party Movie Book, A Complete Guide to the Teen Exploitation Film: 1954–1969*. New York: St. Martin's Press, 1986.

Birmingham, Stephen. *California Rich*. New York: Simon & Schuster, 1980.

Blaine, Hal, and David Goggin. *Hal Blaine and the Wrecking Crew*. Emeryville, Calif.: MixBooks/Act III Publishing, 1990.

Blair, John. *The Illustrated Discography of Surf Music 1961–1965*. Rev. Ed. Ann Arbor, Mich.: Pierian Press, 1985.

Blair, John, and Stephen J. McParland. *The Illustrated Discography of Hot Rod Music 1961–1965*. Ann Arbor, Mich.: Popular Culture Ink, 1990.

Blake, Peter. *God's Own Junkyard*. New York: Holt, Rinehart & Winston, 1964.

Blake, Thomas Edward. *Hawaiian Surfriding: The Ancient and Royal Pastime*. Flagstaff, Ariz.: Northland Press, 1961.

Blake, Tom. *Hawaiian Surfriders, 1935*. Redondo Beach, Calif.: Mountain & Sea, 1983.

Boorstin, Daniel J. *The Americans: The Democratic Experience*. New York: Vintage Books, 1974.

Bottles, Scott L. *Los Angeles and the Automobile: The Making of the Modern City*. Los Angeles: University of California Press, 1987.

Bowers, Darius N. *Seventy Years in Norton County, Kansas, 1987–1942*. Norton, Kans.: Norton County Champion, 1942.

Boy, Billy. *Barbie, Her Life and Times.* New York: Crown Publishers, 1987.

Boyne, Walter J. *The Leading Edge.* New York: Stewart, Tabori & Chang, 1986.

Brodsly, David. *L.A. Freeway, an Appreciative Essay.* Los Angeles: University of California Press, 1983.

Bryant, Keith L. Jr. *History of the Atchison, Topeka and Santa Fe Railway.* Lincoln, Nebr.: University of Nebraska Press (year unknown).

Bugliosi, Vincent, with Curt Gentry. *Helter Skelter: The True Story of the Manson Murders.* New York: Bantam, 1975.

Burt, Rob. *Surf City, Drag City.* New York: Sterling Publishing, 1986.

California Historical Society. *Los Angeles, 1781–1981.* Los Angeles, 1981.

California Magazine. *The Best of California.* Santa Barbara, Calif.: Capra Press, 1986.

Caughey, John and LaRee. *Los Angeles: Biography of a City.* Los Angeles: University of California Press, 1976.

Caughey, John, and Norris Hundley. *California: History of a Remarkable State.* Englewood Cliffs, N.J.: Prentice-Hall, Inc., 1982.

Clarke, Charlotte Bringle. *Edible and Useful Plants of California.* Los Angeles: University of California Press, 1977.

Claxton, William, and Hitoshi Namekata. *Jazz West Coast: Artwork of Pacific Jazz Records.* Tokyo: Bijutsu Shuppa-Sha, Ltd., 1992.

Consumer Reports Editors. *I'll Buy That: 50 Small Wonders and Big Deals That Revolutionized the Lives of Consumers.* Mount Vernon, N.Y.: Consumers Union, 1986.

Conway, John. *Surfing.* Harrisburg, Pa.: Stackpole Books, 1988.

Crump, Spencer. *Ride the Big Red Cars: The Pacific Electric Story.* Glendale, Calif.: Interurban Press, 1983.

Dalley, Robert J. *Surfin' Guitars: Instrumental Surf Bands of the Sixties.* West Jordan, Utah: Surf Publications, 1988.

Darey, David. *True Tales of Old-Time Kansas.* Lawrence, Kans.: University Press of Kansas, 1984.

———. *Entrepreneurs of the Old West.* New York: Alfred A. Knopf, 1986.

Davis, Genevieve. *Beverly Hills: An Illustrated History.* Northridge, Calif.: Windsor Publications, 1988.

Davis, J. Allen. *The Friend to All Motorists: The Story of the Automobile Club of Southern California, 1900–1965.* Los Angeles: Automobile Club of Southern California, 1967.

Diskin, Steve, and Joseph Giovannini. *Los Angeles at 25 MPH*. New York: Van Nostrand Reinhold, 1993.

Dixon, Peter L. *The Complete Book of Surfing*. New York: Coward, McCann & Geoghegan, 1967.

Dunlop, Carol. *California People*. Salt Lake City, Utah: Gibbs M. Smith, 1982.

Edwards, Phil. *You Should Have Been Here an Hour Ago: The Stoked Side of Surfing*. New York: Harper & Row, 1967.

Eliot, Marc. *Walt Disney: Hollywood's Dark Prince*. New York: Birch Lane Press, 1993.

Elliot, Brad. *Surf's Up! The Beach Boys on Record, 1961–1981*. Ann Arbor, Mich.: Pierian Press, 1982.

Emrich, Duncan. *Folklore on the American Land*. Boston: Little, Brown, 1972.

Farmer Cooperative Service. *The Sunkist Adventure*. Washington, D.C.: U.S. Department of Agriculture/U.S. Government Printing Office, 1975.

Federal Writers Project. *The WPA Guide to California*. New York: Random House/Pantheon, 1984. (Originally published in 1939 by Books, Inc., as *California: A Guide to the Golden State*.)

Fein, Art. *The L.A. Musical History Tour: A Guide to the Rock and Roll Landmarks of Los Angeles*. Boston: Faber and Faber, 1990.

Furnas, J. C. *The Americans: A Social History of the United States 1587–1914*. New York: G. P. Putnam, 1969.

Gaines, Steven. *Heroes and Villains: The True Story of the Beach Boys*. New York: Signet Books, 1987, pp. 280–81.

Gebhard, David, and Robert Winter. *Architecture in Los Angeles: A Complete Guide*. Salt Lake City, Utah: Gibbs M. Smith Inc./Peregrine Smith Books, 1985.

———. *L.A. in the Thirties*. Salt Lake City, Utah: Peregrine Smith, 1975.

Gillett, Charlie. *The Sound of the City*. New York: Pantheon Books, New Revised American Edition, 1983.

Giola, Ted. *West Coast Jazz: Modern Jazz in California, 1945–1960*. New York: Oxford University Press, 1992.

Gold, Jeffrey, and David Leaf, eds. *A&M Records: The First 25 Years*. Hollywood, Calif.: A&M Records, Inc., 1987.

Gordon, Robert. *Jazz West Coast: The Los Angeles Jazz Scene of the 1950s*. London: Quartet Books, 1986.

Gregory, James N. *American Exodus: The Dust Bowl Migration and Okie Culture in California.* New York: Oxford University Press, 1989.

Grein, Paul, ed. *Capitol Records: Fiftieth Anniversary, 1942–1992.* Hollywood, Calif.: Capitol Records, Inc., 1992.

Grenier, Judson A., ed. *A Guide to Historic Places in Los Angeles County.* Dubuque, Iowa: Kendall/Hunt Publishing, 1978.

Halberstam, David. *The Powers That Be.* New York: Alfred A. Knopf, 1979.

Hanna, Phil Townsend. *The Dictionary of California Names.* Los Angeles: Automobile Club of Southern California, 1946.

Hart, James D. *A Companion to California.* Los Angeles: University of California Press, 1987.

Hartman, Robert S. *History of Hawthorne.* Hawthorne, Calif.: Hawthorne Chamber of Commerce, 1972.

Heimann, Jim; Rip Georges; and David Gebhard. *California Crazy.* San Francisco: Chronicle Books, 1980.

Henstell, Bruce. *Sunshine and Wealth: Los Angeles in the Twenties and Thirties.* San Francisco: Chronicle Books, 1984.

Hess, Alan. *Googie: Fifties Coffee Shop Architecture.* San Francisco: Chronicle Books, 1985.

Highland, Monica. *Greetings from Southern California.* Portland, Oreg.: Graphic Arts Center.

Hill, Peter and Stephen. *Skate Hard.* Fitzroy, Victoria, Australia: The Five Mile Press, 1988.

Hoover, Mildred Brooke. *Historic Spots in California: Counties of the Coastal Range.* Stanford, Calif.: Stanford University Press, 1937.

Ikuta, Yasutoshi. *Cruise-O-Matic: Automobile Advertising of the 1950s.* San Francisco: Chronicle Books, 1988.

Jackson, Kenneth T. *Crabgrass Frontier: The Suburbanization of the United States.* New York: Oxford University Press, 1985.

Jones, Harvey J. *Mathews: Masterpieces of the Decorative Style.* Layton, Utah: Peregrine Smith Books, 1985.

Jurmain, Claudia K., and James J. Rawls, eds. *California: A Place, a People, a Dream.* San Francisco: Chronicle Books, 1986.

Kahrl, William L. *Water and Power.* Los Angeles: University of California, 1982.

Kaplan, Sam Hall. *L.A. Lost and Found: An Architectural History of Los Angeles.* New York: Crown Publishers, 1987.

Key, Mike, and Tony Thacker. London: Osprey Publishing Ltd., 1987.

Kirker, Harold. *California's Architectural Frontier: Style and Tradition in the 19th Century*. Salt Lake City, Utah: Gibbs M. Smith, 1986.

Kroc, Ray. *Grinding It Out: The Making of McDonald's*. New York: Berkley Publishing, 1977.

Langdon, Philip. *Orange Roofs, Golden Arches: The Architecture of the American Chain Restaurants*. New York: Alfred A. Knopf, 1986.

Leaf, David. *The Beach Boys and the California Myth*. Philadelphia: Courage Books/Running Press, 1985.

Lee, Martin A., and Bruce Shlain. *Acid Dreams: The CIA, LSD and the Sixties Rebellion*. New York: Grove Press, 1985.

Lencek, Lena, and Gideon Bosker. *Making Waves: Swimsuits and the Undressing of America*. San Francisco: Chronicle Books, 1989.

Levine, Lawrence W. *Highbrow—Lowbrow: The Emergence of Cultural Hierarchy in America*. Cambridge, Mass.: Harvard University Press, 1988.

Lewisohn, Mark. *The Beatles Recording Sessions: The Official Abbey Road Studio Session Notes, 1962–1970*. New York: Harmony Books, 1988.

———. *The Complete Beatles Chronicle*. New York: Harmony Books, 1992.

Liebs, Chester H. *Main Street to Miracle Mile: American Roadside Architecture*. Boston: Little, Brown, 1985.

London, Jack. *Learning Hawaiian Surfing: A Royal Sport at Waikiki Beach, Honolulu, 1907*. Honolulu: Boom Enterprises, 1983.

Lueras, Leonard. *Surfing: The Ultimate Pleasure*. New York: Workman Press, 1984.

McClelland, Gordon T., and Jay T. Last. *California Orange Box Labels: An Illustrated History*. Beverly Hills, Calif.: Hillcrest Press, 1985.

McDonough, Jack. *San Francisco Rock: The Illustrated History of San Francisco Rock Music*. San Francisco: Chronicle Books, 1985.

McMinn, Howard E., and Evelyn Maino. *An Illustrated Manual of Pacific Coast Trees*. Berkeley, Calif.: University of California Press, 1981.

McNeil, Alex. *Total Television*. New York: Viking/Penguin, 1984.

McParland, Stephen J. *The Wilson Project*. New South Wales, Australia: Fast Books, 1991.

McPhee, John. *Oranges*. New York: Farrar, Straus and Giroux, 1967.

Maddox, Ben. *The Photography of Max Yavno*. Berkeley, Calif.: University of California Press, 1981.

Makinson, Randell L. *Greene & Greene: Architecture as a Fine Art*. Salt Lake City, Utah: Gibbs M. Smith, 1977.

Malone, Bill. *Country Music U.S.A.* Austin, Tex.: University of Texas Press, 1985.

Manchester, William. *The Glory and the Dream: A Narrative History of America, 1932–1972.* New York: Bantam Books, 1975.

Marchand, Roland. *Advertising and the American Dream: Making Way for Modernity, 1920–1940.* Los Angeles: University of California Press, 1985.

Marquis, Alice Goldfarb. *Hopes and Ashes: The Birth of Modern Times.* New York: The Free Press, 1986.

Marsh, Graham, and Glyn Callingham, eds. *California Cool.* San Francisco: Chronicle Books, 1992.

Milward, John. *The Beach Boys Silver Anniversary.* Garden City, N.Y.: Doubleday/Dolphin Books, 1985.

Moore, Charles, Peter Becker, and Regula Campbell. *The City Observed: Los Angeles, a Guide to Its Architecture and Landscapes.* New York: Vintage Books, 1984.

Mosley, Leonard. *Disney's World.* New York: Stein and Day, 1985.

Mitchell, Pat. *The Fair City: Postcard Views, Hutchinson, Kansas.* Vols. 1 and 2. Topeka, Kans.: Josten's Publications, 1983.

Munz, Philip A. *Shore Wildflowers of California, Oregon and Washington.* Los Angeles: University of California Press, 1964.

O'Brien, Ed, and Scott P. Sayers, Jr. *Sinatra: The Man and His Music: The Recording Artistry of Francis Albert Sinatra—1939–1992.* Austin, Tex.: TSD Press, 1992.

Orbelian, George. *Essential Surfing.* San Francisco: Orbelian Arts, 1982.

O'Reilly, Maurice. *The Goodyear Story.* Elmsford, N.Y.: The Benjamin Company, 1983.

Osborne, Jerry, and Bruce Hamilton. *Popular Rock & Roll Records 1948–1978.* Phoenix, Ariz.: O'Sullivan, Woodside & Co., 1978.

Parker, Robert Miles. *L.A.* New York: Harcourt Brace Jovanovich, 1984.

Patton, Phil. *Open Road: A Celebration of the American Highway.* New York: Touchstone/Simon & Schuster, 1986.

Peck, Abe. *Uncovering the Sixties: The Life and Times of the Underground Press.* New York: Pantheon Books, 1985.

Pelissero, Ellen, and Stan Cornyn. *What a Long, Strange Trip It's Been (An Authorized History of Warner Brothers Records).* Burbank, Calif.: Unpublished, 1980.

Pierson, Robert John. *A Walker's Guide to L.A.'s Beach Communities.* San Francisco: Chronicle Books, 1985.

Poling-Kempes, Lesley. *The Harvey Girls, Women Who Opened the West.* New York: Paragon House, 1989.

Preiss, Byron. *The Beach Boys: The Authorized Biography of America's Greatest Rock and Roll Band.* New York: Ballantine Books, 1979.

Priore, Dominic. *Look! Listen! Vibrate! Smile!* Carlsbad, Calif.: Surfin' Colours Productions, 1989.

————. *The Dumb Angel Gazette* (#3, *Potpourri*). Carlsbad, Calif.: 1990.

Pulos, Arthur J. *The American Design Adventure.* Cambridge, Mass.: The M.I.T. Press, 1988.

Reisner, Marc. *Cadillac Desert: The American West and Its Disappearing Water.* New York: Viking, 1986.

Renneker, Mark, M.D., Kevin Starr, M.D., and Geoff Booth, M.D. *Sick Surfers Ask the Surf Dogs and Dr. Geoff.* Palo Alto, Calif.: Bull Publishing Co., 1993.

Riese, Randall. *Nashville Babylon.* Chicago: Contemporary Books, 1988.

Robinson, W. W. *Land in California.* Berkeley, Calif.: University of California Press, 1948.

Rogan, Johnny. *Timeless Flight: The Definitive Biography of the Byrds.* Rev. ed. London: Square One Books, 1990.

Rolfe, Lionel. *Literary L.A.* San Francisco: Chronicle Books, 1981.

Roth, Ed, and Howie Kusten. *Confessions of a Rat Fink: The Life and Times of Ed "Big Daddy" Roth.* New York: Pharos Books/Scripps Howard Co., 1992.

Sacramento Bee Editors. *California: Past, Present, Future.* Lakewood, Calif.: California Almanac Co., 1971.

Sandburg, Carl. *The American Songbag.* New York: Harcourt Brace Jovanovich, 1970.

Sanjek, Russ. *American Popular Music and Its Business: The First Four Hundred Years.* New York: Oxford University Press, 1988.

Schickel, Richard. *The Disney Version: The Life, Times, Art and Commerce of Walt Disney.* New York: Touchstone/Simon & Schuster, 1985.

Schlebecker, John T. *Wherby We Thrive: A History of American Farming, 1607–1972.* Ames, Iowa: Iowa State University Press, 1975.

Schoneberger, William A. *California Wings: A History of Aviation in the Golden State.* Woodland Hills, Calif.: Windsor Publications, 1984.

Schoneberger, William A., and Robert R. H. Scholl. *Out of Thin Air: Garrett's First 50 Years.* Los Angeles: The Garrett Corp., 1985.

Sculatti, Gene. *The Catalog of Cool.* New York: Warner Books, 1982.

————. *Too Cool*. New York: St. Martin's Press, 1993.

Selvin, Joel. *Ricky Nelson: Idol for a Generation*. Chicago: Contemporary Books, 1990.

Selvin, Joel, and Jim Marshall. *Monterey Pop, June 16–18, 1967*. San Francisco: Chronicle Books, 1992.

Sexton, Richard. *American Style: Classic Product Design from Airstream to Zippo*. San Francisco: Chronicle Books, 1987.

Shannon, Bob, and John Javna. *Behind the Hits: Inside Stories of Classic Pop and Rock and Roll*. New York: Warner Books, 1986.

Shaw, Arnold. *Honkers and Shouters: The Golden Years of Rhythm and Blues*. New York: Macmillan, 1978.

Sherry, Michael S. *The Creation of Armageddon: The Rise of American Air Power*. New Haven, Conn.: Yale University Press, 1987.

Smith, Jack. *The Best of Los Angeles: A Discriminating Guide*. Los Angeles: Rosebud Books, 1980.

Sommer, Robin Langley. *"I Had One of Those"—Toys of Our Generation*. New York: Crescent Books, 1992.

Stanley, Norman. *No Little Plans*. Los Angeles: Los Angeles Chamber of Commerce, 1956.

Stasz, Clarice. *American Dreamers: Charmian and Jack London*. New York: St. Martin's Press, 1988.

Stern, David, and Bill Cleary. *Surfing Guide to Southern California*. Redondo Beach, Calif.: Mountain & Sea, 1984. Originally published by Stern, David H. Malibu, Ca: 1963.

Stevens, Jay. *Storming Heaven: L.S.D. and the American Dream*. New York: Perennial Library, 1988.

Stilgoe, John R. *Borderland: Origins of the American Suburb, 1820–1939*. New Haven, Conn.: Yale University Press, 1988.

Tompkins, Walker A. *Little Giant of Signal Hill*. Englewood Cliffs, N.J.: Prentice-Hall, 1964.

Torrence, Bruce T. *Hollywood: The First One Hundred Years*. New York: New York Zoetrope, 1982.

Weaver, John D. *Los Angeles: The Enormous Village 1781–1981*. Santa Barbara, Calif.: Capra Press, 1980.

Weschler, Lawrence. *Seeing Is Forgetting the Name of the Thing One Sees: A Life of Contemporary Artist Robert Irwin*. Berkeley, Calif.: University of California Press, 1982.

Westphal, Ruth Lilly. *Plein Air Painters of California, the Southland*. Irvine, Calif.: Westphal Publishing, 1982.

Wheeler, Tom. *American Guitars: An Illustrated History.* New York: Harper Perennial, 1990.

Whitburn, Joel. *Top Pop Singles 1955–1990, Compiled from* Billboard. Menomonee Falls, Wis.: Record Research, 1991.

———. *Top Pop Albums 1955–1992, Compiled from* Billboard. Menomonee Falls, Wis.: Record Research, 1993.

———. *Top R&B Albums 1942–1988, Compiled from* Billboard. Menomonee Falls, Wis.: Record Research, 1988.

———. *Top Country Singles 1944–1988, Compiled from* Billboard. Menomonee Falls, Wis.: Record Research, 1989.

———. *Pop Memories 1890–1954, The History of American Popular Music.* Menomonee Falls, Wis.: Record Research, 1986.

White, Forrest. *Fender, The Inside Story.* San Francisco: Miller Freeman Books, 1994.

White, Timothy. *Rock Lives: Profiles and Interviews.* New York: Henry Holt/Owl Books, 1991.

Wincentsen, Edward. *Denny Remembered: Dennis Wilson in Words and Pictures.* El Paso, Tex.: Vergin Press, 1991.

Wolfson Foundation of Decorative and Propaganda Arts. *The Journal of Decorative and Propaganda Arts,* Summer/Fall 1986. Miami, Fla.: 1986.

Worster, Donald. *Dust Bowl: The Southern Plains in the 1930s.* New York: Oxford University Press, 1979.

———. *Rivers of Empire: Water, Aridity and the Growth of the American West.* New York: Pantheon Books, 1985.

Wrobel, Arthur, ed. *Pseudo-Science and Society in 19th Century America.* Lexington, Ky.: University of Kentucky Press, 1987.

Yeager, General Chuck, and Leo Janos. *Yeager: An Autobiography.* New York: Bantam, 1986.

Young, Nat. *Nat Young's Book of Surfing: The Fundamentals and Adventures of Board-Riding.* Sydney, Australia: Reed, 1979.

———. *The History of Surfing.* Palm Beach, New South Wales: Palm Beach Press, 1983.

The author read through hundreds of issues of *Beach Culture, Billboard, California Division of Highways Annual Reports, California Highways and Public Works, California History, Car Craft, Chicago Daily Tribune, Crawdaddy, Daily Breeze, Goldmine, Hawthorne Citizen, Historical Society of Southern Cali-*

fornia Quarterly, Hot Rod, Huntington Beach News, Huntington Beach Pilot, Huntington Beach Post, Hutchinson News, Kicks, L.A. Chamber of Commerce Member's Annual, Los Angeles Daily News, Los Angeles: City and County, Los Angeles Magazine, L.A. Style, Los Angeles Times, L.A. Weekly, Life, Musician, National Geographic, Newsweek, New West, New York Times, Orange Coast Magazine, Orange County Register, Rolling Stone, Skateboarder, Surfer, Surfing, Thrasher, Time, USA-Today, Who Put the Bomp, and innumerable community newspapers and guidebook pamphlets from over the last century for the beach towns along the Southern California coast.

Selected Articles, Periodicals, and Documents

American Federation of Musicians of the United States and Canada, Local Union 47. Brian Wilson, the Beach Boys. February 8, 1962/May 24, 1988. Phonograph Record Contracts.

Bernstein, Laura, and Jill Johnson Keeney. "Surfin' Safari Revisited." *New West* (May 1981).

Brock, Ray. "How Hot Are the Police Specials?" *Hot Rod* (February 1959).

Cahill, Tim. "The Endless Sidewalk: Burgers, Bongos, and the Supreme Challenge of Skating Down Perilous Pavement on a Little, Tiny Board." *Rolling Stone* (July 15, 1976).

Capitol Records Inc. and Brian D. Wilson, Dennis C. Wilson, Carl D. Wilson, and David Marks, Minors. "Order Approving Contract of Minors." Superior Court of the State of California for the County of Los Angeles (No. 805386).

Collins, James H. "Capitol Makes It the 'Big Four.' " *Sales Management Magazine* (November 1, 1951).

Connelly, Chris. "Wilson Phillips: California Girls." *Rolling Stone* (May 2, 1991).

Felton, David. "The Healing of Brother Bri." *Rolling Stone* (November 4, 1976).

Finneran. "The Sunrays: Murry's Suns." *Goldmine* (May 15, 1992).

Francisco, Don. "Desert Stronghold." *Hot Rod* (January 1961).

Gabriel, Trip. "Rolling Thunder." *Rolling Stone* (July 16–30, 1987).

Gari, Brian. "Hal Blaine, Rock 'n' Roll's House Drummer." *Goldmine* (October 5, 1990).

Gilenson, Hal I. "Badlands: Artist-Personal Manager Conflicts of Interest in the Music Industry." *Cardozo Arts and Entertainment Law Journal* (Vol. 9, No. 2, 1991).

Haslam, Gerald. "The Okies: Forty Years Later." *The Nation* (March 18, 1975).

Hoge, Warren. "Skateboard Generation Blooms on City and Suburban Concrete." *The New York Times* (April 2, 1976).

Kent, Nick. "The Last Beach Movie: Brian Wilson 1942– . . . Parts 1, 2 and 3." *New Musical Express* (June–July 1975).

Landy, Eugene. "In the Matter of the Accusation Against: Eugene Landy, Ph.D., Psych. License No. PK-3571, Psych. Exam. Comte." Office of the Attorney General of the State of California before the Psychology Examining Committee Division of Allied Health Professions Board of Medical Quality Assurance, Department of Consumer Affairs, State of California (Case No. D-3745).

Lees, David. "Ride, Ride, Ride the Wild $urf." *Los Angeles* (June 1979).

Love, Frances. "Vs. Michael E. Love." Superior Court of the State of California for the County of Los Angeles (Case No. D626338).

Love, Michael Edward. "Vs. Suzanne Celeste Love, et al." Superior Court of the State of California for the County of Los Angeles (Case No. D 747 057).

McKenna, Kristine. "Revvin' Up the Rat Fink." *Los Angeles Times* (December 20, 1993).

McLellan, Dennis. "Making Waves: 25 Years Later, the Surfer Is Up." *Los Angeles Times* (March 15, 1985).

Miller, Trudi. "CD's Launch: The Hidden History." *Billboard* (September 26, 1992).

Morris, Jan. "Minority Rites." *Saturday Night* (June 1990).

Morse, Steve. "Beach Boys Get Around for the Fourth." *Boston Globe* (July 3, 1990).

Nolan, Tom. "The Beach Boys: A California Saga, Part One." *Rolling Stone* (October 28, 1971).

———. "The Beach Boys: A California Saga, Part Two." *Rolling Stone* (November 11, 1971).

Osborne, Jerry. "Dave Nowlen: A Survivor." *DISCoveries* (October 1989).

Paulsen, Don, and Pam Marchetta. "Are You the Right Girl for the Sunrays?"; "The Beach Boys Have a Midas Touch." *Song Hits* (July 1966).

Petersen, Robert, and the Editors of *Hot Rod*. The Best of Hot Rod: Special Collector's Edition (1986).

Phillips, McCandlish. "Pavement Surfing Makes Splash." *The New York Times* (March 3, 1965).

Reum, Peter. "Collecting Solo Brian Wilson: Beyond the Beach Boys." *Goldmine* (June 1, 1990).

Robicheau, Paul. "Beach Boys Offer—Mostly—Family Fare." *Boston Globe* (August 22, 1994).

Roth, Ed "Big Daddy." "What Ever Happened to the Beatnik Bandit?" *Roth Booklets* (November 1984).

———. "Pinstriping by Roth." *Roth Booklets* (1981).

Severson, John, and the Editors. *The Quarterly Skateboarder* (Vol. 1, No. 1, Winter 1964).

Sharp, Ken. "Love Among the Ruins: The Controversial Beach Boy Speaks His Mind." *Goldmine* (September 18, 1992).

Smith, Richard R. "Early Fender History Re-Examined." *Guitar Player* (December 1984).

Smythe, John. "The History of the World and Other Short Subjects, or From Jan and Dean to Joe Jackson Unabridged." *Skateboarder* (May 1980).

Sorensen, Steve. "Shred Till You're Dead." *San Diego Reader* (February 23, 1984).

Stark, Phyllis. "WNEW: FM's New-Groove Groundbreaker Parties On to Become a New York Classic at 25." *Billboard* (September 12, 1992).

Stein, Seymour. Letter via Fax to Eugene Landy, Sire Records Co. (May 10, 1988).

White, Jack E., Linda Nussbaum, James L. Cantwell, Richard L. Boeth, Tom Curry, and Gina Bellafante. "Special Issue: California, the Endangered Dream." *Time* (November 18, 1991).

White, Timothy. "Hello, Brian . . ."—Checking In with the Bashful Beachcomber." *Crawdaddy* (April 1976).

———. "Van Dyke Parks: I'm Okay/Brian Wilson's Okay." *Crawdaddy* (April 1976).

———. "Little Deuce Coup: Two Beach Boys Sail Solo." *Crawdaddy* (November 1976).

———. "Still Waters Run Deep: A Child Is Father to the Band/The Return of Brian Wilson." *Crawdaddy* (June 1976).

———. "Still Waters Run Deep, Part Two: A Child Is Father to the Band/The Return of Brian Wilson." *Crawdaddy* (July 1976).

————. "Lost Surfari." *Crawdaddy* (September 1976).

————. "Beach Men: We Can Go Our Own Way." *Crawdaddy* (May 1977).

————. "Bet No One Ever Hurt This Bad: Randy Newman Survives an Unhappy Childhood and Blossoms into a Miserable Adult." *Rolling Stone* (November 1, 1979).

————. "Van Dyke Parks and Brer Rabbit Update the Lost Art of the Minstrelsy." *Musician* (February 1985).

————. "The King of Summer Comes Home." *Musician* (August 1985).

————. "Meet Joe Smith: An Anecdotal History of Rock 'n' Roll." *L.A. Style* (November, 1987).

————. "George Harrison Reconsidered: After All Those Years of Mania and Moptops, Dark Suits and Deep Blues, Here Comes the Fun." *Musician* (November 1987).

————. "Back from the Bottom: Beach Boy Brian Wilson." *The New York Times Magazine* (June 26, 1988).

————. "After Innocence: Ex-Eagle Don Henley and Comrade Danny Kortchmar Aim for the Heart of the Matter." *L.A. Style* (February 1990).

————. "Break Away: The Battle for Brian Wilson's Publishing Millions." *Billboard* (October 5, 1991).

————. George Harrison: The Century Award—A Portrait of the Artist." *Billboard* (December 5, 1992).

Wilson, Barbara Carol. "Vs. Dennis Wilson." Superior Court of California, County of Los Angeles (Case No. D834448).

Wilson, Brian D., Dennis C. Wilson, Carl E. Wilson, Michael E. Love, Alan Jardine, et al. "Vs. Capitol Records Inc., a California corporation." Superior Court of the State of California for the County of Los Angeles (Case No. C161 538).

Wilson, Brian. "Vs. Marilyn Wilson." Superior Court of the State of California for the County of Los Angeles (Case No. D 983 605).

Wilson, Brian. "In the Matter of the Conservatorship of Brian Wilson." Superior Court of the State of California for the County of Los Angeles (Case No. SP000008).

Wilson, Brian Douglas. "Plaintiff, vs. Irving Music, Inc., a California corporation; Rondor Music International, Inc., a California corporation; A&M Records, Inc., a California corporation; A&M General Corporation, a California corporation; Almo Music Corporation, a California corporation; and Almo/Irving Music, a California corporation, Defendants."

United States District Court for the Central District of California (Case No. 89 5517 WJR GHKy).

Wilson, Carl D. "Vs. Annie C. Wilson." Superior Court of California, County of Los Angeles (Case No. D000 925).

Wilson, Carole. "Vs. Dennis Carl Wilson, et al." Superior Court of the State of California for the County of Los Angeles (Case No. D711 515).

Wilson, Dennis Carl. "Vs. Carole E. Wilson." Superior Court of the State of California for the County of Los Angeles (Case No. D700 761).

Wilson, Dennis Carl. "Vs. Karen Lamm Wilson." Superior Court of California, County of Los Angeles (Case No. WED 31057).

Wilson, Dennis Carl. "Vs. Karen Lamm Wilson." Superior Court of California, County of Los Angeles (Case No. WE 158).

Wilson, Dennis Carl. "Will of . . ." Superior Court of California, County of Los Angeles (Case No. WEP 19031).

Wilson, Dennis C. "Autopsy Report." Department of Chief Medical Examiner-Coroner of Los Angeles (Case No. 83-16219).

Wilson, Dennis Carl. "In Re. Estate of . . . Deceased." Superior Court of the State of California for the County of Los Angeles, Transferred to the Central District (Case No. WEP 19031).

Wilson, Murry Gage. "In the Matter of the Estate of . . ." Superior Court of the State of California for the County of Los Angeles (Case No. SE 4782).

Wilson, Shawn Love, and Dennis Gage Wilson. "Plaintiffs, vs. Transamerica Occidental Life Insurance Company, Inc." Superior Court of the State of California for the County of Los Angeles (Case No. C 515 935).

Index

LOS ANGELES CHAMBER OF COMMERCE MAP / 1929

Los Angeles County and Southern California constitute a paradise for the motorist. The hundreds of miles of excellent paved highways link together the various communities of the County and make accessible to the motorist all the various points of interest such as mountains, desert and